Decolonisation in the age of globalisation

Manchester University Press

Decolonisation in the age of globalisation

Britain, China, and Hong Kong, 1979–89

Chi-kwan Mark

MANCHESTER UNIVERSITY PRESS

Copyright © Chi-kwan Mark 2023

The right of Chi-kwan Mark to be identified as the author of this work has been asserted in accordance with the Copyright, Designs and Patents Act 1988.

Published by Manchester University Press
Oxford Road, Manchester M13 9PL

www.manchesteruniversitypress.co.uk

British Library Cataloguing-in-Publication Data
A catalogue record for this book is available from the British Library

ISBN 978 1 5261 7132 0 hardback
ISBN 978 15261 9085 7 paperback

First published 2023
Paperback published 2025

The publisher has no responsibility for the persistence or accuracy of URLs for any external or third- party internet websites referred to in this book, and does not guarantee that any content on such websites is, or will remain, accurate or appropriate.

EU authorised representative for GPSR:
Easy Access System Europe – Mustamäe tee 50, 10621 Tallinn, Estonia
gpsr.requests@easproject.com

Typeset by Newgen Publishing UK

Contents

List of abbreviations	*page* vi
Map of Hong Kong	viii
Introduction	1
1 Anglo-Chinese relations, 1979	17
2 Globalisation without decolonisation? Hong Kong, 1979–81	44
3 Not for (re)turning: Thatcher meets Deng Xiaoping, 1982	75
4 Bargaining for sovereignty and administration, 1982–83	99
5 Negotiating autonomy and continuity, 1984	130
6 Anglo-Chinese interactions and globalisation, 1985–86	165
7 Democratisation and its limits, 1985–89	198
Conclusion	232
Bibliography	247
Index	261

Abbreviations

AHKA	All Hong Kong Alliance in Support of the Patriotic Democratic Movement in China
BDTC	British Dependent Territories Citizen
BLO	Bodleian Library, University of Oxford, Oxford, UK
BN(O)	British National (Overseas)
CAAC	Civil Aviation Administration of China
CAC	Churchill Archives Centre, Churchill College, Cambridge, UK
CCP	Chinese Communist Party
CLP	China Light and Power Company
COCOM	Coordinating Committee for Multilateral Export Controls
DTI	Department of Trade and Industry
DXN	*Deng Xiaoping nianpu*
DXW	*Deng Xiaoping wenxuan*
EEC	European Economic Community
FCO	Foreign and Commonwealth Office
GATT	General Agreement on Tariffs and Trade
GDL	GATT Digital Library 1947–94, Stanford Libraries, Stanford University
GEC	General Electric Company
HK	Hong Kong
IMF	International Monetary Fund
MFA	Multi-Fibre Arrangement
MoD	Ministry of Defence
MTF	Margaret Thatcher Foundation, UK
NCNA	New China News Agency
NPC	National People's Congress
PLA	People's Liberation Army
PRC	People's Republic of China
PRO	Public Records Office, Kwun Tong, Hong Kong
SAR	Special Administrative Region of Hong Kong

SDI	Strategic Defence Initiative
SEZ	Special Economic Zone
SJC	St. John's College, Cambridge, UK
TNA	The National Archives, Kew, Surrey, UK
UMELCO	Unofficial Members of the Executive Council and the Legislative Council
ZZW	*Zhao Ziyang wenji*

Map of Hong Kong

Introduction

Between 31 January and 2 February 2018, Theresa May, then British prime minister, made an official visit to the People's Republic of China (PRC). She spelt out her aims in the *Financial Times* before setting off, stating that as 'a global trading nation', Britain would be 'deepening co-operation' with China on key global and economic issues.[1] She hoped to intensify the 'golden era' of Sino-British relations, first proclaimed by Chinese President Xi Jinping and May's predecessor, David Cameron, in 2015. May had succeeded Cameron as prime minister in 2016, following his resignation after the British voted to leave the European Union, yet she lost the Conservative majority in a snap general election the following year. She went to China in 2018 with the aim of promoting a 'Global Britain' – 'a country with the self-confidence and the freedom to look beyond the continent of Europe and to the economic and diplomatic opportunities of the wider world'.[2] The Foreign and Commonwealth Office (FCO) defined 'Global Britain' as being 'open, inclusive and outward facing', 'free trading', supportive of 'the rules-based international system', and, insofar as China was concerned, being proactive in building 'a strong economic and global partnership'.[3]

In 1982, more than thirty-five years before May's visit, Margaret Thatcher, the first female prime minister in British history and also a Tory herself, had journeyed to the People's Republic. Although her primary objective was to negotiate for the future of Hong Kong, Thatcher also intended to explore trade opportunities with China's paramount leader, Deng Xiaoping, who was launching a policy of reform and opening up. In a sense, Thatcher, like her Conservative successors decades later, held the vision of 'Global Britain', a power that would actively advance its economic interests and political influence in an increasingly globalised world. In the FCO's assessment of the objectives of her visits to China and Japan, the prime minister could demonstrate that 'Britain as world power has a role to play in an area of great strategic importance and in relations with two great Asian powers'.[4]

This book is about Britain's policy and relations with China and Hong Kong in the 1980s, exploring the twin themes of globalisation and decolonisation.

Thatcher, globalisation, and decolonisation

Margaret Thatcher came to power amid the 'crisis' of seventies Britain.[5] She was determined to reverse Britain's 'long-term economic decline' by offering a free-market alternative to the welfare state model of James Callaghan.[6] Externally, the 1979 Conservative manifesto declared 'a strong Britain in a free world' as one of the five main tasks of the government.[7] Thatcher envisioned that the United Kingdom (UK) should not merely aspire to a European future or accept a post-imperial fate. As she declared in a speech in 1981, 'Europe may be central to our foreign policy but it is very far from being the whole of that policy'. Rather, Britain's role 'remains world-wide', aiming 'to strengthen security, to extend liberty, and to promote prosperity' across the globe.[8]

In spreading democracy and prosperity to other countries, Thatcher found a close partner in United States (US) President Ronald Reagan. What united Thatcher and Reagan was a neoliberal worldview, where 'anticommunism, free enterprise and freedom were inextricably linked'. The pair worked together to create 'an open world economic order – for open markets, free trade and the free movement of capital'.[9] The origin of neoliberalism can be traced back to the 1920s, when, after the breakup of the Hapsburg Empire, a group of neoliberal thinkers contemplated a project of global market integration.[10] Neoliberalism was 'a theory of political economic practices that proposes that human well-being can best be advanced by liberating individual entrepreneurial freedoms and skills within an institutional framework characterized by strong private property rights, free markets, and free trade'. Rather than simply rolling back the state, neoliberalism held that the state had a crucial role to 'create and preserve an institutional framework appropriate to such practices'.[11] Moreover, neoliberalism saw 'the need for the *global capitalist system to continue to expand*'.[12]

Globalisation was 'a planetary process or set of processes involving increasing *liquidity* and the growing multidirectional *flows* of people, objects, places and information'.[13] It did not emerge suddenly in the 1980s or the 1990s; rather, it took different forms at different times – 'archaic, proto, modern, and post-colonial'.[14] The post-colonial or contemporary phase of globalisation began around 1950, thanks to the role of the United States in the global Cold War, the collapse of European empires, and the technological and information revolution.[15] The 1970s were a pivotal decade for the advent of finance-led globalisation. The end of the Bretton Woods system of pegged exchange rates, the shift to post-Fordist flexible manufacturing, and the rise of the service sector highlighted the limits of state power and the importance of economic interdependence.[16] In the United States, think tanks funded by wealthy corporations and Republican politicians, including presidential hopeful Reagan, promoted a neoliberal order, which championed free markets, to replace the 'New Deal order', based on Franklin Roosevelt's version of social democracy.[17] In Britain, neoliberal think tanks like the Institute of Economic Affairs advised Thatcher on how to deal with the 'crisis' of managed capitalism and to make a bid for the premiership.[18] The so-called offshore world of 'archipelago capitalism' also became a site of free-market globalisation. From Panama and Malta to Singapore and Switzerland, low taxation and light regulation turned these places into offshore tax havens, financial centres, and foreign trade zones.[19] Nevertheless, it was the 1980s that witnessed 'the breakthrough of neoliberal policies with the governments of Reagan and Thatcher'.[20] Globalisation entered an intensified phase due to the convergence of a host of new personalities and developments: Reagan's economic policy and military build-up in order to make the world safe for capitalism;[21] the debt crisis in the Third World, which propelled many developing countries of Latin America, Asia, and Africa to accept the International Monetary Fund (IMF)-imposed economic adjustment measures – or the so-called 'Washington Consensus' – as a precondition for loans;[22] and, as this book argues, Thatcher's promotion of neoliberalism worldwide and Deng Xiaoping's engagement with the global economy.

During the 1980s, Thatcher and her officials 'did not use the politicized language of globalization with any frequency'. (The concept did not become a buzzword until the 1990s.) Nevertheless, they 'took growing international economic integration as given, and within that talked a lot about the need to improve British *competitiveness*' as a result of 'the increasing internationalization of the economy'.[23] 'We have to compete in the world markets', Thatcher declared in an interview with the *Daily Mail* in 1989. Britain needed to compete with the goods from Japan, the United States, Singapore, Hong Kong, and so forth.[24] The problem was that since the mid-1970s, Britain appeared to have lost its competitive advantage, falling behind other advanced industrialised countries.[25] Britain's relative economic decline was manifested in the manufacturing industry rather than the services industry.[26] To reverse the decline, Thatcher wanted a return to 'the free-trading, liberal, globally oriented economy'.[27] In promoting economic globalisation, Thatcher could not afford to ignore the Far East, which contained 'some of the fastest growing economies in the world'. Thatcher held the conviction that East Asian countries like Japan and China 'have to be fully integrated into a global free-trading economy if [British] industries are to compete effectively'.[28] In short, Thatcher saw Britain's identity as a global, not purely European or post-imperial, trading nation.

Deng Xiaoping's opening up of China since 1979 presented Britain and other Western powers with great opportunities for trade and investment.

Anglo-Chinese relations had flourished since the establishment of full diplomatic relations in 1972. In the 1980s, Britain engaged with China more closely than ever, not least due to the political necessity of discussing Hong Kong's future. Thatcher looked beyond economics in her promotion of globalisation. It was the neoliberal assumption that free markets and liberal democracy were inextricably linked, and that economic globalisation would lead to political liberalisation in China.[29] As Thatcher perceived in 1984: 'The Chinese belief that the benefits of a liberal economic system can be had without a liberal political system seems to me false in the long term.'[30] Rather, '[i]n due course communism *will* fail in China'.[31] Nevertheless, Thatcher and the FCO 'invested hope in long-term reform of the communist system rather than in its imminent demise'.[32] As a 'pragmatic neoliberal', Thatcher adopted a gradual and instrumental approach to democratic promotion worldwide. 'I wanted to see the fall of communism – not just in eastern Europe and the Soviet Union but in every corner of the globe – but I wanted to see this achieved peacefully', she recollected.[33]

What of Deng Xiaoping's attitude towards globalisation? During the 1980s, Deng 'did not refer to "globalization" per se, but he advocated China's adaptation to the "world-wide technological revolution"'.[34] To become a key player in the global economy, China joined the IMF and the World Bank in 1980, and declared its intention of resuming its status at the General Agreement on Tariffs and Trade (GATT) in 1986. To stimulate trade and foreign investment, Deng first established special economic zones in southern China, and then opened coastal cities across the country. 'By mid-1984', as Samuel Kim observes, 'the concept of global interdependence and one world market emerged as an important component of Chinese reformers' world peace and development line'.[35] Nevertheless, Deng's concept was one of 'independent globalization' or a strategy that seamlessly combined an 'open door' policy with the principle of 'self-reliance', according to Ronald Keith. Deng adopted 'a rational response to globalization, which was designed to seize the opportunities for foreign investment and technology transfer while controlling for those political aspects of globalization that undercut state sovereignty'.[36] In embracing economic globalisation, Deng's primary aim was to build 'socialism with Chinese characteristics'.[37] In short, Deng's vision of 'independent globalisation', which stressed sovereignty and socialism, was fundamentally different from Thatcher's neoliberal variant.

The clash of visions between Thatcher and Deng played out most prominently in the question of Hong Kong, which was partly ceded and partly leased by treaties in the course of the nineteenth century. While the British acquired Hong Kong Island and the Kowloon Peninsula in perpetuity, their hold on the New Territories was based on a ninety-nine-year lease, which was due to expire on 30 June 1997. Rejecting the three 'unequal treaties' governing Hong Kong's status, Deng was determined to recover the whole of Hong Kong in 1997. With her aversion to socialism and her pride in capitalist Hong Kong, Thatcher was eager to extend British rule beyond 1997. Between September 1982 and 1984, diplomatic talks over Hong Kong's future took place in Beijing, culminating in Thatcher's agreement to concede both sovereignty and administration to China. The Iron Lady was 'for (re)turning'.

Britain, China, and Hong Kong: a global, diplomatic, and imperial history

This book, then, is about how Britain actively engaged with China in order to promote globalisation and manage Hong Kong's decolonisation. It commences with Thatcher's rise to power and Deng Xiaoping's adoption of reform in 1979. It ends with the 1989 Tiananmen Square crackdown, which dashed all Western hopes for the emergence of a democratic China and renewed the crisis of confidence in Hong Kong. Two central questions drive the analysis. What role did Britain play in China's globalisation and reforms? Why did Thatcher resist the decolonisation of Hong Kong in 1982, but change her mind two years later? In answering these questions, this study interrogates such key concepts as 'globalisation', 'decolonisation', and 'appeasement'. While focusing on British perspectives and policy, the book does not ignore the Chinese side of the relationship. By bridging the divide among studies of globalisation, Anglo-Chinese relations, and Hong Kong's decolonisation, the book is at once a study of global history, diplomatic history, and imperial history.

Although the term was rarely used by officials and scholars alike until the 1990s, 'globalisation' was not merely a contemporary and Western phenomenon. A. G. Hopkins and Jürgen Osterhammel, to name just two, have examined the trajectory of globalisation from a long-term historical perspective.[38] Some scholars regard the 1970s as a crucible of late twentieth-century globalisation.[39] Others focus on the significance of the 1980s, particularly concerning the global spread of democracy.[40] This book aims to historicise 1980s globalisation by bringing together three crucial players – Britain, China, and Hong Kong, an externally oriented economy with strong global connections. On China, a number of major biographies of Deng Xiaoping have appeared in the past decade, providing valuable insights into the economic revolution he unleashed in China.[41] On the international sources of Deng's reform, Julian B. Gewirtz explores the influence of Western and foreign economists on the Chinese government, particularly reform-minded officials like Zhao Ziyang.[42] Among foreign countries, the United States undoubtedly played the most important role in enmeshing China in the global economy.[43] Nevertheless, the unique contribution made by Britain to China's modernisation and globalisation is little known. Not only did Thatcher attach importance to China's integration into the global economy, but the imperative of managing Hong Kong's decolonisation also made Anglo-Chinese interactions both necessary and frequent. This study intends to fill the void in the existing literature, but with one caveat: the primary focus is on the diplomacy, not economics, of globalisation – that is, how Thatcher and British diplomats promoted free trade and economic cooperation during meetings with Chinese leaders and officials.

To its advocates, globalisation was a progressive, homogenising, and inevitable force. The adoption of free markets was linked to the development of democracy, which in turn contributed to world peace. By late 1989, the global spread of free-market capitalism and liberal democracy, argues Francis Fukuyama, marked the 'end of history' and the 'triumph' of the United States in the Cold War.[44] The case of China seems to suggest otherwise, however. While the communist party states in Eastern Europe collapsed one after another in 1989, the Chinese Communist Party (CCP) survived the Chinese student protests culminating in the Tiananmen Square crackdown and, with hindsight, the Western powers' imposition of (limited) sanctions on China in its aftermath. All this demonstrates that there existed more than one version of globalisation in world history.[45] As Martin Jacques and Odd Arne Westad both argue, throughout the nineteenth and twentieth centuries (and beyond), China wanted to search for its own path to modernity, which was shaped by and helped shape the Western capitalist model.[46]

This book is primarily a diplomatic history of Britain's policy towards China and Hong Kong during the Thatcher era. It builds on the new historiography of Thatcher and 'Thatcherism'. There are now excellent biographies of the Iron Lady[47] and overall assessments of 1980s Britain.[48] Thatcher's foreign policy has been relatively under-studied, with former British diplomats providing valuable insider accounts[49] and most secondary works focusing on the Anglo-American 'special relationship' and the end of the superpower Cold War.[50] Thus far, there has been a conspicuous absence of research on Anglo-Chinese relations during the Thatcher period. According to the revisionist scholarship, 'Thatcherism' was a vague set of principles and values rather than a fixed blueprint and rigid doctrines. A complicated character, Thatcher was at once a strong-willed and pragmatic person.[51] According to Jonathan Aitken, there were 'two sides of her personality': the 'emotional Margaret Thatcher' and the 'realistic Prime Minister'.[52]

When it came to British foreign policy, pragmatism was often associated with 'appeasement'. As R. Gerald Hughes argues: '[A]ppeasement did not disappear from British foreign policy formulation after 1945 ... In actual fact, the appeasement "tradition" continued throughout the postwar era (often under the banner of "pragmatism") and its employment was seen by its Foreign Office proponents as something to be proud of.'[53] He further stresses that 'collective memory' is not quite the same as 'history'. Ever since the 1938 Munich Conference, during which Neville Chamberlain's Britain acquiesced in Nazi Germany's annexation of the Sudeten German territory of Czechoslovakia in order to avert war, the word 'appeasement' has been endowed with negative connotations in British public opinion.[54] The collective memory of Munich does not sit comfortably with the revisionist historiography of Chamberlain's 'appeasement' policy in the 1930s, which portrays Chamberlain not as the 'guilty man' dictated by Britain's 'economic decline', but as a realistic leader who opted for appeasing the German aggressor since alternative policies were deemed impractical and too risky.[55] Insofar as Anglo-Chinese relations were concerned, the historical memory of the 1793 Macartney Embassy to Qing China might have lingered whenever the question of engagement or confrontation with China came up for debate. George Lord Macartney had failed in his mission to develop trade and diplomatic intercourse with China, partly because he refused to perform the ritual of 'kowtow' (kneeling on both legs and bowing the forehead to the ground) during his imperial audience.[56] Almost two centuries later, the Thatcher government's refusal to stand firm on China over the Tiananmen crackdown led to accusations of 'kowtowing' to Beijing in Parliament, the media, and society at large. In the words of Christopher Meyer, who had served as Foreign Secretary Geoffrey Howe's press secretary and later the British ambassador in Washington, China presented the FCO with the dilemma of 'kowtow versus the gunboat' (the Royal Navy being an instrument of Victorian gunboat diplomacy against Qing China).[57] British diplomats were acutely aware that being too soft or too tough with regard to China carried both benefits and pitfalls.

Edward Heath, the former Conservative prime minister, writes of appeasement in his memoir: '[N]egotiation is not appeasement. Appeasement involves a sacrifice of a moral principle in order to avert aggression. Negotiation requires some change on the status quo in order to make progress, without giving up any basic point of principle.'[58] While seeing Heath as her lifelong political rival, Thatcher probably agreed that negotiation was no 'appeasement' because the main purpose of diplomatic talks was to change 'the status quo', be it the attitude or policy of the other party. Significantly, this book argues that, in pursuing a diplomacy of engagement with China, and during the negotiations over Hong Kong's future, Thatcher and the FCO aimed to 'educate' Deng Xiaoping about the nature of free-market capitalism and the rules-based international order. To 'educate' meant to spread new knowledge and to reshape Chinese preconceptions and behaviour. The notion of 'educating' China had a long history in the British official mind, albeit with different meanings over time. During the nineteenth century, Victorian Britain undertook a 'pedagogical project' of influencing the declining Qing empire through a mix of coercion and enticement, with the aim of teaching China about how to 'behave properly' in the age of European imperialism.[59] During the Cold War a century later, British diplomats assessed the pros and cons of China's admission to the United Nations (UN), which could be boiled down to 'Education of China versus Disruption of the U.N.', regarding 'the aim of trying to teach China to become a more normal and co-operative member of international society' as paramount.[60] In the 1980s, the FCO and Thatcher continued to talk about 'educating' China. With the full normalisation of Anglo-Chinese relations, the process of 'education' was conceived in terms of a diplomacy of engagement, negotiation, and cooperation. That said, it might be wishful thinking on the part of Thatcher and FCO mandarins that Britain had the ability to 'change' China in its image. Ironically, while Thatcher hoped to 'educate' the Chinese leaders about Hong Kong, it was the Iron Lady who might need educating on the colony's realities in the first place.

Focusing on imperial history, this book discusses the decolonisation of Hong Kong at length. The protracted Anglo-Chinese negotiations over Hong Kong's future have been the subject of writing by former British diplomats,[61] Western journalists,[62] British and Chinese historians,[63] and former Chinese communist officials responsible for Hong Kong affairs.[64] While informative and still valuable in many ways, these works have not benefited from the declassified British archives relating to the Thatcher period. In the second volume of his authorised biography of Thatcher, Charles Moore touches upon Hong Kong by utilising the hitherto unpublished Thatcher papers and countless interviews with his protagonist and former British ministers and diplomats.[65] Moore provides valuable insights into Thatcher's personality, arguing that her occasional 'unreasonableness' made real negotiation possible and ultimately fruitful.[66] In his general account of Hong Kong and China from 1979 to 2020, Michael Sheridan, using British archival sources, devotes a chapter to Thatcher's China visit and another to the 1982–84 negotiations (the latter of which is rather short on detail and documentation).[67] This book is at once more comprehensive and more limited than the existing publications. At one level, it draws upon the newly declassified British documents more thoroughly than any other work, thus allowing the reader to grasp how Thatcher and British diplomats sought to 'educate' the Chinese during the Hong Kong negotiations.[68] At another level, this book stops short of providing a blow-by-blow account of the Hong Kong talks in order to make space for discussion of Anglo-Chinese bilateral relations.

More importantly, it aims to unravel the dynamics of Hong Kong's decolonisation by placing the 1982–84 negotiations within a historical and global context. It is necessary to recall how imperial historians define and explain the phenomenon of decolonisation.

To John Darwin, British imperialists imagined and constructed different kinds of empire across the world, including White Dominions, Crown Colonies, the Indian Raj, and informal empires – all of which constituted a 'British world-system'. Just as Britain's empire building was a diverse and haphazard process, so too was decolonisation the result, not of a grand design, but of the interplay between metropolitan politics, colonial resistance, and international changes. Decolonisation concerned not only the legal-constitutional event of a transfer of sovereignty, but also the weakening of economic, social, and cultural ties between Britain and its colonies.[69] Nevertheless, the legal-constitutional and the socio-economic–cultural aspects of decolonisation did not necessarily go hand in hand, if at all. On the one hand, the moment of independence when sovereignty was transferred to indigenous people with the hoisting of the new national flag (or 'flag independence') would represent only the first 'wave' or 'process' of decolonisation if the former colonial power continued to exercise influence over the newly independent nation.[70] On the other, the gradual loosening of socio-economic-cultural ties might long precede the formal severing of constitutional links. This was particularly so after 1945, when goods, ideas, and people could move more easily beyond territorial boundaries in an increasingly globalised world. In this regard, there has been a 'global turn' in the study of imperial history – that is, how empire/decolonisation interacted with the process of globalisation.[71] Anthony Hopkins, for one, contends that 'decolonization was a response to changes in the process of globalization after the Second World War'. The 'profound changes to the world economy reduced the value of colonial forms of integration', which were 'vertical' in nature and were characterised by political domination and a racial hierarchy that ranked Anglo-Saxons above other peoples. In other words, empire had no place in the age of intensified globalisation or 'post-colonial globalisation'.[72] Likewise, Martin Thomas and Andrew S. Thompson argue that 'colonial rule is widely regarded as an obstacle to globalization that had to be removed'.[73]

In Hong Kong's case, the relationship between decolonisation and globalisation is more complicated. By the early 1980s, Hong Kong transformed itself into what might be called a 'global city': a British colony that was well connected with the global economy. At first glance, empire did not seem to pose an obstacle to Hong Kong's economic globalisation. Nevertheless, as Thomas and Thompson succinctly observe, decolonisation can be defined not just as 'a prior condition to globalization', but also as 'a phenomenon propelled by globalization' and 'a globalizing force in its own right'.[74]

The decolonisation of Hong Kong in the mid-1980s was facilitated by its emergence as a 'global city', which in turn played a key role in globalising the world, notably in integrating reforming China in the global economy. Although its constitutional links with the UK remained intact until 1 July 1997, Hong Kong had indeed experienced 'decolonisation' of sorts since the 1960s, thanks to its growing economic prosperity and its administrative autonomy from London. In the age of intensified globalisation, Britain could not take the imperial connection for granted when it came to trade and commerce with Hong Kong. Against the backdrop of Hong Kong's 'long decolonisation' and economic globalisation, Thatcher and British diplomats deliberated over its future during 1982–84. It was not Hong Kong's economic value to Britain per se that was uppermost in their mind. When she signed the Joint Declaration in December 1984, Thatcher felt confident that the maintenance of Hong Kong's capitalist system after 1997 would contribute to economic globalisation, so essential to the prospects for 'Global Britain'. By defining 'decolonisation' as a complicated phenomenon encompassing constitutional, economic, and cultural aspects, and by recognising the inherent tensions between empire and globalisation, we can better understand why Thatcher wanted to hold on to Hong Kong in 1982, but she was 'for (re)turning' by 1984.

Book outline

The book is organised chronologically, with Chapters 1 and 6 devoted exclusively to Anglo-Chinese bilateral relations and Chapters 2, 4, and 5 to Hong Kong's decolonisation. Chapters 3 and 7 each address both Anglo-Chinese relations and Hong Kong in different sections. Chapter 1 focuses on Anglo-Chinese relations during the Callaghan–Thatcher transition and the first eight months of the Thatcher premiership. It begins by outlining Thatcher's diplomatic approach and Deng Xiaoping's opening policy, concluding with the state visit to Britain by Premier Hua Guofeng in late 1979, which set the stage for a long-term relationship between Britain and China. Chapter 2 turns to Hong Kong between 1979 and 1981. Set against the backdrop of Hong Kong's 'long decolonisation' or growing autonomy from London since the late 1950s, the first section explores how the Callaghan and then Thatcher governments took soundings about Hong Kong's future. The second section examines the interaction between globalisation and decolonisation, showing how Hong Kong's emergence as a 'global city' had eroded the imperial links with Britain, at a time when Hong Kong and China became more interdependent economically. Chapter 3 focuses on Thatcher's visit to China in September 1982. The first section looks at how Thatcher and Deng

Xiaoping discussed, and disagreed over, Hong Kong's future, and the second section examines how Thatcher seized every opportunity to advance British trade prospects in China.

Chapter 4 examines the Anglo-Chinese negotiations over Hong Kong between October 1982 and the end of 1983. Thatcher's negotiating objectives and strategies were the polar opposite of Deng Xiaoping's, which can be boiled down to free-market capitalism versus national sovereignty. The chapter details how Thatcher was pulled in different directions by FCO diplomats and Hong Kong's unofficial members, and how her pragmatism got the better of her. In Chapter 5, we follow the difficult Hong Kong talks in 1984, when Britain's negotiating objectives shifted to securing the highest degree of autonomy for Hong Kong and continuity of its systems after 1997. Yet the Chinese remained sensitive to any issues that had to do with sovereignty. This chapter highlights how the British saw the negotiations as a way of 'educating' the Chinese about Hong Kong's capitalist system, culminating in the signing of the Joint Declaration.

In Chapter 6, we return to Anglo-Chinese bilateral relations, covering the years from late 1984 to 1986. With the resolution of the Hong Kong question, the Thatcher government hoped to capitalise on the good political atmosphere to deepen economic relations with China This chapter details the high-profile visits of Premier Zhao Ziyang and General Secretary Hu Yaobang to Britain, and that of Queen Elizabeth II to China. The last section examines China's attempts to seek GATT membership, and assesses the degree of China's integration into the global economy by the close of 1986. Finally, Chapter 7 explores the Thatcher government's approach to democratic promotion in China and Hong Kong. The first section examines how Britain responded to the Tiananmen crackdown in 1989. The second section focuses on the development of representative government in Hong Kong since 1984 and the drafting of the Basic Law (the city's mini-constitution after 1997), illustrating how Britain and China reconciled the two processes. In the Conclusion, I will first discuss the progress of China's application for GATT membership in 1989, before summarising the arguments of the book from global, imperial, and diplomatic perspectives. An overarching theme running through the book is that Thatcher's neoliberalism drove Britain to involve China in free-trade globalisation and to 'educate' the Chinese in Hong Kong's capitalist system. Yet Thatcher was a 'pragmatic neoliberal', who was willing to work with the equally pragmatic Deng Xiaoping to manage Anglo-Chinese relations and Hong Kong issues, yielding mixed results.

Finally, a note on sources. This book makes extensive use of the declassified British archives held in the National Archives at Kew, including the Prime Minister's Office files (PREM 19), the records of the Cabinet Defence and Overseas Policy Committee's Sub-Committee on Hong Kong (CAB 148), and the Foreign and Commonwealth Office files on China (FCO 21) and Hong Kong (FCO 40). They are supplemented by the private papers of Thatcher, Cradock and others, the oral interview transcripts of former British diplomats and Hong Kong officials, and digital archives such as the GATT Digital Library. The rights of British materials created in a government role are retained by the Crown, and they are quoted here under the Open Government Licence. Material from the Cradock papers is cited by permission of the Master and Fellows of St John's College, Cambridge. British newspapers, such as *The Times* and *Guardian*, were accessed through ProQuest. On Chinese sources, the chronicles and writings of PRC leaders and the memoirs of former Chinese communist officials responsible for Hong Kong affairs are used to illuminate China's perspectives and policies.

Earlier versions of parts of Chapters 2 and 3 have been published respectively in 'Decolonising Britishness? The 1981 British Nationality Act and the Identity Crisis of Hong Kong Elites', *Journal of Imperial and Commonwealth History*, 48: 3 (2020), 565–90, and 'To "Educate" Deng Xiaoping in Capitalism: Thatcher's Visit to China and the Future of Hong Kong in 1982', *Cold War History*, 17: 2 (June 2017), 161–80.

Notes

1. Theresa May, 'The global trading system works when we all play by the rules', *Financial Times* (30 January 2018), www.ft.com/content/17209dce-05b3-11e8-9e12-af73e8db3c71.
2. House of Commons, Foreign Affairs Committee, 'Global Britain', Sixth Report of Session 2017–19, HC 780 (12 March 2018), 6, https://publications.parliament.uk/pa/cm201719/cmselect/cmfaff/780/780.pdf.
3. FCO memo, March 2018, appended in *ibid.*, 19–28.
4. The National Archives, Kew, Surrey, UK (hereafter TNA), PREM 19/788, Acland to Armstrong, 7 July 1982.
5. Niall Ferguson, 'Introduction: Crisis, What Crisis?', in Niall Ferguson, Charles S. Maier, Erez Manela, and Daniel J. Sargent (eds), *The Shock of the Global: The 1970s in Perspective* (Cambridge, MA: Harvard University Press, 2010), 8–11; Jim Tomlinson, 'Thrice Denied: "Declinism" as a Recurrent Theme in British History in the Long Twentieth Century', *Twentieth Century British History*, 20: 2 (2009), 235–6.
6. Margaret Thatcher, *The Downing Street Years* (London: HarperCollins, 1993), 9.
7. Bodleian Library, University of Oxford, Oxford, UK (hereafter BLO), Conservative Party Archive, Conservative Central Office, PUB 156/4, 'The Conservative manifesto 1979', April 1979.

8 Margaret Thatcher Foundation (hereafter MTF), Thatcher's speech to Diplomatic and Commonwealth Writers Association at New Zealand House, London, 8 April 1981, www.margaretthatcher.org/document/104613.
9 James E. Cronin, *Global Rules: America, Britain and a Disordered World* (New Haven, CT: Yale University Press, 2014), 122, 149.
10 Quinn Slobodian, *Globalists: The End of Empire and the Birth of Neoliberalism* (Cambridge, MA: Harvard University Press, 2020).
11 David Harvey, *Neoliberalism: A Brief History* (Oxford: Oxford University Press, 2007), 2; Damien Cahill and Martijn Konings, *Neoliberalism* (Cambridge: Polity Press, 2017), 10.
12 George Ritzer and Paul Dean, *Globalization: The Essentials*, 2nd edition (Hoboken, NJ: Wiley-Blackwell, John Wiley & Sons, 2019), 42 (original emphasis).
13 *Ibid.*, 2 (original emphasis).
14 A. G. Hopkins, 'Introduction: Globalization – An Agenda for Historians', in A. G. Hopkins (ed.), *Globalization in World History* (London: Pimlico, 2002), 3.
15 Alfred E. Eckes, Jr. and Thomas W. Zeiler, *Globalization and the American Century* (Cambridge: Cambridge University Press, 2003), Chapters 6–7.
16 Daniel J. Sargent, *A Superpower Transformed: The Remaking of American Foreign Relations in the 1970s* (New York: Oxford University Press, 2015).
17 See Gary Gerstle, *The Rise and Fall of the Neoliberal Order: America and the World in the Free Market Era* (New York: Oxford University Press, 2022), 107–40.
18 Ben Jackson, 'The Think-tank Archipelago: Thatcherism and Neo-liberalism', in Ben Jackson and Robert Saunders (eds), *Making Thatcher's Britain* (Cambridge: Cambridge University Press, 2012), 43–61.
19 Vanessa Ogle, 'Archipelago Capitalism: Tax Havens, Offshore Money, and the State, 1950s–1970s', *American Historical Review*, 122: 5 (December 2017), 1431–58.
20 Slobodian, *Globalists*, 23.
21 Hal Brands, *Making the Unipolar Moment: U.S. Foreign Policy and the Rise of the Post-Cold War Order* (Ithaca, NY: Cornell University Press, 2016), 172–223; Gerstle, *The Rise and Fall of the Neoliberal Order*, 129–30.
22 Odd Arne Westad, *The Global Cold War: Third World Interventions and the Making of Our Times* (Cambridge: Cambridge University Press, 2005), 359–63.
23 Jim Tomlinson, *Managing the Economy, Managing the People: Narratives of Economic Life in Britain from Beveridge to Brexit* (Oxford: Oxford University Press, 2017), 93 (original emphasis).
24 MTF, Margaret Thatcher interview for *Daily Mail*, 17 May 1989, www.margaretthatcher.org/document/107477.
25 Nicholas Crafts, 'Economic Growth during the Long Twentieth Century', in Roderick Floud, Jane Humphries, and Paul Johnson (eds), *The Cambridge Economic History of Modern Britain*, vol. 2: *1870 to the Present* (Cambridge: Cambridge University Press, 2014), 26–59.

26 Nick Crafts, 'Reversing Relative Economic Decline? The 1980s in Historical Perspective', *Oxford Review of Economic Policy*, 7: 3 (Autumn 1991), 84.
27 David Edgerton, *The Rise and Fall of the British Nation: A Twentieth-Century History* (London: Allen Lane, 2018), 268.
28 Thatcher, *The Downing Street Years*, 501.
29 G. John Ikenberry, *A World Safe for Democracy: Liberal Internationalism and the Crisis of Global Order* (New Haven, CT: Yale University Press, 2020), 263; Brands, *Making the Unipolar Moment*, 220; Martin Jacques, *When China Rules the World: The End of the Western World and the Birth of a New Global Order*, 2nd edition (London: Penguin Books, 2012), 12, 16.
30 Thatcher, *The Downing Street Years*, 494–5.
31 Margaret Thatcher, *Statecraft: Strategies for a Changing World* (London: HarperCollins, 2003), 178 (original emphasis).
32 Richard Vinen, 'Thatcherism and the Cold War', in Jackson and Saunders (eds), *Making Thatcher's Britain*, 211.
33 Thatcher, *The Downing Street Years*, 801.
34 Ronald Keith, *Deng Xiaoping and China's Foreign Policy* (Abingdon: Routledge, 2018), 207.
35 Samuel S. Kim, 'Thinking Globally in Post-Mao China', *Journal of Peace Research*, 27: 2 (May 1990), 197.
36 Keith, *Deng Xiaoping and China's Foreign Policy*, 56–7.
37 *Deng Xiaoping wenxuan* [The Selected Works of Deng Xiaoping] (hereafter *DXW*), vol. 3 (Beijing: Renmin chubanshe, 1993), 29.
38 Hopkins (ed.), *Globalization in World History*; Jürgen Osterhammel and Niels P. Peterson, *Globalization: A Short History* (Princeton, NJ: Princeton University Press, 2005).
39 Ferguson, Maier, Manela, and Sargent (eds), *The Shock of the Global*; Sargent, *A Superpower Transformed*.
40 Samuel P. Huntington, *The Third Wave: Democratization in the Late Twentieth Century* (Norman, OK: University of Oklahoma Press, 1993); Edward Friedman (ed.), *The Politics of Democratization: Generalizing East Asian Experiences* (Boulder, CO: Westview Press, 1994).
41 Ezra F. Vogel, *Deng Xiaoping and the Transformation of China* (Cambridge, MA: Harvard University Press, 2011); Michael Dillon, *Deng Xiaoping: The Man who Made Modern China* (London: Tauris, 2015); Alexander V. Pantsov with Steven I. Levine, *Deng Xiaoping: A Revolutionary Life* (New York: Oxford University Press, 2015).
42 Julian B. Gewirtz, *Unlikely Partners: Chinese Reformers, Western Economists, and the Making of Global China* (Cambridge, MA: Harvard University Press, 2017).
43 Harry Harding, *A Fragile Relationship: The United States and China since 1972* (Washington, DC: Brookings Institution Press, 1992); David M. Lampton, *Same Bed Different Dreams: Managing U.S.-China Relations 1989–2000* (Berkeley, CA: University of California Press, 2001).
44 Francis Fukuyama, *The End of History and the Last Man* (London: Penguin, 1992).

45 Stephen D. King, *Grave New World: The End of Globalization, the Return of History* (New Haven, CT: Yale University Press, 2017), 7; Hopkins (ed.), *Globalization in World History*.
46 Jacques, *When China Rules the World*, 13–15; Odd Arne Westad, *Restless Empire: China and the World Since 1750* (London: The Bodley Head, 2012), 15.
47 Charles Moore, *Margaret Thatcher: The Authorized Biography*, vol. 1: *Not for Turning* (London: Allen Lane, 2013); *Margaret Thatcher: The Authorized Biography*, vol. 2: *Everything She Wants* (London: Allen Lane, 2015); *Margaret Thatcher: The Authorized Biography*, vol. 3: *Herself Alone* (London: Allen Lane, 2019); Jonathan Aitken, *Margaret Thatcher: Power and Responsibility* (London: Bloomsbury, 2013); Robin Harris, *Not for Turning: The Life of Margaret Thatcher* (London: Bantam Press, 2013); David Cannadine, *Margaret Thatcher: A Life and Legacy* (Oxford: Oxford University Press, 2017).
48 Jackson and Saunders (eds), *Making Thatcher's Britain*; Richard Vinen, *Thatcher's Britain: The Politics and Social Upheaval of the 1980s* (London: Pocket Books, 2010); Dominic Sandbrook, *Who Dares Wins: Britain, 1979–1982* (London: Penguin, 2020).
49 Percy Cradock, *In Pursuit of British Interests: Reflections on Foreign Policy under Margaret Thatcher and John Major* (London: John Murray, 1997); Robin Renwick, *A Journey with Margaret Thatcher: Foreign Policy under the Iron Lady* (London: Biteback Publishing, 2013).
50 James Cooper, *Margaret Thatcher and Ronald Reagan: A Very Political Special Relationship* (London: Palgrave, 2012); Richard Aldous, *Reagan and Thatcher: The Difficult Relationship* (London: Arrow Books, 2013); Archie Brown, *The Human Factor: Gorbachev, Reagan, and Thatcher, and the End of the Cold War* (Oxford: Oxford University Press, 2020).
51 Moore, *Margaret Thatcher*, vol. 2, 91; Vinen, *Thatcher's Britain*, 290; Sandbrook, *Who Dares Wins*, xxv.
52 Aitken, *Margaret Thatcher*, 424.
53 Hughes, R. Gerald, *The Postwar Legacy of Appeasement: British Foreign Policy since 1945* (London: Bloomsbury Academic, 2014), 183.
54 Ibid., 1–19.
55 For a historiographical overview, see Sidney Aster, 'Appeasement: Before and After Revisionism', *Diplomacy & Statecraft*, 19: 3 (2008), 443–80.
56 James L. Hevia, *Cherishing Men from Afar: Qing Guest Ritual and the Macartney Embassy of 1793* (Durham, NC: Duke University Press, 1995).
57 Christopher Meyer, *Getting Our Way: 500 Years of Adventure and Intrigue: The Inside Story of British Diplomacy* (London: Phoenix, 2010), 164.
58 Edward Heath, *The Course of My Life: My Autobiography* (London: Hodder and Stoughton, 1999), 653.
59 James L. Hevia, *English Lessons: The Pedagogy of Imperialism in Nineteenth-Century China* (Durham, NC: Duke University Press, 2003).
60 TNA, FO 371/187052, Hopson to de la Mare, 31 January 1966.
61 Percy Cradock, *Experiences of China* (London: John Murray, 1994); Geoffrey Howe, *Conflict of Loyalty* (London: Macmillan, 1994).

62 Robert Cottrell, *The End of Hong Kong: The Secret Diplomacy of Imperial Retreat* (London: John Murray, 1993); Mark Roberti, *The Fall of Hong Kong: China's Triumph and Britain's Betrayal* (New York: John Wiley & Sons, Inc., 1996).
63 Steve Tsang, *Hong Kong: An Appointment with China* (London: I.B. Tauris, 1997); Qi Pengfei, *Deng Xiaoping yu Xianggang huigui* [Deng Xiaoping and the Return of Hong Kong] (Beijing: Xinhua chubanshe, 2004); Chen Dunde, *Xianggang wenti tanpan shimo* [Negotiations for the Hong Kong Question From Beginning to End] (Hong Kong: Chung Hwa Book (HK) Company, 2009).
64 Li Hou, *Huigui de lichen* [The Journey of Retrocession] (Hong Kong: Joint Publishing (HK), 1997); Wong Man Fong, *China's Resumption of Sovereignty over Hong Kong* (Hong Kong: The David C. Lam Institute for East-West Studies, Hong Kong Baptist University, 1997); Lu Ping (with the collaboration of Qian Yijiao), *Lu Ping koushu Xianggang huigui* [Lu Ping Speaks on the Return of Hong Kong] (Hong Kong: Joint Publishing (HK), 2009); Zhang Chunsheng and Xu Yu, eds, *Zhou Nan jiemi GangAo huigui – ZhongYing ji ZhongPu tanpan taiqian muhou* [Zhou Nan's Leaks about the Return of Hong Kong and Macao to their Motherland – Sino-British and Sino-Portuguese Talks and their Background] (Xianggang: Zhonghua chubanshe, 2012).
65 Moore, *Margaret Thatcher*, vol. 2, 9–19, 95–103.
66 *Ibid.*, 19.
67 Michael Sheridan, *The Gate to China: A New History of the People's Republic & Hong Kong* (London: William Collins, 2021), Chapters 4–5.
68 I first developed the theme of 'educating' China in 'To "Educate" Deng Xiaoping in Capitalism: Thatcher's Visit to China and the Future of Hong Kong in 1982', *Cold War History*, 17: 2 (June 2017), 161–80.
69 John Darwin, *Britain and Decolonisation: The Retreat from Empire in the Post-War World* (London: Palgrave, 1988); *Unfinished Empire: The Global Expansion of Britain* (London: Allen Lane, 2012); *The Empire Project: The Rise and Fall of the British World-System* (Cambridge: Cambridge Press, 2009).
70 Martin Thomas and Andrew S. Thompson, 'Rethinking Decolonization: A New Research Agenda for the Twenty-First Century', in Martin Thomas and Andrew S. Thompson (eds), *The Oxford Handbook of the Ends of Empire* (Oxford: Oxford University Press, 2018), 1–26.
71 On the relationship between the British Empire and globalisation, see Gary B. Magee and Andrew S. Thompson, *Empire and Globalisation: Networks of People, Goods and Capital in the British World, c.1850–1914* (Cambridge: Cambridge University Press, 2010). On the American Empire's role in globalisation, see A. G. Hopkins, *American Empire: A Global History* (Princeton, NJ: Princeton University Press, 2018).
72 A. G. Hopkins, 'Rethinking Decolonization', *Past and Present*, 200 (August 2008), 215–16.
73 Thomas and Thompson, 'Rethinking Decolonization', 16.
74 *Ibid.*, 18.

1

Anglo-Chinese relations, 1979

On 13 March 1972, Britain and China reached an agreement on the establishment of full diplomatic relations. Until this point, despite London's diplomatic recognition of the PRC as early as January 1950, Beijing had refused to reciprocate due to a number of factors: Chinese representation in the UN, Taiwan's status, and the issue of Hong Kong (which could be exploited to split the Anglo-American alliance during the Cold War). Only when the British no longer insisted on the 'undetermined' status of Taiwan did China agree to exchange ambassadors.[1] A new chapter was opened in Anglo-Chinese relations, characterised by frequent ministerial visits, increased bilateral trade, and cultural exchanges during the 1970s. Foreign Secretary Alec Douglas-Home visited China between 29 October and 2 November 1972, and his Chinese counterpart, Ji Pengfei, reciprocated in June 1973. Britain's exports to China more than doubled, from £31.5 million in 1972 to about £80 million the following year.[2] The London Philharmonic Orchestra gave a notable performance in China in March 1973, and a Chinese exhibition of archaeological discoveries opened at the Royal Academy in London in September of that year.[3]

After Harold Wilson started his second spell as prime minister in March 1974, Anglo-Chinese political relations cooled because of his eagerness to seek détente with the Soviet Union. But James Callaghan, succeeding Wilson in April 1976, took a more critical stance towards Moscow.[4] The death of Premier Zhou Enlai in January that year, and of Chairman Mao Zedong in September, created political uncertainty in China. Not until after the announcement of a modernisation programme by Premier Hua Guofeng, Mao's designated successor, in February 1978 did the prospects for Anglo-Chinese relations improve. In late July, the British ambassador to China, Percy Cradock, filed a long report on Anglo-Chinese relations to the FCO. By helping to make China 'a more Western-oriented and even a slightly more open society', he argued, Britain would turn China into 'a major factor for Asian and world stability'. Now that Chairman Mao had gone, 'a favourable moment for stable Chinese development and good Sino/UK relations' had arrived.[5]

This chapter examines Anglo-Chinese relations during the Callaghan–Thatcher transition and the first eight months of the Thatcher premiership, starting in May 1979. It is necessary to start with an overview of Thatcher's diplomatic approach and Deng Xiaoping's opening-up policy.

Thatcher and British diplomacy

Margaret Hilda Roberts was born in Grantham, Lincolnshire, on 13 October 1925. Her father was the owner of a local grocery shop and a devout Methodist, who instilled a strong work ethic and a sense of civic duty in his daughter. After graduating from Somerville College, Oxford, with a chemistry degree in 1947, Margaret Roberts worked briefly as a research chemist. In 1951 she married Denis Thatcher, a successful businessman whose wealth enabled Mrs Thatcher, as Margaret Roberts was renamed, to train and then practise as a barrister.[6] In October 1959, Thatcher was elected for the safe Conservative seat of Finchley. In 1961, Thatcher was appointed to the junior ministerial post of parliamentary secretary at the Ministry of Pensions and National Insurance under Harold Macmillan's premiership. When the Tories returned to power after six years of Labour rule in late 1970, Prime Minister Edward Heath promoted Thatcher to secretary of state for education and science. Five years later, however, Thatcher challenged Heath's party leadership, and saw off other competitors to become the leader of the opposition during Harold Wilson's second Labour government.[7] By exploiting the so-called 'winter of discontent' and promising a free-market alternative to the Keynesian model, Thatcher defeated James Callaghan's Labour in the general election on 3 May 1979.[8]

While pledging to roll back the welfare state and to rescue Britain's long-term economic decline, Thatcher herself did not have 'an intellectually orderly mind'. Rather, she borrowed (and implemented) 'the ideas of others',[9] for example, those of Keith Joseph, Friedrich Hayek, and Milton Friedman. Over time, there emerged 'Thatcherism', a vague set of principles and values characterised by free markets, monetarism, low taxation, weak union power, privatisation, democracy, and the rule of law.[10] Thatcher was not only a conviction politician, but also an effective public performer,[11] skills that would help her win a second term in 1983 and a third in 1987. Thatcher had a dominant leadership style, concentrating as much power as possible in her hands and intimidating ministers whom she deemed 'wet'.[12]

Thatcher's diplomatic approach was shaped by her strong beliefs in freedom, law, and progress. She attached importance to the Anglo-American 'special relationship', which had been the cornerstone of British foreign policy since 1947, thanks to common interests, shared language and tradition, and personal trust. In the 1980s, Thatcher enjoyed a 'special personal relationship' with President Ronald Reagan, with the pair sharing a neoliberal ideology of anti-communism, free enterprise, and freedom across the globe.[13] Given her strong conviction in capitalism, Thatcher regarded 'the growing Soviet threat' as one of the main challenges facing Britain.[14] On Europe, Thatcher was a reluctant pro-marketeer: she demanded 'getting our money back' from the European Community in the form of a significant budget rebate.[15] Although, in 1986, Thatcher signed the Single European Act in the hope of creating a genuine single market in Europe, her vision for Europe was 'a Community of open trade, light regulation and freely co-operating sovereign nation-states' rather than a supranational entity as envisioned by socialist François Mitterrand of France and Christian Democrat Helmut Kohl of West Germany.[16] Rather than confining itself to Europe, Thatcher saw Britain as a global trading nation, and, for that matter, China as an important player in economic globalisation.

Thatcher's first encounter with China can be dated back to April 1977. As leader of the opposition, Thatcher visited China between 7 and 13 April as part of her Far Eastern trips. Due to her strong anti-Soviet stance, Thatcher was accorded a warm reception by the Chinese leaders, who 'wanted to see Britain and Western Europe support the United States in balancing Soviet power'. She received an audience with Party Chairman and Premier Hua Guofeng, who succeeded the late Mao Zedong in late 1976. During their talks, Hua stressed the theme of denouncing the Soviet Union and the Gang of Four. Besides Beijing, Thatcher travelled to Suzhou, Hangzhou, and Shanghai, where she visited factories and academic institutions.[17] It appeared that Thatcher did enjoy a trek to the famous Great Wall. After climbing the wall, Thatcher jokingly asked Douglas Hurd, her parliamentary private secretary who accompanied her to China: 'Did I get to the top quicker than Ted [Heath]?'[18] Back in 1974, Hurd had accompanied Edward Heath, then leader of the Conservative Party, on a trip to China. Unlike Heath's fascination with the Middle Kingdom, Thatcher 'did not feel at home at all', and instead found the Chinese approach 'wholly alien' to her.[19] As Hurd recollected, Thatcher 'disliked the Chinese system' and was particularly 'appalled' at the 'efficiently imposed uniformity of thought' of the Chinese people.[20] Thatcher's impression of Hua's China exemplified her aversion to socialism.

During her first term as prime minister (1979–83), Thatcher was preoccupied with economic matters. Lacking foreign affairs experience, she could not but rely on Foreign Secretary Lord Carrington, with whom she developed 'an occasionally stormy but generally successful relationship'.[21]

Thatcher had a far less harmonious relationship with her second foreign secretary, Francis Pym, following Carrington's resignation as a result of the Falklands War in early April 1982. Geoffrey Howe, who succeeded Pym in June 1983, was able to form a close partnership with Thatcher. Following her landslide victory in the 1983 general election, Howe was chosen as foreign secretary because Thatcher regarded 'his preference for negotiation and discussion ... over making decisions' as a good fit for her leadership style.[22] Howe's diplomatic style was characterised by 'patient and lawyerly negotiation leading to incremental advance and well-crafted compromise'.[23]

The formulation of China policy fell within the responsibility of the FCO. While the prime minister and the Cabinet made decisions, the specialists in the Far Eastern and the Hong Kong Departments, together with the British diplomats in China, drafted policy papers and offered advice that informed those decisions. In particular, Percy Cradock, UK ambassador in China between 1978 and 1983, was the formidable figure behind Britain's China/Hong Kong policy during the Thatcher years. A Cambridge graduate who had worked as a law tutor at his alma mater before joining the Foreign Office, Cradock became a Sinologist by studying Mandarin in Hong Kong. During his posting to the British Chargé d'Affaires Office in Beijing in the mid-1960s, Cradock had survived the Red Guards' harassment resulting from the Chinese Cultural Revolution.[24] Between October 1982 and late 1983, Cradock was the chief British negotiator at the Anglo-Chinese talks over Hong Kong's future. Cradock had earned Thatcher's trust, so much so that he was appointed as her foreign policy adviser at 10 Downing Street in 1984 and, a year later, simultaneously as chairman of the Joint Intelligence Committee. During 1984, Cradock continued to oversee the Hong Kong negotiations in his capacity as deputy under secretary in the FCO. The 'good working relationship' between Thatcher and Cradock helped strengthen the links between Number 10 and the FCO.[25]

To Cradock, China was 'of critical importance to Britain in the Hong Kong context'.[26] Indeed, Britain's China policy was inextricably linked with its Hong Kong policy. Both set of policies were formulated by a 'Cold War generation of diplomatic Sinologists' centred on Cradock.[27] These FCO mandarins shared a similar educational background and China experiences, as well as a similar mindset about how diplomacy should be conducted. Murray MacLehose, an Oxford graduate and a Chinese linguist, had served in the British consulate in Hankou in the late 1940s and headed the Foreign Office's Far Eastern Department in the mid-1960s, becoming the Hong Kong governor between 1971 and 1982. David Wilson, who had also attended Oxford, studied Chinese, and served in the British mission in Beijing, was appointed as MacLehose's political adviser in 1977. (Coincidentally, both MacLehose and Wilson were Scots or 'Scottish Mafia'.)[28] Edward Youde, who received Chinese training at London's School of Oriental and African Studies (where Wilson got his doctorate) and had been involved in negotiations with the Chinese communists during the 1949 *Amethyst* crisis, was the British ambassador in China from 1974 to mid-1978. In mid-June 1978, Cradock succeeded Youde as ambassador. In mid-1982, Youde succeeded MacLehose as Hong Kong governor, and served until his sudden death in early December 1986. In April 1987, Wilson was appointed as the new governor. Such was Cradock's network of Sinologists involving Wilson, MacLehose, and Youde. As Kerry Brown, himself a former British diplomat who has served in China, observes: 'For people like Cradock, diplomacy was never about moral considerations. It was about their definition of a world of hard and fast facts and clearly designed interests.'[29] To Cradock, the aim was 'to negotiate quietly but tenaciously with China in pursuit of Hong Kong's interests, to press as hard as [Britain] could, but not to enter on trials of strength [Britain] could only lose and to avoid defiance and open breaches'.[30] The Sinologists played a vital role in guiding the Thatcher government towards a pragmatic policy towards China.

In Britain, China policy was not a matter for bureaucratic infighting and domestic politics. While the Ministry of Defence and the Treasury, for example, might not always see eye to eye with the FCO over China issues that had wider military and financial implications, any differences could normally be resolved through interdepartmental consultation. In Parliament, the prime minister and the foreign secretary were seldom subjected to intense pressure, partly because the Labour opposition, no matter whether under Michael Foot (1980–83) or Neil Kinnock (1983–92), was 'politically ineffective'.[31] While respecting tradition and the constitution, Thatcher's decision-making style was such that she was inclined to marginalise Parliament, particularly after securing large majorities in the House of Commons in 1983 and 1987.[32] Nevertheless, during the Hong Kong negotiations, Thatcher and Howe found it 'important to keep influential MPs closely informed'. It was not because there was a constitutional need to consult Parliament first, although the government would need to secure the enactment of the necessary implementing legislation before ratification of an agreement. Rather, Thatcher realised that Parliament was interested in obtaining (if not how to obtain) a settlement that was genuinely acceptable to Hong Kong people, lest the government would face domestic criticism and,[33] worse still, an exodus of Hong Kong citizens to Britain.

Non-governmental organisations with a stake in China played a role in Anglo-Chinese relations. The Sino-British Trade Council, founded in 1954 by the five representative bodies of the British industry, including the China Association, with official support helped British companies to crack into the China market. Its operations included briefing British trade missions to China on request, publishing a monthly English-language bulletin about Sino-British trade, and maintaining links with the Office of the Chinese Commercial Counsellor in London. In its trade promotion activities, the Sino-British Trade Council maintained close contact with officials in the Department of Trade (where a China unit was set up in late 1978 to coordinate Whitehall's efforts) and with diplomats in the British Embassy in Beijing.[34] The '48 Group of British Traders with China', which emerged out of the 1952 Moscow International Economic Conference, was dedicated to promoting trade between Britain and China, albeit that it was more left-leaning than the Sino-British Trade Council and was not endorsed by the government.[35] British organisations that facilitated cultural exchanges with China included the Great Britain–China Centre, inaugurated in 1974. To seize the initiative from the left-wing Society for Anglo-Chinese Understanding, in 1972 the FCO had established the Great Britain–China Committee, consisting of ex-diplomats, politicians, and businessmen like Malcolm MacDonald, Michael Stewart, and John Keswick,[36] which evolved into the centre two years later. The Great Britain–China Centre received an annual grant of £25,000 from the FCO, and administrative support from the British Council.[37] It sponsored visits to the mainland, entertained distinguished Chinese visitors, administered the Educational Trust for funding academic exchanges, and ran a regular programme of talks and film shows.[38]

Deng Xiaoping and China's opening policy

Deng Xiaoping was born to a landlord family in Guang'an, Sichuan Province, on 22 August 1904. It was the time when China under the Qing dynasty was on the brink of collapse amid Western imperialism and Chinese revolutionary activities. In the early 1920s, after China became a republic, Deng studied and worked in France, before leaving for the Soviet Union to study communism. After seven years abroad, Deng returned to China to join the Chinese Communist Party (CCP). Accused of being a leader of the 'Mao [Zedong] faction', in 1931 Deng was purged by the pro-Moscow elements within the party. In retrospect, this would be the first of Deng's 'thrice banished, thrice rehabilitated' experiences in his long political career.[39] After the founding of the PRC on 1 October 1949, Deng assumed regional party leadership roles in Tibet and southwest China. Between 1952 and the mid-1960s, Deng, who had been transferred back to Beijing, served as vice premier and general secretary of the Party Central Committee. In the wake of Mao's disastrous Great Leap Forward campaign, Deng along with President Liu Shaoqi stepped in to inaugurate a programme of economic readjustment. This turned out to be the origin of Deng's second purge, this time by Chairman Mao. Shortly after the outbreak of the Chinese Cultural Revolution in 1966, Deng, accused of being a 'capitalist roader', fell into disgrace. Starting from 1973, Deng was gradually rehabilitated by Mao. By early 1975, Deng was vice chairman of the Party Central Committee, vice premier of the State Council, vice chairman of the Central Military Commission, and chief of the general staff of the People's Liberation Army (PLA). However, the death of Premier Zhou Enlai on 8 January 1976 and, three months later, the outburst of protests by students and workers at Tiananmen Square resulted in Deng being purged for the third time on the grounds of masterminding the 'counter-revolutionary riots'.[40] On 9 September of that year, Mao passed away at the age of eighty-two. Shortly afterwards, Premier Hua Guofeng, supported by army and party veterans, arrested the Gang of Four, thus paving the way for Deng's third political comeback.

At the Third Plenum of the Tenth Party Central Committee on 16–21 July 1977, a resolution was passed to restore Deng's party, government, and military positions.[41] The Eleventh Party Congress held the following month further elected Deng as vice chairman of the CCP, while Hua Guofeng was party chairman and chairman of the Central Military Commission.[42] Behind the scenes, however, the struggle for supremacy between Hua, a 'whateverist' who stubbornly followed whatever policy decisions Mao made, and Deng, a pragmatist who was planning for reform, was underway. At the Third Plenum of the Eleventh Party Central Committee on 18–22 December 1978, Deng's policy of reform and opening up was approved.[43] During 1980 and 1981, Deng strove to out-manoeuvre Hua by building a reform-oriented 'nuclear core' centred on him. In September 1980, Zhao Ziyang took over the premiership; and in July 1981, Hu Yaobang became chairman (renamed general secretary in September 1982) of the CCP. Deng preferred not to hold formal titles himself. He stepped down as vice premier in 1980, and in 1987 he took 'voluntary retirement' from all party posts, retaining only the chairmanship of the Central Military Commission.[44] But there is no doubt that Deng was China's paramount leader from 1979.

New research has shown that the stirrings of reform could be traced back to the pre-Deng Xiaoping era. Under Mao Zedong's rule, communist traders and diplomats, or 'market Maoists', had made deals with foreign capitalists with the aim of strengthening the Chinese state.[45] In view of the economic chaos caused by the Great Leap Forward, in 1961 communist cadres in Bao'an County (which would later become the City of Shenzhen – discussed below) had carried out 'exceptional policies' to facilitate cross-border trade with capitalist Hong Kong.[46] After China had normalised relations with the United States, Japan, and Western European countries in the early 1970s,

Premier Zhou Enlai (with Vice Premier Deng) advocated, in his 1975 government work report, 'the comprehensive modernization of agriculture, industry, national defence, and science and technology'. In February 1978, Party Chairman Hua Guofeng (despite his 'whateverism') unveiled an ambitious ten-year modernisation programme for the period 1976–85 (despite a two-year lapse). It concentrated on heavy industry through the importation of Western technology and turnkey plants.[47] Not until after Deng's ascendancy, however, did the reform gather momentum and China fully embrace 'a new Third Way promoting an outwardly oriented, consultative economic paradigm'.[48] Economically, Deng was a pragmatist, as captured by his famous 'cat theory': 'Whether black cat or white cat, as long as it catches mice it is a good cat'.[49]

In 1979, Deng had no master plan for reform. Consequently, Guangdong provincial officials, such as First Party Secretary Xi Zhongxun and Second Party Secretary Yang Shangkun, took the initiative to allow Guangdong to 'go one step ahead' of the rest of China.[50] Early that year, Beijing agreed to the establishment of the 'Shekou Industrial Zone', located within the City of Shenzhen to the north of Hong Kong, as the first 'export processing zone'. Indeed, the idea originated from a suggestion by the China Merchants Company in Hong Kong to create a site in Shekou for recycling old Chinese vessels.[51] On 15 July, the Party Central Committee and the State Council approved Xi and Yang's proposal for the adoption of a 'special policy' with 'flexible measures' in Guangdong and Fujian.[52] On 26 August 1980, the 'special economic zones' (SEZs) were officially inaugurated in Shenzhen, Zhuhai, Shantou, and Xiamen. Deng had chosen these places due to their geographical proximity to Hong Kong or Taiwan, whose wealthy and enterprising Chinese diasporas were encouraged to support China's reform. By providing tax breaks, tariff incentives, and a cheap labour force, Deng hoped that the SEZs would play a pivotal role in attracting foreign investment and technology and in promoting China's exports.[53]

But Deng's reform got off to a tough start. Hua Guofeng's ambitious modernisation programme had caused macroeconomic imbalances, trade deficits, and high inflation. This necessitated a policy of three-year 'readjustment' (April 1979 to 1981) as proposed by Chen Yun, a conservative party elder.[54] Worrying about the impact of external opening on the domestic economy and particularly state-owned enterprises, Chen insisted on the policy cycles of 'two steps forward, one step back'. At the heart of the differences between conservatives and reformers was the relative importance of plan and market. Since 1979, China's gradual departure from the command economy had been characterised by a 'dual-track system' or 'the coexistence of a traditional plan and a market channel'. A two-tier pricing system was created for most goods, with a normally lower state-set price and a typically higher market price.⁵⁵ To Chen, a 'planned economy' was 'fundamental' and 'primary', while a 'market mechanism' was 'necessary' but 'secondary'.⁵⁶ In justifying the reform, Deng queried why socialist countries could not practise a 'market economy', which he insisted was not the same as 'capitalism'. Regarding a 'planned economy' as 'the fundamental', albeit with the addition of a 'market economy', Deng aimed to build a 'socialist market economy'.⁵⁷ In Deng's view, both the planned economy and market economy were means to build socialism rather than defining characteristics of different social systems.⁵⁸

If Deng was a pragmatist in economic terms, he remained dogmatic when it came to political reform. In late 1978, Beijing students and residents put up dazibaos or 'big-character posters' at the Democracy Wall in Xidan in support of the Four Modernisations. A former Red Guard named Wei Jingsheng penned a dazibao calling for 'the Fifth Modernisation: Democracy'.⁵⁹ Against this backdrop, on 30 March 1979, Deng delivered a speech to party cadres: 'We must persistently uphold the Four Cardinal Principles: defend the socialist path, the dictatorship of the proletariat, the leadership of the party, and Marxism-Leninism and Mao Zedong Thought.'⁶⁰ The Democracy Wall was closed down as a result. While advocating economic reform, Deng had no intention of weakening the political dominance of the CCP. As such, China's reform since 1979 was characterised by a recurrent pattern of oscillation between 'soft Leninism' and 'hard Leninism', or a *'fang-shou* cycle'.⁶¹ Economic reform flowed (*fang*) and ebbed (*shou*) between market-oriented and state-oriented policies in response to the socio-economic-political problems that emerged in China at the time.⁶²

From a wider perspective, Deng pursued a strategy of 'independent globalisation', which combined seamlessly an 'open door' with the principle of 'self-reliance'.⁶³ It symbolised China's 'independent opening', in that Beijing would hold the initiative of determining the degree and pace of engagement with the outside world.⁶⁴ In Deng's assessment, 'peace' and 'development' were replacing wars and 'struggles' as the major themes of the 1980s.⁶⁵ Yet in 1979 and 1980, Deng observed that the international situation had not been 'relaxed' but had become 'more tense'. 'Hegemonism' was 'the most dangerous source of war in the world', with the Soviet Union posing the main threat to China.⁶⁶ In view of the revived Soviet threat, Deng decided to expedite the negotiations over Sino-American normalisation, which resulted in the establishment of diplomatic relations on 1 January 1979. While forming a de facto strategic alliance with the United States, Deng basically followed Mao Zedong's Theory of the Three Worlds, arguing that China permanently belonged to the Third World.⁶⁷ Deng regarded a 'strong and united' Europe – the Second World – as crucial to the maintenance of a peaceful international environment.⁶⁸ Western Europe, including Britain, figured prominently in China's strategy of opposing Soviet hegemonism, promoting European integration, and seeking advanced technology and capital for the Four Modernisations.[69]

Anglo-Chinese relations during the Callaghan–Thatcher transition

During the Callaghan–Thatcher transition, several decisions and events had policy implications for the future Thatcher government: preliminary discussions with the Chinese about the sale of Harrier aircraft; the conclusion of an ambitious agreement on Anglo-Chinese economic cooperation; and a convergence of strategic views on the Soviet Union in the light of the Sino-Vietnamese Border War. The early 1970s had witnessed significant British strategic exports to China, including the sales of thirty-five Trident aircraft by Hawker Siddeley and contracts with Rolls-Royce for the manufacture of Spey 202 aero-engines in China. Since then, the Chinese had demonstrated interest in the Harrier (a vertical take-off and landing fighter), marine gas turbines, communications equipment for ships, and so forth.[70] In the 1970s, the Chinese air force consisted mainly of the J-6 fighter, a version of the Soviet MiG-19. After resuming his position in the Central Military Commission in mid-1977, Deng Xiaoping found it imperative to modernise the Chinese air force due to frequent plane accidents, inadequate training, and poor aircraft quality.[71] Thus, Chinese officials and aviation experts attended the British Army Equipment Exhibition in June 1978 and the Farnborough Air Show in September of that year in order to scrutinise the latest British military technologies.[72] The Chinese also made shopping trips to France and West Germany because by that time the United States was unwilling to sell arms to China.[73]

In April 1978, the FCO and the Ministry of Defence (MoD) produced a joint paper setting out the general considerations and political implications of selling Harriers to China. From a commercial point of view, in 1976 British exports of goods to China totalled US$125 million, as compared with German exports worth US$623 million and French exports worth US$335 million. Although China had 'never made any open or even implied link between civil and military sales', the paper noted, a successful conclusion of one or more military deals could lead to certain further related civil exports. As for the strategic arguments, British defence sales would increase China's offensive capability, enable Beijing to increase military assistance to Third World countries, and provoke an adverse reaction from Moscow. But the strategic advantages outweighed the disadvantages: defence sales would increase China's ability to defend itself against the Soviet Union, benefit British industry and employment, and have a positive political impact on

British interests in Hong Kong. Concerning the attitude of the Coordinating Committee for Multilateral Export Controls (COCOM), strategic exports to China were being treated on the same basis as those to the Soviet Union. But since December 1977, special procedures had allowed member countries to argue for particular military sales that would not prejudice the strategic interest of the West. In sum, the joint paper recommended arms sales to China 'within the limits of what the British Government believe to be acceptable in strategic terms' and of what main COCOM partners would agree, while reserving the right to go ahead despite COCOM opposition 'unless the general political or commercial objections appear to outweigh the advantages of the sale'.[74]

James Callaghan's government had to consider the attitudes of both Moscow and Washington. By 1978, Anglo-Soviet relations had fallen away from the high point of détente, symbolised by the 1975 Helsinki Act, due to growing Soviet military strength and Moscow's support for Cuban intervention in Angola and the Horn of Africa. Callaghan hoped to rejuvenate the détente with the Soviet Union, not least to avoid an arms race.[75] It was to Britain's advantage to maintain 'good relations' with both the Soviet Union and China.[76] The Soviets, for their part, were determined to sabotage any British defence sales to China, thanks to deteriorating Sino-Soviet relations, which in turn were influenced by China's growing tensions with Vietnam (which allied itself with Moscow). On 20 November 1978, Leonid Brezhnev sent a personal message to Callaghan, warning that defence sales to China were 'a dangerous development' that should be 'stopped, and stopped in time, without delay'.[77] In view of the revived Soviet threat, by early 1978 US President Jimmy Carter had shifted from a policy of 'even-handedness' towards both the Soviet Union and China, as advocated by Secretary of State Cyrus Vance, to a pro-China 'tilt' proposed by National Security Adviser Zbigniew Brzezinski. Over Vance's objection, Carter was prepared to transfer advanced civilian and dual-purpose technology to China on a case-by-case basis. Although the ban on US arms sales to China remained in force, Washington announced in mid-1978 that it would no longer object to defence sales by Western European allies.[78] With the establishment of Sino-American diplomatic relations in 1979, Carter's position on the Harrier sale was such that Washington would 'neither encourage nor discourage the sale of defensive weapons' to China.[79] On 16 January, Callaghan announced in Parliament that the British government was ready to negotiate with China the sale of the Harrier, which was 'essentially a defensive aircraft', provided this was 'balanced by substantially increased trade in other fields which would bring significant benefit to our civilian export industries'.[80]

Callaghan's mention of 'civilian export industries' was significant, for he saw defence sales as part of a larger trade package in order to foster a strong economic relationship with China. Back in November 1978, Wang Zhen, Chinese vice premier, had visited Britain. During his meeting with Callaghan on the 16th, Wang revealed that the Four Modernisations adopted by Premier Hua Guofeng 'represented a new Long March towards the achievement of the great goal which China had set herself'. In this regard, China welcomed the proposed efforts by both countries to 'achieve the target of a level of trade of between $8-$10 billion by 1985', particularly the supply of modern industrial equipment and technology by Britain. Callaghan fully agreed, believing that the target should be $10 billion. He proposed to conclude an agreement on economic cooperation, a draft of which was handed over to the Chinese.[81]

During the visit, Wang and Foreign Secretary David Owen signed an agreement on scientific and technological cooperation. Accordingly, both countries agreed to promote, on the basis of equality and mutual benefit, exchanges and cooperation between British and Chinese scientists, scholars, researchers, postgraduate students, and technicians in the field of science and technology.[82] Secretary of State for Industry Eric Varley accepted Wang's invitation to visit China in early 1979 to sign an economic cooperation agreement.[83] But before Varley set off for China, Deng Xiaoping had decided to launch an attack on Vietnam.

The Sino-Vietnamese Border War between 17 February and 16 March 1979 was triggered by Vietnam's invasion of Cambodia in late 1978 to topple the pro-Beijing Khmer Rouge regime. Yet Deng approached what he called China's 'self-defence counter-attack' from a wider geopolitical and domestic political perspective. The Vietnamese occupation of Cambodia, intensified Sino-Vietnamese border clashes, and Hanoi's alignment with Moscow: all were seen within the global context of the Soviet efforts to 'encircle' China. In countering the growing Soviet threat and Vietnamese regional ambitions, Deng found a golden opportunity to consolidate China's new strategic alliance with the United States and his domestic political position. During his high-profile visit to the United States in late January/early February 1979, Deng obtained from President Carter the 'green light' to wage a limited war against Vietnam.[84]

During the Sino-Vietnamese Border War, Britain demonstrated a degree of strategic convergence with China. While calling for both sides to cease fighting, Britain felt reassured that China's action was 'a limited one' and 'would not last long or cover a wide area'.[85] On the other hand, Britain was frustrated with Vietnam's refusal to withdraw from Cambodia, while expressing concern about the Vietnamese refugee problem and particularly Hanoi's apparent attempts to 'export its unemployment and other difficulties to the poor and developing countries in South East Asia'.[86] On 5 March 1979, China announced its military withdrawal from Vietnam.[87]

Although the PLA's operational performance on the battlefield had been poor, Deng's sense of victory lay in his assessment of the geopolitical outcomes: he had taught the Vietnamese a 'bitter lesson', while demonstrating China's strategic value to the United States.[88] While not supporting any arms sales to China in the midst of the war, Callaghan 'had some sympathy with the Chinese objective of ensuring that the longstanding Soviet aim of trying to organise South East Asia did not come to anything'.[89] In the opinion of H. A. H. Cortazzi, deputy under secretary of state at the FCO, although China was fighting the Vietnamese, 'the action was in fact hitting at the Soviet Union' in order to 'deal a heavy blow to the USSR for instigating the Vietnamese to launch hegemonic expansion in South East Asia'. The Sino-Vietnamese conflict coincided with Secretary of State for Industry Eric Varley's visit to China. The fact that Varley's visit went ahead as planned 'showed that the British Government was not easily blown off course'.[90]

The Callaghan government had set 'ambitious objectives' for Varley's trade mission to China from 24 February to 5 March. While the signing of the agreement on economic cooperation was 'one of the main objectives', the 'prime objective' of the visit concerned 'obtaining of contracts, letters of intent, or agreements in principle over a number of industrial sectors so as to produce a substantial balanced package'.[91] As Vice Premier Wang Zhen's guest, Varley led a party of twenty-nine officials, industrialists, and journalists. He had an intensive programme, featuring talks with Premier Hua Guofeng, Vice Premiers Li Xiannian and Wang Zhen, eight ministers including Minister of Foreign Trade Li Qiang, and representatives of the Bank of China and the State Planning Commission.[92]

Varley met with Wang Zhen on his first full day in China. Referring to the prime minister's comment the previous year (1978) that the two countries should have 'a balanced relationship in all respects – political, commerce and economic, defence and cultural', Varley hoped that the visit would lead to 'the closest possible UK involvement in China's modernisation'. Wang brought up the draft economic cooperation agreement provided by the British. He recalled, during his previous visit to Britain, that the two sides had agreed to make reference to a figure of US$10 billion as the target of trade up to 1985. However, Britain now proposed US$20 billion, although China regarded US$10 billion as 'more realistic'. Wang confided to Varley that the French figure of US$14 billion, according to the 1978 Sino-French economic cooperation agreement, was 'really too large'. Besides, Wang raised the issue of technology transfer. China was ready to undertake 'many projects where advanced technology, reasonable price, and favourable terms were offered'. Although sometimes the asking price might be too high, 'if terms were roughly equal, Britain would be at the forefront of China's consideration'. Varley replied that 'British equipment was fully competitive', and that Britain was in a position to help China to develop its exports to third markets.[93]

On 4 March, Varley was received by Premier Hua Guofeng. Concerning the draft economic cooperation agreement, Hua said that although some of his colleagues 'had had misgivings about agreeing a high figure because of the problem of "insolvency"', he thought that the figure of US$14 billion might be 'reached and exceeded'. But Hua also sounded a note of caution about the prospects for Sino-British economic relations. In the initial stages, 'the pace of trade and cooperation might not be fast but should move forward steadily on a solid footing'. Although China hoped to import at an accelerating rate, it had to contemplate 'the problem of disbursement' and the 'problem of the assimilation of imported equipment'.[94]

Following the Hua–Varley meeting, a signing ceremony was held at the Great Hall of the People, where Varley and Li Qiang put their signatures to the agreement on economic cooperation. Accordingly, Britain and China should 'take all possible measures to create favourable conditions for strengthening economic co-operation' and for 'bringing about a rapid increase in their economic ties', so that 'the total value of joint economic activity shall as far as possible reach US dollars 14 billion' during the period from 1979 to 1985. The two countries should 'expand economic co-operation and exchanges involving technology transfers, manufacturing equipment and products' in the following sectors: agriculture, textile industry, consumer goods industry, food processing and packaging industry, machine-building industry, coal industry, oil and natural gas industry, aerospace industry electronics, telecommunications, consultancies, and so forth. The agreement should enter into force on the day of signature, and remain in force until 31 December 1985.[95]

Reporting to the FCO, Ambassador Percy Cradock regarded Varley's mission as a 'substantial success'. The economic cooperation agreement was accompanied by an exchange of letters, stipulating the British provision of a credit facility of US$5 billion up to 31 March 1985. Given the Chinese desire for not over-committing themselves to their modernisation drive, together with the limits of time, Cradock acknowledged that it was impracticable for the British to sign any specific contracts or letters of intent in the course of the visit. Nevertheless, Cradock believed that Britain was now 'in a position to gain major benefit from the Chinese market', although it needed to 'remain commercially competitive' and to ensure 'resolute follow-up by firms in each field'.[96] Callaghan agreed that Varley's was 'clearly a very good visit'.[97]

However, Callaghan could not reap the political benefits of Varley's trade mission as he lost the general election of 3 May 1979 to Margaret Thatcher.

Thatcher and Hua Guofeng's visit to Britain

The main thrust of the Conservative government's policy towards defence sales to China did not depart much from its Labour predecessor's. According to a brief for the Cabinet Defence and Overseas Policy Committee in early June 1979, 'the Chinese have shown considerable interest in virtually the whole range of British defence equipment'. Foreign Secretary Lord Carrington recommended the approval of certain categories of defence sales, which would create no 'substantial impact on the military balance, vis-à-vis the Soviet Union' and which would raise no objection in principle from COCOM partners but would bring about substantial 'commercial, industrial and employment benefits' to Britain.[98] When the Defence and Overseas Policy Committee convened on 11 June, Carrington pointed out that six specific items, including the Harrier, were now ready for formal approval by the government. He drew ministers' attention to the fact that if clearance for these items was sought through COCOM, the United States would veto them; but if Britain proceeded outside the formal COCOM machinery, the Americans would be prepared to tacitly acquiesce in their sales. As Thatcher summarised the discussion, Britain should inform its COCOM partners of its intentions without seeking their concurrence. British companies, in close consultation with the government, should proceed with negotiations with the Chinese over the Harrier and other non-offensive items.[99]

A small team from British Aerospace arrived in Beijing in early July to submit the detailed technical proposals for the Harrier. The initial Chinese response was that 'the price was too high', and the proposed escalation formula was unacceptable. Moreover, the Chinese expressed 'strong disappointment at the absence of an offer to supply BL 755 Cluster Bomb' in the package.[100] As a matter of fact, the basic price of seventy Harrier aircraft was about £350 million, with an additional £105 million for estimated price escalation and £130 million for spares. The value of the licence and parts for manufacturing Harriers in China would amount to £150–200 million.[101] As for the BL 755 cluster bomb, the MoD held that it was classed as 'a highly lethal weapon', and that sensitivity about its sales to the likes of China and Arab states 'derived partly from their potential use in internal repression'. Nevertheless, given China's demand and the FCO's lobbying, the MoD later agreed that the BL 755 cluster bomb was 'equipment associated with Harrier supply', and its sale to China would 'not remotely upset the strategic balance, or threaten the security of the Soviet Union'.[102]

In late August, British Aerospace was informed that a Chinese evaluation team would visit Britain in October to evaluate the Harrier aircraft and its equipment. Yet the Chinese were still unable to give a definite number of Harriers they wanted to buy.[103] As it turned out, no Chinese evaluation team arrived in Britain that month. Worse still, there was an apparent absence of discussion between the Chinese and British Aerospace for the rest of 1979, prompting the company's deputy chairman to conclude in February 1980 that 'the line seemed to have gone dead over Harriers'. Michael Palliser, permanent under secretary of state at the FCO, believed that the Chinese hesitation about the Harrier sale was related to fierce competition between the British and US arms industries. While concern about the British price might be one factor, Palliser suspected that the Chinese 'hoped, in the light of their developing relationship with the United States, that before too long they might be able to get American aircraft on more favourable terms'.[104] True, Washington adopted a more relaxed attitude towards defence sales to China during 1979 in view of the rapidly changing international environment, from the overthrow of the pro-US Shah in Iran early in the year (which resulted in the loss of intelligence facilities there) to the Soviet invasion of Afghanistan in December (which elevated the value of the US–China strategic alliance). In early January 1980, just before leaving office, President Carter authorised the sale of 'non-lethal' military equipment to China on a case-by-case basis, although it remained official policy not to sell arms to that country.[105]

In essence, China's lack of interest in the Harrier sale by 1979 had to do with its three-year economic readjustment policy.[106] Due to Hua Guofeng's rush for modernisation through the importation of technology and turnkey industrial plants, there was an imbalance between industrial and agricultural development (the latter of which had been relatively neglected) and within the industrial sector (heavy industry had been privileged over light industry). In April, the Chinese government adopted the principles of 'readjustment, reform, consolidation, [and] improvement' to develop the economy in the next three years.[107] Facing a shortage of foreign exchange, together with defence as a low priority in the Four Modernisations, China found it imperative to bargain over price and to buy a smaller number of Harriers than had originally been envisaged.[108] By March 1980, Beijing had in mind an initial purchase of twelve Harriers, with possible subsequent orders of twelve more.[109] Eventually, the Harrier negotiations collapsed amid China's continuing austerity programme.[110]

The Thatcher government faced not only China's haggle over the Harrier's price, but also stiff competition from other countries, such as Japan, the United States, and West Germany, in terms of civilian trade with China.[111] Since the establishment of full diplomatic relations in 1972, Anglo-Chinese trade had flourished, but by 1978 China still occupied an insignificant share of Britain's total exports and imports. In 1973, the value of Britain's exports to China (mainly aircraft, electrical machinery, textiles, and iron and steel) jumped nearly threefold from that of the previous year to £84.8 million, representing 0.7 per cent of its total exports. Britain's imports from China (mainly foodstuffs and raw materials) totalled £47.8 million, or 0.3 per cent of its total imports, thus yielding a favourable trade balance. Since 1976, Britain began to suffer from a trade deficit with China, and the China share in both Britain's total exports and imports remained about 0.3 per cent.[112]

Given her eagerness to promote free-trade globalisation, Thatcher attached importance to the visit to Britain by Premier Hua Guofeng between 28 October and 3 November 1979. Hua's visit represented 'the climax of a series of exchanges in the political, commercial and cultural fields which China has developed with Britain, and more generally with the West', since Mao Zedong's death.[113] As part of his European tour, including stops in France, West Germany, and Italy, Hua's was the first ever visit to Britain by a Chinese premier. According to the FCO, the British objectives were to 'impress Premier Hua with Britain as a stable prosperous society'; 'reaffirm the importance we attach to Sino-British relations and to the development of a stable, responsible and prosperous China'; 'establish a working understanding with the Chinese Government at the highest level'; 'promote our commercial interests' in China; and 'develop our understanding with the Chinese over Hong Kong'. The British were to accord Hua, who was not formally head of state of the PRC,[114] 'a reception corresponding in most respects to Head of State treatment', including a guard of honour at the welcoming ceremony, luncheon given by the Queen, and substantive talks with the prime minister and other key ministers. A carefully planned programme for Hua's strong delegation featured visits to the facilities of British transport, energy, and agriculture industries and cultural entertainment.[115]

On 29 October at Downing Street, Thatcher held the first plenary session with Hua, concentrating on international issues. Hua first expressed a complimentary comment on Thatcher: 'In China she was very much respected as a leader, for her insight into the international situation.' Given her anti-Soviet stance, Thatcher talked of a world with 'many limited areas of tension' – Southeast Asia, Iran, the Horn of Africa, and southern Africa particularly Rhodesia – and wondered 'whether all these formed part of a grand design or whether they represented opportunism by the Soviet Union making trouble where it could'. She suggested that the two sides should begin with Southeast Asia because of 'the tragedy taking place there': over half a million refugees had fled Vietnam. Thatcher revealed that she had raised the issue with Soviet Premier Alexei Kosygin, who was asked to 'use his influence with the Vietnamese authorities to dissuade them from turning so many people out'. Contrary to Kosygin's claim that 'all those leaving were drug addicts, criminals or spies', Thatcher believed that their expulsion was 'deliberately designed to hurt the refugees themselves, to hurt those countries which received them and to cause instability in South East Asia'.

Hua professed that, after the end of the Vietnam War, the Hanoi leadership aimed to build 'an Indochina Federation', with 'the backing of the Soviet Union', in order to achieve 'regional hegemony'. Hua then gave his rendering of Soviet global strategy. He asserted that 'in the West there was Cuba and in the East there was Vietnam', and that both countries 'acted on behalf of the Soviet Union'. He criticised the 'Soviet meddling' in the affairs of Afghanistan, Iran, and (with Cuba) South Yemen. While the Soviet Union was increasing its pressure on Western Europe (for example, by deploying SS20 intermediate missiles in Eastern Europe), 'its strategic design seemed to be to encircle Europe from its periphery', with a particular interest in the oil-producing countries in the Middle East. Thatcher expressed her general agreement with Hua, feeling 'confident that both the US and Western Europe would hold fast in the West, and looked to China and Japan to do so in the East'.[116]

On the next day, the discussions focused on trade issues. Accompanied by a group of ten British businessmen, Secretary of State for Trade John Nott called on Premier Hua at Claridge's. Hua said that China was 'a vast market with its population of 900 million', and hoped to 'buy as much advanced technology from British firms as early as possible'. At the time, China was 'adjusting its economy', and it was 'still poor and still a developing country'. But Hua believed that there was still 'wide scope for the expansion of Sino-British trade'. Nott asked each British businessman in turn to give a presentation on his industry. Lord Nelson of Stafford, chairman of General Electric Company and president of the Sino-British Trade Council, summarised the role of the council in promoting trade and the company's electric power equipment and experience in power transmission over long distances. Allen Greenwood, deputy chairman of British Aerospace, talked of aircraft and anti-tank missiles. Hua interjected by acknowledging that Britain was 'in the lead in the list of countries with whom China co-operated in the field of civil aviation'. As for other British companies, Wogen Buckton Group concentrated on compensation trade, the British Agricultural Export Council on agricultural cooperation, and the '48 Group' on joint ventures.[117]

On the same day, Nott along with Secretary of State for Industry Keith Joseph held separate talks with Vice Premier Yu Qiuli. The two secretaries sought to impress upon the Chinese the achievement of the British industries. Joseph said that Britain had 'great experience in coal mining', and was willing to help China develop coal mines 'with a full transfer of technology and perhaps under joint ventures'. He enquired about the purchase of a nuclear power station by the Guangdong provincial authorities, highlighting that Britain's 'safety record was second to none'. Nott, referring to Britain as 'a major maritime nation', hoped to reach an agreement on modernisation of port facilities at Shanghai. Although Britain was 'an urban society', he stressed, it was considered to have 'the most efficient agriculture in Europe'. In response, Yu said that as China needed to carry out 'the re-adjustment of the national economy', which was linked with agricultural development, there was scope for cooperation in relation to farming equipment, insecticides, and poultry. Besides, China, facing a worldwide fuel problem, wanted to buy know-how to renovate its energy industry, such as coal extraction. When discussing the issue of civil aviation, the two sides had some disagreement. After several years of negotiation, an air services agreement had been initiated in July, but there was a dispute over the choice of airport in London. Although Nott hoped to begin air services immediately, it was the British government's 'firm rule that no new services were allowed to use Heathrow'. He recommended the use of Gatwick, but Yu insisted on Heathrow.[118]

On 1 November, Thatcher held a second round of talks with Hua at Downing Street, focusing on bilateral economic issues. She began with the topic of Hong Kong's immigration problems, and raised the issue of Hong Kong's future at the end of the meeting (see Chapter 2). On Sino-British trade, Thatcher said that Britain was ready to supply China with a wide range of defence equipment, including the Harrier, despite pressure from Moscow. Praising the prime minister for 'taking a far sighted political view of the problem', Hua argued that if China achieved the modernisation of national defence, it would be 'in a better position to serve as a restraint on the Soviet Union'. To Hua, Britain had 'advanced technology in this field', and 'its munitions industry could produce more advanced equipment than Britain needed'. Britain could 'go into joint production with China, whose needs were greater'. Turning to civilian trade, Thatcher assured Hua that China would 'receive all cooperation possible on the development of commercial relations', such as coal mining and power generation. Hua mentioned that China now had total offers of 20 to 30 billion dollars of credit, but it was important to be prudent and to consider its ability to pay for what it really wanted. Concerning the unsigned air services agreement, John Nott said that if Heathrow was to be opened to new airlines, the British government would try its best to get the Civil Aviation Administration of China (CAAC), the Chinese state airline, in. But he insisted that Gatwick was 'the better airport', while hoping that air services would begin no later than April 1980. Vice Foreign Minister Zhang Wenjin said that if Heathrow was opened to new airlines, CAAC should be 'the first on the list'. Thatcher confirmed with Hua that the air services agreement would be signed at end of the meeting. During an informal conversation just before signature, the two sides decided that the agreement would be signed 'on the understanding that, if Heathrow was opened to new airlines, CAAC would be given priority; but that this would not be a formal condition of signature, and that the British Government could not commit themselves to putting China top of the list'. In the presence of Thatcher and Hua, Nott and Yu inked the air services agreement.[119]

Thatcher and Hua, moreover, witnessed the signing of an agreement on education and cultural exchange by their foreign secretaries on the same day. Indeed, since the visit to China of the then secretary of state for education, Shirley Williams, in July 1978, the British government had agreed to a greatly expanded programme of exchanges with China. It focused mainly on the placing in Britain of up to 1,000 Chinese researchers and postgraduate students a year in the field of science and technology, and the recruitment of English-language teachers for key institutions in China. Other areas of cultural exchange included the strengthening of links between British and Chinese scientific societies and institutions (such as the Royal Society and the Chinese Academy of Sciences); provision of postgraduate scholarships for Chinese students in Britain; and exploration of British cooperation with the Chengdu University of Science and Technology.[120] According to the new education and cultural exchange agreement, Britain and China would adopt all necessary measures to promote cooperation and exchanges in the fields of education, culture, arts, publishing, health, youth, and sports.[121]

At 9:30 am on 3 November 1979, Hua's party took off from Heathrow, flying to Italy as the final leg of his European tour. Ambassador Cradock reported to the FCO that the visit was 'a very great success'. After the meetings between Hua and Thatcher, the Chinese had told him that 'they knew they could speak more freely in London than in Paris or Bonn'.[122] According to Deputy Under Secretary Cortazzi, the visit 'should have helped to encourage moderate, outward-looking policies in China'. During the numerous conversations, the British had demonstrated that the UK was 'eager to help China develop its economy', while expecting China to 'assume its responsibilities as a major world power'. That said, Cortazzi had not formed a high opinion of the personality of Hua, who was 'detached, impassive and impersonal' and who lacked 'the sureness of touch of a Mao or a Zhou'. Nevertheless, Britain could not afford to 'ignore China's growing political, economic and commercial weight'. Britain's 'long-term commercial prospects' would 'depend on the progress of China's modernisation programme and on the competitiveness of British firms'. With Hua's visit being 'a useful first step', Britain should be able to 'establish a reasonable and mutually advantageous relationship with China over the next 20 years and beyond'.[123]

Cortazzi was right to be optimistic about Anglo-Chinese economic relations as Deng Xiaoping was the main architect of China's reform.

Conclusion

In May 1979, Thatcher came to power with the aim of reversing Britain's relative economic decline and restoring its power and influence abroad. With her neoliberal belief in free-market capitalism, she saw the globalisation of free trade as essential to her vision of 'Global Britain'. The policy of economic reform and opening up launched by Deng Xiaoping in late 1978 provided a golden opportunity for Britain to integrate China into the global economy. By helping its modernisation, the Thatcher government hoped to 'educate' China in its responsibilities as a major power in the liberal international order. In Deng's vision, though, China was pursuing 'independent globalisation' with an emphasis on sovereignty and socialism, different from Thatcher's neoliberal variant. Under the influence of conservatives like Chen Yun, the Chinese government created a dual-track system by using both the plan and market to guide the transition from the command economy. Deng's initial reform took a step back in April 1979, when a three-year readjustment policy was inaugurated. While being pragmatic in economic terms, Deng had no intention of embracing Western-style democracy – hence the shutdown of the Democracy Wall and the upholding of the Four Cardinal Principles.

During 1979, Anglo-Chinese relations were enhanced and institutionalised by reciprocal high-level visits and the conclusion of a series of agreements on economic cooperation, cultural and science exchanges, and air services. Hua Guofeng's high-profile visit to Britain in October/November was of symbolic significance. As Thatcher stated in the return dinner held at the Chinese Embassy in London, Hua's was a 'historic visit' that 'raised our common interests to a new level' and 'laid a solid foundation for the further development of these interests in the future'.[124] Nevertheless, the lack of progress in the Harrier negotiations (which eventually collapsed) and the modest level of Britain's trade with China raised a few question marks over the competitiveness of British companies. In an increasingly globalised world, Thatcher, considering the Chinese as 'one of the world's most enterprising peoples',[125] realised that Britain had to compete with West Germany, France, the United States, and Japan in the China market. How to restore Britain's status as a global trading nation was one of the main challenges she faced. Meanwhile, Thatcher and the FCO were confronted with the question of Hong Kong's future.

Notes

1 See Chi-kwan Mark, *The Everyday Cold War: Britain and China, 1950–1972* (London: Bloomsbury Academic, 2017).
2 Wang Weimin, *Bainian zhongying guanxi* [A Century of Sino-British Relations] (Beijing: Shiji zhishi chubanshe, 2006), 277–9, 281–2; TNA, FCO 21/1226, Addis to Douglas-Home, 'China: Annual review for 1973', 31 December 1973.
3 Robert Bickers, *Out of China: How the Chinese Ended the Era of Western Domination* (London: Allen Lane, 2017), 367–9.
4 Wang, *Bainian zhongying guanxi*, 280–1.
5 TNA, FCO 21/1611, Beijing to FCO, nos. 469, 470, and 471, 31 July 1978.
6 Dean Palmer, *The Queen and Mrs Thatcher: An Inconvenient Relationship* (Stroud, Gloucestershire: The History Press, 2016), 55–6.
7 Cannadine, *Margaret Thatcher*, 9–23.
8 John Shepherd, *Crisis? What Crisis? The Callaghan Government and the British 'Winter of Discontent'* (Manchester: Manchester University Press, 2013).
9 Moore, *Margaret Thatcher*, vol. 1, 302.
10 Saunders, '"Crisis? What Crisis?" Thatcherism and the Seventies', in Jackson and Saunders (eds), *Making Thatcher's Britain*, 25–42.
11 Moore, *Margaret Thatcher*, vol. 1, 302.
12 Brown, *The Human Factor*, 100.
13 Cronin, *Global Rules*, 122, 149.
14 Thatcher, *The Downing Street Years*, 9.
15 Renwick, *A Journey with Margaret Thatcher*, 93–6.
16 Thatcher, *The Downing Street Years*, 536.
17 Margaret Thatcher, *The Path to Power* (London: Harper Press, 2011), 388–91 (quote on 390); Churchill Archives Centre, Churchill College, Cambridge, UK (hereafter CAC), Papers of Baroness Thatcher, THCR 1/10/7, 'Itinerary for the visit of Mrs Thatcher, leader of the British Conservative Party'.
18 Moore, *Margaret Thatcher*, vol. 1, 365.
19 *Ibid*.
20 Douglas Hurd, *Memoirs* (London: Abacus, 2004), 144.
21 Aitken, *Margaret Thatcher*, 283.
22 Moore, *Margaret Thatcher*, vol. 2, 68.
23 'Obituaries: Lord Howe: Faithful Conservative chancellor and foreign secretary under Margaret Thatcher who later rebelled against her leadership style', *The Sunday Telegraph* (11 October 2015).
24 See Mark, *The Everyday Cold War*, Chapter 4.
25 Cradock, *In Pursuit of British Interests*, 26; Sherard Cowper-Coles, *Ever the Diplomat: Confessions of a Foreign Office Mandarin* (London: HarperCollins, 2012), 86.
26 Cradock, *In Pursuit of British Interests*, 203.
27 Kerry Brown, *What's Wrong with Diplomacy? The Future of Diplomacy and the Case of the UK and China* (Melbourne: Penguin Group (Australia), 2015), 16.

28 CAC, British Diplomatic Oral History Programme, GBR/0014/DOHP 83, Interview with David Clive Wilson (Lord Wilson of Tillyorn), 19 September 2003, p. 32.
29 Brown, *What's Wrong with Diplomacy?*, 16–17.
30 The Library, St. John's College, Cambridge (hereafter SJC), Papers of Percy Cradock, Cradock/B/8, Cradock to Major, 17 November 1992.
31 Anthony Seldon, with Jonathan Meakin and Illias Thoms, *The Impossible Office? The History of the British Prime Minister* (Cambridge: Cambridge University Press, 2021), 159.
32 *Ibid.*, p. 133.
33 TNA, PREM 19/1057 Part 8, Note of meeting on 5 September 1983; FCO 40/1737, Burrows to Hum, 8 October 1984.
34 BLO, Uncatalogued Papers of Lord Callaghan, Box 280, Research Department note: 'General information on the People's Republic of China', enclosed in Wye memo, August 1979; TNA, BT 241/3201, Lord Nelson of Stafford to Caines, 28 October 1982.
35 Shao Wenguang, *China, Britain and Businessmen: Political and Commercial Relations, 1949–1957* (London: Macmillan, 1991), 153–4.
36 CAC, Papers of Michael Stewart, STWT 10/1/7, 'Great Britain–China Committee', 23 March 1972.
37 Priscilla Roberts, 'Bringing the Chinese State Back In: The Role of Quasi-Private Institutions in Britain and the United States', in Priscilla Roberts and Odd Arne Westad (eds), *China, Hong Kong and the Long 1970s: Global Perspectives* (London: Palgrave Macmillan, 2017), 308–9; Tom Buchanan, *East Wind: China and the British Left, 1925–1976* (Oxford: Oxford University Press, 2012), 209.
38 BLO, Uncatalogued Papers of Lord Callaghan, Box 280, Brooke to Callaghan, 6 August 1986.
39 On Deng's first purge, see 'Deng Xiaoping: Gaige shi Zhongguo de dierci geming' bianxie zu, *Deng Xiaoping: Gaige shi Zhongguo de dierci geming* [Deng Xiaoping: Reform is China's Second Revolution] (Beijing: Taihai chubanshe, 2017), 1–5.
40 *Deng Xiaoping nianpu, 1975–1997* [A Chronicle of Deng Xiaoping, 1975–1997] (hereafter *DXN*), vol. 1 (Beijing: Zhongyang wenxian chubanshe, 2004), 149–50.
41 *Ibid.*, 162–3.
42 *Ibid.*, 185.
43 *Ibid.*, 454–6.
44 Lu Ning, *The Dynamics of Foreign Policy Decisionmaking in China* (Boulder, CO: Westview Press, 1997), 156–9, 162.
45 Jason M. Kelly, *Market Maoists: The Communist Origins of China's Capitalist Ascent* (Cambridge, MA: Harvard University Press, 2021).
46 Taomo Zhou, 'Leveraging Liminality: The Border Town of Bao'an (Shenzhen) and the Origins of China's Reform and Opening', *Journal of Asian Studies*, 80: 2 (May 2021), 337–61.

47 Lawrence C. Reardon, *A Third Way: The Origins of China's Current Economic Development Strategy* (Cambridge, MA: Harvard University Asia Center, 2020), 18–19.
48 Ibid., 33.
49 Deng had uttered the 'cat theory' as early as 1962, although by that time he referred to a 'yellow', not 'white', cat. Ruan Ming, *Deng Xiaoping: Chronicle of an Empire* (Boulder, CO: Westview Press, 1994), 4–5.
50 *Xi Zhongxun wenji* [The Collected Works of Xi Zhongxun], vol. 1 (Beijing: Zhonggong dangshi chubanshe, 2013), 506–17.
51 Shenzhen shi shizhi bangongshi (ed.), *Zhongguo Gongchandang Shenzhen lishi dashiji, 1921–2011* [A Historical Record of Key Events of the Chinese Communist Party in Shenzhen, 1921–2011] (Shenzhen: Shenzhen baoye jituan chubanshe, 2012), 175; Li Lanqing, translated by Ling Yuan and Zhang Siying, *Breaking Through: The Birth of China's Opening-up Policy* (New York: Oxford University Press, 2009), 73–87.
52 Gu Mu, *Gu Mu huiyilu* [Memoir of Gu Mu] (Beijing: Zhongyang wenxian chubanshe, 2009), 323–5.
53 Vogel, *Deng Xiaoping and the Transformation of China*, 399–406.
54 Zhonggong Zhongyang wenxian yanjiushi (ed.), *Chen Yun duiwai kaifang sixiang xingcheng he fazhan* [The Formation and Development of Chen Yun's Thinking about External Opening] (Beijing: Zhongyang wenxian chubanshe, 2013), 82, 93.
55 Barry Naughton, *The Chinese Economy: Transitions and Growth* (Cambridge, MA: The MIT Press, 2007), 91–2, 97–8; Bao Pu, Renee Chiang, and Adi Ignatius (eds. and trans.), *Prisoner of the State: The Secret Journal of Zhao Ziyang* (London: Pocket Books, 2010), 95–6.
56 *Chen Yun wenxuan* [The Selected Works of Chen Yun], vol. 3 (Beijing: Renmin chubanshe, 1995), 245.
57 *DXW*, vol. 2, 231–6.
58 Su Xing (et al.), *Deng Xiaoping shehuizhuyi shichang jingji lilun yu Zhongguo jingji tizhi zhuangui* [Deng Xiaoping's Theory of Socialist Market Economy and the Changing Trajectory of China's Economic Institution] (Beijing: Renmin chubanshe, 2008), 46.
59 *DXN*, vol. 1, 501–3.
60 *DXW*, vol. 2, 158–84.
61 David Shambaugh, *China's Leaders: From Mao to Now* (Cambridge: Polity Press, 2021), 23.
62 Alvin So and Yin-Wah Chu, *The Global Rise of China* (Cambridge: Polity, 2015), 20. Also see Yang Jisheng, *Gaige niandai de zhengzhi douzheng* [Political Struggles during the Reform Years] (Hong Kong: Excellent Culture Press, 2004).
63 Keith, *Deng Xiaoping and China's Foreign Policy*, 56–7.
64 Zheng Bijian (et al.), *Jingji quanqiuhua yu Zhongguo jingji jueqi* [Economic Globalisation and the Economic Rise of China] (Beijing: Zhonggong zhongyang dangxiao chubanshe, 2006), 106.

65 Shu Guang Zhang, *Beijing's Economic Statecraft during the Cold War, 1949–1991* (Washington, DC: Woodrow Wilson Centre Press, 2014), 262.
66 *DXN*, vol. 1, 490–1.
67 *Ibid.*, 200–1.
68 *Ibid.*, 389, 467.
69 Harish Kapur, *Distant Neighbours: China and Europe* (London: Pinter Publishers, 1990), 143, 170; Martin Albers, *Britain, France, West Germany and the People's Republic of China, 1969–1982: The European Dimension of China's Great Transition* (London: Palgrave Macmillan, 2016), 173–5.
70 TNA, PREM 16/1535, Far Eastern Department steering brief: 'Defence sales', 20 April 1978.
71 John Wilson Lewis and Xue Litai, *Imagined Enemies: China Prepares for Uncertain War* (Stanford, CA: Stanford University Press, 2006), 218–20.
72 David Crane, 'The Harrier Jump-Jet and Sino-British Relations', *Asian Affairs*, 8: 4 (March–April 1981), 230.
73 Kapur, *Distant Neighbours*, 144–6.
74 TNA, PREM 16/1535, 'British defence sales to China', 16 March 1978.
75 TNA, PREM 16/1535, Cartledge to Prendergast, 20 March 1978.
76 TNA, PREM 16/1535, Limited Circulation Annex (5 May 1978), CM(78)17th Conclusions, 4 May 1978.
77 TNA, PREM 16/1536, Brezhnev to Callaghan, 20 November 1978.
78 Harding, *A Fragile Relationship*, 88–9.
79 Crane, 'The Harrier Jump-Jet and Sino-British Relations', 240.
80 *Hansard*, House of Commons Debates, vol. 960, 16 January 1979, col. 1497.
81 TNA, PREM 16/1536, Record of Callaghan's discussion with Wang Zhen on 16 November 1978.
82 Wang Hongxu, *Qishi niandai yilai de ZhongYing guanxi* [Sino-British Relations since the 1970s] (Harbin: Heilongjiang jiaoyu chubanshe, 1996), 87–8.
83 TNA, PREM 16/1536, Department of Industry press notice: 'Big increase in UK-Chinese trade planned', 17 November 1978.
84 See Xiaoming Zhang, *Deng Xiaoping's Long War: The Military Conflict between China and Vietnam, 1979–1991* (Chapel Hill, NC: The University of North Carolina Press, 2015), 40–66; James Mann, *About Face: A History of America's Curious Relationship with China, from Nixon to Clinton* (New York: Random House, 1999), 98–100.
85 TNA, FCO 21/1701, FCO to Beijing, no. 181, 20 February 1979.
86 TNA, FCO 21/1701, FCO to Hanoi, no. 41, 19 February 1979; FCO to Hanoi, no. 43, 19 February 1979.
87 TNA, FCO 21/1704, Beijing to FCO, no. 283, 5 March 1979.
88 Zhang, *Deng Xiaoping's Long War*, 138–40.
89 TNA, FCO 21/1704, 'The Prime minister's telephone conversation with Chancellor Schmidt on 6 March 1979'; Beijing to FCO, no. 283, 5 March 1979.
90 TNA, FCO 21/1703, Record of call by Chinese ambassador on minister of state for foreign and Commonwealth affairs, 4 p.m., 26 February 1979.
91 TNA, FCO 21/1710, Department of Trade to Beijing, no. 36, 8 February 1979.

92 TNA, FCO 21/1710, Cradock to Owen, 12 March 1979.
93 TNA, FCO 21/1710, Duguid note: 'Varley's opening discussions with Wang Zhen on 25 February 1979 at 8:30 am', February 1979.
94 TNA, FCO 21/1710, Note of meeting between Varley and Hua Guofeng on 4 March 1979.
95 TNA, FCO 21/2687, Agreement on economic cooperation between the government of the UK and the government of the PRC, 4 March 1979.
96 TNA, FCO 21/1710, Cradock to Owen, 12 March 1979; Varley to Callaghan, 6 March 1979.
97 TNA, FCO 21/1710, Private Secretary at Downing Street to Duguid, 12 March 1979.
98 TNA, DEFE 69/662, Secretary of state for defence brief for Cabinet Defence and Overseas Policy Committee meeting, 8 June 1979.
99 TNA, FCO 21/1723, Extract from OD(79)2nd meeting on 11 June 1979.
100 TNA, FCO 21/1723, Smith to Masefield, 11 July 1979.
101 TNA, FCO 21/1721, Cotterill to Kelley, 19 January 1979.
102 TNA, FCO 21/1723, Cheesman to Fursland, 9 August 1979; Fursland to Cheesman, 23 July 1979.
103 TNA, FCO 21/1723, Fozard to Chandler, 31 Aug 1979; Parker to Fan Chunchui, 3 September 1979.
104 TNA, FCO 21/1820, Palliser to McLaren, 5 February 1980.
105 Harding, *A Fragile Relationship*, 92; Hugo Meijer, 'Balancing Conflicting Security Interests: U.S. Defense Exports to China in the Last Decade of the Cold War', *Journal of Cold War Studies*, 17: 1 (Winter 2015), 7–12.
106 Crane, 'The Harrier Jump-Jet and Sino-British Relations', 245. Kapur, *Distant Neighbours*, 148–9.
107 *DXN*, vol. 1, 497, 505–6.
108 TNA, FCO 21/1820, McLaren to Cradock, 26 February 1980; Beijing to FCO, no. 202, 5 March 1980.
109 TNA, FCO 21/1820, Beijing to FCO, no. 232, 18 March 1980; Smith to Miles, 7 March 1980.
110 TNA, FCO 21/1904, Cradock to Carrington, 'China: Annual review for 1980', 6 January 1981.
111 On the comparative trade figures, see Albers, *Britain, France, West Germany and the People's Republic of China*, 300–1.
112 TNA, PREM 16/1535, 'Annex II: Statistics on British defence sales to China', 16 March 1978, enclosed in Prendergast to Cartledge, 13 April 1978.
113 BLO, Uncatalogued Papers of Lord Callaghan, Box 280, 'Visit of Chinese Premier Hua Guofeng, 28 October–3 November 1979', enclosed in Fursland to Sharpe, 23 October 1979.
114 Ye Jianying, one of the founding marshals of the PLA and a supporter of Deng Xiaoping, served as China's head of state in his capacity as chairman of the Standing Committee of the NPC.

115 TNA, FCO 21/1712, Cortazzi to Cradock, 29 November 1979; Jiang Enzhu, *Daguo jiaoliang: ZhongOu guanxi yu Xianggang huigui qinli* [Great Power Contest: Witnessing Sino-European Relations and the Return of Hong Kong] (Beijing: Zhongxin chuban jituan, 2016), 127.
116 TNA, FCO 21/1711, Record of discussion between Thatcher and Hua Guofeng on 29 October 1979.
117 TNA, FCO 21/1711, Hampson note, 30 October 1979.
118 TNA, FCO 21/1712, Hampson note, 30 October 1979.
119 TNA, FCO 21/1712, Record of discussion between Thatcher and Hua Guofeng on 1 November 1979.
120 TNA, BW 23/60, Llewellyn to Blaker, 9 July 1979; Sedgwick-Jell to Hull, 27 December 1979.
121 Wang, *Qishi niandai yilai de ZhongYing guanxi*, 77.
122 TNA, FCO 21/1712, Beijing to FCO, no. 969, 7 November 1979.
123 TNA, FCO 21/1712, Cortazzi to Cradock, 29 November 1979.
124 Jiang, *Daguo jiaoliang*, 128.
125 Thatcher, *Statecraft*, 164.

2

Globalisation without decolonisation? Hong Kong, 1979–81

Hong Kong history to 1979

During the nineteenth century, Hong Kong was established as a British Crown Colony in three stages. After Britain had defeated Qing China in the First Opium War (1839–42), the Treaty of Nanking (Nanjing) of 1842 ceded Hong Kong Island to the UK in perpetuity. After another Chinese defeat, this time by Anglo-French forces, in the Second Opium War (1856–60), Britain acquired the Kowloon Peninsula under the 1860 Convention of Peking (Beijing). During the so-called 'scramble for concessions' in China, Britain obtained a ninety-nine-year lease of the New Territories according to the 1898 Convention of Peking. The three treaties gave colonial Hong Kong a land area of approximately 391 square miles, including some two hundred islands.[1] The British acquired Hong Kong not for the sake of territorial ambitions (Foreign Secretary Lord Palmerston once dismissed Hong Kong as 'a barren island', although pre-colonial Hong Kong had been a settled community with different sorts of economic activities) or exploitation of its natural resources (which did not exist, except for its deep harbour).[2] Nor did the colonial founders' vision of 'Anglo-China' turn into an ambitious 'civilising mission'. (Instead, early British Hong Kong was plagued with crime and racial discrimination.)[3] Rather, Hong Kong was seen primarily as a staging ground for the promotion of British economic interests in China, although Shanghai, opened as a treaty port in 1842, turned out to be the hub of Britain's informal economic empire in China during the nineteenth and early twentieth centuries.[4]

The colonial system of Hong Kong was defined by the Letters Patent and the Royal Instructions. The governor ruled through an Executive Council, comprising ex-officio and appointed members (the latter of whom were drawn mainly from the corporate and professional services sectors), and a Legislative Council, a wholly appointed body (until 1985). The British Empire in Hong Kong survived the collapse of Qing China in 1911 and the Guangzhou–Hong Kong strike boycott in 1925–26, but not Japan's invasion in December 1941, after which Hong Kong was occupied for three years and eight months. Following Japan's defeat in the Second World War, in September 1945 the British returned to Hong Kong, taking advantage of US President Harry Truman's subordination of anti-colonialism to Anglo-American relations and Chiang Kai-shek's preoccupation with the impending Chinese civil war. After the founding of the PRC on 1 October 1949, the British were relieved to learn that the Chinese communists were willing to leave Hong Kong alone, thanks to its strategic and economic value in the Cold War against the United States. While not recognising the legality of the three 'unequal treaties', China adopted a policy of 'long-term planning, full utilisation' towards Hong Kong.[5]

After 1945, Hong Kong's politics, economy, and society could not be immune from events and developments in Britain, China, and the wider world. Politically, Governor Mark Young contemplated constitutional reform, focusing on an elected Municipal Council, in the hope of developing a sense of citizenship among Hong Kong Chinese. The Young Plan, however, received a cool reception from the unofficial members of the Legislative Council. Alexander Grantham, who succeeded Young in mid-1947, proposed instead an enlarged Legislative Council, which would have a majority of unofficial members and be partly elected by a limited franchise. By September 1952, both Grantham and the British Cabinet decided to abandon all plans for constitutional reform, fearing that the CCP–Guomindang struggle would be extended to local elections and believing that the majority of the Hong Kong population was uninterested in democracy.[6] Not until the mid-1960s, during David Trench's governorship, did the British re-examine the issue, this time concentrating on local administration.[7] But when large-scale leftist riots, inspired by the Chinese Cultural Revolution, broke out in May 1967, any proposed changes to local government were brought to a halt. Prior to the riots, China had stated more than once that it would not tolerate 'a self-governing Hong Kong', which was seen as a prelude to independence.[8] Fear or assumptions of China's opposition to democratic reform,[9] together with the (perceived) political apathy of the local people,[10] meant that the Hong Kong government remained a 'benevolent autocracy' until the early 1980s.

If Hong Kong's political system remained unchanged for three decades after 1945, this was not the case for its economy and society. Since 1842, Hong Kong had served as a primary node for the flow of goods, people, and ideas between China and the rest of the world.[11] It was an important entrepôt for trade with China. The imposition of US and UN embargoes on China as a result of the 1950–53 Korean War, and China's economic reorientation towards the Soviet bloc, significantly reduced the volume of entrepôt trade.[12] China, however, continued to supply essential foodstuffs to, and receive overseas Chinese remittances through, Hong Kong. Another consequence of the Chinese civil war and the Cold War was the influx of Chinese refugees, including both entrepreneurs from Shanghai and unskilled peasants from Guangdong, to Hong Kong in the late 1940s and beyond. The trade embargoes on China propelled Hong Kong to the path of industrialisation, a process that had begun in the 1930s and was now intensified by the expertise of Shanghai textile industrialists and the availability of Cantonese refugees as a cheap labour force.[13] Besides, Hong Kong benefited economically from its position within the Sterling Area, which allowed preferential access to the Commonwealth markets, and from its maintenance of a free dollar market to facilitate entrepôt trade with East and Southeast Asia, which, however, created a 'dollar gap' that contravened London's exchange controls.[14] By the late 1950s, Hong Kong's export-oriented industrial economy began to take off, with textiles and garments being its main pillar and the United States becoming its largest export market. Hong Kong's economic success was such that the textile industry was forced to accept, in 1959, 'voluntary restrictions' over the export of textiles and garments to Britain and the United States. In 1961–62, such 'voluntary restrictions' were formalised as first short-term and then long-term government-to-government agreements regarding international trade in cotton textiles, the latter of which would twice be extended until 1973. By 'protecting free trade' against Western protectionism, Hong Kong's economy, paradoxically, became more prosperous.[15]

Besides the growth of industrial exports, Hong Kong became 'the premier Asian financial centre'. By 1965, its foreign exchange market, gold market, and banking system were 'global in scope and impact', while its stock market was 'primarily regional'. Hong Kong's competitive advantage as a regional and later international financial centre included: its sophisticated banking and financial institutions that had been developed to service trading activities since the nineteenth century; its geographical position within a time zone that enabled twenty-four-hour global trading; and its light regulatory environment that attracted foreign capital.[16] Philip Haddon-Cave, Hong Kong's financial secretary between 1971 and 1981, used the term 'positive non-interventionism' to describe, and justify, the government's laissez-faire approach. Rather than embracing the virtues of nineteenth-century liberalism, however, the colonial government chose to selectively intervene in the economy, such as in housing and education.[17] At times, Hong Kong was caught up in the international financial turmoil. In November 1967, the British government's devaluation of sterling by 14 per cent resulted in a loss of £56 million for Hong Kong (which needed to hold its huge sterling reserves in London) and a similar devaluation of the Hong Kong dollar against the US dollar. But within days, the Hong Kong government was able to increase by 10 per cent the value of the Hong Kong dollar against the pound, and in mid-1968 to secure from London an agreement on exchange guarantees for Hong Kong's sterling reserves in the event of future devaluation.[18] On 15 August 1971, the Nixon administration announced the end of convertibility of the US dollar into gold – the so-called 'Nixon shock' – in order to restore the United States' primacy in the global economy. In June 1972, the British government decided to float the pound against the US dollar, thus effectively dismantling the Sterling Area. The following month, the Hong Kong government responded by pegging the Hong Kong dollar to the US dollar. From 1 January 1973, Hong Kong abolished all exchange controls, and from 26 November 1974, the Hong Kong dollar was allowed to float independently.[19]

The severing of monetary links with sterling should be seen in the wider context of Hong Kong's 'long decolonisation' between the late 1950s and the 1970s.[20] At a time when the Cold War and decolonisation were intensifying across the globe, the UK–Hong Kong relationship underwent subtle transformation. As early as 1949, London had concluded that Hong Kong was indefensible against a Chinese attack. It was feared that Beijing would attack Hong Kong in the context of a wider Sino-American war over Korea, Indochina, or Taiwan.[21] The imperative of making defence cuts, together with the lack of a firm US military commitment, prompted Prime Minister Harold Macmillan to consider 'abandoning Hongkong' in 1957.[22] During the 1960s, Britain accelerated the decolonisation of Africa, decided to withdraw all its forces from east of Suez, and made two (unsuccessful) bids for entry into the European Economic Community (EEC). While remaining constitutionally a Crown Colony, Hong Kong gained financial and administrative autonomy from London, thanks to its geographical remoteness and financial position, shrinking resources within Whitehall, and lack of parliamentary interest. The colonial government could draw up its own budget and raise loans while bargaining with London over defence contribution and sterling reserves.[23] During the anti-colonial riots in 1967, the Harold Wilson government became so despondent that it undertook contingency planning for an evacuation from Hong Kong, while conducting a long-term study of its future. By 1969, the final version of the long-term study concluded that 'Hong Kong's future must eventually lie in China', and that Britain's objective 'must be to attempt to negotiate its return, at a favourable opportunity, on the best terms obtainable for its people and for [British] material interests there'.[24]

During the 1970s, the constitutional relationship between the UK and Hong Kong became increasingly anomalous. In early March 1972, four months after the PRC's admission to the UN, Beijing requested the UN Committee on Decolonisation to remove Hong Kong, which was a 'part of

Chinese territory', from the list of 'colonial territories' under the committee's terms of reference. In November, the UN General Assembly adopted the committee's resolution on decolonisation, removing Hong Kong and Macao from the list of non-self-governing territories.[25] With the establishment of Anglo-Chinese ambassadorial relations in early 1972 and Britain's entry into the EEC in 1973, Hong Kong's status could not but become a political embarrassment for London.[26] Governor Murray MacLehose was determined to uphold Hong Kong's administrative autonomy. While carrying out a massive programme of housing, new towns, education, and anti-corruption, MacLehose resisted the left-wing Labour government's demands for a rapid expansion of social services (like introduction of minimum wages).[27]

Against the backdrop of Britain's retreat from empire and embrace of Europe on the one hand, and on the other Hong Kong's growing economic prosperity and administrative autonomy, the future of Hong Kong emerged as an urgent issue for the Labour and then Conservative governments in 1979. That year, the process of globalisation was given a boost by Margaret Thatcher's coming to power and Deng Xiaoping's adoption of an open-door policy. The twin processes of decolonisation and globalisation interacted in a subtle manner in Hong Kong's case.

First soundings about Hong Kong's future

As of 1979, the retention of Hong Kong offered a number of advantages and disadvantages to Britain. According to a FCO study, in the post-Mao Zedong era, Hong Kong was 'a very positive factor in the development of relations between Britain and China'. Economically, Hong Kong was 'an increasingly important market for British goods', and a commercial gateway to the Far East for British companies. From a military point of view, although Hong Kong was deemed indefensible against an (unlikely) attack from China, the 1975 defence costs agreement stipulated that the Hong Kong government met 75 per cent of the total costs of the garrison, with the possibility of negotiating a further small increase after the expiry of the agreement in 1982. Hong Kong, moreover, provided 'a welcome, and increasingly rare opportunity for British units to serve outside Europe', particularly the Brigade of Gurkhas.

As for disadvantages, the UK–Hong Kong relationship was 'inherently difficult and increasingly anomalous'. Given China's long-held suspicion that development of representative government was a normal path to independence, the British had contemplated, but did not introduce, democracy in Hong Kong. As time went by, it would become 'increasingly embarrassing for the British Government to have to defend in Parliament the maintenance of a paternalistic, oligarchic and essentially undemocratic system of government'. Besides, Hong Kong could cause London 'increasing international embarrassment' when it was 'pursuing interests which conflict with those of the UK', such as trade matters. The FCO concluded that on balance the advantages Britain derived from Hong Kong appeared to be greater than the disadvantages. Indeed, a withdrawal from Hong Kong was 'not a realistic option for the foreseeable future' unless 'by agreement with the Chinese'. A unilateral withdrawal would lead to the 'collapse of one of the world's leading financial centres', which would seriously damage British financial interests and would trigger an exodus of Hong Kong people to Britain.[28] In this vein, the FCO's main concern was less about the value of empire but more about the cost of premature decolonisation.

In late 1978, a window of opportunity seemed to have been opened for Britain to resolve the question of Hong Kong, whose New Territories Lease was due to expire in 1997. As Hugh Cortazzi, FCO deputy under secretary of state, observed of events in the past months, China had made it plain that 'Chinese interests will require the maintenance of the status quo [in Hong Kong] for the foreseeable future'. The PRC and its local agencies had made 'substantial investment' in the city.[29] A new water agreement had been signed, providing for a 30 per cent increase in annual water supply over the next four years.[30] Besides, the local branch of the New China News Agency (NCNA), China's de facto embassy in the territory, had demonstrated an eagerness to cultivate a more direct relationship with the Hong Kong governor. On 7 September 1978, its newly arrived head, Wang Kuang, called on Governor Murray MacLehose – the first time for such high-level contact.[31] On 13 December, MacLehose reciprocated by holding a lunch for Wang, accompanied by Second Director Li Jusheng. During the lunch meeting, the Chinese 'persistently pushed at [MacLehose] an invitation to visit Peking'. Li talked of 'Hong Kong's part in the modernisation programme'. Wang said that if MacLehose visited Beijing, 'our leaders would receive you'.[32]

The suggestion that Hong Kong had a role to play in China's modernisation was conveyed by a more authoritative Chinese official. On 14 December, Li Qiang, minister of foreign trade, arrived in Hong Kong as a transit stop before his return to China a week later. While in Hong Kong, Li met a large number of Chinese and foreign business people, visited the Far East Stock Exchange, and gave a press conference. He revealed that China was now eager to accept different forms of international trading practice, including government-to-government loans and joint ventures. Significantly, Li asserted that 'Hong Kong has an important role to play in the modernisation of China as a centre of communications, an entrepot and a source of expertise on business and industry'. When the governor invited him to

Flagstaff House for tea on the 19th, Li was 'very positive about the role which Hong Kong could play in the "four modernisations" policy', claiming that China 'had a great deal to learn from Hong Kong'.[33]

In early 1979, James Callaghan's Labour government considered whether the Hong Kong governor should accept the invitation to visit China and, for that purpose, raise the question of land leases in the New Territories. All land in Hong Kong was owned by the Crown, and was leased by paying the government a premium. The usual term of land leases in the New Territories was seventy-five years from 1 July 1898, with a right of renewal for a further term of twenty-four years less the last three days.[34] The British ambassador to China, Percy Cradock, proposed an approach to the Chinese at the next favourable opportunity: 'Though there is never an ideal time, the next one or two years, with Deng [Xiaoping] at the height of his power, are likely to be as good as we shall get.'[35] Foreign Secretary David Owen agreed that MacLehose should accept the invitation. Indeed, the FCO had been planning for Owen's own visit to China.[36] Cradock suggested that MacLehose should go before Owen, for the governor, 'a very experienced China hand', would be in a better position to sound out the Chinese about the technical question of land leases.[37] On 9 February, Li Qiang issued a formal invitation to MacLehose and his wife for 'a friendly visit' some time in the spring.[38] MacLehose accepted Li's invitation the following month.[39]

The British decided that the NCNA should be given an advance hint that MacLehose would want to say something about the New Territories leases during the visit.[40] The Chinese, for their part, indicated to the FCO their desire to arrange a meeting between the governor and Deng Xiaoping, although they were unable to commit 'in view of Deng's heavy programme'.[41] On 17 March, Deng approved a report by the Ministry of Foreign Affairs and the Ministry of Foreign Trade recommending him to receive the Hong Kong governor during the visit.[42] By that time, however, the question of Hong Kong was not on the agenda of the Chinese government. Despite the establishment of the Hong Kong and Macao Affairs Office within the State Council under Liao Chengzhi in April 1978, there was no plan for taking any initiative on Hong Kong's future: Deng regarded reunification with Taiwan as his top priority. On the New Year's Day of 1979, the Standing Committee of the National People's Congress (NPC) had issued an important message to the compatriots in Taiwan about 'striving to reunify the motherland peacefully'. The message coincided with the establishment of full diplomatic relations between China and the United States.[43] After Sino-American normalisation, Deng regarded the international environment as 'favourable' to the prospect of Taiwan's return to the motherland, declaring national reunification as one of the three main tasks of the 1980s (the other two being maintenance of world peace and China's Four Modernisations).[44]

According to the FCO, the main objective of MacLehose's China visit was to 'remove the significance of the 1997 deadline before its approach starts to undermine confidence'. The governor should aim to 'secure the future of Hong Kong in the medium term', which was related 'specifically to land leases in the New Territories'.[45] As all land leases granted in the New Territories would expire three days before 1 July 1997, the gradual run-down of existing leases, together with the inability of the Hong Kong government to grant new leases lasting beyond 1997, would 'fairly soon begin to deter major new investment, and create problems of confidence'. The FCO was acutely aware of the official Chinese position on Hong Kong – that 'Hong Kong is Chinese territory temporarily occupied by Britain', and that the three treaties under which Hong Kong was ceded or leased to Britain were 'unequal' and 'invalid'. Thus, it was imperative to separate the long-term issue of Hong Kong's future from the short- and medium-term practical problem of the New Territories leases. On the latter, the governor should propose 'to issue future leases in the New Territories without a fixed term, valid "for so long as Her Majesty may administer the Territories", and to convert existing leases into indeterminate leases of the same kind'. The British proposal would not require any modification of China's formal position on Hong Kong.[46] On 22 March, Owen submitted a memorandum to the Cabinet Defence and Overseas Policy Committee. Callaghan saw no objection to his proposed action concerning MacLehose's visit.[47]

The first Hong Kong governor to pay an official visit to the PRC, MacLehose was accompanied by David Wilson, his political adviser, and Yuet-keung Kan, senior unofficial member of the Executive Council, and was joined by Ambassador Cradock in Beijing. On 27 March, Li Qiang met with the governor. Li pointed out that the current emphasis of China's economy was on building up such basic industries as energy, transport, communications, and steel and non-ferrous metals. This required the import of technology and management skills from abroad. On the latter, Li attested that 'the Chinese had much to learn from Hong Kong'. MacLehose was pleased that Hong Kong might 'play a role' in China's modernisation, adding that 'both Hong Kong and Guangdong could benefit from a division of labour'.[48]

The highpoint of MacLehose's visit was his interview with Deng Xiaoping at the Great Hall of the People at 10 am on 29 March. To MacLehose's surprise, Deng seized the initiative by raising the question of Hong Kong's future. Deng asserted that 'China had a consistent policy: sovereignty over Hong Kong belonged to China', but 'Hong Kong had her own special status'. Although Hong Kong residents were concerned about the future of the

New Territories in 1997, this was 'still 18 years away'. Deng indicated that any solution of the status of the New Territories should be based on the 'prerequisite that Hong Kong was part of China', but China would 'respect the special status of Hong Kong' and would 'never affect investments' there. Deng then mentioned China's policy towards Taiwan: after reunification with the motherland, 'Taiwan could still enjoy a special status and local autonomy, and even her own armed forces'. In response, MacLehose, recalling his conversation with Li, said that 'Hong Kong was of benefit to socialist construction' in China. But MacLehose stated that Hong Kong 'faced an immediate problem' – the tens of thousands of land leases in the New Territories issued with a validity lasting only until June 1997. He worried that the steadily shortening of the time of the leases would deter investment. MacLehose stressed that 'the matter was not relevant to the Chinese position on Hong Kong'.[49]

MacLehose then raised the subject of Chinese immigration to Hong Kong. Prior to 1978, the number of illegal immigrants from the mainland (who had 'touched base' in the urban areas and thus were allowed to stay in Hong Kong) and legal immigrants (who carried China-issued exit permits) was roughly in balance with the level of Hong Kong residents' emigration to third countries.[50] But that year saw an influx of illegal Chinese immigrants to Hong Kong due to a mix of push and pool factors: poor living conditions in Guangdong and job opportunities in capitalist Hong Kong.[51] In the first three months or so of 1979, the number of illegal immigrants arrested and repatriated by the Hong Kong government reached 8,352, which was higher than the already high figure of 8,192 for the whole of 1978. With an estimated evasion ratio of 1:4, tens of thousands of illegal immigrants were thought to have successfully entered the city.[52] During his interview with Deng, MacLehose lamented that 'too many people were coming with or without permits', but he believed that 'in principle the matter could be solved' after further discussion with the Guangzhou authorities. Deng offered his solution in two ways: first, China would adopt 'more effective measures' to reduce pressure on Hong Kong; second, 'it would be advisable for private investors to put more money into Guangdong and raise living standards there so that it was not necessary for people to go to Hong Kong'. Seeing illegal immigration to Hong Kong as both 'a long term and a short term problem', MacLehose agreed with Deng that investors should be encouraged to invest in Guangdong.

The subject reverted to the New Territories leases. Deng 'formally requested the Governor to ask investors to put their hearts at ease'. 'It was China's long term policy to regard Hong Kong as a special case, no matter what political solution was reached by 1997', Deng said. MacLehose responded that 'the problem could not be overcome by generalised assurances'. He proposed 'replacing the leases valid to 1997 with leases valid as long as Britain administered the New Territories', a move that would 'get rid of the date'. Deng brushed off MacLehose's proposal by stressing that 'it would be best to avoid wording which mentioned continuing British administration'. Deng claimed that 'in this century and in the beginning of the next century ..., Hong Kong would be continuing with a capitalist system, while China was continuing with a socialist system'. 'By 1997 China might take over Hong Kong', Deng continued, but 'this would not affect her economy'. Thus ended the one-hour-long meeting.[53]

On the afternoon of the same day, MacLehose met with Foreign Minister Huang Hua. To ensure that there was 'no misunderstanding' on Deng's part, MacLehose reiterated his proposal for the New Territories leases, which would 'not affect China's basic position [on Hong Kong] in any way' and would not require the Chinese government to 'say or do anything'. Rather, it was 'a question of adjusting British land law' by 'removing the date and having something less specific'. Huang opined that '[t]ime was not pressing', for there were still eighteen years before the New Territories Lease expired. He added that China would study the British proposal.[54] In short, neither Deng nor Huang specifically endorsed MacLehose's proposal about the New Territories leases, although they did not reject it outright.

Upon his return to Hong Kong, MacLehose held a one-hour press conference before a large group of local and overseas journalists on 6 April.[55] To pre-empt questions about Hong Kong's future, MacLehose first emphasised that his was 'a goodwill visit' – 'not a negotiating visit or a visit to draft agreements'. Its 'principal significance' was simply that 'the invitation was issued and that the visit took place'. Nevertheless, the visit 'marked a more normal and franker relationship, and recognition that this would be to our mutual benefit'. In revealing the discussions in Beijing, MacLehose mentioned 'the long-standing Chinese position on Hong Kong': 'it is part of China and a problem that will be solved when the time is ripe'. He noted 'the importance which the Chinese leaders attach to the value of Hong Kong, to the contribution that it could make to the modernisation programmes, [and] to the importance of maintaining investment and confidence in Hong Kong'. Significantly, MacLehose stated that Deng had 'formally requested [him] to "ask investors in Hong Kong to put their hearts at ease"'. Deng had also asked for 'encouragement of investment' in Guangdong and the rest of China. To MacLehose, Deng's statement was 'a frank statement of China's needs' and 'a most encouraging message'.[56]

In offering his post-mortem on MacLehose's visit, Cradock believed that Deng 'kept his options open' about the time when China would resume sovereignty over Hong Kong. As for the next step, Cradock proposed that Britain should 'wait a little and see what reactions come in', and should 'clarify matters if the Chinese appear to have misunderstood the [British] position' on land leases.⁵⁷ To the FCO's Hong Kong and General Department, the visit was 'as successful as we could reasonably have hoped'. It would have been 'too much to expect an immediate and positive response' from Deng, but at least the British proposal was 'now on record with the Chinese'.⁵⁸ In reporting to Callaghan on 9 April, Owen wrote that 'Deng himself raised the issue of the future of Hong Kong', reaffirming the Chinese view on sovereignty over Hong Kong. But on the specific question of land leases in the New Territories, Deng 'evidently found it difficult to grasp the English legal concepts involved but appeared to accept that all that was proposed was the removal of the terminal date in leases, and that this required no Chinese action and did not conflict with the Chinese position'. Owen agreed with Cradock that Britain should now 'let matters rest for a while' so as to give China 'reasonable time to absorb and consider' the British ideas.⁵⁹

Owen could not but wait. Back on 28 March, after the Scottish National Party's withdrawal of support for the Scotland Act of 1978, a vote of no confidence had been passed by one vote, forcing Callaghan to call a general election. In preparation for the general election, Owen had to postpone his planned visit to China in April. In his memoir, Owen recollected that the Chinese 'might have shown more willingness to tackle the [Hong Kong] issue' had he been 'able to engage Deng Xiaoping's mind over the problem that April', given 'the extremely good relations' between Britain and China.⁶⁰ It was not to be.

On 3 May, Margaret Thatcher defeated Callaghan with a parliamentary majority of forty-three seats. The coming to power of the Tories did not fundamentally change the ongoing deliberations over Hong Kong's future within Whitehall. The FCO had been contemplating the legal steps to eliminate the date of 1997 from existing land leases in the New Territories, and to grant new ones extending beyond 1997. First, legislation in Hong Kong was needed since land leases of undetermined length were unknown under Common Law. Besides, a covering Order in Council in the UK about the governor's powers to administer the New Territories after 1997 was required in order to reduce the risk of legal challenge in local courts.⁶¹ But as Deng had taken issue with mentioning 'continuing British administration' in the British proposal about the New Territories leases, both MacLehose and Cradock suggested that the British should issue a statement about the legal steps to allay Chinese suspicions.⁶² Accordingly, the Chinese government should be informed that Britain intended to remove 'the legal limitation' on the period of land ownership in the New Territories. The Hong Kong government would pass a law to 'remove the date from existing leases, and issue new leases without a fixed date'. Similarly, the British government would address the 'legal problem about the governor's powers to administer the New Territories' by issuing an Order in Council. Such an order would be 'purely permissive': 'its only effect would be to permit such administration to continue under British law if, at the time, the Chinese government so wished'. Above all, both legal steps 'were entirely without prejudice to the Chinese position on Hong Kong, and did not commit either the present or future Chinese governments to any particular course of action with regard to the future of the territory'.[63]

In a memorandum to Thatcher dated 2 July, Foreign Secretary Lord Carrington said that the ever-shortening period of land leases was 'beginning to affect investment decisions' in Hong Kong. Although the problem of 'confidence' was 'not yet acute', 'now is a particularly good time to tackle' the land lease question, given the 'good' Anglo-Chinese relationship and Deng's expressed desire for 'Hong Kong's contribution to China's modernisation'. Referring to MacLehose's China visit, Carrington said that as the governor had 'deliberately put the matter in general terms and treated it in a low key', the Chinese leaders might 'not have fully understood what we are intending to do'. Thus, Carrington suggested that the FCO would make a private approach to the Chinese about the British legal steps. After reading Carrington's memorandum, Thatcher took note of his suggestion.[64]

On 5 July, Cradock called on Assistant Foreign Minister Song Zhiguang. Cradock talked of the proposed British legal steps, and left a copy of his statement with Song. He added orally that what was being proposed 'required no action on the part of the Chinese authorities'; but if asked, Britain would say that it had informed China in advance of the British actions. Song's immediate response was to recall Deng's position on Hong Kong, stressing that Deng 'had indicated "the degree to which [China] can go"'. Cradock replied that what Britain had in mind was 'not the New Territories Lease of 1898 but the thousands of individual land leases in the New Territories'. But to him, it was unclear 'whether there was any confusion in Song's mind since the Chinese term he used could be either singular or plural', with his interpreter making it 'single in English'.[65]

It took over two months for Beijing to respond to Cradock's initiative. On 24 September, Cradock was summoned to the Chinese Foreign Ministry by Song Zhiguang, who read out the Chinese reply (and handed Cradock a copy). The Chinese government's position on Hong Kong was 'consistent and clear' and was 'well known to the British government'. Deng's remarks to MacLehose 'were of great weight and should serve to stabilize the confidence of the investors'. Thus, China considered the British legal steps as 'unnecessary and inappropriate', while urging Britain to 'desist from taking the proposed actions'. But Song said that both sides should 'maintain close contact', adding that if the British had any views or suggestions, they should put them forward to China.[66] To Cradock, this was 'a disappointing reply and a more thorough rejection' than he personally had envisaged. Cradock suggested to the FCO that it was imperative to 'keep a dialogue going and keep this rebuff secret'.[67] In reporting to Thatcher in early October, Carrington said that Britain needed to maintain secrecy about the approach, since a leak could be 'very damaging as well as embarrassing'.[68] He argued that the Chinese premier's forthcoming visit to Britain would provide an opportunity to remind China of the problem of the New Territories leases.

As discussed in Chapter 1, Hua Guofeng visited Britain as part of his West European tour. When meeting with Hua on 1 November, Thatcher briefly raised the issue of land leases. Invited by the prime minister to address the issue, Carrington said that 'as 1997 approached, uncertainty about new leases [in the New Territories] grew'. Acknowledging that Britain would not pursue its previous proposals which China found 'unacceptable', Carrington nonetheless hoped that 'Premier Hua could give thought, or cause thought to be given, to the problem of maintaining confidence in Hong Kong's future'. Thatcher echoed Carrington's request by saying that 'the British Government did not expect an answer on the spot, but were asking the Chinese Government to give thought to the question'. Hua replied that the Chinese government indeed 'had given serious thought to this question, and had given their reply to the British Government'. Yet it had to be 'very careful about what was said about Chinese territory'. Hua concluded that China enjoyed 'very good relations' with both the British and Hong Kong governments at the moment, and would 'keep in touch' with London.[69]

Quiet but persistent prompts, 1980–81

Having been rebuffed by Deng Xiaoping in 1979, the British decided to go slow about the question of the New Territories leases during 1980. In his communication with Cradock on 22 February, MacLehose wrote that there was 'no question of confidence breaking at least for the next year or two', but 1982 would be 'a potentially critical year'. As the length of a standard mortgage was fifteen years, confidence in the value of land leases in the New Territories would begin to fade from 1982 onwards, with the result that investment would dry up and a flow of capital overseas would damage the value of the Hong Kong dollar. MacLehose proposed that Britain should seek to 'thicken out Deng's assurance to investors', by obtaining confirmation that 'investors could have confidence that leases issued for periods that passed 1997 would be respected'.[70] Cradock supported MacLehose's idea, believing that Deng was 'speaking honestly when he indicated that no decisions had been made about the future of Hong Kong'.[71] In April, the FCO

Hong Kong, 1979–81   57

decided that in order to 'avoid another rebuff', any approach to the Chinese should concentrate on 'the leases question' rather than 'continued British administration'. The aim was to get them to 'expand Deng's assurances in a form that could be publicly quoted'.⁷²

The British sensed an opportunity to take soundings of China's attitude in June, when Liao Chengzhi, who was entrusted by Deng to devise Hong Kong policy, was recuperating in Hong Kong after a medical operation in the United States.⁷³ Rather than inviting such a high-level Chinese official to the Government House, which would be too politically sensitive, MacLehose visited Liao at his guest house on the Peak on 13 June. MacLehose said that the length of individual land leases in the New Territories now lasted for seventeen years only, and investors would start to move their money elsewhere in two to three years' time if new leases beyond 1997 were not issued. Liao asserted that the problem of Hong Kong 'had to be considered from the international strategic point of view' since events were 'interlinked'. He brought up the subject of Sino-Russian relations, claiming that '1.5 million sq.kms which the Russians had grabbed from China could be put aside, but there were a further 30,000 sq.kms which should be returned'. Liao said that 'China approved very much of the strong attitude towards the Soviet Union taken by Mrs Thatcher', with Britain and China having 'a common interest in this problem'. 'The solution to Hong Kong should be considered in this wider context', he stressed, and '[n]othing should be done which would endanger Sino-British relations'. Liao did acknowledge that there should be 'a discussion of concrete problems'.⁷⁴ In assessing the significance of Liao's comments, MacLehose was pleased that 'Liao's long stay here should thus, at the least, have contributed towards educating the decision-makers in Peking about the problems we, and they, must face'.⁷⁵

The British continued to underscore the problem of land leases when Foreign Minister Huang Hua visited Britain in early October.⁷⁶ Although Huang, like Liao, was reluctant to expand on Deng's assurances over Hong Kong, the repeated British prompts about land leases were not without effect on Beijing. While Deng regarded resumption of sovereignty over Hong Kong as a foregone conclusion, how to achieve it, and particularly how to maintain Hong Kong's prosperity and stability, was thought to be a challenging task. The Chinese government needed more 'investigation and research' (*diao yan*) about Hong Kong before coming up with any proposal of its own.⁷⁷ In mid-February 1981, Deng decided to 'put the Hong Kong question on the agenda', requesting Liao to study the issue in order to produce 'clear guidelines'.⁷⁸ In March, Liao chaired a meeting of representatives from the Hong Kong and Macao Affairs Office and the Foreign Ministry. They discussed two options of resolving the Hong Kong question. The first option was to maintain the status quo of Hong Kong until the conditions were ripe, by following the Macao model (continuing Portuguese administration under China's sovereignty) adopted by China and Portugal when establishing diplomatic relations in 1979. The other was to take back Hong Kong in 1997, but China would need to find the best way to maintain its stability and prosperity after retrocession.[79] While Hong Kong was now up on the agenda of the Chinese government, Deng's main preoccupation remained peaceful unification with Taiwan, as demonstrated in his remarks to the British foreign secretary during his much-postponed trip to China in April.

Back in September 1975, Carrington, then leader of the opposition in the House of Lords, had first visited China. He was 'impressed by the confidence and courtesy' of Deng Xiaoping, who had recently been rehabilitated as vice premier.[80] On 3 April 1981, Carrington met Deng again in Beijing. He raised the Hong Kong issue by highlighting the problem of confidence. 'Because the British relied (perhaps over-much) on concepts of legality', Carrington said, 'the date of 1997 was beginning to cause uncertainty in the minds of the Hong Kong people in spite of the assurances which the Vice-Chairman had given'. He wondered if Britain and China would be able to discuss the problem. Deng replied that 'at present China was not in a position to make much comment on the matter'. But 'the assurances he had given [in 1979] represented the formal and dependable position of the Chinese Government'. Importantly, Deng asked Britain to 'study China's policies towards Taiwan' when considering Hong Kong's future. China had proposed a solution to the Taiwan question, whereby Taiwan's 'way of life' and 'political set-up' would not be changed after national reunification. At this juncture, Deng brought up the issue of Tibet. (As first secretary of the CCP Southwestern Bureau in the early 1950s, Deng had been in charge of the negotiations over the 1951 Seventeen Point Agreement, which allowed Tibet to maintain its political-economic-religious system under China's sovereignty.)[81] Referring to the 1951 agreement between China and the Dalai Lama over Tibet, Deng said that China had promised that 'for a considerable period there would be no reform in Tibet'. Only when the Dalai Lama had 'betrayed his country' and fled to India in 1959 (as a result of the failed Lhasa uprising) did China begin reform in Tibet, thus speaking volumes about the fact that 'China would not show bad faith'. Finally, Deng reiterated that Carrington could tell investors to 'set their minds at ease', but China 'could not say much' since it had 'one billion people' to consider.[82]

To Deng, Hong Kong was closely linked to the Taiwan question. On 30 September 1981, on the eve of the thirty-second anniversary of the founding of the PRC and at the approach of the seventieth anniversary of the 1911 Revolution, Marshal Ye Jianying, chairman of the Standing Committee of the NPC, made a major speech about peaceful reunification with Taiwan, which became known as Ye's 'nine points'. Recalling the 1979 New Year's Day message to the compatriots in Taiwan, Ye aimed to elaborate on China's Taiwan policy. First, in order to 'bring an end to the unfortunate separation of the Chinese nation as early as possible', Beijing proposed talks between the CCP and the Guomindang 'on a reciprocal basis'. Second, it proposed that the two sides should 'make arrangements to facilitate the exchange of mails, trade, air and shipping services and visits by relatives, tourists, academics and athletics'. Ye proclaimed that, after reunification with the motherland, Taiwan would 'enjoy a high degree of autonomy as a special administrative region' and 'retain its armed forces'. Besides, Taiwan's current socio-economic system and its way of life would 'remain unchanged'. Ye also made a reference to Hong Kong: China hoped that 'our compatriots in Hong Kong and Macao and Chinese nationals residing abroad will continue to act in the role of a bridge and contribute their share to the reunification of the motherland'.[83] In fact, Deng was the chief architect of China's Taiwan policy. The 'nine points' delivered in Ye's name were 'in effect one country, two systems'.[84]

In assessing Ye's statement, Cradock opined that China tended to 'put Taiwan, Hong Kong and Macao in the same bracket'. Although Beijing would not necessarily give the same concessions as it promised to Taiwan, Cradock believed that a similar offer in Hong Kong terms would be 'continuation of British administration for a negotiable period in return for recognition of Chinese sovereignty over the whole colony'.[85] Writing to Thatcher on 15 December 1981, Carrington said that although the Chinese were 'in no hurry to come to grips with the problem', it was still important that Britain tried to 'induce the Chinese to look at the problem realistically while guarding against euphoria in Hong Kong leading to disillusionment'. Thatcher's proposed visit to China (as a return for Premier Hua's 1979 visit to Britain), he argued, would be 'an excellent move in the context of our relations with China and our international position as a whole'.[86]

Globalisation and Hong Kong–Britain–China relations

At a time when the British government was contemplating the question of Hong Kong's political future, the economic relationship between the UK and Hong Kong was evolving within the context of globalisation. The contemporary phase of globalisation started in 1945, and particularly accelerated since the 1970s, and was driven by the United States. With the United States becoming its principal export market in 1959, Hong Kong was part and parcel of US-led globalisation.[87] By the early 1980s, Hong Kong exhibited many striking features of a 'global city' – a centre of global trade, an international financial centre, a communications hub, and a city of cosmopolitan and enterprising people.[88] From textiles and clothing in the 1950s, Hong Kong's industrial exports were diversified into plastics, toys, and electronics from the 1960s onwards. Between 1970 and 1980, there was an increase of over 450 per cent in Hong Kong's exports of goods, or an annual growth rate of 18.6 per cent.[89] As an international financial centre, Hong Kong hosted fifty-eight offices of foreign banks in 1980, ranking fifth among world cities (New York occupied the top spot, with eighty foreign banks).[90] Also that year, Hong Kong overtook Japan's Kobe as the world's third busiest container port; by 1987, it replaced the Netherlands' Rotterdam as the world's number one container port.[91] Hong Kong's Kai Tak Airport, one of the busiest airports in the world, contributed to the globalisation of tourism. In 1980 the number of inbound tourists reached 2.3 million, an increase of 148 per cent from 1970.[92]

After 1945, empire was inherently incompatible with globalisation: the former depended on vertical hierarchy and integration, while the latter was characterised by horizontal connections and networks.[93] As Hong Kong's economy became globalised, Britain could not take the imperial connection for granted but rather had to compete with other countries for access to the Hong Kong market. Since 1975, Britain had suffered from a consistently large visible trade deficit with Hong Kong, although it enjoyed a fluctuating surplus in invisibles (including private sector profits and official transactions). In 1979, Britain's exports to Hong Kong, mainly manufactured goods like electrical machinery and transport equipment, amounted to £442 million, representing a massive growth rate of 46.2 per cent from the previous year. Its imports from Hong Kong, such as clothing, textiles, and electrical products, increased by 54.3 per cent to £691 million. The following year, Britain's exports to Hong Kong increased further to £559.4 million, while its imports from Hong Kong saw an even more significant leap to £850.3 million.[94] To put these figures in perspective, in 1980 Hong Kong was Britain's second largest export market in Asia, although it ranked only nineteenth in the league of Britain's export markets worldwide. On the other hand, Britain occupied sixth place in the share of Hong Kong's total imports, which was a long way behind Japan, China, and the United States. It was Hong Kong's third most important export market.[95] As Secretary of State for Trade John Nott told Lord Carrington in early 1980, '[t]he much vaunted "British link" clearly does not extend to commercial decisions', and it was largely the responsibility of British companies themselves to sell to Hong Kong.[96] To Carrington, Hong Kong was 'an important market', albeit 'one of the most competitive markets anywhere in the world'. Thus, UK exporters would 'need to grasp the opportunities vigorously' in order to increase the British share of Hong Kong's imports of manufactured goods.[97]

Trade in textiles and clothing was particularly competitive in the age of globalisation. Although Hong Kong was one of the world's largest exporters of clothing, Cecil Parkinson, minister of trade, lamented that 'not enough of that clothing is made from British cloth'. In 1979, for instance, Britain had gained a market share of under 1 per cent of Hong Kong's imports of textile fabrics.[98] As mentioned earlier, Hong Kong had been forced to accept 'voluntary restrictions' on textile exports to the UK as early as 1959. In 1974, the Multi-Fibre Arrangement (MFA), which covered trade in textile products of cotton, man-made fibres, wool, and blends, was concluded. It was renewed in 1977 for a further four years.[99] During the negotiations over the MFA renewal under the auspices of GATT in 1981, the EEC pressed for tighter restrictions and quotas on so-called 'dominant suppliers' like Hong Kong on the grounds of giving more favourable treatment to smaller less developed countries and newcomers to the textile trade.[100] Although Margaret Thatcher was committed to the principle of free trade, Britain needed to follow the common commercial policies of the EEC. Pressure from the UK textile and clothing industries, which faced the prospect of losing 100,000 jobs in 1981, propelled the Thatcher government to resort to protectionist measures against low-cost suppliers.[101]

From the Hong Kong government's perspective, 'the UK textile industries' main problem' lay in 'their inability to compete with their EEC counterparts', and thus restricting imports from less developed countries suppliers offered 'no solution to that problem'.[102] Given its financial and administrative autonomy from London, Hong Kong conducted its own external commercial relations within the framework of 'a basically free trade policy'.[103] In international trade negotiations, Hong Kong officials, with the presence of a FCO official in their delegation, carried out their own talks.[104] Hong Kong's negotiating strategy regarding the MFA renewal was to seek coordination with other developing countries in order to preserve their common interests.[105] On 22 December 1981, an agreement was reached to renew MFA for another four years,[106] after the EEC had made some concessions, including no unilateral action to cut back Hong Kong's quotas.[107] As usual, Hong Kong needed to 'protect free trade' by itself rather than counting on the sovereign.

The UK–Hong Kong economic links could also be measured in terms of direct foreign investment. As of early 1980, UK investment in Hong Kong was valued at about £16 million, covering some thirty-six British establishments and representing 7 per cent of total foreign investment in the territory. While ranking third, Britain was a long way behind the United States and Japan, which constituted 47 per cent and 19 per cent of Hong Kong's total foreign investment, respectively. A little over half of UK direct overseas investment (not including portfolio) was in non-manufacturing sectors, such as finance, insurance, commerce, and real estate.[108]

UK firms managed to secure a number of lucrative public works contracts in Hong Kong. The construction of the mass transit railway was one such example. After obtaining contracts worth over £290 million for the first-stage Kwun Tong line, in 1979 UK firms, such as Metro Cammell, General Electric Company (GEC) Rectifiers, and Cable and Wireless, were successful in getting a substantial share of the contracts for the Tsuen Wan extension.[109] Another example was the Castle Peak power station, co-built by China Light and Power Company (which supplied electricity to Kowloon and the New Territories) and Esso (a US oil company). In the late 1970s, UK companies like GEC Turbine Generators and Balfour Beatty were awarded hardware contracts worth £350 million for the building of the Castle Peak 'A' Station, a four 350-megawatt dual coal/oil-fired station.[110] In early 1981, the British were interested in the Castle Peak 'B' Station, a four 660-megawatt coal-fired station. As Secretary of State for Industry Keith Joseph argued, the contract worth £550 million would be 'the largest power plant export order ever won by the United Kingdom' and thus 'a major boost for our power plant industry'.[111] The contracts with British companies were signed in August 1981.[112] Although the imperial connection might have caused the Hong Kong government to favour UK companies over foreign enterprises, the tender system meant that the British were not always successful in bidding for Hong Kong's projects. To the FCO's Hong Kong and General Department, the main determining factors were 'financial flexibility' and 'the performance of firms in fulfilling existing contracts'. A bid by B.A.I./Halcrow for the master consultancy plan for a new airport at Chek Lap Kok was unsuccessful, while GEC lost the order for the construction of the Hong Kong Electric Company's Lamma Island power station to a Japanese firm.[113]

Even the long-established British expatriate firms in Hong Kong, such as the Hong Kong and Shanghai Bank, Jardine Matheson, Swire Pacific, and the Kadoorie Group,[114] put their own business interests above those of the UK. Indeed, at a time of economic globalisation, the British *hongs* in Hong Kong basically became multinational corporations, thus raising question marks over their 'British' credentials.[115] An example of the inherent conflict between metropolitan interests and local interests was the breakup of the British Airways' monopoly on the London–Hong Kong route in late 1980. Although the British Civil Aviation Authority had initially rejected its application, the Cathay Pacific Airways, a 'local airline' owned by Swire Pacific, supported by the colonial governor, made a strong case that Hong Kong's economic well-being and global demands for open skies justified its operation of the route.[116] In short, Hong Kong's economic value to Britain per se was difficult to discern in the age of globalisation.[117] The fact of the matter was that Britain 'receives no revenue from Hong Kong',[118] unlike the extraction or 'drain' of resources from its former colonies like India.[119]

If the UK–Hong Kong economic relationship was eclipsed by intensified globalisation, Hong Kong's traditional role as an intermediary in trade between China and the rest of the world assumed renewed prominence as a result of Deng Xiaoping's opening policy. In 1979, Hong Kong's re-exports to China of goods imported from the rest of the world rose by 514 per cent to £124 million, and by a further 244 per cent to £233 million in the first eight months of 1980. The majority of these re-exports were textile yarn, fabrics, man-made fibres, and television receivers originating from Taiwan, Japan, and the United States. However, goods of UK origin were valued at just £4.3 million in 1979, and a miniscule £3.5 million in 1980.[120] Hong Kong's direct exports to China (mainly textile products, electrical machinery, and telecommunications equipment) grew from US$17 million in 1978 to US$121 in 1979, and further to US$323 million in 1980. Hong Kong's imports from China had been substantial prior to Deng's opening policy. Since 1979, on top of the steady increase in Hong Kong's retained imports from China (mainly foodstuffs and raw materials), re-exports of China origin (chiefly clothing, crude vegetable materials, and miscellaneous manufactured articles) increased from US$781 million in 1978 to US$1,132 million the following year, and to US$1,687 million in 1980. The balance of trade was strongly in China's favour: a visible trade surplus of some US$2,654 million in 1979 and US$3,171 million in 1980. Hong Kong took up 26 per cent of China's total exports in 1979, and the Hong Kong share remained more or less the same throughout the 1980s. The earnings from Hong Kong in the form of direct exports, re-exports, and remittances constituted a third of China's total foreign exchange earnings. China ranked third among Hong Kong's main trading partners in 1979 and 1980, moving to the top spot in 1985.[121]

Hong Kong, moreover, played the key role of financier in China's reform. Due to Hong Kong's geographic proximity and cultural ties with Guangdong Province, Hong Kong compatriots became the main source of foreign direct investment in the Pearl River Delta. In the first few years of China's opening up, Hong Kong business people invested mainly in tourism, real estate, and compensation trade projects. By January 1981, about 490 enterprises involving some form of foreign investment had been established in the Shenzhen SEZ, 80 per cent of which were by Hong Kong capital.[122] From 1984, Hong Kong entrepreneurs of light manufacturing industries, such as clothing, handbags, and plastic products, relocated their assembly and processing operations to the mainland, taking advantage of the cheap labour force and preferential tax and land policies there. Over time, they employed as many as three million Chinese workers in the Pearl River Delta.[123] By establishing a subcontracting network of small and medium-sized firms in China, Hong Kong contributed to the globalisation of production – a post-Fordist, flexible mode of production that connected Hong Kong capital and know-how with Chinese labour and overseas markets.[124] In the 1980s, Hong Kong was responsible for almost 60 per cent of contracted foreign investment in China as a whole, followed by the United States as a poor second (around 11 per cent) and Japan (7 per cent).[125]

Improvement of transport facilitated the movement of people between Hong Kong and Guangdong.[126] A direct through train passenger service between Kowloon and Guangzhou, suspended more than thirty years earlier, was resumed on 4 April 1979. Governor MacLehose, ending his historic visit to China, boarded the first direct train at Guangzhou for Hong Kong.[127] Through bus services started between Hong Kong and Guangzhou in April 1981, and were extended to other towns in Guangdong thereafter. Passenger ferry services to Guangzhou and to other destinations in Guangdong were opened. It was estimated that the passenger traffic at Lo Wu increased from about 2.8 million in 1978 to 6.1 million in 1979, and to 7.7 million in 1981.[128]

In short, since 1979 the flows of goods, capital, and people between Hong Kong and China had increased to such an extent that by 1983 'the two economies are inter-dependent', according to the Hong Kong government.[129] In the global economy, Hong Kong exploited its comparative advantage by relocating its light manufacturing operations to southern China, while concentrating on its role as provider of services and finance. China, short of capital but not of labour and land, participated in, and benefited from, the global production system that Hong Kong investors created.

British Nationality Act and Hong Kong immigration

If Deng's opening policy enabled people to move back and forth between Hong Kong and China, the passage of the British Nationality Act in 1981 showed how the Thatcher government strove to shut the door to immigrants from Hong Kong.[130] Intended to bring nationality law in line with immigration policy, the 1981 Act replaced 'Citizen of the United Kingdom and Colonies' (CUKC) with three separate categories of citizenship – 'British Citizen', 'British Overseas Citizen', and 'British Dependent Territories Citizen' (which covered Hong Kong). Influenced by racial considerations and domestic politics, Thatcher and Home Secretary William Whitelaw imagined 'a narrowly conceived domestic community of Britishness based firmly within the United Kingdom'.[131]

The origin of restrictions over 'coloured' immigrants could be traced back to 1962. The Commonwealth Immigrants Act abolished, in effect, free access to the UK by non-white CUKCs, which had hitherto been guaranteed by the 1948 British Nationality Act, through the introduction of a voucher system. The Immigration Act of 1971 reinforced immigration restrictions by introducing the racially discriminatory concept of 'patriality': only 'patrials' with a 'close connection' to Britain (defined as those who had been born in Britain or who had at least one parent or grandparent who were born there, and who had already taken up residence in Britain) enjoyed the right to settle, while 'non-patrials' were treated as 'aliens' who required a work permit for entry to Britain. In April 1977, James Callaghan's Labour government published a green paper proposing the creation of two separate citizenships to replace CUKC – British Citizens (persons with the right of abode in Britain) and British Overseas Citizens (persons without the right of abode in Britain).[132] Building on Labour's green paper, the Thatcher government took up the task of enacting a new nationality bill, which aimed to prevent Britain from being 'swamped' by immigrants from the colonies and the Commonwealth who were deemed to have no close connection with the UK.

The majority of Hong Kong residents did not intend to migrate to the UK and, for that matter, nor did they aspire to become 'white Britons'. Despite the trend of inhabitants of the New Territories seeking employment in the 1950s and early 1960s, the total number of Hong Kong immigrants in Britain was relatively small. In 1981, it was just 58,917.[133] Still, being the largest of the remaining British Dependent Territories with 2.6 million CUKCs (out of a total population of about five million), Hong Kong would be most affected by the proposed nationality bill. At a time when the approach of 1997 was creating uncertainty in Hong Kong, the unofficial members of the Executive Council and the Legislative Council feared that the UK was distancing itself from the territory. The unofficials thus played an active role in lobbying London during the passage of the nationality bill.[134] At last, the Thatcher government agreed to create 'a three-tier citizenship' to accommodate some of Hong Kong's concerns.[135]

On 30 October 1981, the British Nationality Act received Royal Assent.[136] Accordingly, British subjects in Hong Kong became 'British Dependent Territories Citizens' (BDTC), who enjoyed the right of abode in Hong Kong (but not in Britain) and whose status could be transmitted to the next generation. By the time the 1981 Act came into effect on 1 January 1983, however, the Anglo-Chinese negotiation over Hong Kong's future had already started (albeit making little progress), thus casting serious doubt on the continuation of Hong Kong's BDTC status after 1997.

The passage of the British Nationality Act demonstrated that Thatcher was opposed to the free movement of people, or the globalisation of migration, due to racial stereotypes and domestic politics. Although the 1981 Act was not initially designed to tackle the 1997 question, Britain was, in effect, 'decolonising' Hong Kong through nationality legislation. The bond between the British nation and the Hong Kong populace, already weakened by the 1962 and 1971 immigration restrictions, was further eroded by the Act.

Conclusion

In 1979, the British sensed a window of opportunity for discussing Hong Kong's future with the Chinese. As China desperately needed the capital and expertise of Hong Kong to carry out its modernisation programme, Governor MacLehose accepted the invitation to visit Beijing. His plan was to raise the short-term issue of individual land leases in the New Territories. By securing Chinese agreement to extend the leases beyond 1997, Britain could bypass the thorny question of sovereignty. During his interview with MacLehose, however, Deng Xiaoping seized the initiative by asserting that China possessed sovereignty over Hong Kong, although the latter's special status would be respected after 1997. Having been rebuffed by Deng, the British government, under Margaret Thatcher since May 1979, decided to take a go-slow approach to China. The immediate objective was to keep reminding the Chinese of the problem of the New Territories leases and, hopefully, to get them to expand on Deng's assurances. In 1979, and throughout 1980 and 1981, Deng regarded Taiwan, not Hong Kong, as his top priority of national reunification: the formula of what would later be called 'one country, two systems' was being devised for that purpose. Nevertheless, Britain's persistent prompts about Hong Kong did create a sense of urgency on Deng's part by late 1981, so much so that Hu Yaobang and other officials responsible for Hong Kong affairs were asked to come up with concrete proposals for resolving the issue.

The deliberations over Hong Kong's future took place against the backdrop of intensified globalisation in the 1980s. Hong Kong's emergence as a 'global city' transformed, and created strains on, the relationship between the metropole and the colony. At a time when goods, money, and to a lesser extent people were moving freely across borders due to economic globalisation, the UK government found it increasingly difficult to balance metropolitan interests against Hong Kong's demands and needs, such as the textile trade and London–Hong Kong air services. The value of empire had been eclipsed by Hong Kong's connectivity with the global economy.

Foreign Secretary Carrington was acutely aware that Hong Kong was one of the most competitive markets in the world. In 1981, for instance, Britain's share of Hong Kong's total imports had dropped from 7.9 per cent a decade ago to 4.5 per cent.[137] The UK government could not 'coerce' Hong Kong into buying more British goods and services than the competitiveness of UK companies would allow. Nor did London extract revenue from Hong Kong. While the Callaghan and then Thatcher governments resisted *de jure* decolonisation by trying to get round the 1997 deadline, the process of *de facto* decolonisation in terms of UK–Hong Kong economic ties (amid growing economic interdependence between Hong Kong and China) and sentimental bond (with the 1981 British Nationality Act denying the right of abode in Britain to Hong Kong people) was well underway.[138]

As the year 1981 drew to a close, Thatcher, who had been preoccupied with domestic economic matters, had yet to make up her mind on Hong Kong's future. In September 1982, she flew to Beijing to commence the Hong Kong talks.

Notes

1 On the history of colonial Hong Kong, see Steve Tsang, *A Modern History of Hong Kong: 1841–1997* (London: I.B. Tauris, 2003); John Carroll, *A Concise History of Hong Kong* (Hong Kong: Hong Kong University Press, 2007).

2 Stephen Platt contends that the First Opium War, which resulted in the seizure of Hong Kong Island, was motivated by free-trade interests and drug profiteering. Stephen Platt, *Imperial Twilight: The Opium War and the End of China's Last Golden Age* (London: Atlantic Books, 2019).

3 Christopher Munn, *Anglo-China: Chinese People and British Rule in Hong Kong, 1841–1880* (Hong Kong: Hong Kong University Press, 2008). It is worth noting that although every colonial power might claim to have a 'civilising mission', Britain was not enthusiastic about 'exporting' British culture (like cricket) or assimilating local Chinese as far as the colonisation of Hong Kong was concerned.

4 Tsang, *A Modern History of Hong* Kong, 20–3; Robert Bickers, 'The Colony's Shifting Position in the British Informal Empire in China', in Judith Brown and Rosemary Foot (eds), *Hong Kong's Transitions, 1842–1997* (London: Macmillan, 1997), 33–61.

5 Chi-kwan Mark, *Hong Kong and the Cold War: Anglo-American Relations 1949–1957* (Oxford: Oxford University Press, 2004), 26–9; William Roger Louis, 'Hong Kong: The Critical Phase, 1945–1949', *American Historical Review*, 102: 4 (October 1997), 1052–84.

6 Steve Yui-sang Tsang, *Democracy Shelved: Great Britain, China, and Attempts at Constitutional Reform in Hong Kong, 1945–1952* (Hong Kong: Oxford University Press, 1988).

7 Norman Miners, *The Government and Politics of Hong Kong*, 2nd edition (Hong Kong: Oxford University Press, 1977), 192–3.
8 TNA, CO 1030/1674, Wallace to Poynton, 2 December 1963; Note: 'Status of Hong Kong – Chinese attitude', *ibid.*
9 Suzanne Pepper, *Keeping Democracy at Bay: Hong Kong and the Challenge of Chinese Political Reform* (Lanham, MD: Rowman & Littlefield, 2008), 139, 144–5.
10 Gordon Matthews, Eric Kit-wai Ma, and Tai-lok Lui, *Hong Kong, China: Learning to Belong to a Nation* (London: Routledge, 2008), 27–35.
11 David R. Meyer, *Hong Kong as a Global Metropolis* (Cambridge: Cambridge University Press, 2000).
12 Mark, *Hong Kong and the Cold War*, 143–58.
13 Wong Siu-lun, *Emigrant Entrepreneurs: Shanghai Industrialists in Hong Kong* (Hong Kong: Oxford University Press, 1988).
14 Catherine R. Schenk, 'Closing the Hong Kong Gap: The Hong Kong Free Dollar Market in the 1950s', *Economic History Review*, 47: 2 (May 1994), 335–53.
15 Lawrence Mills, *Protecting Free Trade: The Hong Kong Paradox, 1947–97* (Hong Kong: Hong Kong University Press, 2012).
16 Catherine Schenk, *Hong Kong as an International Financial Centre: Emergence and Development, 1945–65* (London: Routledge, 2001), 133–7, 159.
17 For a critique of Hong Kong's 'positive non-interventionism', see David W. Clayton, 'From Laissez-faire to "Positive Non-Interventionism": The Colonial State in Hong Kong Studies', *Social Transformations in Chinese Societies*, 9: 1 (2013), 1–20.
18 Catherine R. Schenk, 'The Empire Strikes Back: Hong Kong and the Decline of Sterling in the 1960s', *Economic History Review*, 57: 3 (August 2004), 568–77.
19 Lu Dong Qing and Lu Shou Cai, *Xianggang jingji shi* [A History of Hong Kong Economy] (Hong Kong: Joint Publishing (HK), 2002), 172.
20 See Chi-kwan Mark, 'Lack of Means or Loss of Will? The United Kingdom and the Decolonization of Hong Kong, 1957–1967', *International History Review*, 31: 1 (March 2009), 45–71; 'Development without Decolonisation? Hong Kong's Future and Relations with Britain and China, 1967–1972', *Journal of the Royal Asiatic Society*, 24: 2 (2014), 315–35; 'Crisis or Opportunity? Britain, China, and the Decolonisation of Hong Kong in the Long 1970s', in Roberts and Westad (eds), *China, Hong Kong and the Long 1970s*, 257–77.
21 See Mark, *Hong Kong and the Cold War*, Chapter 2.
22 National Archives and Records Administration, College Park, Maryland, US, Record Group 59, Records of the Executive Secretariat, Conference Files, 1949–63, Box 127, Continuation of memo of dinner conversation, 20 March 1957.
23 Leo F. Goodstadt, *Uneasy Partners: The Conflict between Public Interest and Private Profit in Hong Kong* (Hong Kong: Hong Kong University Press, 2005), 49–70.

24 TNA, CAB 134/2945, Stewart memo for Ministerial Committee on Hong Kong, 28 March 1969.
25 Huang Hua, *Qinli yu jianwen: Huang Hua huiyilu* [Experience and Observation: Memoir of Huang Hua] (Beijing: Shiji zhishi chubanshe, 2007), 193.
26 On the impact of Britain's entry to the EEC on Hong Kong, see James Fellows, 'Britain, European Economic Community Enlargement, and "Decolonisation" in Hong Kong, 1967–1973', *International History Review*, 41: 4 (2019), 753–74.
27 Ray Yep and Tai-Lok Lui, 'Revisiting the Golden Era of MacLehose and the Dynamics of Social Reforms', *China Information*, 24: 3 (2010), 249–72.
28 TNA, FCO 21/1735, Hong Kong and General Department, 'Hong Kong in the 1980s', March 1979.
29 TNA, FCO 40/957, Cortazzi to PS/PUS, 9 November 1978.
30 TNA, FCO 40/1634, Wilson to McLaren, 4 December 1978.
31 TNA, FCO 40/946, Hong Kong (hereafter HK) to FCO, no. 1103, 15 September 1978.
32 TNA, FCO 21/1634, MacLehose to McLaren, 15 December 1978.
33 TNA, FCO 21/1634, Wilson to Samuel, 21 December 1978; Wilson to Samuel, 29 December 1978.
34 TNA, CO 129/624/6, HK to Secretary of State for the Colonies, no. 1009, 16 September 1950.
35 TNA, FCO 21/1734, Beijing to FCO, no. 16, 4 January 1979.
36 TNA, FCO 21/1734, FCO to HK, no. 60, 17 January 1979.
37 TNA, FCO 21/1734, Walden to Far Eastern Department, 26 January 1979.
38 TNA, FCO 21/1735, Li Qiang to MacLehose, 9 February 1979.
39 TNA, FCO 21/1735, MacLehose to Li Qiang, 5 March 1979.
40 TNA, FCO 21/1735, McLaren to Cortazzi, 19 March 1979.
41 TNA, FCO 21/1735, Beijing to HK, no. 22, 19 March 1979.
42 *DXN*, vol. 1, 493.
43 Qian Jiang, *Deng Xiaoping yu ZhongMei jianjiao fengyun* [Deng Xiaoping and the Winds and Clouds of Establishing Sino-American Diplomatic Relations] (Beijing: Zhonggong dangshi chubanshe, 2005), 191–5.
44 *DXW*, vol. 2, 185–8, 239–73.
45 TNA, FCO 21/1734, McLaren to Murray, 29 January 1979.
46 TNA, FCO 21/1735, McLaren to Murray, 2 March 1979; MacLehose to McLaren, 21 December 1978.
47 TNA, PREM 16/2093, Cartledge to Wall, 26 March 1979.
48 TNA, FCO 21/1735, Record of meeting between MacLehose and Li Qiang on 27 March 1979.
49 TNA, FCO 21/1736, Record of conversation between MacLehose and Deng Xiaoping on 29 March 1979; *DXN*, vol. 1, 500–1.
50 TNA, FCO 21/1711, Hong Kong and General Department, 'Essential facts', 31 October 1979.

51 Xi Zhongxun zhuzheng Guangdong bianweihui (ed.), *Xi Zhongxun zhuzheng Guangdong* [Xi Zhongxun Governs Guangdong] (Beijing: Zhonggong dangshi chubanshe, 2007), 78; Florence Mok, 'Chinese Illicit Immigration into Colonial Hong Kong, c. 1970–1980', *Journal of Imperial and Commonwealth History*, 49: 2 (April 2021), 339–67.
52 TNA, FCO 21/1736, Wilson to McLaren, 9 May 1979; LIC Assessment: 'Chinese measures to control legal emigration', enclosed in note for the governor's security committee, 9 May 1979.
53 TNA, FCO 21/1736, Record of conversation between MacLehose and Deng Xiaoping on 29 March 1979.
54 TNA, FCO 21/1735, Record of meeting between MacLehose and Huang Hua on 29 March 1979.
55 TNA, FCO 21/1735, HK to FCO, no. 444, 6 April 1979.
56 TNA, FCO 21/1735, Text of opening remarks at press conference, attached in HK to FCO, no. 445, 6 April 1979.
57 TNA, FCO 21/1736, Cradock to McLaren, 23 April 1979.
58 TNA, FCO 21/1736, Quantrill to Murray, 20 April 1979.
59 TNA, PREM 16/2093, Owen to Callaghan, 9 April 1979.
60 David Owen, *Time to Declare* (London: Penguin Books, 1992), 407–8.
61 TNA, FCO 21/1736, Wilson to McLaren, 9 May 1979; FCO 21/1737, Draft Order-in-Council; FCO 21/1736, Quantrill to Murray, 26 April 1979.
62 TNA, FCO 21/1737, Beijing to FCO, no. 445, 14 May 1979; Beijing to FCO, no. 443, 14 May 1979.
63 TNA, FCO 21/1737, HK to FCO, no. 899, 30 June 1979.
64 TNA, PREM 19/789 Part 1, Carrington to Thatcher, 2 July 1979; Cartledge to Wall, 5 July 1979.
65 TNA, FCO 21/1738, Beijing to FCO, no. 622, 6 July 1979.
66 TNA, PREM 19/789 Part 1, Beijing to FCO, no. 826, 24 September 1979; Beijing to FCO, no. 825, 24 September 1979.
67 TNA, PREM 19/789 Part 1, Beijing to FCO, no. 827, 24 September 1979.
68 TNA, PREM 19/789 Part 1, Carrington to Thatcher, 9 October 1979.
69 TNA, FCO 21/1712, Record of discussion between Thatcher and Hua Guofeng on 1 November 1979.
70 TNA, FCO 40/1162, MacLehose to Cradock, 22 February 1980.
71 TNA, FCO 40/1162, Cradock to MacLehose, 8 April 1980.
72 TNA, FCO 40/1162, FCO to HK, no. 340, 25 April 1980.
73 Wang Junyan, *Liao Chengzhi Zhuan* [Biography of Liao Chengzhi] (Beijing: Renmin chubanshe, 2006), 540.
74 TNA, FCO 40/1162, Record of meeting between MacLehose and Liao Chengzhi at 2 Barker Road, Hong Kong, on 13 June 1980.
75 TNA, FCO 40/1162, MacLehose to McLaren, 8 July 1980.
76 TNA, FCO 40/1164, Record of conversation between Carrington and Huang Hua on 1 October 1980.
77 Wong, *China's Resumption of Sovereignty over Hong Kong*, 12, 27.
78 *DXN*, vol. 2, 715.

79 Chen, *Xianggang wenti tanpan shimo*, 54–7.
80 Lord Carrington, *Reflect on Things Past: The Memoirs of Lord Carrington* (London: Collins, 1988), 268.
81 Qi, *Deng Xiaoping yu Xianggang huigui*, 217–20.
82 TNA, FCO 40/1288, Extract from conversation between Carrington and Deng Xiaoping on 3 April 1981; *DXN*, vol. 2, 729.
83 TNA, FCO 40/1290, Beijing to FCO, no. 594, 30 September 1981; *Ye Jianying nianpu, 1897–1986* [A Chronicle of Ye Jianying, 1897–1986], vol. 2 (Beijing: Zhongyang wenxian chubanshe, 2007), 1200–2.
84 *DXN*, vol. 2, 797.
85 TNA, FCO 40/1290, Beijing to FCO, no. 603, 6 October 1981.
86 TNA, FCO 40/1291, Carrington to Thatcher, 15 December 1981.
87 On US–Hong Kong economic relations through the lens of US-oriented Hong Kong business elites, see Peter E. Hamilton, *Made in Hong Kong: Transpacific Networks and a New History of Globalization* (New York: Columbia University Press, 2021).
88 On the characteristics of global cities, see Greg Clark, *Global City: A Short History* (Washington, DC: Brookings Institution Press, 2016); Saskia Sassen, *The Global City: New York, London, Tokyo* (Princeton, NJ: Princeton University Press, 2001). On Hong Kong in particular, see Stephen Chiu and Tai-Lok Lui, *Hong Kong: Becoming a Chinese Global City* (London: Routledge, 2009); Meyer, *Hong Kong as a Global Metropolis*.
89 Lu and Lu, *Xianggang jingji shi*, 226.
90 Schenk, *Hong Kong as an International Financial Centre*, 125.
91 Lu and Lu, *Xianggang jingji shi*, 278.
92 Ibid., 234.
93 Hopkins, 'Rethinking Decolonization'. It must be noted that in the nineteenth century, the British Empire was a powerful force of (imperial) globalisation – see Magee and Thompson, *Empire and Globalisation*. Nevertheless, as Niall Ferguson argues in his general account of the contest between hierarchies and networks across history, although the British Empire was 'hierarchical' in 'theory', 'its practice was to delegate considerable power to local rulers and private networks'. Niall Ferguson, *The Square and the Tower: Networks, Hierarchies and the Struggle for Global Power* (London: Penguin Books, 2018), 163.
94 TNA, FCO 40/1286, 'Hong Kong: Economic importance to the UK', attached in Exeter to Williamson, 6 January 1981; CAB 133/528, FCO brief: 'Hong Kong's economic relations with UK, EC, US and Japan', 1982; Hong Kong Government, *Hong Kong 1980: A Review of 1979*, 238; Hong Kong Government, *Hong Kong 1981: A Review of 1980*, 258.
95 TNA, FCO 40/1304, March to Youde, 15 April 1981; FCO 40/1304, Searle memo, 31 March 1981; CAB 133/528, FCO brief: 'Hong Kong's economic relations with UK, EC, US and Japan', 1982.
96 TNA, FCO 40/1157, Nott to Carrington, 19 February 1980.
97 TNA, FCO 40/1157, Carrington to Nott, 28 February 1980.

98 Public Records Office, Kwun Tong, Hong Kong (hereafter PRO), HKRS 70-8-356, Press release: 'Minister backs British textiles in mission to Hong Kong', 30 July 1980; Press release: 'Main points of speech by minister of state and leader of textile mission, Cecil Parkinson, MP', 5 September 1980.

99 Mills, *Protecting Free Trade*, 73–84, 105–8; David Clayton, 'Constructing Colonial Capitalism: The Public Relations Campaigns of Hong Kong Business Groups, 1959–1966', in David Thackeray, Andrew Thompson, and Richard Toye (eds), *Imagining Britain's Economic Future, c.1800–1975: Trade, Consumerism and Global Markets* (Cham: Palgrave Macmillan, 2018), 231–51.

100 PRO, HKRS 545-1-133-12, Hong Kong Government Office, London, 'UK textiles under MFA II and the prospects for MFA III', March 1982.

101 TNA, FCO 40/1157, Textiles brief for minister of state's visit to Hong Kong, 30 August–5 September 1980; PRO, HKRS 70-8-356, 'Showdown over the textile agreement', *Hong Kong Standard* (19 February 1981).

102 PRO, HKRS 70-8-356, Hong Kong Government Office, London, 'UK textiles under the MFA: What next?', April 1983.

103 Hong Kong Government, *Annual Report for the Year 1978*, 16.

104 Mills, *Protecting Free Trade*, 134–5.

105 Hong Kong Government, *Hong Kong 1983: A Review of 1982*, 23.

106 Hong Kong Government, *Hong Kong 1982: A Review of 1981*, 25.

107 PRO, HKRS 545-1-133-2, Statement by Lawrence Mills, Commissioner of Trade, on his return from MFA negotiations in Geneva, 23 December 1981; Mills, *Protecting Free Trade*, 116.

108 TNA, FCO 40/1157, Brief for secretary of state for trade's visit to Hong Kong 26–30 January 1980; FCO 40/2036, Hong Kong Government Office, London to FCO.

109 TNA, FCO 40/1304, Williamson to Sullivan, 30 January 1981; FCO 40/1157, Brief on railway projects for secretary of state for trade's visit to Hong Kong, 26–30 January 1980.

110 TNA, CAB 133/528, Department of Industry brief, 7 September 1982; FCO 40/1157, Department of Trade/Overseas Projects Group brief, January 1980.

111 TNA, PREM 19/785 Part 2, Armstrong to Thatcher, 20 January 1981.

112 China Light and Power Company, *Annual Report 1982*, 7.

113 TNA, FCO 40/1304, Williamson to Sullivan, 30 January 1981.

114 See Feng Bangyan, *Xianggang yingzi caituan, 1841–1996* [British Business Groups in Hong Kong, 1841–1996] (Hong Kong: Joint Publishing (HK), 1996).

115 On a critical analysis of the 'British credentials' of the four largest British *hongs* in Hong Kong, see Goodstadt, *Uneasy Partners*, 168–79.

116 John D. Wong, 'Hong Kong Breaking into the International League: Cathay Pacific's Extension to Long-haul Routes, 1970s–1980s', *International Journal of Asian Studies* (2021), 1–20.

117 In the postwar period, successive British governments had undertaken so-called 'cost-benefit' analyses of Hong Kong and other colonies (for example, in 1957). Despite being one of the largest holders of sterling in the Sterling Area (which was disbanded after June 1972), there was no definite answer to Hong Kong's

economic value to the UK. Tony Hopkins, 'Macmillan's Audit of Empire, 1957', in Peter Clarke and Clive Trebilcock (eds), *Understanding Decline: Perceptions and Realities of British Economic Performance* (Cambridge: Cambridge University Press, 1997), 234–60; Goodstadt, *Uneasy Partners*, 231–3.

118 TNA, FCO 21/2214, 'Future of Hong Kong', attached in Clift to Donald, 23 July 1982.
119 See Shashi Tharoor, *Inglorious Empire: What the British Did to India* (London: Penguin Books, 2017), Chapter 1.
120 TNA, FCO 40/1303, 'Hong Kong and UK-China trade', December 1980; FCO 40/1286, 'Hong Kong: Economic importance to the UK', attached in Exeter to Williamson, 6 January 1981; PRO, HKRS 1687-1-82, 'Hong Kong's re-exports to China by major commodities', EIC631/7/1.
121 TNA, FCO 40/1301, Political Adviser's Office, HK, 'Notes on Hong Kong's economic links with China', 3 February 1981; Lau Pui-king, 'Economic Relations between Hong Kong and China', in Joseph Y. S. Cheng (ed.), *Hong Kong in Transition* (Hong Kong: Oxford University Press, 1986), 238, 241; Lu and Lu, *Xianggang jingji shi*, 295.
122 TNA, FCO 40/1301, Political Adviser's Office, HK, 'Hong Kong's economic relations with Guangdong', 22 January 1981; Political Adviser's Office, HK, 'Shenzhen: Progress report', 25 June 1981.
123 Chiu and Lui, *Hong Kong*, 134.
124 So and Chu, *The Global Rise of China*, 5, 50–1.
125 Yun-wing Sung, *The China-Hong Kong Connection: The Key to China's Open-Door Policy* (Cambridge: Cambridge University Press, 1991), 18, 100.
126 TNA, FCO 21/1833, Memo for Executive Council, 9 April 1980.
127 Deng Kaisong and Lu Xiaomin (et al.), *Yue Guang guanxi shi 1840–1984* [A History of Guangdong-Hong Kong Relations 1840–1984] (Hong Kong: Qilin shuye youxian gongsi, 1997), 346.
128 TNA, FCO 40/1269, Government Information Services, 'Sea and land links between China and Hong Kong', February 1981; PRO, HKRS 1642-1-24, Summary note of lunch for Vice-Governor Liu Tianfu on 13 November 1980; PRO, HKRS 1642-1-41, Deputy political adviser to members of the Hong Kong-China Economic Committee, 6 May 1982.
129 TNA, FCO 40/1472, Economic Services Branch, HK, 'Hong Kong's economic value to China', June 1983.
130 For details, see Chi-kwan Mark, 'Decolonising Britishness? The 1981 British Nationality Act and the Identity Crisis of Hong Kong Elites', *Journal of Imperial and Commonwealth History*, 48: 3 (2020), 565–90.
131 Kathleen Paul, *Whitewashing Britain: Race and Citizenship in the Postwar Era* (Ithaca, NY: Cornell University Press, 1997), 183, 189.
132 David Dixon, 'Thatcher's People: The British Nationality Act 1981', *Journal of Law & Society*, 10: 2 (Winter 1983), 166–7.
133 Gregor Benton and Edmund Terence Gomez, *The Chinese in Britain, 1800–Present: Economy, Transnationalism, Identity* (Basingstoke: Palgrave Macmillan, 2008), 51.

134 As in the British archives, 'unofficials' and 'unofficial members' are used interchangeably in this book.
135 Mark, 'Decolonising Britishness?'.
136 TNA, FCO 40/1337, Home Office news release, 30 October 1981.
137 Mo Kai, 'Xiandai maoyi tixi de chengzhang licheng' ['The Course of Development of the Modern Trading System'], in Wang Gungwu (ed.), *Xianggang shi xinbian* [Hong Kong History: New Perspectives], vol. 1 (Hong Kong: Joint Publishing (HK), 1997), 309.
138 Although, in 1982, the majority of Hong Kong residents preferred British rule to China's takeover, Mark Hampton argues that Hong Kong Chinese 'Britishness' was more instrumental than affective in nature, and only a small number of them (mainly elites) had emotional identification with the UK. Mark Hampton, *Hong Kong and British Culture, 1945–1997* (Manchester: Manchester University Press, 2017), Chapter 6.

3

Not for (re)turning: Thatcher meets Deng Xiaoping, 1982

On 22 September 1982, Margaret Thatcher arrived in Beijing to discuss Hong Kong's future with Deng Xiaoping.[1] She was determined to retain both British sovereignty and administrative rights over Hong Kong. Nevertheless, Deng saw the Hong Kong issue in the wider context of Taiwan and, for that matter, Sino-American relations. After Sino-American normalisation in 1979, Deng had hoped that Taiwan would be peacefully reunified with the motherland in the not-so-distant future. By late 1981, however, the Taiwan question re-emerged as the main irritant in Sino-American relations, thanks to the Ronald Reagan administration's inclination to increase arms sales to Taiwan. In October, Premier Zhao Ziyang raised the issue with Reagan, who, however, wanted Beijing to make a statement on renunciation of force against Taiwan.[2] To Deng, how to achieve national unification with Taiwan was entirely a matter of China's 'internal affairs'.[3]

Not until 17 August 1982 did the United States and China sign a joint communiqué, according to which the Reagan administration would gradually reduce its arms sales to Taiwan, leading over a period of time to a final resolution.[4] Although the immediate crisis over arms sales was over, as the CCP's mouthpiece the *People's Daily* warned, the 'fundamental obstacle to the development of Sino-American relations is the U.S. "Taiwan Relations Act"', a law passed by Congress in April 1979 authorising the administration to maintain non-diplomatic relations with Taiwan and ensure its self-defence capabilities.[5] In other words, the United States still posed a potential threat to China's sovereignty claims over Taiwan.[6] The controversy over US arms sales to Taiwan, together with the perceived changing strategic balance between the United States and the Soviet Union in the former's favour, prompted Deng to proclaim China's 'independent foreign policy'. At the Twelfth Party Congress on 1 September, Deng talked at great length about the fundamental principle of 'independence and self-reliance'. While China would 'unswervingly follow a policy of opening to the outside world', the government should ensure that '[w]e, the Chinese people, have our national self-respect and pride'.[7]

It is clear that Deng's nationalist feelings had been stirred by the United States. Against the international backdrop of Sino-American disagreement over Taiwan, Deng saw the imperative of resolving the Hong Kong question. Now that Taiwan's reunification with China appeared to be a more complicated task than he might have thought three years ago, Deng shifted his priority to Hong Kong, which, if successfully handled, could serve as a showcase of what would later be known as 'one country, two systems'. During her visit to Beijing, Thatcher thus found that Deng's views on Hong Kong were the polar opposite of hers. She did secure Deng's agreement to open diplomatic talks on Hong Kong's future, though. As a fervent believer in free-trade globalisation, Thatcher also seized the opportunity to promote British economic interests in China.

Preparations for the visit

On 15 December 1981, Deng instructed Party Chairman Hu Yaobang and other colleagues responsible for Hong Kong affairs to come up with more than two proposals for resolving the Hong Kong question within two to three months.[8] In January 1982, a joint policy task force consisting of five members, including Liao Chengzhi (who was placed in overall charge), Lu Ping of the State Council's Hong Kong and Macao Affairs Office (who became the team leader), and representatives of the Hong Kong branch of the NCNA, was established. They spent several months on *diao yan* (investigation and research), paying several visits to Hong Kong and drafting twenty-plus reports. By March, Liao's team submitted to the Party Central Committee a preliminary plan for resolving the Hong Kong question, including the suggestion that Hong Kong's capitalist system and free port status should be maintained.[9] On 21 March, Deng approved the preliminary plan in principle, but wanted to seek further opinion on concrete proposals.[10]

Deng was eager to hear first-hand the views of Hong Kong compatriots, particularly business people. This was part of his strategy of constructing a 'patriotic united front of the new era'.[11] Indeed, the Chinese communists had a long history of wooing wealthy capitalists in Hong Kong, and the local branch of the NCNA had been playing an active role.[12] (When Xu Jiatun became NCNA director in the midst of the Hong Kong negotiations in mid-1983, he intensified the united front work.) Between mid-March and mid-June 1982, Deng received more than ten groups of visitors from Hong Kong, from business tycoons such as Li Ka-shing and Fok Ying-tung to academic leaders like Hong Kong University Vice Chancellor Rayson Huang and newspaper executives like Dr Louis Cha of *Ming Pao*. Deng's main purpose was not to enquire whether China should recover Hong Kong in

1997, which to him was a foregone conclusion. Rather, he wanted to solicit their views about how to maintain prosperity and stability in Hong Kong, a more challenging task.[13]

On 16 September, Deng convened a meeting with Hu Yaobang, Party Vice Chairman Li Xiannian, Li Hou, deputy director of the Hong Kong and Macao Affairs Office, and others at his residence. The main subjects of discussion were Hong Kong's current financial situation in view of an internal report suggesting a massive outflow of capital from the territory, and the British prime minister's upcoming visit to China. Li Hou along with representatives of the Bank of China confirmed that there had been no massive capital outflow of late, but only normal movement of capital in and out of Hong Kong. In response, Deng asserted that the policy of recovering Hong Kong in 1997 was a 'correct' one. But during the fifteen-year transition, China should prepare for possible turbulence in Hong Kong, and, in the event of 'serious disturbance', it should 'reconsider the timing and method of recovering Hong Kong'. Thatcher's visit would provide a good opportunity for China to stress its principle and to seek British cooperation over Hong Kong.[14] Negotiation with the British would be 'a complicated [and] long-term struggle'.[15]

From the perspective of the FCO, Thatcher's visit to China, as part of her Far Eastern tour, would be in return for the 1979 visit to Britain of Hua Guofeng, and would bring the prime minister in line with the majority of the heads of government of Britain's major European partners who had sojourned in the PRC (such as France and West Germany).[16] In early January 1982, Humphrey Atkins, the Lord privy seal, travelled to Beijing in preparation for Thatcher's visit. When receiving Atkins on 6 January, Premier Zhao Ziyang spelt out China's general stand on Hong Kong – that 'China would safeguard her sovereignty', and the prosperity of Hong Kong would be maintained. After recalling Ye Jianying's 'nine points' on Taiwan, Zhao said that there was as yet 'no specific formula' for Hong Kong, but the problem 'would not be put on the shelf until 1997'.[17] On 9 March, Foreign Secretary Lord Carrington sent a detailed minute to Thatcher about the meeting: while 'the Chinese have not moved on essentials', it was encouraging that they 'recognise the existence of the problem as well as the need for it to be solved before 1997'. Although the Chinese had stated that they wanted to 'see Hong Kong remain a free port and a commercial and financial centre', Carrington suspected that they had yet 'fully grasped the ways in which confidence could be threatened or maintained'. To Carrington, 'Confidence in the Territory, particularly among investors, is likely only to be maintained if autonomy is guaranteed by the administration continuing on the same lines, ie through the British'. Aware of the legal reality that Hong Kong was partly ceded and partly leased, Carrington argued that

Britain could 'only maintain sovereign powers in the New Territories up to 1997' and 'the rest of the Territory is not viable on its own' after that date. If Britain and China could come to 'an arrangement whereby [Britain] made some sort of recognition of Chinese sovereignty over the rest of the Territory (ie Hong Kong Island and Kowloon) while still retaining the right to administer the Territory beyond 1997', it would represent a 'real foreign policy success'.[18] Thatcher read but made no comment on the substance of Carrington's minute, but hoped to discuss the matter with him in the coming weeks.[19]

Deng Xiaoping used a former prime minister to communicate an important message to London. In early April, Edward Heath, an old 'friend of China' due to his role in Sino-British normalisation, visited China for the fifth time.[20] In response to Heath's query about how China would handle the Hong Kong question, Deng asserted that China possessed 'sovereignty over Hong Kong'. Referring to Ye's 'nine points' on Taiwan, which could be applied to Hong Kong, Deng stated that the new Chinese constitution (to be approved by the NPC later in the year) would make provision for the creation of 'special administrative zones', according to which Hong Kong would be permitted to keep its 'various systems'. Under such an arrangement, Deng claimed, Britain 'might suffer a loss of taxation revenue from Hong Kong', but 'trade and commerce would not suffer'.[21] As the FCO assessed the interview, what Deng had suggested was, in essence, 'the Taiwan solution' for Hong Kong.[22] From the British Embassy in Beijing, Percy Cradock believed that Deng had used 'the visit of a distinguished, but non-government, visitor, to put forward what is in effect a tentative offer in advance of the Prime Minister's visit'. Cradock was deeply concerned that Deng had shown 'continued misunderstanding of the way the Hong Kong economy works and what investors will accept', including 'the delusion that the UK Treasury receives taxation revenue from Hong Kong'. 'We must correct Chinese misconceptions', he recommended to the FCO.[23] In other words, Britain should 'educate' China on the nature of Hong Kong's free-market capitalism.

The Deng–Heath meeting came just days after Argentina had invaded the Falkland Islands on 2 April 1982. Preoccupied with commanding what would become a ten-week-long war, Thatcher was unable to see the record of the conversation until mid-July.[24] Only after the end of the Falklands War could she devote time to the Hong Kong question. Notwithstanding the euphoria of victory, Thatcher was 'well aware' that China was not Argentina and Hong Kong was not the Falkland Islands, 'both from the military and the legal viewpoints'.[25] With her conviction in free-market capitalism, Thatcher believed that Hong Kong's economic success owed much to 'a British framework of political and financial institutions'.[26] Indeed, Hong Kong was 'more British in character than Britain itself during the heyday of postwar Welfare State consensus'.[27] In the early 1980s, Hong Kong embodied many features of 'Thatcherism': a free-market economy (with selective government intervention), fiscal conservatism (with no or minimal external debt), low taxation (which was conducive to foreign investment), the rule of law (which guaranteed personal freedom if not democracy), and weak union power (which ensured rare industrial conflicts). What was uppermost in Thatcher's mind was not Hong Kong's economic value to Britain per se. As discussed in Chapter 2, globalisation had eroded the value of the imperial connection, and Britain had to 'compete on level terms' with other countries in terms of visible trade with Hong Kong. Although Britain regarded Hong Kong as a vital export market in Asia, and UK companies valued the dynamic city as a commercial gateway to the Far East, some of the 'economic and commercial benefits derived from Hong Kong by the UK' could still continue even without 'the present system of administration'.[28] After all, Hong Kong was a free port open to all countries: the United States and Japan, for example, did not need empire to advance their respective commercial interests in the territory. The main concern of the Thatcher government was that a unilateral withdrawal from Hong Kong would create 'serious problems' for the UK, such as the loss of British investment and a possible exodus of Hong Kong residents to Britain.[29]

Besides, Thatcher found it morally wrong to hand over capitalist Hong Kong to communist China. She felt strongly for the Hong Kong people, who treasured British administration and the capitalist way of life. (In early 1982, three comprehensive opinion surveys, conducted by the Reform Club, the Baptist College, and the Hong Kong Observers, respectively, showed 85 to 93 per cent of respondents favouring the status quo of continual British administration in Hong Kong.)[30] That said, Thatcher's sense of moral obligation was compromised by her aversion to Hong Kong immigration to Britain, as manifested in the passage of the 1981 British Nationality Act.

Thatcher's China visit was scheduled for 22–26 September, followed by a two-and-a-half-day visit to Hong Kong. Primarily a working visit, Thatcher would lead a small party including Assistant Under Secretary Alan Donald, Hong Kong Governor Edward Youde, her private secretary, John Coles, and a few FCO officials – but not the foreign secretary. According to the FCO, the 'main objectives' of the visit were to 'demonstrate Britain's willingness to develop through exchanges at the top level an enduring and balanced relationship with China' and to 'take such limited opportunities as may arise to further our commercial interests'. But the 'dominant objective' was to 'seek agreement on the opening of discussions on the future of the Territory after 1997' and to 'reaffirm our wish to see a major Hong Kong contribution to China's economic development'.[31]

On 28 July, Thatcher chaired a meeting at Downing Street with the foreign secretary, the British ambassador in Beijing, the Hong Kong governor, and other officials. Following the line of argument previously used by Carrington (who had resigned over the Falklands War), Thatcher asserted that 'there appeared to be a fundamental lack of comprehension on the Chinese side as to what was needed to maintain confidence in Hong Kong', and the proposals they had so far put forward 'would in themselves bring about a collapse of confidence'. Thatcher suggested the idea of a 'management contract' – a device that would leave the administration of Hong Kong in British hands, while allowing China to claim that it had recovered sovereignty. But she stressed that 'we should not start by assuming that we shall have to give up sovereignty'. Cradock, however, reminded the prime minister that 'the alternative, if we clung to sovereignty, was a confrontation with China'. Thatcher also raised the sensitive issue of British nationality and Hong Kong immigration. To her, 'citizenship was linked to sovereignty': if sovereignty was transferred to China, the inhabitants of Hong Kong could no longer have British passports. In this regard, it was essential that there was 'no danger of a mass influx of Hong Kong citizens' to Britain as a result of an agreement with China.[32]

After the Downing Street meeting, the FCO constituted a special group under Lord Belstead, minister of state responsible inter alia for Asian affairs, with the aim of producing a full study of all aspects of the Hong Kong problem.[33] The study, titled 'The Future of Hong Kong: A Special Study', was completed in late August.[34] In a minute to Thatcher dated 3 September, Foreign Secretary Francis Pym summarised the study's conclusion that 'the likeliest way of reconciling our position and that of the Chinese while meeting the interests of the people of Hong Kong as a whole would be some form of "management contract"'. Any such arrangement should provide 'very firm guarantees for the continuation of British administration beyond 1997', and only 'on that basis could any acknowledgement of Chinese sovereignty be considered'. With the immigration issue in mind, Pym added that a 'management contract' would 'be saleable in this country both in Parliament and to public opinion', and, by maintaining confidence in Hong Kong's future, would 'discourage people in Hong Kong from trying to leave and come to this country'.[35]

Thatcher hoped to gauge the 'climate of opinion' in Hong Kong before her China trip. On 8 September, she invited the Hong Kong governor and five unofficial members of the Executive Council and the Legislative Council (UMELCO) to lunch in Downing Street. (This would be the first of a series of UMELCO delegations to London during the Hong Kong negotiations.) Having a disposition to 'suddenly propose something dramatic and impractical' in policy deliberations,[36] Thatcher asked whether those present would welcome 'independence' if it were a 'genuine option' for Hong Kong. Lydia Dunn, a member of both councils and an executive at Swire Pacific, replied that 'independence', if feasible, would be 'preferable to absorption of China', although 'the wish of the people of Hong Kong' would be maintenance of the British system. Sze-yuen Chung, senior unofficial member of the Executive Council and a successful industrialist, said that it was widely believed that China would not allow Hong Kong to become independent. Thatcher then floated the idea of continuing British administration 'in exchange for a sovereignty which was merely titular'. Dunn replied that 'at first blush the Chinese might regard titular sovereignty as inadequate', but they were 'pragmatic' and might be reconciled to the British standpoint '[o]nce they had been educated to see that prosperity flowed from British administration'. Sceptical about their 'pragmatic' character, Thatcher claimed that the Chinese were 'Marxist' and their system was 'centralist'. The Chinese 'did not understand what was necessary to maintain confidence'. Finally, Thatcher reassured her guests that Britain's 'duty lay with the five and a half million people of Hong Kong'.[37]

On 13 September, Thatcher chaired a small ministerial meeting, during which the foreign and home secretaries and the attorney general endorsed her negotiating approach.[38] In Beijing, Thatcher would employ the tactics of playing up the 'confidence factor' and of stressing Britain's moral responsibility to Hong Kong rather than the latter's economic value.

'Steel factory' confronts the Iron Lady[39]

Arriving by the Royal Air Force VC10 in the early afternoon of 22 September, Thatcher's party was greeted at Beijing Airport by Vice Foreign Minister Zhang Wenjin. A formal welcoming ceremony was arranged outside the Great Hall of the People, where Thatcher inspected a guard of honour. There followed the first round of talks between Premier Zhao Ziyang and Thatcher, focusing on China's relations with the superpowers.[40] At night, a welcoming banquet in the prime minister's honour was given by Zhao in the Great Hall for some two hundred guests. Apparently hoping to create a good atmosphere for tomorrow's talks on Hong Kong, Thatcher gave a speech about the long history of Anglo-Chinese 'friendship', quoting a Tang poem to illustrate that '[geographical] distances mean very little' to 'friendship'.[41]

During the second session with Zhao Ziyang on 23 September, Thatcher first made a statement conveying the crucial message about how capitalist Hong Kong worked. Hong Kong was 'a unique example of successful Sino/British co-operation', and the problem faced by Britain and China at the moment was 'how to agree about its future while maintaining its prosperity'. Thatcher asserted that 'the prosperity of Hong Kong depends on confidence', which in turn depended not only on 'good relations between Britain and China' but also on other things – 'a stable and internationally respected currency'; 'a financial and tax regime favouring business enterprise and which is not liable to sudden change' (and one from which 'Britain derives no revenue'); 'a formal and internationally respected system of law'; 'the maintenance of public order'; and 'the freedom of its political and economic system'. Referring to the 'general assurances' given by China that 'the present local systems will be preserved', Thatcher said that they would 'not be enough by themselves to maintain confidence'. Rather, she reiterated that '[c]onfidence in Hong Kong, and thus its continued prosperity, depend on British administration'. On the 'delicate' issue of sovereignty, Thatcher stated that the Chinese position was 'well-known' to the British government, but it was 'politically difficult' for her to agree to China's assertion of sovereignty over Hong Kong. The latter would 'involve Britain abrogating by Act of Parliament the treaties under which the British administer Hong Kong'.

After listening very carefully to Thatcher's statement, Zhao remarked that the Hong Kong question was 'an issue left over from history', and that the time had come when China would 'recover its sovereignty over Hong Kong in 1997 – and no later'. Claiming that China was 'not bound by treaties signed between the British Government and the Ching dynasty', Zhao asserted that the recovery of the entire Hong Kong (Hong Kong Island and Kowloon being 'inseparable' from the New Territories) was 'an issue concerning Chinese sovereignty, territorial integrity and the national feelings of the Chinese people'. After the resumption of sovereignty, China would pursue 'special policies' in Hong Kong. If it came to 'a choice between the two', Zhao warned, 'China would put sovereignty above prosperity and stability' because '[s]overeignty was a matter of principle'. Zhao was optimistic that Chinese investors would stay if China pursued a policy of maintaining prosperity in Hong Kong, asking rhetorically where else they could go. Sensing Zhao's apparent ignorance of global capitalism, Thatcher immediately suggested Singapore, the Philippines, or even New York.

After stressing the 'confidence factor', Thatcher underscored the legality of the three treaties governing Hong Kong's status – or, more precisely, the legal implications of abrogating international treaties. By 1997, 'the legal basis for the British Administration of the new territories would end: the British Government honoured its agreements'. Yet 'the legal basis for British retention of Hong Kong and Kowloon would continue as a matter of international law'. Although the Chinese wanted these treaties to be abrogated, Thatcher hoped that they would 'recognise that abrogation would have to be achieved through a law passed by the British Parliament'. If Beijing insisted on abrogating one agreement 'valid at international law', she wondered 'what assurance could there be that they would keep any other agreement'.[42] In countering Zhao's emphasis on sovereignty, Thatcher, too, stressed a 'principle' which 'ran strongly throughout the British character' – the 'duty to those who for 140 years had put their faith, their future and their investment in Hong Kong under British administration'. It was because of the people of Hong Kong that the British government had a moral obligation to reach agreement through consultation with the Chinese government.[43]

The highlight of the visit was Thatcher's interview with Deng Xiaoping at the Great Hall of the People on 24 September. While understanding 'how important the principle of sovereignty was to China', Thatcher said that 'sovereignty was also a difficult issue for her': 'she had to convince the British Parliament and Mr. Deng had to convince the Chinese people'. Claiming that the British and Chinese governments shared the 'common objective' of 'maintaining the prosperity and stability of Hong Kong', Thatcher spelt out her position on resolution of the 1997 question. If the two governments could agree 'definite arrangements about the future administration and control of Hong Kong', and if she was satisfied that they would work and 'command confidence' in the British Parliament and among the people of Hong Kong, Thatcher would 'consider the question of sovereignty' and recommend the outcome to Parliament accordingly. As there was 'no time in the present short visit to reconcile the differences' over Hong Kong, Thatcher proposed that, before her departure from Beijing, both sides should announce that further talks would take place.

Deng underscored China's basic position on Hong Kong in three aspects – sovereignty, prosperity, and the question of how to 'avoid turbulence' in Hong Kong between now and 1997. First and foremost, 'sovereignty was not a matter which could be discussed': 'in 1997 China would certainly recover sovereignty over Hong Kong'. It was 'under this pre-condition', Deng stressed, that China and Britain would hold talks to discuss the 'formulae for the future of Hong Kong' and the 'policies for maintaining Hong Kong's prosperity'. With the 'century of humiliation' in mind, Deng warned that if Hong Kong was not returned to China in 1997, the Chinese government 'would not be able to account for it to the Chinese people', who would think that 'the new China was like the China of the Ching dynasty and the present leaders were like Li Hongzhang' (who had signed the 'unequal treaties'). Significantly, Deng revealed that in 'no more than one or two years time', the Chinese government would formally announce its decision to recover Hong Kong. He had postponed an announcement because China needed time to solicit widespread views from various circles in Hong Kong and to conduct consultation with Britain. Referring to Thatcher's remarks about the 'difficulties' of returning Hong Kong to China, Deng offered his personal view that Hong Kong's retrocession would 'bring a much bigger benefit because it meant that the period of colonialism would have ended in Britain'.

Unimpressed by Deng's comments on the nature of British colonialism, Thatcher replied that it was Britain's 'normal policy' to bring former colonies to independence, but that Hong Kong was exceptional 'because of the complications of the lease from China'. To correct the Chinese misunderstanding of the UK–Hong Kong relationship, Thatcher stressed that 'the British Government derived no revenue from Hong Kong, and Hong Kong received no aid' from London. She insisted that 'Britain was not a colonialist country', and it 'simply wanted to carry out her moral duty to Hong Kong'. Thatcher later added that 'every survey' showed that Hong Kong residents 'wished the British system of administration to be maintained'.

On the question of maintaining prosperity and stability, Deng said that China 'hoped to enjoy the co-operation of Britain', but that 'did not mean that the prosperity of Hong Kong could be maintained only under British administration'. Rather, it 'depended fundamentally on the policy pursued by China towards Hong Kong' after 1997. If there were 'very large and serious disturbances' in the next fifteen years, Deng warned, 'the Chinese Government would be forced to consider the time and formula relating to the recovery of its sovereignty over Hong Kong'. He added that any 'major disturbances' would be 'man-made (artificial), not natural'. When queried by Thatcher that 'all disturbances were created by man', Deng clarified that the disturbances 'would be created, not by Governments, but by individuals, some Chinese, some British'. He cited the example of the Hong Kong and Shanghai Bank: 'No-one knew how many banknotes it had issued'. Governor Youde corrected Deng by saying that the colonial authorities knew. Deng agreed, but insisted that the Hong Kong people he talked to did not know. Deng professed that the British and Chinese governments should 'prevent some businessmen from doing things which were detrimental to the prosperity and stability of Hong Kong'.

Towards the end of the meeting, Deng suggested that the two sides should agree to start discussions through diplomatic channels on the 'precondition' that 'in 1997 China would recover sovereignty over Hong Kong'. 'Under this pre-condition', he said, they would 'discuss how to ensure a good transitional period of fifteen years and what would be done after fifteen years'. After some discussion of the wording, the two sides agreed to issue the following statement:

> Today the leaders of both countries held far reaching talks in a friendly atmosphere on the future of Hong Kong. Both leaders made clear their respective

positions on this subject. They agreed to enter talks through diplomatic channels following the visit with the common aim of maintaining the stability and prosperity of Hong Kong.[44]

After an 'abrasive' meeting with the 'cruel' Deng,[45] Thatcher, leaving the Great Hall of the People, walked down the steps but unfortunately slipped and fell to her knees. (She had recently had an operation on her varicose veins in a UK hospital.)[46] The moment of Thatcher's slip, captured by television cameras, would become the collective memory of Hong Kong people.

The following day, Thatcher departed Beijing for Shanghai and then Guangzhou, before travelling to Hong Kong. In Hong Kong, Thatcher's main objectives were to reassure the Hong Kong people that Britain's commitment to the territory was 'as strong as ever', to confirm that the 'common objective' of Britain and China was to 'maintain Hong Kong's prosperity and stability', and to 'promote British commercial interests'.[47] Upon arrival on 26 September, Thatcher first gave the Hong Kong governor and his senior officials a brief rundown on the Beijing talks.[48] When meeting with some thirty UMELCO the following day, Thatcher could not but express her frustration with the perceived Chinese ignorance of capitalism. The Chinese leaders 'thought they could run a capitalist society but they did not know what it meant'. To Thatcher, Deng's 'pragmatism counted for little compared with his Marxist-Leninism'. Assuming that the Chinese leaders had not heard 'the truth about what made Hong Kong a success from local personalities who had been invited to Peking', Thatcher requested the unofficial members' help in getting across the basic message that Hong Kong's prosperity depended on British administration.[49]

The public reaction to Thatcher's visit was generally positive. While the content of Thatcher's discussions with the Chinese leaders was kept secret, Hong Kong residents had been encouraged by the joint statement on opening talks, and by Thatcher's remarks at the press conference to the effect that Britain stood by the treaties and had a moral responsibility to Hong Kong people.[50] However, disturbed by Thatcher's comments, the Chinese Ministry of Foreign Affairs and the NCNA responded with statements and articles emphasising China's sovereignty over Hong Kong.[51] Against this backdrop, the Hang Seng Index in the Hong Kong Stock Exchange fell for consecutive days, from over a thousand points on 26 September to 862.06 points when it closed on the 29th.[52]

Thatcher returned from China convinced that Deng had a poor understanding of the nature of capitalism in Hong Kong: he assumed that London derived taxation revenue from Hong Kong, and asked the British to prevent investors from withdrawing capital from the territory. Thatcher believed that the Chinese 'would need to be educated slowly and thoroughly in how it worked if they were to keep Hong Kong prosperous and stable'.[53] In early October, the FCO proposed a number of ways to 'educate further the Chinese in the realities of Hong Kong'. It was important to convince Beijing that 'continuity of British administration and ultimate control from London' were 'essential to the maintenance of confidence' in Hong Kong not because 'the British have expertise in administration which the Chinese lack'. Rather, the reason lay in the fact that 'the British connection' was 'valued ... as an insurance against interference from Peking on major domestic and external issues'. The FCO, nonetheless, recognised that this would be 'a very difficult message to get across both frankly and without causing offence'. As for the channels to convey the message, the British government could consider Hong Kong residents, especially 'people of influence in business and the professions', or 'friendly foreign governments', such as the United States (Secretary of State George Shultz had already offered to help). The process of 'educating' the Chinese could also be conducted by the British diplomats in Beijing, major British companies operating in China, and the FCO itself through communication with the Chinese Embassy in London.[54] Thatcher, regarding the FCO's proposals as 'too general in nature', wanted 'more specific ideas' to 'carry the education process forward'.[55]

Anglo-Chinese economic relations

Another objective of Thatcher's China visit was to promote British commercial interests on the mainland. Since the signing of the agreement on Anglo-Chinese economic cooperation in March 1979, which set an ambitious target for increasing economic exchanges to the total value of US$14 billion by 1985, Anglo-Chinese bilateral trade had reached its best-ever level, but then began to decline. During 1979, Britain's visible exports to China had increased more than twofold, from £91 million in 1978 to the all-time high of £213 million the following year. Its imports from China increased slightly, from £110 to £138 million, thus resulting in a trade surplus of £75 million.[56] Nevertheless, no sooner had the economic cooperation agreement been signed than the Chinese government, in April 1979, adopted a policy of 'economic readjustment' to tackle the problems brought about by Hua Guofeng's ambitious ten-year modernisation programme.[57] Consequently, China suspended or cancelled contracts for the import of foreign turnkey projects and foot-dragged on the purchase of defence equipment (like the Harrier). This did not mean a u-turn for Deng Xiaoping's reform; on the contrary, the four SEZs were officially inaugurated in 1980. Rather, under the influence of conservatives led by Chen Yun, the policy cycle had shifted in favour of state planning at the expense of market forces.

In January 1982, Chen Yun warned against the problem of smuggling activities in the coastal regions and particularly Guangdong, where most joint ventures were located. By April, his warnings resulted in the adoption by the Central Committee and the State Council of a campaign to 'strike hard against serious economic crimes', which then 'turned into a campaign against economic liberalization'.[58] In the course of the fifth session of the Fifth NPC in December, Chen vividly likened the relationship between the market and the plan to that between a bird and a cage: 'You mustn't hold the bird in your hands too tightly, or it would be strangled. You have to turn it loose, but only within the confines of the cage.'[59] In the early 1980s, neither Deng, who still considered Chen as 'the primary decision maker on economic issues',[60] nor Premier Zhao Ziyang, who appeared to be 'an extremely cautious reformer',[61] challenged Chen's imposition of economic orthodoxy.

Owing to the effects of economic 'readjustment', British exports to China (primarily textile fibres and machinery, mining machinery, chemicals, and scientific and telecommunication equipment) declined, while their imports from China (mainly clothing, foodstuffs, and chemicals) increased. From a high of £213 million worth of exports with a surplus of £75 million in 1979, Britain's exports were reduced to £126 million with a deficit of £46 million in 1981. In the first half of 1982, its exports were down to £45 million and its deficit up to £55 million. The volume of Anglo-Chinese trade declined not just in absolute terms, but also in relation to the growth of Britain's main competitors, notably Japan, the United States, and the Federal Republic of Germany. Due to historical links, economic performance, and geopolitical factors, Japan and the United States were the top two trading partners of China, and were a long way ahead of Britain in terms of the value and share of both exports and imports.[62] Within the EEC, Britain was outperformed by West Germany and even by France and Italy in some years. West Germany was a highly industrialised nation with sophisticated technology, particularly concerning the motor industry and heavy machinery. Bonn's pursuit of *Ostpolitik* with the Soviet Union meant that while the German federal government avoided strategic cooperation with Beijing (in order to avoid provoking Moscow), the regional government and politicians used every opportunity to develop trade with China. As for France, the state was actively involved in promoting trade (and cultural exchange) with China through logistical and, where possible, financial support. As the first major Western power to establish diplomatic relations with the PRC (in 1964), France enjoyed a 'privileged' political position in Beijing's eyes.[63]

In 1979, Britain was ranked seventh in terms of its share of China's visible imports, and was lower than only West Germany (which ranked third) among the EEC countries. In 1981, however, Britain, whose ranking tumbled to eleventh, was overtaken by both France (ranked eighth) and Italy (ranked tenth), not to mention West Germany (which dropped slightly to fourth place). Overall, Britain's share of the China market was very small, and only 3.2 per cent even when it enjoyed the highest figure of exports in 1979 (see Table 3.1).[64] On the other hand, China's position in the UK's export market was insignificant, declining from sixty-fifth place in 1977 to forty-fourth by 1983.[65]

Britain's poor export performance was down to a host of factors. According to the Sino-British Trade Council's 1981 operations report, many British companies faced difficulties in 'identifying valid enquiries, firm projects, and authoritative trading partners in China'.[66] Potential investors and traders had been put off by a lack of clarity in the regulations governing the SEZs, problems with bureaucracy, and poor communications.[67]

Major British companies operating in China lamented that the Chinese were 'very anxious to secure the keenest possible price', had the tendency to 'ask for detailed technical specifications', and were 'acutely slow in reaching decisions'.[68] To Percy Cradock and his staff in the commercial section of the Beijing Embassy, China was 'a competitive market', and the Chinese were, 'in general, skilful negotiators'. In order to secure valuable contracts with the Chinese, aspiring British exporters needed preparatory work, advance publicity, and above all persistence. Unlike Britain's major competitors, such as France and West Germany, there was no joint commission to review bilateral trade on an annual basis: Cradock had proposed establishing a Sino-British commission, but the Department of Trade and Industry (DTI) opposed it on financial grounds. Besides, the UK was 'among the least generous of China's Western trading partners with regard to aid'. While it had established a modest technical cooperation programme, the British government could not afford to provide soft loans to British companies bidding for projects in China. Nevertheless, Cradock was optimistic that, given the experience and expertise of UK companies, Britain was 'well placed' to respond to China's development priorities, notably energy, communications, transport, and industrial innovation.[69]

A possible source of energy for China was nuclear power. The General Electric Company (GEC), 'one of the most stable, respected and profitable companies in the United Kingdom' that employed 150,000 people in 1980,[70] was interested in the Guangdong nuclear power station project. Back in early 1979, senior Chinese officials of Guangdong Province had approached GEC representatives in Hong Kong about the import of nuclear plant. Lawrence Kadoorie, a Hong Kong-born businessman of Baghdadi Jewish descent who held a UK passport and received a life peerage in 1981, was chairman of China Light and Power Company (CLP). He was enthusiastic about the construction of a nuclear power station near the border of

Table 3.1 Trade with China (£ million)

	1978	1979	1980	1981	1982
Britain:					
Exports	91	213	169	126	103
Imports	110	138	153	172	193
Balance	−19	+75	+16	−46	−90
Share of China's total imports:					
Percentage	2.71	3.2	2.77	1.55	1.37
Ranking	8	7	7	11	12
West Germany:					
Exports	516	704	491	501	
Imports	190	252	347	379	
Balance	+326	+452	+144	+122	
Share of China's total imports:					
Percentage	9.44	11.09	6.83	7.93	5.11
Ranking	2	3	3	3	5
France:					
Exports	103	160	130	135	
Imports	117	154	201	250	
Balance	−14	+6	−71	−115	
Share of China's total imports:					
Percentage	2.26	2.59	1.61	1.88	1.22
Ranking	9	8	9	8	14
Italy:					
Exports	98	131	110	159	
Imports	104	186	188	197	
Balance	−6	−55	−78	−38	
Share of China's total imports:					
Percentage	1.75	1.97	1.28	1.6	1.69
Ranking	11	9	12	10	9
Japan:					
Exports	1,569	1,725	2,169	2,505	
Imports	1,054	1,390	1,859	2,630	
Balance	+515	+335	+310	−125	
Share of China's total imports:					
Percentage	28.45	25.16	26.5	27.73	20.64
Ranking	1	1	1	1	2

(*continued*)

Table 3.1 (Cont.)

	1978	1979	1980	1981	1982
United States:					
Exports	429	813	1,614	1,776	
Imports	169	279	455	934	
Balance	+260	+534	+1,159	+842	
Share of China's total imports:					
Percentage	6.61	11.85	19.64	22.59	22.7
Ranking	3	2	2	2	1

Hong Kong. To the Department of Industry in Britain, if CLP 'retained its pro-British purchasing policy', the project would be 'the largest Sino-British venture at least since the Revolution with potential UK hardware orders of about US$1300 m[illion]'.[71] In early 1980, the Guangdong Electricity Company and CLP agreed to undertake a feasibility study on the project, led by Dr Walter Marshall, deputy chairman of the UK Atomic Energy Authority.[72] Completed in November, the feasibility study recommended the commissioning of a two 900-megawatt pressurised water reactor nuclear power station in one of the two recommended sites adjacent to Hong Kong (Daya Bay was eventually chosen), and the establishment of a joint venture in Guangdong, with shareholding split between the Guangdong Electricity Company and a new Hong Kong nuclear investment company under CLP's management. The feasibility report envisaged separate nuclear and conventional islands. If all things were equal, preference would be given to Britain for the supply of the conventional island. As for the nuclear island, the options included the United States' Westinghouse, France's Framatome, and West Germany's Kraftwerk Union.[73]

From the outset, Thatcher had acquired an interest in the Guangdong nuclear project due to her close relationship with Kadoorie.[74] In March 1982, a technical mission from the Guangdong Electricity Company and CLP visited Britain to discuss the project. In July of the same year, the British were invited to present to the Chinese an equipment package, together with a supporting financial package, which included a nuclear island by Westinghouse/National Nuclear Corporation (the latter being a British firm); a GEC conventional island; fuel supplies and processing by British Nuclear Fuels Ltd.; and technical support services by the Central Electricity Generating Board and the UK Atomic Energy Authority.[75] But there were controversaries over the possible supplier of the nuclear island. Although the Chinese preferred the US option (which was deemed more technologically advanced) to the French option, the US administration was concerned about the issue of nuclear non-proliferation and safeguards. Foreign Secretary Francis Pym, however, argued that 'non-proliferation concerns' were outweighed by 'the economic and political advantages of co-operation with the PRC on a project of this scale' – for example, export opportunities for Britain up to US$2 billion and benefits to long-term relations between Britain and China and between China and Hong Kong.[76] Against the background of the uncertainty over the Guangdong nuclear project, Thatcher visited China in September 1982 to explore business opportunities besides discussing the Hong Kong question. In its brief for the prime minister, the Department of Trade suggested making the point that 'Britain has great expertise in China's economic priority sectors such as energy, transport, communications and agriculture', and thus 'there should be much more scope for mutually beneficial co-operation in these and other areas'.[77]

When meeting with Zhao Ziyang on 23 September, Thatcher endeavoured to 'sell' British goods and services to China. She raised the Guangdong nuclear project, in which Britain was 'deeply interested' and was 'ready to work with any nuclear partner of China's choice'. She expressed her gratitude that the Chinese had indicated that 'GEC would be competent to make turbine island'. Zhao said that '[i]f the prices and agreed terms were favourable', China was 'planning to use French-made reactor equipment and British generating equipment'. Thatcher asked whether this was a 'decision', for she understood that the Guangdong Power Company had also been 'considering the Americans as the partner in the project'. Zhao confirmed that the company was 'not pursuing formal contacts with the United States'. Thatcher said that Britain 'shared China's wish to maximise trade'. Zhao replied that although Sino-British trade was 'not yet on a large scale', there was 'a broad prospect for further advances'. In the coming twenty years, the Chinese 'wished to exploit their energy resources, to develop transport and communications, and to modernise their existing production capacity in a planned way'. But Zhao hoped that the British would 'try to be competitive, since increases in cooperation on these matters depended not only on Government collaboration but on the competitiveness of businessmen'. Zhao requested Britain to 'provide low rate long-term loans in the interests of promoting exports and cooperation in economic and technological matters'.

Turning to specific projects, Zhao regarded the ongoing discussions between Pilkingtons and the Ministry of Building Materials over the joint venture of a float glass plant in Shanghai as 'promising'. So were the prospects of British involvement in offshore oil exploration in the Yellow Sea and the South China Sea. Nevertheless, not all negotiations between the British and Chinese had gone smoothly, one example of which was the refitting of two Luda-class Chinese destroyers by Marconi. Zhao highlighted 'a problem about the clause covering fluctuations and costs', and hoped that Thatcher 'could help in finding a way of overcoming this problem'. Thatcher undertook to look into it. Finally, Zhao sought Thatcher's assistance about the sending of Chinese students to Britain, whose numbers had decreased 'because of the level of fees'. He referred to the assistance given by the US government in the form of provision of materials and bursaries. Thatcher promised to explore some form of technical cooperation with the Chinese government.[78]

On the morning of 25 September, Zhao enthusiastically made a farewell call on Thatcher at Diaoyutai Guest House before she left Beijing for Shanghai. Zhao said that the prime minister's visit was 'a great success', and there were 'broad prospects for Sino-British cooperation in the economic, technological and trade fields'. But as China was still 'an underdeveloped and relatively poor country', Zhao hoped that Britain would 'help to surmount the obstacle which high rate loans and high prices put in the way of expanded Sino-British relations'. Thatcher, having seen 'great changes' in China since her last visit in 1977, expressed confidence that China would 'grow steadily' over the next twenty years. In response to Zhao's repeated emphasis on British prices, Thatcher advised that while China would 'drive a hard bargain in any trade negotiations', she wanted the premier to appreciate that 'the best products were often worth a higher price'. Some international negotiators tended to ignore the fact that '[g]oods that were more expensive at first tended to last longer and be a better buy in the long run'.[79] Clearly, Thatcher wanted to drive home the message that Britain was a competitive player in the global economy.

Shortly after Zhao's farewell call, Thatcher travelled to Shanghai. She visited the British Petroleum office and a biochemistry research institute. Given her Oxford degree in chemistry, she deeply impressed the Chinese scientists with her knowledge. As the climax of her Shanghai visit, Thatcher launched a ship built for Hong Kong's shipping magnate, Y. K. Pao, naming it 'World Goodwill'.[80] Pao was not just her close friend, but also the golfing partner of Denis Thatcher.[81]

The following day, Thatcher rounded off her visit with a brief stop in Guangzhou. Curious about the SEZs, Thatcher asked Governor Liu Tianfu 'what special powers Guangdong Province had'. She was told that Guangdong along with Fujian could 'pursue specific policies and flexible measures', and the two provinces were 'even more open to the outside world than China as a whole'. Thatcher alluded to the telecommunications link between Hong Kong and Guangdong established by the Cable and Wireless Company. Liu regarded Cable and Wireless as 'a very good company', which had 'a long history of cooperation' with Guangdong. Thatcher brought up the subject of the Guangdong nuclear power station, which was 'an enormous example of possible cooperation between Britain, Hong Kong and Guangdong Province'. She talked of 'her close friendship with Sir Walter Marshall', head of the Central Electricity Generating Board, who had lately visited Guangzhou to discuss the project. Liu praised Lord Kadoorie of CLP for 'his great enthusiasm for the project'. When Liu revealed that Guangdong was 'quite rich in offshore oil' but it would take time to exploit, Thatcher suggested that 'Britain's North Sea experience could be very useful to Guangdong'.[82]

Economic gesture for Hong Kong talks

The China visit was deemed a success by the Thatcher government. In deliberating on follow-up measures, Thatcher and the FCO explored the possibility of linking Hong Kong's future with Anglo-Chinese economic relations to Britain's advantage. They considered whether Britain's 'negotiating hand with the Chinese over Hong Kong [could] be strengthened by making, in the right way and at the right time, one or more gestures in the field of Anglo/Chinese relations' that were 'conditional on the satisfactory outcome of the talks'.[83] By early October 1982, the FCO came up with some initial ideas about possible gestures to the Chinese. It was assumed that the 'pragmatism' of Deng Xiaoping had 'definite limits', and the Chinese could not 'easily retreat from their public position on the resumption of sovereignty'. Thus, the Chinese 'national pride' would 'prevent their accepting any "sweeteners" which could too obviously appear as bribes'. Although Britain should not make 'any gesture conditional on the satisfactory outcome of the [Hong Kong] talks', the FCO still found 'gestures' useful in two respects. First, the Chinese, and particularly Premier Zhao, had made it clear that they would 'welcome easier terms for British goods and projects'. While the FCO was under no illusion that Britain would 'get a direct political return', it might 'improve the atmosphere of the talks by economic means' – for example, using aid/trade provision funds to support British companies' bids for projects in China, or strengthening scientific and technological links and English-language teaching. Second, if, during the Hong Kong talks, China was prepared to compromise over 'continued British administration', Britain might 'make such a compromise more palatable by improving the economic benefits to China of a continuing triangular relationship' among Britain, Hong Kong, and China. In this regard, the British government might use the Guangdong nuclear project as a possible gesture by offering 'a partly tied soft loan' to support it. Nonetheless, the FCO recognised that some of these initiatives would be 'expensive', particularly finding aid funds for China. In the event that China was receptive to the idea of strengthening triangular economic cooperation, Britain might present it as 'part of a package' by offering to negotiate 'a new Treaty with China', characterised by 'formal establishment of new era of Anglo-Chinese relations on basis of friendship, equality, etc' and 'continuing British administration of Hong Kong'. Francis Pym found these ideas 'worth considering and developing further'. But he believed that Britain 'should not assume that the Chinese position would be susceptible to change through financial inducement', and that any 'gesture involving financial expenditure' would need to be carefully justified.[84]

After considering the FCO's initial ideas, Thatcher held that 'the goal of "improving the atmosphere of the talks"' was 'too vague to be worth spending money on' – unless Britain could find a gesture that would 'positively promote a solution on Hong Kong'. She regarded the idea of a 'Treaty of Friendship and Co-operation' as 'worth refining on a contingency basis, since it might help the Chinese to accept a solution which would otherwise be unpalatable'.[85]

Conclusion

In September 1982, Thatcher travelled east to China with the aim of extending British rule in Hong Kong beyond 1997. Her negotiating strategy was to play up the 'confidence factor' by arguing that only British administration could maintain confidence and thus prosperity in Hong Kong. Believing that the three treaties governing Hong Kong's status remained valid (albeit that Britain could hold onto less than 10 per cent of the territory of Hong Kong after the expiry of the New Territories Lease in 1997), Thatcher cautioned against any unilateral action to abrogate international treaties. In response to Deng Xiaoping's criticism of British colonialism, she took pains to emphasise that Britain derived no revenue from Hong Kong, but it had a moral obligation to its people. Thatcher confided to Deng that if satisfactory arrangements could be made about the future administration of Hong Kong, she would 'consider the question of sovereignty' and recommend the outcome to Parliament accordingly. In her innermost thoughts, though, the most Britain was willing to concede to China was 'titular sovereignty', whereby Britain would continue to maintain effective control over Hong Kong under a 'management contract'. To eradicate all the legacies of the 'century of humiliation', Deng was determined to recover both sovereignty and administration over the entire of Hong Kong by 1997. With his nationalist feelings stirred by the Americans due to arms sales to Taiwan, Deng regarded the principle of sovereignty as non-negotiable. He insisted that it was under the 'precondition' of China resuming sovereignty over Hong Kong that China and Britain would hold talks to discuss Hong Kong's future.

While in China, Thatcher seized every opportunity to advance British commercial interests. Although the conclusion of the economic cooperation agreement in 1979 had raised high hopes for expanded Anglo-Chinese trade, by 1982 Britain suffered from a trade deficit and its share of China's total imports remained small. Beijing's policy of three-year economic readjustment since April 1979 was one factor behind Britain's rather disappointing export performance, but so was the competitiveness of British companies in the global economy. Thatcher believed that the UK had a competitive advantage over other countries in the fields of energy, communications, transport, and industrial innovation. Thus, Thatcher endeavoured to impress upon Zhao Ziyang and Guangdong officials the experience and expertise of UK companies. She was anxious to secure the contract for the conventional island of the Guangdong nuclear power station. Zhao was optimistic about the prospects for Sino-British economic cooperation. However, he requested Thatcher to offer competitive prices and technical aid to British companies' bids for projects in China.

In Beijing, Thatcher was taken aback by Deng's apparent ignorance of capitalism. It was thus essential to 'educate' the Chinese about how capitalist Hong Kong worked in forthcoming talks. For her part, Thatcher failed to understand Deng's sense of history and the strength of Chinese nationalism as far as the recovery of Hong Kong was concerned. The clash of their views would play out in the Hong Kong negotiations.

Notes

1 This chapter draws partly on Chi-kwan Mark, 'To "Educate" Deng Xiaoping in Capitalism: Thatcher's Visit to China and the Future of Hong Kong in 1982', *Cold War History*, 17: 2 (June 2017), 161–80.
2 Harding, *A Fragile Relationship*, 112–15.
3 *Deng Xiaoping junshi wenxuan* [The Selected Military Works of Deng Xiaoping], vol. 3 (Beijing: Renmin chubanshe, 1993), 151–2.
4 Harding, *A Fragile Relationship*, 383–5.
5 David Shambaugh, *Beautiful Imperialist: China Perceives America, 1972–1990* (Princeton, NJ: Princeton University Press, 1991), 265.
6 M. Taylor Fravel, *Strong Borders, Secure Nation: Cooperation and Conflict in China's Territorial Disputes* (Princeton, NJ: Princeton University Press, 2008), 254.
7 Editorial Committee for Party Literature, CCP Central Committee (ed.), *Selected Works of Deng Xiaoping, vol. 3: 1982–1992* (Beijing: Foreign Languages Press, 1994), 13–16.
8 *DXN*, vol. 2, 91; Qi, *Deng Xiaoping yu Xianggang huigui*, 250.
9 Lu, *Lu Ping koushu Xianggang huigui*, 17–21; Wong, *China's Resumption of Sovereignty over Hong Kong*, 17–19.

10 *DXN*, vol. 2, 805; Lu, *Lu Ping koushu Xianggang huigui*, 17.
11 Wei Wei and Liu Ke, *Deng Xiaoping lilun fazhan shi* [A History of the Development of Deng Xiaoping Theory] (Beijing: Shanghai renmin chubanshe, 2004), 305–6.
12 Cindy Yik-yi Chu, *Chinese Communists and Hong Kong Capitalists: 1937–1997* (New York: Palgrave Macmillan, 2010).
13 *DXN*, vol. 2, 805, 824, 827–8; Li, *Huigui de lichen*, 76–7; Wong, *China's Resumption of Sovereignty over Hong Kong*, 22–3.
14 *DXN*, vol. 2, 849; Li Hou, *Huigui de lichen*, 88; Chen, *Xianggang wenti tanpan shimo*, 94–8.
15 Zhang and Xu (eds), *Zhou Nan jiemi GangAo huigui*, 117.
16 MTF, Lyne to Alexander, 9 July 1981, www.margaretthatcher.org/document/122659.
17 TNA, PREM 19/789 Part 1, Beijing to FCO, no. 18, 8 January 1982.
18 TNA, PREM 19/789 Part 1, Carrington to Thatcher, 9 March 1982.
19 TNA, PREM 19/789 Part 1, Coles to Holmes, 15 March 1982.
20 *Deng Xiaoping ji waiguo shounao huitan lu* [A Record of Deng Xiaoping's Meetings with Foreign Heads] (Beijing: Taihai chubanshe, 2011), 93–9.
21 TNA, PREM 19/789 Part 1, Beijing to FCO, no. 202, 6 April 1982; *DXN*, vol. 2, 812–13.
22 TNA, FCO 21/2212, FCO to HK, no. 254, 15 April 1982.
23 TNA, PREM 19/789 Part 1, Beijing to FCO, no. 209, 7 April 1982.
24 TNA, PREM 19/789 Part 1, Fall to Coles, July 21, 1982.
25 Thatcher, *The Downing Street Years*, 259.
26 Thatcher, *The Path to Power*, 584.
27 Hampton, *Hong Kong and British Culture*, 176.
28 TNA, FCO 21/2214, Clift to assistant private secretary, 16 July 1982.
29 TNA, FCO 21/2214, 'Future of Hong Kong', attached in Clift to Donald, 23 July 1982.
30 Sze-Yuen Chung, *Hong Kong's Journey to Reunification: Memoirs of Sze-Yuen Chung* (Hong Kong: Chinese University Press, 2001), 50–1.
31 TNA, PREM 19/788, Acland to Armstrong, 7 July 1982.
32 TNA, PREM 19/789 Part 1, Note of meeting, 28 July 1982.
33 TNA, PREM 19/789 Part 1, Coles to Thatcher, 29 July 1982.
34 TNA, PREM 19/792, FCO, 'The future of Hong Kong: A special study', August 1982.
35 TNA, PREM 19/789 Part 1, Pym to Thatcher, 3 September 1982; Coles to Thatcher, 6 September 1982.
36 Moore, *Margaret Thatcher*, vol. 1, 681.
37 TNA, PREM 19/789 Part 1, Holmes to Coles, 6 September 1982; PREM 19/790 Part 2, Record of discussion, 8 September 1982.
38 TNA, PREM 19/790 Part 2, Coles to Holmes, 13 September 1982.
39 Deng was nicknamed 'steel factory' by Mao Zedong, who considered him to be as tough and strong as steel. Zhang and Xu (eds), *Zhou Nan jiemi GangAo huigui*, 123.

40 TNA, PREM 19/962 Part 2, Note of meeting, 22 September 1982.
41 MTF, Thatcher speech, 22 September 1982, www.margaretthatcher.org/document/105022.
42 TNA, PREM 19/962 Part 2, Record of conversation, 23 September 1982.
43 TNA, PREM 19/962 Part 2, Record of conversation between Thatcher and Zhao Ziyang, 23 September 1982.
44 TNA, PREM 19/962 Part 2, Record of meeting between Thatcher and Deng Xiaoping, 24 September 1982; *DXW*, vol. 3, 12–15.
45 Cradock, *Experiences of China*, 179.
46 Moore, *Margaret Thatcher*, vol. 2, 13.
47 TNA, CAB 133/528, Hong Kong steering brief by FCO, 7 September 1982.
48 MTF, Record of meeting, 26 September 1982, www.margaretthatcher.org/document/122625.
49 MTF, Record of meeting, 27 September 1982, www.margaretthatcher.org/document/122627.
50 TNA, PREM 19/790 Part 2, Clift to Giffard, 30 September 1982; Cottrell, *The End of Hong Kong*, 92–3.
51 TNA, PREM 19/790 Part 2, Beijing to FCO, no. 613, 30 September 1982; HK to FCO, no. 1105, 1 October 1982; Beijing to FCO, no. 616, 4 October 1982.
52 TNA, PREM 19/790 Part 2, Clift to Giffard, 30 September 1982; Holmes to Coles, 1 October 1982.
53 Thatcher, *The Downing Street Years*, 262.
54 TNA, PREM 19/791 Part 3, Bone to Coles, 11 October 1982.
55 TNA, PREM 19/791 Part 3, Coles to Bone, 13 October 1982.
56 TNA, FCO 21/2694, FCO Far Eastern Department, 'UK/China trade relations', 26 January 1984.
57 *DXN*, vol. 1, 497, 505–6.
58 Bao, Chiang, and Ignatius (eds), *Prisoner of the State*, 103–4.
59 Quoted in Gewirtz, *Unlikely Partners*, 112–13.
60 Bao, Chiang, and Ignatius (eds), *Prisoner of the State*, 96.
61 Barry Naughton, *Growing Out of the Plan: Chinese Economic Reform, 1978–1993* (Cambridge: Cambridge University Press, 1995), 178.
62 See Akira Iriye, *China and Japan in the Global Setting* (Cambridge, MA: Harvard University Press, 1998), Chapter 3; Harding, *A Fragile Relationship*, Chapters 3–5.
63 Albers, *Britain, France, West Germany and the People's Republic of China*, 175–82, 189–99.
64 TNA, CAB 133/528, Department of Trade brief: 'China: commercial issues (other than Guangdong nuclear)', 7 September 1982; FCO 21/2694, Hallett to Davies, 20 March 1984.
65 TNA, FCO 21/2695, Ashton to Smith, 23 October 1984.
66 TNA, BT 241/3201, 'Sino-British Trade Council 1981 operations report', 8 January 1982.
67 TNA, FCO 98/2439, FCO brief: 'China's foreign trade', July 1985.

68 TNA, PREM 19/962, Note of meeting between Thatcher and Association for British Commerce in China on 23 September 1982.
69 TNA, FCO 21/2694, Cradock to Pym, 28 November 1983.
70 TNA, PV12/20, 'UK turbine generator expertise for the Guangdong nuclear project', enclosed in Brown to Abrahams, 6 October 1980.
71 TNA, PV12/20, Brown to PS/Lord Trenchard, 7 October 1980.
72 TNA, AB 65/1565, 'CLP/KEC feasibility study', 27 October 1980, enclosed in Gardiner to Lawson, 28 October 1980.
73 TNA, FCO 21/1834, 'Guangdong nuclear project', enclosed in McLaren to Youde, 31 October 1980; PV 13/50, Kadoorie to Thatcher, 4 March 1982.
74 TNA, PV 12/20, FCO to Beijing, no. 525, 2 October 1980.
75 TNA, CAB 133/528, Department of Industry brief: 'Guangdong nuclear power station project', 7 September 1982.
76 TNA, PREM 19/785 Part 2, Pym to Thatcher, 28 July 1982.
77 TNA, CAB 133/528, Department of Trade brief: 'China: commercial issues (other than Guangdong nuclear)', 7 September 1982.
78 TNA, PREM 19/962, Record of conversation between Thatcher and Zhao Ziyang on 23 September 1982.
79 TNA, PREM 19/962, Note of conversation at the farewell call of Zhao Ziyang on Thatcher on 25 September 1982.
80 TNA, PREM 19/962, Cradock to Pym, 7 October 1982.
81 On Pao's life, see Anna Pao Sohmen, *Y K Pao: My Father* (Hong Kong: Hong Kong University Press, 2013).
82 TNA, PREM 19/962, Record of meeting between Thatcher and Liu Tianfu and Liang Lingguang on 27 [sic] September.
83 TNA, PREM 19/790 Part 2, Coles to Holmes, 4 October 1982.
84 TNA, PREM 19/791 Part 3, Bone to Coles, 11 October 1982.
85 TNA, PREM 19/791 Part 3, Coles to Bone, 13 October 1982.

4

Bargaining for sovereignty and administration, 1982–83

Negotiating approaches and teams

Deng Xiaoping set the resumption of both sovereignty and administration over Hong Kong as the principal objective of the Sino-British negotiation. What guided his policy of national unification with Hong Kong – and Taiwan and Macao – was the concept of 'one country, two systems',[1] which evolved in several stages. The first stage began around the time of the Third Plenum of the Eleventh Party Central Committee in December 1978, when the idea of 'peaceful unification' with Taiwan emerged to replace the slogan of armed liberation. The second stage was symbolised by the announcement on 30 September 1981 of Marshal Ye Jianying's 'nine points' on Taiwan and the NPC's adoption on 4 December 1982 of the new Chinese constitution, whose article 31 made provision for the creation of 'special administrative region/zone'. By mid-1983, during the third phase, Deng made the notion of 'one country, two systems' more comprehensive, systematic, and theoretical, by formulating the 'six points' for Taiwan and the 'twelve points' for Hong Kong.[2] In 1984, when the Sino-British talks over Hong Kong's future reached a critical juncture, Deng formally enunciated the concept of 'one country, two systems' when receiving delegations from Hong Kong and visitors from abroad.[3]

The essence of the concept of 'one country, two systems' was twofold. On the one hand, it provided the foundation for China's resumption of sovereignty over the whole of Hong Kong on 1 July 1997. On the other hand, the coexistence of the mainland's socialist system and Hong Kong's capitalist system would help ensure stability and prosperity in the Hong Kong Special Administrative Region (SAR). Underlying the thinking about 'one country, two systems' was the principle of 'one China'. Deng was determined to achieve national unification and to eradicate the legacies of the 'century of humiliation'. But taking into account Hong Kong's unique history and realities, Deng was willing to allow Hong Kong people to enjoy a high degree of autonomy and maintain their way of life. Nevertheless, the 'main body' of 'one country, two systems' ought to be socialism, and China with a population of one billion would not be affected by a capitalist enclave of five million people at its southern tip.[4]

In terms of negotiating style, the Chinese were used to negotiating through 'principles'.[5] From the outset, they insisted that the British side should accept the premise that sovereignty over Hong Kong should revert to China in 1997, before any detailed discussion could take place. Indeed, to Deng, sovereignty was not a matter for discussion. What is more, sovereignty and administration were deemed indivisible: China vehemently opposed the exchange of sovereignty for continuing British administration. While being firm in principle, China was flexible enough to recognise British interests in Hong Kong and to seek their cooperation, particularly during the transitional period. Deng saw the Hong Kong negotiation as 'a complicated, long-term struggle'. Yet, at the age of 78 in 1982, Deng believed that the talks should not be without a time limit. He set a 'deadline' whereby China would unilaterally announce its plans for Hong Kong if no agreement was reached in one or two years' time. To Deng, the Hong Kong question was a bilateral issue between the Chinese and British governments. As such, he strove to prevent the people of Hong Kong from becoming a third party in the diplomatic talks – or creating a 'three legged stool'.[6] That said, Deng was keen to rally support from Hong Kong compatriots through direct personal communication and propaganda work. By inviting and receiving delegations of business people, professionals, and media workers from Hong Kong, Deng aimed to present China's resumption of sovereignty over Hong Kong as a fait accompli, while 'selling' the 'one country, two systems' formula to Hong Kong residents. In this way, Beijing hoped to construct a 'patriotic united front of the new era'.[7] In negotiations with foreigners, the Chinese were used to complementing formal proceedings with 'megaphone diplomacy'. By briefing newspaper correspondents and making public statements on their own position on Hong Kong, they hoped to exert pressure on the British.

Deng was the chief architect of China's negotiating strategy and indeed its Hong Kong policy. The Hong Kong and Macao Affairs Office within the State Council was involved in drafting policy papers and giving advice to the Politburo and the Central Committee. Liao Chengzhi served as director of the office from 1978 until his death on 10 June 1983, when Ji Pengfei succeeded him. Li Xiannian, the party elder who led the Central Foreign Affairs Leading Small Group and was appointed President of the PRC in mid-1983, took overall charge of Hong Kong and Macao affairs. To Li, the Hong Kong question was not just about resuming the exercise of Chinese sovereignty, but also about how to maintain stability and prosperity in Hong Kong and to better serve China's Four Modernisations. As the Hong Kong talks were conducted through diplomatic channels, the Chinese Foreign Ministry was charged with the day-to-day task of negotiation.[8] During the preliminary talks between October 1982 and June 1983, Zhang Wenjin, vice foreign minister responsible for West European affairs, was the chief negotiator. When the plenary session started in July 1983, Yao Guang, a former ambassador to France, headed the Chinese delegation consisting of Li Jusheng, deputy director of the Hong Kong branch of the NCNA, and Lu Ping, an adviser at the Foreign Ministry's West European Department, among others. Xu Jiatun became the director of the local NCNA from 30 June 1983 onwards. As a serving member of the Party Central Committee and a former party secretary of Jiangsu Province, Xu was the most senior figure ever to be appointed to Hong Kong. During the negotiations, he played a proactive role in undertaking united front and propaganda work in Hong Kong.[9]

The British approached the Hong Kong talks very differently. Margaret Thatcher's personality and leadership style were such that Britain should start the negotiation from first principles and exhaust all alternative solutions before conceding (if at all) to China as the FCO tended to favour.[10] As of October 1982, the British negotiating objective was that Thatcher would 'consider' making a recommendation to Parliament on sovereignty if Britain and China could make satisfactory administrative arrangements for post-1997 Hong Kong, which should be acceptable to both Parliament and the people of Hong Kong. But any concession Thatcher had in mind was merely 'titular sovereignty', with administration of Hong Kong kept firmly in British hands under a new 'management contract'. In other words, it was to 'abandon sovereignty's form in return for keeping its substance'.[11] Significantly, Thatcher and the FCO saw negotiation with the Chinese as the 'most effective means of education' about how capitalist Hong Kong worked – in particular, how the British link was vital to maintaining confidence and prosperity in Hong Kong.[12] As such, the British wanted to 'put down the maximum amount of detail about how Hong Kong was run' in the final agreement, which slightly resembled 'the *Encyclopedia Britannica*' according to David Wilson, who was involved in the final stage of the negotiation. This was in stark contrast to China's desire for 'the shortest possible agreement, if possible just the declaration'.[13]

The FCO assumed primary responsibility for supervising the Hong Kong talks on a day-to-day basis. Until January 1984, when he took up the position of the prime minister's foreign affairs adviser, Ambassador Percy Cradock headed a five-member negotiating team, comprising Hong Kong Governor Edward Youde and Richard Evans (who succeeded Cradock as chief negotiator in 1984). Trusted by Thatcher, Cradock, in his capacity as deputy under secretary of state in the FCO, continued to oversee the Hong Kong negotiations in 1984. Thatcher was heavily involved in policy-making concerning Hong Kong: she 'saw all the key telegrams and other papers', and 'worked extremely hard'.[14] In early October 1983, a sub-committee on Hong Kong, under the Cabinet Defence and Overseas Policy Committee, was set up to 'keep under review all aspects of the conduct of the negotiations with the Chinese Government of the future of Hong Kong'. Chaired by the prime minister, it consisted of key ministers such as the foreign secretary and the minister of state, the home secretary, the chancellor of the exchequer, and the defence secretary, with the attendance of the Hong Kong governor and the British ambassador in China when necessary.[15]

From the outset, the Hong Kong governor made the case for briefing and consulting the unofficial members of the Executive Council about the talks. As Edward Youde reminded the FCO, under the Letters Patent and the Royal Instructions, the governor was required to consult the Executive Council on all important issues of policy. Sze-yuen Chung, senior unofficial member of the council, 'felt a strong responsibility to the wider community which [the unofficials] were appointed to represent on [all Hong Kong] issues'.[16] To Chung, the future of Hong Kong was 'plainly a matter of life or death to Hong Kong's British subjects', and as such there was 'a vital requirement for the total involvement of the Executive Council in the formulation of HMG's position and the conduct of the negotiation'.[17] The FCO and particularly Cradock were less enthusiastic about involving the unofficial members due to career diplomats' dislike of any external interference in the conduct of diplomacy. It was important to 'avoid letting the Unofficials believe that they can expect a "blow by blow" account of all that passes between the Chinese and British Governments during negotiations, and a right of veto on detailed points'.[18] Cradock called it the 'First Law of Diplomacy' – 'often it is much harder to deal with disputes among your own side [Hong Kong and the Beijing Embassy] than to deal with the other side [China]'.[19] It was incumbent upon the prime minister to reconcile the conflicting views between Cradock/FCO and the unofficials/governor. With her conviction in free-market capitalism, Thatcher found it morally wrong to hand over Hong Kong to communist China, particularly so because the majority of Hong Kong residents treasured British rule.[20] Thatcher felt strongly for the unofficial members, whom she had first invited to 10 Downing Street for consultation in September 1982 and whose support she was eager to secure throughout the Hong Kong negotiations.

Talks on talks

Following Thatcher's China visit, Percy Cradock wasted no time in kick-starting the Hong Kong negotiation. In a telegram to the FCO on 30

September, Cradock proposed to approach Vice Foreign Minister Zhang Wenjin to discuss arrangements for substantive talks. It was imperative that the joint statement issued by Thatcher and Deng in Beijing should form the basis of the formal talks.[21] Indeed, the joint statement was 'a modest British triumph since it omitted any mention of a return to Chinese sovereignty'.[22] The FCO agreed that Britain should avoid accepting any other basis for the substantive talks than the joint statement, particularly 'any Chinese precondition on the discussion of sovereignty'.[23]

On 5 October, Cradock held the first preliminary talks with Zhang Wenjin. Cradock suggested that the substantive talks be conducted in the first instance by a small British team with the possible attendance of the Hong Kong governor, and that the content be kept confidential. Zhang said that although China was 'greatly concerned about prosperity and stability in Hong Kong', 'sovereignty came first', and the two sides should first of all discuss the 'premise' in the substantive talks. 'On the premise that China would recover sovereignty not later than 1997', he continued, China would 'seek the cooperation of the British side on the questions of how to maintain stability and prosperity' in Hong Kong. Zhang added that it was 'not possible subjectively to separate sovereignty from administration', the latter being 'one form of exercise of sovereignty by a country'. To counter Zhang's suggestion, Cradock said that the Chinese position was 'very clear' to Britain, but so was the prime minister's – that Thatcher 'could not contemplate making recommendations to Parliament on sovereignty unless she was fully satisfied about the arrangements for administering Hong Kong after 1997'. Unconvinced, Zhang asserted that if the British side persisted with the idea of 'British administration', then 'differences of principle would emerge and it would be hard for the talks to proceed'. Cradock recalled the Thatcher–Deng joint statement, which was drafted in such a way that 'reflected the fact that there were differences of view on basic points'. Thus, to insist on Britain's acceptance of 'preconditions not expressed in the joint statement' would be 'inconsistent' with its aim.[24] As Private Secretary John Coles reported to Thatcher, the meeting was 'not very encouraging', but the Chinese might 'move later if [the British] adopt the right approach'.[25]

On 19 October, Cradock called on Zhang to deliver a message. Cradock first pointed out that Thatcher regarded the joint statement as 'the basis for the talks', with no implication that the Chinese would be 'giving up their position'. Recalling Deng's agreement that the talks should cover, among other matters, 'arrangements for the period after 1997', Cradock proposed that the first step should be 'an exchange of views on the practical arrangements for administration' so as to enable the prime minister to determine whether she could make recommendations on sovereignty to Parliament. Zhang responded that the Chinese government would study the British proposal and reply later. In his assessment, Cradock believed that the second meeting was a 'more relaxed occasion' than the first, not least because Zhang 'did not choose to rehearse the theme of sovereignty'. He was optimistic that Britain would receive a positive reply on substantive talks in the near future.[26]

In reality, the Chinese were in no hurry to start substantive talks. Instead, during November, they were more interested in communicating directly to Hong Kong compatriots about China's policy. Wang Kuang, head of the local NCNA, had dinner with a group of Hong Kong property developers, and Xi Zhongxun, vice chairman of the NPC and a former governor of Guangdong, received a delegation of the Hong Kong Trade Development Council. As the FCO assessed it, Beijing's main objective was to 'encourage Hong Kong people to accept the inevitability of a benevolent Chinese assumption of sovereignty'.[27] In late November, the Hong Kong governor drew Whitehall's attention to reports by local newspapers on Liao Chengzhi's meeting with a visiting delegation from the Hong Kong Manufacturers Association, during which Liao allegedly said that 'China would recover Hong Kong no later than 1997' and that 'sovereignty and administrative control were inseparable'.[28] After reading the governor's report, Thatcher lamented that the Chinese had been conducting 'a massive and rather impressive publicity campaign for their own position on Hong Kong', while Britain had yet to find any convincing means of carrying out 'an intensive educational campaign'. She wanted 'a suitable response to the current manipulation by the Chinese of public opinion'.[29]

It took more than a month for the Chinese to get in touch with the British again. In their meeting over lunch on 4 December, Zhang first said that the British could expect a reply to Cradock's proposal shortly. Zhang explained that the delay had to do with a major reshuffle in the Foreign Ministry – that he would leave Beijing to become Chinese ambassador to the United States by the end of the year, and Yao Guang, currently ambassador in Paris, would take up the post of vice foreign minister responsible for Western Europe. Besides, Foreign Minister Huang Hua had retired last month.[30] As 1982 gave way to 1983, the British had yet to receive a Chinese reply. On 26 January 1983, Cradock called on Vice Foreign Minister Yao Guang, who simply confirmed that a reply was being prepared and would be delivered as soon as possible. But 'the precise timing was not very important', Yao said. What was important was that Britain should have 'a better understanding of the Chinese stand on Hong Kong'.[31] As Foreign Secretary Francis Pym told Thatcher, the Chinese continued to 'sidestep' the talks and to 'concentrate on a direct approach to people in Hong Kong, presenting their basic plan as a foregone conclusion'.[32]

The Chinese reply finally came on 9 February, when Cradock was requested to call at the Foreign Ministry. Reading from a piece of paper (which was handed over to the British later), Yao made a number of points, notably that 'Hong Kong was part of China and must be returned'. He said that diplomatic consultations on Hong Kong should consist of 'confirmation of the recovery of sovereignty by China by 1997' and, on that basis, exploration of 'how to effect a smooth transition' and 'how Britain would cooperate with China in maintaining prosperity and stability'. Cradock asked if 'acceptance of Chinese sovereignty' was 'an absolute pre-condition for talks'. Yao insisted that there should be 'a premise', and once Britain had confirmed it, 'discussions on specific issues' could go ahead.[33] As Cradock reported to the FCO, Yao's reply was 'unforthcoming but not unexpected'.[34]

In a memorandum for Thatcher dated 16 February, Pym argued that without a signal to the Chinese that Britain was 'prepared to consider a package which if agreed would include recognition of their sovereignty over the whole of Hong Kong', substantive talks would never get started. As for the options open to Britain, Pym laid down three main categories, namely to continue with the present negotiating strategy, to secure continuing British administration beyond 1997 but by different means, and to accept the Chinese position on recovering both sovereignty and administrative control while seeking the best possible deal for Hong Kong. Seeing Pym as a 'wet' Conservative, Thatcher handwrote at the top of his paper that what was being proposed was 'pathetic' and amounted to a 'sell-out'.[35]

In a meeting at Downing Street on 7 March, Thatcher said that 'the worst feature of the present situation was the absence of negotiations'. To float a radical idea, Thatcher wondered whether Britain 'could not move Hong Kong fairly rapidly down the path towards independence, though stopping short of that final point'. Britain might consider 'launching a process of putting Hong Kong Chinese in positions where they could run the affairs of Hong Kong', which should be completed in five years. Thatcher stressed that it was not her intention that 'Hong Kong should become independent', just that Hong Kong could acquire 'a status more like that possessed by Bermuda'. Governor Edward Youde, who had returned to London for consultation, agreed that 'Hong Kong should move along the path of self-determination'. Indeed, 'a good deal of progress' in local elites' political participation had already been made. But Youde was sceptical about the introduction of 'full democratic elections' in Hong Kong, which would lead to the involvement of political parties and propel China to 'disrupt the system'.

The main challenge for Britain was how to persuade the Chinese to open substantive talks without a premature surrender on sovereignty. In view of the Chinese insistence on 'sovereignty as a pre-condition for talks', Cradock came up with an imaginative idea: that Britain should 'try to find ways of finessing the sovereignty issue', while seeking to 'avoid confrontation'.

He suggested that Thatcher should send a personal message to her Chinese counterpart to the effect that if satisfactory arrangements for Hong Kong's future administration could be made, she 'would make recommendations to Parliament on sovereignty'.[36] As Pym highlighted the significance of the proposed letter, the formula used was 'still unconditional' and entailed 'no commitment' by the British government before the terms of future arrangements had been agreed. Yet the letter strengthened what Thatcher had offered to Deng Xiaoping back in September 1982, which was merely that she would 'consider' making recommendations on sovereignty.[37] On 10 March, the Cabinet confirmed the decision to send a message to Premier Zhao, with a view to getting substantive talks started and preventing Beijing from using the occasion of the NPC meeting in June to announce its plan for Hong Kong.[38]

On 23 March, Cradock called on Yao Guang to deliver Thatcher's letter to Zhao dated 10 March. Employing the rhetoric of what Cradock would later call the 'first finesse', Thatcher first expressed 'great disappointment' that six months had lapsed since their last meeting, but there was still 'no real progress' in substantive talks on Hong Kong. Although the British 'fully understand the importance the Chinese Government attach to the matter of sovereignty', 'it is not constitutionally in [her] power as Prime Minister acting alone to agree to the transfer of sovereignty'. Rather, it was 'Parliament which alone has the power to decide'. Nevertheless, Thatcher now 'strengthened' her previous 'assurance' on Hong Kong:

> Provided that agreement could be reached between the British and Chinese Governments on administrative arrangements for Hong Kong which would guarantee the future prosperity and stability of Hong Kong, and would be acceptable to the British Parliament and to the people of Hong Kong as well as to the Chinese Government, [she] would be prepared to recommend to Parliament that sovereignty over the whole of Hong Kong should revert to China.

Towards the end of the letter, Thatcher said that if a solution to the Hong Kong question could be reached, it would be 'a great contribution to the development of friendly relations between Britain and China'.[39] After reading out Thatcher's letter, Cradock added as a personal comment that 'the assurance in the message represented the limit of what the prime minister was empowered under the British constitution to agree to on her own authority'. Britain hoped that China would see the message as 'a sign of our sincerity' in seeking to resolve the Hong Kong question through 'friendly discussions'. Moreover, Cradock stressed that the content of the letter and indeed its existence should be 'kept strictly confidential by both sides'. In response, Yao revealed that Premier Zhao 'attached importance to this

Bargaining for sovereignty and administration 107

question', although he had been busy with overseas journey and domestic matters. He was confident that Zhao would reply to Thatcher shortly.[40]

Despite Cradock's request for confidentiality, the Chinese appeared to deliberately leak the content of Thatcher's letter, portraying it as a British concession. In early April, Youde reported to Whitehall that the local NCNA had told the editor of *South China Morning Post* that Thatcher had sent a personal message to Zhao to the effect that 'Britain would concede sovereignty over Hong Kong if the package was right'. The FCO was aware that Liao Chengzhi had likewise given a pretty full account of Thatcher's letter to a visiting MP, Hal Miller. In the FCO's assessment, 'the main aim of these breaches of confidence by the Chinese is to spread the idea publicly that we are prepared to concede sovereignty, in order to make it impossible for us to withdraw from this position'.[41]

In the wake of Thatcher's message, the Chinese finalised their blueprint for Hong Kong and refined their negotiating strategy. In late March, the Hong Kong and Macao Affairs Office under Liao Chengzhi submitted its revised plan for resolving the Hong Kong question to the Central Committee.[42] On 4 April, Deng studied the plan and recommended the Politburo to discuss it.[43] An extended Politburo meeting took place on 22 April, during which the 'twelve points' were adopted as the basic guidelines for negotiation with the British over Hong Kong.[44] The 'twelve points' included: establishment of the Hong Kong SAR after the handover; a high degree of autonomy for Hong Kong, with the exception of diplomatic and defence matters; independent judiciary; Hong Kong people ruling Hong Kong; no change in Hong Kong's socio-economic system and way of life; protection of British interests in Hong Kong; and the drafting of a Basic Law for Hong Kong.[45] At the meeting, Deng made it plain that in future talks the British should first confirm the 'premise' that China would recover Hong Kong in 1997, which was 'non-negotiable'. Then, the two sides should discuss how to maintain Hong Kong's prosperity after 1997, and finally how to ensure no disturbance in Hong Kong during the transitional period. To Deng, the negotiation might succeed or fail. In the event of failure, China would unilaterally announce its recovery of Hong Kong in 1997.[46]

Zhao's reply to Thatcher was delivered by Yao when he met Cradock on 9 May. In his letter dated 28 April, Zhao first reiterated Deng's stand on Hong Kong. Recalling Thatcher's letter in which the prime minister had 'given an assurance that [she was] prepared at a certain stage to recommend to Parliament that sovereignty over the entire Hong Kong area should revert to China', Zhao agreed to hold formal talks as soon as possible with 'the common aim of maintaining the prosperity and stability of Hong Kong'. The two sides should start 'substantive discussions on the form of transference of sovereignty as well as on the related questions of how China and Britain can cooperate during the transitional period between now and 1997 and after 1997'. Zhao noted that a settlement of the Hong Kong question would not only 'erase the historical trauma', but also 'give a tremendous impetus' to the development of friendly relations between Britain and China.[47] As Yao had conveyed Zhao's message via a Chinese interpreter, Cradock said that the premier's reply was 'given in a positive spirit', but he wanted to clarify one point which might be 'just a matter of translation'. While Zhao's letter had mentioned Thatcher's assurance that she was prepared at a certain stage to recommend that sovereignty revert to China, Cradock stressed that the prime minister would make such a recommendation 'provided certain conditions were met'. As Zhao seemed to have bypassed the significance of conditionality in Thatcher's letter, Cradock continued, it was essential to hold substantive talks on 'how the conditions might be met to enable transference of sovereignty to take place'. Yao replied that his rendering of Thatcher's offer was 'not a direct quotation'. He suggested that the two sides should meet to discuss the agenda and the composition of delegations for the substantive talks.[48]

In Cradock's opinion, Zhao's was 'a positive response', which had 'broken the deadlock'. But Cradock also discerned pitfalls in Zhao's reply, which did 'not accurately represent the prime minister's letter': Zhao had blurred or even removed 'the essential precondition' that Thatcher was prepared to recommend transfer of sovereignty to Parliament.[49] Nevertheless, Cradock was eager to keep up the momentum by proposing the format of substantive talks. On the agenda, Cradock was inclined to discuss the three subjects in Zhao's letter, albeit in reverse order. He hoped to discuss arrangements for Hong Kong after 1997 first, followed by how to handle the transitional period, and finally how to effect transfer of sovereignty.[50] At a Cabinet meeting on 12 May, ministers found the general tone of Zhao's letter 'friendly'. They agreed that the British position on a transfer of sovereignty was 'fully protected by the conditions which we had laid down, including the agreement of the British Parliament and the people of Hong Kong'.[51]

Zhou Nan, assistant foreign minister responsible for West European affairs, was tasked with discussing the format of substantive talks with Cradock. A fluent English speaker and a cultivated man of Chinese poetry, Zhou had served in the PRC's permanent delegation to the UN for over a decade, becoming ambassador from late 1980 to 1981.[52] Obviously, Beijing valued Zhou's diplomatic and English-language skills in negotiation with the British. When meeting with Cradock on 2 June, Zhou said on a personal basis that China was ready to accept the British preferred order of discussion – namely, arrangements after 1997, arrangements pre-1997, and sovereignty – but the three items should be formally included in the text of the agenda. Specifically, China wanted a reference to 'transfer of sovereignty' in the agenda. Cradock hoped to find neutral wording for the agenda formula in order to preserve the conditionality implied in Thatcher's letter to Zhao. But the use of definite or indefinite article became a sticking point between the two sides. While Zhou proposed the phrase 'the factors relating to the transfer of sovereignty', Cradock disliked the definite article before 'transfer of sovereignty', which to him would have no significance in the Chinese text since the Chinese language did not have articles.[53] It took three weeks, after several informal exchanges,[54] to resolve the impasse over the agenda formula. At an informal meeting with Cradock on 23 June, Zhou proposed that, 'as the only possible way out', both sides should 'delete the articles, definite and indefinite, and have simply "matters relating to transfer of sovereignty"'.[55] After hearing of the breakthrough, Thatcher, who had recently won a landslide in the general election, commented that 'Sir Percy handled this conversation very well indeed'.[56]

Why did China make a gesture of goodwill to Britain? As Deng told a group of Hong Kong delegates to the NPC and the Political Consultative Conference two days later, China agreed to begin substantive talks with the item 'arrangements after 1997' in order to 'enable the British to back down with grace'. In negotiations, China was firm in principle but flexible in tactics. Once agreement was reached on the first and second items, Deng believed there would not be much to be ironed out on the last item about sovereignty. China intended to 'take care of British interests' in Hong Kong. On the other hand, Deng said that the recent slide of the Hong Kong dollar could be attributed to 'human factors'. China would ensure that Britain should 'assume responsibility' for 'not doing things harmful to Hong Kong'.[57]

On 28 June, Cradock and Yao finalised the details of the first plenary session. It was agreed that on 1 July the Chinese and British governments would make simultaneous press announcements that a 'second phase of talks' on the future of Hong Kong would begin in Beijing on 12 July.[58] The use of the phrase 'second phase' was meant to signify a departure from the hitherto procedural wrangling between the two sides.

Exchanging sovereignty for administration

In formulating Britain's negotiating strategy for the second phase of the talks, the FCO aimed to continue 'the process of education of the Chinese by encouraging examination in more detail of various aspects of Hong Kong administration in order to point up the importance of the British link'.[59] Britain was prepared to exchange sovereignty for administration if the essence of the latter could be guaranteed. On 4–5 July, a week before the first round of talks, Thatcher invited a group of unofficial members of Hong Kong's Executive Council to 10 Downing Street for consultation. In his opening statement, Senior Unofficial Sze-yuen Chung noted six matters of importance, including consultation by London and participation by the governor in the talks. On the British negotiating objective, Chung ascertained that the great majority of people in Hong Kong wanted continuing British administration. But to secure a Chinese agreement for that purpose, Chung realised that a 'price' might have to be paid. If it meant simply 'handing over titular sovereignty in order to save China's face', he believed that the majority of the local population would accept that. But any final arrangement for continuing British administration should contain 'an element of effective insulation from Chinese turmoil and interference'.[60]

On the morning of 12 July at a state guest house of the Foreign Ministry in Beijing, formerly the Austro-Hungarian legation building,[61] the first plenary session opened. As agreed, the two sides made opening statements, to be followed by comments on the second day of talks. Declaring that 'Hong Kong was an integral part of China' and China 'never recognized the three unequal treaties', Yao Guang said that China would recover the entire of Hong Kong by 1997 at the latest. China would 'never accept any separation of administrative power from sovereignty'. Yao concluded that it would not be difficult to reach an agreement on Hong Kong if there was 'a real desire for a settlement', adding that a settlement would 'heal the historical trauma and contribute to a further development of Sino-British relations'.[62] Cradock, recalling Thatcher's March letter to Zhao, said that the prime minister 'fully understood the importance the Chinese government attached to the matter of sovereignty'. But it was 'not within the constitutional limits of her powers as prime minister acting alone to agree to the transfer of sovereignty': that was a matter for Parliament to decide. Besides, such a transfer of sovereignty would need to be 'part of the overall package of measures guaranteeing the future stability and prosperity of Hong Kong'. Cradock proposed that the best way forward was to 'conduct a joint examination of the present arrangements for the administration of Hong Kong' in the second round, where the Hong Kong governor would join the negotiations. The two sides would review the 'factors' that contributed to the present level of stability and prosperity in Hong Kong, particularly 'the crucial importance of confidence'. Cradock stressed that '[u]nilateral declarations or general expressions of hope or good intention' by China would 'not suffice' to inspire confidence. Rather, it required 'very special arrangements' to ensure that 'capitalist Hong Kong is insulated from socialist China' after 1997. Such arrangements should allow for 'the continuation of the British administrative role in Hong Kong', albeit that there would be 'increased scope for Hong Kong people to take part' in administration.[63]

On the second day, Li Jusheng, deputy director of the local NCNA, made a few points about what he regarded as Hong Kong's dissatisfaction with British rule and its desire for reunification with China. The 'overwhelming majority' of Hong Kong residents had applied for 'compatriot return permits' and thus 'recognised the People's Republic of China as their motherland'. The socialist system in China 'had not harmed Hong Kong but benefited it' since 1949, thus discrediting the argument that Hong Kong should be 'insulated' from China after 1997. At present, Hong Kong people had a feeling of unease, 'not so much due to 1997 as to the social conditions in Hong Kong', such as the 'high crime rate' and the recent 'tax increases'. Li noted that although monetary deposits had been moved from Hong Kong dollars into other currencies, this did not mean that 'capital was leaving the territory' or that there was 'a crisis of confidence'; it only reflected 'the lifting of the interest withholding tax which meant discrimination against Hong Kong dollar deposits'. In response, Cradock pointed out 'many striking examples of misinformation about Hong Kong on the Chinese side'. Governor Youde said that Hong Kong indeed had imported more from the mainland than the other way round, thus benefiting China, and that 'monetary deposits' should not be confused with 'investments', with a large amount of financial movement in Hong Kong being offshore.[64] At last, Cradock and Yao agreed on the dates of the second and the third plenary sessions (25–26 July and 2–3 August, respectively), which would commence agenda item one (arrangements after 1997). In the next round, Cradock proposed to first explore present-day Hong Kong in order to see 'what made for its prosperity', with the British side delivering a preliminary presentation.[65] The first plenary concluded with a press statement that the two sides had had 'useful and constructive talks' and would resume discussions on 25 July.[66]

In reviewing the British negotiating strategy, Cradock intended to intensify 'the educative process' by passing to the Chinese 'as much factual and educative material as possible about Hong Kong and the importance of the British link'. He was, however, pessimistic that China would find the British arguments for 'continuing the administrative status quo without modification' persuasive. Geoffrey Howe, who replaced Pym as foreign secretary after the cabinet reshuffle, agreed that the Chinese were 'very unlikely' to agree to 'any deal in which purely formal sovereignty would be traded for the continuation of the status quo, and in particular to the continuation of a controlling link with London after 1997'. Nevertheless, these were still early days in the negotiations, and it would be wrong to concede to China before Britain had 'tested the water much more thoroughly'. Howe believed that Deng was 'certainly a pragmatist', albeit that he would 'stick to principle'.[67] Thatcher generally shared Howe's views, but wondered 'what modifications to the administrative status quo' Britain could accept.[68]

During the second plenary session on 25–26 July, Governor Youde first gave a presentation on how capitalist Hong Kong worked. Covering international trade, the convertibility of the currency, the legal system, and so forth, Youde argued that the link between Hong Kong and the UK, and the British role in administration, contributed to Hong Kong's transformation from an entrepôt and commercial centre into a diversified and externally oriented economy.[69] In response, Yao Guang made it plain that China would 'never accept an arrangement whereby China had symbolic sovereignty and Britain retained administration'. He gave a detailed account of China's 'special policies' towards Hong Kong after 1997. He claimed that what China did in Hong Kong was its 'internal affair', but 'in view of a friendly Sino-British relationship and the common desire to maintain stability and prosperity' in Hong Kong, China had chosen to notify Britain before making its policies public.[70] Yao rebuffed Cradock's claims about 'the need for Parliamentary approval' of Hong Kong's administrative arrangements, depicting it as 'Britain's affair' which had 'nothing to do with China'. Li Jusheng stated that Hong Kong's prosperity depended on a number of factors, such as 'policies and hard work of the Chinese residents of Hong Kong', Hong Kong's 'geographical position', and the 'consistent support of the Chinese government over the last 30 years' – 'factors' that would remain after 1997 even 'without British administration'. He acknowledged that the British 'had made some positive contribution' to Hong Kong's development, but a number of policies had 'not been successful', such as 'high land prices' and 'the rise in electricity prices'. Significantly, Li claimed that Britain had 'very large economic interests in Hong Kong', including invisibles, special air traffic rights, and certain utility monopolies by British companies. As Britain obviously 'enjoyed special privileges in Hong Kong', Li argued that the Thatcher government should cease talking about a 'moral obligation' to Hong Kong residents.[71]

After the meeting, a press statement was released, noting 'two more useful days of talks' (but without the word 'constructive' as used in the first communiqué) and the date of the next round, which would take place the next week on 2–3 August.[72] Cradock noted in his assessment of the session that Yao was 'firmer' and used 'tougher language' than in the first round, and Youde's presentation on how Hong Kong worked seemed to have 'no detectable impact' on the Chinese position.[73] Anthony Parsons, a special adviser to the prime minister on foreign affairs, recommended that Britain should maintain its negotiating approach for as long as possible. If Britain conceded to the Chinese demands prematurely, it would cause 'an immediate crisis of confidence in Hong Kong'.[74]

During the third plenary session in early August, as part of 'the educative process', Cradock and Youde introduced the four papers on the legal, economic, monetary, and financial systems of Hong Kong, and handed them over to the Chinese.[75] Yao gave a review of the second phase of the talks so far, which 'had failed to make due progress'. Although China had decided to accommodate the British side about the order of discussion in the agenda, in the first two rounds Britain's 'only purpose in continuing to talk solely about the present systems in Hong Kong was to argue for the continuation of British administration, so that China should have sovereignty only in name'. Yao could not but criticise Britain for 'evading the question of fundamental principle'.[76] For his part, Cradock expressed his frustration about 'the Chinese erection of barriers of "principle"'. At the end of the meeting, a press statement was released, stating merely that talks had taken place and would resume on 22–23 September after a recess.[77] In Hong Kong, the financial markets responded negatively to the absence of the adjectives 'useful' and 'constructive' in the press statement. The Hang Seng Index fell by thirty-six points, or almost 5 per cent, on 4 August, and the Hong Kong dollar plunged to below $7.5 to the US dollar the following day.[78]

During the summer recess, China took stock of its negotiating strategy. Chairing a meeting of the Central Foreign Affairs Leading Small Group on 17 August, Li Xiannian listened to Yao Guang's report on the Hong Kong talks. Li asserted that in view of the British scheme to 'exchange sovereignty for administration', it was important to mobilise government officials and propaganda specialists to counter the British arguments. Li calculated that the talks might succeed or fail, and China should prepare for no agreement rather than backing down.[79] In another meeting on 20 September, Li talked of the importance of 'Hong Kong people ruling Hong Kong'. He deemed it vital to conduct '[united front] work among the masses' in order to persuade Hong Kong people of China's policy. Economically, it was vital to preventing the outflow of capital from Hong Kong. At the next round of talks, the Chinese side should counter the argument that the falling value of the Hong Kong dollar represented a 'confidence crisis', and instead should point out that it was 'caused by the British'.[80] To step up propaganda efforts, the Foreign Ministry issued statements on Hong Kong, while the *People's Daily* published articles about China's position on the territory.[81] In Hong Kong, the newly appointed NCNA director, Xu Jiatun, intensified united front work to co-opt local residents from all walks of life.[82]

Deng Xiaoping was personally involved in influencing the Hong Kong talks. He used the occasion of Edward Heath's visit to China on 10 September to send a strong message to London. In a nearly two-hour meeting, Deng first said that there were 'no contradictions between Britain and China except for Hong Kong, which was not difficult to resolve'. On Hong Kong, Deng asserted that the 'British aim of exchanging sovereignty and administration was not possible'. He hoped that when the talks resumed on 22 September, the British 'would not get stuck on the issue of administration', lest China be obliged to issue a unilateral declaration on Hong Kong. Deng called for the Thatcher government to adopt a 'wise policy', so that Britain and China could issue a 'joint declaration' about Hong Kong's future. Heath agreed that a joint declaration would be 'beneficial' to both Britain and China, and would 'have a big influence on international opinion on Taiwan, and particularly in the United States'. Concerning Taiwan, Deng claimed that he had 'gone beyond' Ye Jianying's 'nine points' by proposing that, after reunification with China, Taiwan would also be allowed to 'buy weapons for its forces' (albeit that by that time it 'would not need many weapons'). Deng hinted that Hong Kong was similar to Taiwan: 'China would recover sovereignty, but everything else would remain the same'. During the transitional period, Deng stressed that there should be 'no disturbances or damage' in Hong Kong, and that 'Hong Kong people should play an increasing role, though not as yet the main role, in running Hong Kong, so that they would know how to govern Hong Kong in 1997'. To recapitulate, Deng asserted that when the Hong Kong talks resumed, there should be 'no further fuss over sovereignty or the right of administration'.[83]

As for Britain, Thatcher reviewed the negotiating strategy at a Downing Street meeting, attended by Howe, Cradock, Youde, and others, on 5 September. In summarising the first three rounds of talks, Cradock said that they had achieved at least the British objective of beginning 'a process of educating the Chinese in the complexities of Hong Kong'. But he discerned no sign that Beijing's basic attitude had changed, and there was 'a danger of deadlock'. A particular problem was that the Chinese might exert pressure on the British by simply refusing to announce the date of the next meeting at the end of one session, a scenario that would have 'a bad effect on confidence in Hong Kong'. Youde echoed the point on confidence by mentioning that the Hong Kong dollar was slowly drifting down, despite the territory's good export performance. Thatcher deemed it vital to keep the talks going and avoid a breakdown, lest there be a risk that China would 'foment disturbances in Hong Kong'. She said that her March letter to Premier Zhao had already 'shown considerable flexibility' with respect to the sovereignty issue, and a further concession would 'simply be pocketed by the Chinese' and make Britain 'appear to be weak'. Howe regarded the Hong Kong talks as 'one of the most difficult diplomatic tasks ever attempted', wondering if the current British objective was 'unattainable'. The meeting concluded that Britain should maintain its present negotiating position.[84] On 20 September, the FCO instructed Cradock to insist on the need for British administration, while inviting the Chinese to provide further details of their proposals.[85]

During the fourth round on 22–23 September, after Cradock had made a statement, Yao Guang said that China had hoped for a 'change of attitude' on the British part after the recess, only to find that they still 'clung obstinately to [their] unreasonable demand for continued British administration'. Britain's insistence on administration 'amounted to out and out insistence on colonial rule': it tried to 'replace the old unequal treaties with a new one', thus demonstrating 'an imperialist attitude'. All this led China to question Britain's 'sincerity in seeking a negotiated settlement'. Equally disappointed, Cradock said that the British side had hoped that the four papers on Hong Kong's systems handed over at the last session would have enabled the Chinese to get down to 'an objective factual study which [Britain] believed was the pre-requisite of success' for Hong Kong. However, not only had Yao failed to make at least some reference to the papers, but his statement had 'simply reiterated principles and demands which apparently had to be met before worthwhile negotiations could begin'. Cradock assured Yao that Britain was 'sincere' about reaching an agreement with China, and Deng's comments to Heath were being 'carefully studied'. Yao confirmed that China had studied the four papers 'very carefully', but had concluded that their main theme was to 'argue the case for continued British administration'.[86] The fourth round ended with a press statement, which only noted the date of the next meeting, 19–20 October.[87]

The absence of any reassuring words in the press statement intensified the crisis of confidence in the Hong Kong dollar. Since the summer of 1983, the exchange rate of the local currency against the US dollar had been under pressure. During the five-day week between 16 and 23 September, the exchange rate had fallen dramatically from 7.78 to 8.73 per US dollar, or a depreciation of the Hong Kong dollar by 10.8 per cent. On 24 September, dubbed 'Black Saturday', the Hong Kong dollar plunged further to 9.5 per US dollar. The Hang Seng Index, too, dropped from 916 to 786 points during that week. There was panic buying in Hong Kong. Although, by 27 September, the exchange rate had stabilised somewhat after the Hong Kong government's intervention in the foreign exchange markets, the crisis of confidence did not dissipate.[88]

The financial crisis reflected not only the political uncertainty over Hong Kong's future, but also the laxity of monetary control by the colonial government, famous for its philosophy of 'positive non-interventionism'.[89] Until mid-1972, when the pound was floated and the Sterling Area was disbanded, the two note-issuing banks, the Hongkong Bank and the Chartered Bank, were required to back the issue of currency by depositing sterling with the Exchange Fund in return for certificates of indebtedness. Since 1974, after a brief peg to the US dollar, Hong Kong operated a floating exchange rate system.[90] In view of the sharp plunge of the Hong Kong dollar in September 1983, the Hong Kong government explored new schemes to stabilise the exchange rate.[91] On 4–5 October, the chief economic adviser to the Bank of England, Charles Goodhart, and the assistant secretary in the balance of payments division of the Treasury, David Peretz, flew to Hong Kong to offer technical advice. After extensive discussions, it was agreed that pegging the local currency to the US dollar would offer the most feasible and effective solution.[92] Announced by Financial Secretary John Bremridge on 15 October, with effect from 17 October, the Hong Kong dollar would be pegged at a fixed rate of 7.8 to the US dollar.[93] The financial markets responded positively to the new measures in the next four days, putting a halt to the crisis of confidence, at least temporarily.[94]

Finessing the British link

While the Hong Kong government and the UK Treasury were finding ways to stabilise the local currency, Cradock and the FCO considered the strategy for the fifth round of talks. In a telegram to Whitehall on 24 September, Cradock wrote that the talks had now 'reached a critical juncture', with two paths for Britain to follow – 'confrontation' with China or 'seeking to negotiate the best possible arrangements for Hong Kong as a special administrative region of China'. He predicted that if the British line was not changed, the breakdown of negotiations would occur during the next round.[95] When meeting with Chinese Foreign Minister Wu Xueqian in New York for the UN General Assembly on 27 September, Geoffrey Howe got the impression that the Chinese remained adamant on the question of sovereignty.[96] In early October, the FCO prepared a paper for ministerial consideration, setting out the options open to Britain about Hong Kong's future.[97] According to Howe, there were four policy options, including to continue the present negotiating approach and to accept the Chinese premise that both sovereignty and administration would pass to China in 1997. The option that Howe recommended was to 'maintain our present view that continued British administration is the best way to maintain confidence, but to seek a further formula through which we could explore what flexibility there might be in the Chinese concept of administration, and what guarantees, including continuing British links, the Chinese would be prepared to build into their plan'. What Howe had in mind was to extend 'the conditional formula deployed over sovereignty' in Thatcher's March letter to Zhao to 'the right of administration'. Accordingly, Thatcher would send another message to Zhao that, if arrangements could be agreed which would ensure Hong Kong's stability and prosperity, the British government would be prepared to recommend to Parliament a bilateral agreement conferring both sovereignty and the right of administration to China in 1997. But the British government would retain the right to reject any package that proved to be unacceptable after exploration with the Chinese.[98] That is to say, Howe hoped to 'finesse' the British link as the prerequisite for an agreement by considering and, if they were acceptable, incorporating the Chinese ideas of administration.

When discussing Howe's policy options in a Downing Street meeting on 5 October, Thatcher wondered whether Britain could pin China down on what the latter was apparently willing to offer in regard to the future system of Hong Kong, particularly 'the concept of a 50-year period of autonomy starting in 1997'. Thatcher had in mind 'a Singapore-type autonomy for Hong Kong preserved by a treaty lasting for 50 years'. Arguing that the British had employed 'a conditional formula in respect of sovereignty', which however was portrayed by Chinese propagandists as Britain's surrender of sovereignty, Thatcher did not look with favour on the suggestion that Britain should now concede 'the right of administration' to China. Instead, 'the right of administration should pass to the residents of Hong Kong': that was 'what autonomy meant'. A somewhat emotional Thatcher asserted that Britain 'still had sovereignty in perpetuity over Hong Kong and Kowloon', and could still 'bring the people close to independence by 1997'. Nevertheless, the pragmatic Howe was swift to remind the prime minister that any future arrangements for Hong Kong would 'depend crucially on China's consent and acquiescence', and that Britain had the right to sovereignty over only 8 per cent of the territory after 1997. Cradock agreed that it was only through cooperation, not confrontation, that Britain and China could reach an agreement 'in the interests of the people of Hong Kong'. In sum, Howe believed that now was the time to discuss 'what elements of administration' should be preserved in order to guarantee stability and prosperity in Hong Kong after 1997. China's 'special policies' accompanied by 'a 50-year guarantee', together with 'credible elements of a British presence', might offer the best solution.[99]

After the Downing Street meeting, Thatcher was thinking more in terms of the 'realistic Prime Minister' than the 'emotional Margaret', which reflected the 'two sides of her personality'.[100] When receiving a delegation of unofficial members of Hong Kong's Executive Council to London on 7 October, Thatcher first spelt out the British objective of keeping the Hong Kong talks going and probing the Chinese proposals, while avoiding confrontation with China. Howe, referring to China's objection to the retention of British administration, said that Britain was seeking 'a formula which would make some move towards the Chinese but without any prejudice to our ultimate right to take decisions'. Sze-yuen Chung responded that it was the unofficials' unanimous view that British administration should continue after 1997. He put it bluntly: 'the British link between HMG and the Governor was inseverable and anything else could be discussed'. Notwithstanding

Hong Kong's financial crisis of late (by that time, the Hong Kong government had yet to announce the Hong Kong–US dollar peg), Chung argued that the exchange rate of the Hong Kong dollar, the state of the securities market, and the reactions of the Hong Kong people to the Chinese plan would 'eventually influence the Chinese position on the future of Hong Kong'. While not underestimating 'the grave consequences of stalemate or breakdown' of the talks, Chung optimistically believed that Hong Kong 'could survive such turbulence'. Feeling less complacent, Thatcher pointed out that a collapse of currency 'meant a collapse of society as well', with the Weimar Republic in the 1930s being an obvious example. Thatcher admitted that a deal had to be struck now. After the expiry of the New Territories Lease in July 1997, China would obtain both sovereignty and administration over the bulk of Hong Kong by 'just sitting and waiting', while the British position in Hong Kong Island and Kowloon 'might only last for a few months'. Britain had to consider 'ways of saving China's face'. After a long discussion, the unofficials were eventually persuaded to endorse the British negotiating approach.[101]

On 14 October, Cradock called on Yao Guang, conveying a message from Thatcher to Zhao Ziyang – a manoeuvre that Cradock termed the 'second finesse'. After recalling her March letter, Thatcher noted that in the talks so far the British had maintained that 'a continuation of British administration is the best and surest basis for the continued stability and prosperity of Hong Kong', and this view had 'not changed'. However, Thatcher was aware that the Chinese had made 'certain proposals on the arrangements they envisage for Hong Kong after 1997'. Britain was 'particularly interested in those elements which, with adequate safeguards might ensure autonomy for the Hong Kong people, the preservation of their existing freedoms, … a continuing important role for Britain, and a guarantee that these special arrangements for Hong Kong would last for at least 50 years'. Thatcher proposed that the two sides should discuss 'what other effective methods' might be devised to maintain stability and prosperity in Hong Kong, and should 'explore further the Chinese ideas'. If, on the basis of the Chinese proposals, the two sides could agree on 'arrangements of lasting value to the people of Hong Kong', the British government would be prepared to recommend to Parliament a bilateral agreement enshrining such arrangements.[102]

After reading out Thatcher's letter, Cradock offered his personal observations that the message represented 'a sincere effort to accommodate Chinese views on sovereignty and administration', while reflecting 'the constitutional constraints on the prime minister's freedom of action as far as a transfer of sovereignty was concerned'. Yao first rehearsed the Chinese 'premise', and then asked what the phrase 'other effective methods', in Thatcher's letter, really meant. Cradock replied that the word 'other' was very important, meaning 'other than British administration'. He added that the British side would not put forward a 'new method' at the next meeting, but rather hoped to 'learn more of the Chinese proposals and build on them'. Cradock further clarified that 'for the purposes of our discussions', Britain was 'no longer insisting on British administration as the prerequisite', but would seek to build on the Chinese proposals.[103]

Cradock's 'second finesse' could not deceive Beijing. The following day, Li Xiannian held a meeting with officials from the Foreign Ministry, the Hong Kong and Macao Affairs Office, and the local NCNA to discuss Thatcher's letter to Zhao. Li argued that while the prime minister's message should be affirmed, China should simultaneously expose its 'deficiencies and ambiguities'. In the next round, the British should be asked to clarify what so-called 'participation', 'link', and 'continuing important role' meant. Li suggested that the joint statement issued at the end of the next session could include some positive words. Besides, China should specify its 'twelve-point' policy for Hong Kong. After the meeting, Li reported its conclusions to Deng Xiaoping, who gave his approval.[104]

During the fifth plenary session on 19–20 October, Yao Guang asked the British to clarify the exact meaning of 'other effective measures', 'the nature and form of a future British role', and any difference between 'the British link' to which Cradock referred now and the one used in the past. Cradock confirmed that the phrase 'other effective measures' meant 'methods other than those which [Britain] had hitherto advocated' – that is, 'other than British administration'. On 'a future British role', Cradock said that this would be the subject for discussion in the talks. His reference to 'a British link' was merely 'a shorthand phrase for the very close relations in many spheres between the UK and Hong Kong', and detail about that future relationship would emerge from further talks. In short, Cradock stated that the British side no longer insisted on continuing British administration as a 'prerequisite', and hoped to explore the Chinese proposals in order to find out what could be built on them. Still unsure, Yao asked if the British could explicitly recognise Chinese sovereignty. At last, Yao agreed to issue a press statement, describing the talks as 'useful and constructive' and proposing to hold the next meeting a few weeks later on 14–15 November.[105]

In Cradock's assessment of the fifth round, he noted that the Chinese had made 'no further threat to break off the talks', but it was 'still hard to judge the precise extent of the progress'.[106] Cradock proposed that Britain should provide the Chinese with working papers about the various aspects of Hong Kong's administration after 1997, beginning with its legal and financial systems, as a basis for discussion within the framework of the Chinese proposals.[107] Howe supported Cradock's proposal.[108] At the first meeting of the Sub-Committee on Hong Kong of the Cabinet Defence and Overseas Policy

Committee, which was set up to review all aspects of the negotiations, on 25 October, Howe said that it was important to 'maintain momentum in the negotiations and avoid the Chinese retreating from their more forthcoming posture'. The British would put forward working papers on different sectors of Hong Kong's administration, designed to explore and expand on Chinese ideas. The committee endorsed Howe's approach.[109]

For all the nuances in Thatcher's second message to Zhao and Cradock's further clarification, the Chinese remained deeply suspicious of the British motives in the talks. In an interview with the Spanish foreign minister in late October, Deng Xiaoping talked of the similarities and differences between the Hong Kong question and the Gibraltar question. He criticised that the British no longer talked about 'administrative rights', but about 'a certain degree of participation [and] management', which China found unacceptable. The earlier depreciation of the Hong Kong dollar was 'caused by the British'. To Deng, China would not be intimidated. If the Hong Kong situation became uncontrollable in the coming years, it would reconsider the timing and formula of recovering Hong Kong.[110] At an informal meeting with Cradock on 8 November, Yao mentioned the recent remarks made by Thatcher at a BBC World Service 'phone-in' programme, during which she had allegedly said that 'the British link is very important indeed, because it is partly responsible for the kind of success' witnessed in Hong Kong. Yao wondered how Thatcher's comments could be reconciled with Cradock's suggestion that the negotiations would be held 'on the basis of the Chinese proposals'.[111]

In his report to the FCO, Cradock wrote that 'the Chinese still harbor deep suspicion of our motives'. He believed that the British government should be prepared to make at least a general, formal statement to the effect that Britain envisaged 'no link of authority between post-1997 Hong Kong and the UK', subject to the same 'conditionality' as that in previous messages.[112] The Hong Kong governor, however, had strong reservations about Cradock's suggestion, which would be 'tantamount to implicit affirmation of the Chinese premise'.[113] Howe, too, did not recommend ruling out an authoritative British link for the time being.[114] Nevertheless, the outcome of the sixth plenary session on 14–15 November tilted the balance of arguments in Cradock's favour. During the discussions, Yao reiterated 'the extreme importance of the premise', and regarded both 'continued British administration after 1997' and 'any form of co-administration' as 'absolutely unacceptable'. He drew a 'distinction' between the policies that China would adopt after 1997, which were 'China's internal affair [sic]', albeit that British suggestions would be welcome, and 'matters concerning British interests in Hong Kong and Sino-British co-operation', where China hoped to have detailed discussion with the British. Referring to the two working papers on legal and financial systems that the British had handed over, Yao lamented that they were, 'in places, inconsistent with the Chinese premise and in other places went into excessive detail in fields that would be a function of the future SAR government'.[115] Although the tone of the meetings remained 'very friendly', and the agreed press statement described the sixth round as 'useful and constructive',[116] Cradock could not but feel that the Chinese position had 'hardened', possibly as a result of Deng's personal intervention. To dispel Chinese suspicions, Cradock strongly recommended that in the next round he should state that the British side would make 'no proposal on a British link or role which conflicts with the transfer of both sovereignty and the right of administration to China'.[117]

When the Sub-Committee on Hong Kong convened on 17 November, Howe pointed out that the outlook following the sixth round looked 'bleak', given the Chinese unwillingness to enter into detailed discussion about matters they regarded as 'their own internal policy'. Unless they were told that Britain would 'make no proposal on a British link or role which conflicted with the transfer of both sovereignty and the right of administration to China', there was a risk that the Chinese might 'break off the negotiations', which would in turn 'precipitate a breakdown of confidence in Hong Kong'. In discussion, ministers were acutely aware of the dilemma faced by Britain. The option of turning Hong Kong into 'a self-governing territory on the Singapore model' was deemed 'unworkable' in view of China's possible 'hostile reaction', while giving Hong Kong a 'greater measure of internal self-government in the meantime' would run 'the risk that the Chinese could believe that the United Kingdom intended to move the colony towards independence'. Besides, Hong Kong was indefensible against China's forceful takeover, and it would not be right to 'sacrifice British lives' in an attempt to defend the colony. In a word, 'the Chinese in the last analysis held all the cards'. The Sub-Committee concluded that since it was impossible to prevent China from acquiring both sovereignty and administration, the British negotiating tactics should be to find ways of 'smoothing the transition to Chinese rule and seeking the strongest possible assurances of autonomy for Hong Kong after the transition'. Thatcher remarked that an explicit affirmation of no British link was essential to avoiding a breakdown of the talks. She deemed it vital that the unofficial members of Hong Kong's Executive Council should understand 'the realities of the negotiating situation'. Besides, the government should explain its position both to Conservative members in Parliament and to the leaders of the Labour Party and the Liberal and Social Democratic Parties.[118] Once again, pragmatism got the better of Thatcher.

On 28 November, Cradock called on Yao to make a statement to the effect that the British government envisaged 'no link of authority' between

Britain and Hong Kong after 1997. He stressed that this communication, together with Thatcher's October message, should have 'removed any remaining doubts about British intentions' on the Chinese part. Yao said personally that Cradock's message 'deserved full attention' and was 'needed because the question of the future link was a sensitive issue and one of major concern to the Chinese government'. Yao assured Cradock that the Chinese would comment on the working papers received so far and on future ones.[119]

During the seventh round on 7–8 December, the Chinese, for the first time, entered into detailed discussions on the three working papers, which covered Hong Kong's legal and financial systems and its external economic relations. Yao commented on the working papers in accordance with China's 'twelve-point' plan.[120] As Howe reported to Thatcher, the seventh round was conducted in a 'significantly improved atmosphere'.[121] At the third meeting of the Cabinet Sub-Committee on Hong Kong on 13 December, Howe stated that the Chinese comments on the working papers had revealed a 'measure of common ground' between China's and Britain's positions. He argued that the British should make the Chinese proposals 'more acceptable and workable'. The Sub-Committee endorsed Howe's suggestion that, before the next round in January 1984, the unofficial members of Hong Kong's Executive Council should be invited to London to review the progress.[122]

Conclusion

Through a close reading of the declassified British archives along with Chinese material, this chapter has shown that Britain and China had polar-opposite views on Hong Kong's future, which could be boiled down to free-market capitalism versus national sovereignty. To Deng Xiaoping, sovereignty was not a matter for discussion. When preliminary talks started in October 1982, the Chinese insisted that the British side should explicitly affirm their 'premise' on sovereignty before substantive talks could commence. The Chinese stuck to this fundamental principle during the 'second phase' of the talks between July and November 1983, refusing any detailed discussion of administrative arrangements for post-1997 Hong Kong. On the other hand, Thatcher firmly believed that Hong Kong's success owed much to its capitalist system. Thus, the British aimed to seek 'detailed discussion without preconditions, with the hope of educating the Chinese on the complexity of Hong Kong and bringing them to realise the necessity for a strong British administrative element and reliable political insulation from the mainland if the essential features of Hong Kong are to be preserved after the expiration of the New Territories Lease in 1997'. Unlike the Chinese who put a premium on sovereignty, the British regarded 'means of assuring continued prosperity' as the 'objective' of the talks, while 'transfer of sovereignty' was the 'corollary'.¹²³

Having resisted the Chinese premise for some five months, in March 1983 Cradock sought to achieve a breakthrough by making what would become the 'first finesse', in the form of a letter by Thatcher to Zhao Ziyang. The aim was to finesse the Chinese precondition for formal talks by suggesting that Thatcher would be prepared to (rather than simply 'consider') recommend to Parliament a transfer of sovereignty if satisfactory administrative arrangements for Hong Kong could be made. In effect, Thatcher's letter symbolised a conditional concession on sovereignty. It was conditional in the sense that Thatcher did not commit herself to transfer of sovereignty unless Parliament and the Hong Kong people accepted it. As a concession to China for the opening of substantive talks, the Thatcher government now focused on exchanging sovereignty for continuing British administration in Hong Kong. Throughout the first six rounds of formal talks, Cradock and Governor Youde sought to 'educate' the Chinese in the working of Hong Kong, arguing that only British administration could maintain confidence and thus prosperity in Hong Kong. Nevertheless, the Chinese saw sovereignty and administrative rights as indivisible. Meanwhile, they finalised the 'twelve-point' plan for Hong Kong, revealing its key ideas to Cradock in the confidential talks and to Hong Kong visitors and foreign journalists in public. The Chinese believed that their proposals for a high degree of autonomy, the maintenance of Hong Kong's socio-economic system, and so forth would suffice to inspire confidence among Hong Kong residents.

With the two sides at loggerheads and the prospect of a breakdown in negotiations, the crisis of confidence intensified in Hong Kong. The Hong Kong dollar plunged to a new low after the fourth round, prompting the Hong Kong government to introduce a system of pegging with the US dollar. It became clear to Cradock that Britain needed to change its negotiating tactics, lest China unilaterally announce its plan for Hong Kong. With Thatcher's endorsement, on 14 October Cradock made the 'second finesse' – this time, by finessing the 'British link' as the prerequisite for transferring administrative rights and sovereignty. In conveying Thatcher's message to Zhao, Cradock said that the British were eager to explore the Chinese proposals and, on that basis, to build 'arrangements of lasting value' for Hong Kong. But Cradock still insisted on the conditionality of Thatcher's offer: any recommendation to Parliament on a transfer of sovereignty and administrative rights was contingent on satisfactory exploration of the Chinese proposals, and on the continuation of the 'British link' with post-1997 Hong Kong. To Beijing, any suggestion of the 'British link' was nothing but colonial rule in disguise, reflecting London's half-hearted affirmation of China's sovereignty over Hong Kong. Eventually, Cradock and Howe convinced Thatcher that the British government should envisage 'no link of authority' between the UK and Hong Kong after 1997. Accordingly, Cradock informed Yao of this in late November, after which the Chinese agreed to detailed discussions of the working papers on Hong Kong's systems.

The wrangling over the issues of sovereignty and administration in the preliminary talks and in the first six plenary sessions revealed mutual misunderstanding and mistrust between the two sides. Whereas the Chinese regarded Britain as being hypocritical in claiming a moral obligation to the Hong Kong people while extracting economic benefits from the colony, the British lacked faith in China's 'twelve-point' plan. The British were annoyed by the Chinese propensity to leak the content of the confidential talks. Within the British camp, there were different strands of opinion over negotiating objectives and tactics. On the one hand, Cradock, the seasoned Sinologist, was always mindful of the limits of Britain's bargaining power and the danger of confrontation with China. On the other hand, the unofficial members of Hong Kong's Executive Council pressed for the continuation of British rule. At first, Thatcher was determined not to concede to China prematurely. She held that Hong Kong's economic success owed much to the British link, such as the rule of law, personal freedom, and above all free-market capitalism. But the spectre of the breakdown of talks, together with the advice of Howe and Cradock, finally changed her mind: the 'emotional Margaret' gave way to the 'pragmatic Thatcher'. This demonstrated that although Thatcher might have disliked the FCO as an institution, she valued the talent and diplomatic skills of the likes of Cradock, who would be appointed as her foreign affairs adviser at Downing Street in 1984. Nevertheless, Thatcher's agency should not be lightly brushed aside: her active involvement in policy deliberations and consultation with the unofficials suggested that she was not simply led by the nose by FCO diplomats. Thatcher's tough approach, and at times her 'unreasonable' demands (like bringing Hong Kong to a status closer to independence), at the onset of negotiations were not without significance. As Charles Moore, her authorised biographer, writes: 'Because of her stubbornness, both parties had time to adjust and discuss ... By a paradox, Mrs Thatcher's "unreasonableness" made real negotiation possible in a way that conventional diplomatic behavior would not have done.'[124] The real test would come in 1984.

Notes

1 The origins of Deng's ideas about 'one country, two systems' can be traced back to 1950–51, when Deng, as first secretary of the CCP Southwestern Bureau, was in charge of the negotiations with the Dalai Lama government concerning the 'peaceful liberation' of Tibet. The resultant Seventeen Point Agreement allowed

Tibet to maintain its political-economic-religious system under China's sovereignty. The high degree of autonomy that Tibet enjoyed between 1951 and 1959 (when the Lhasa uprising propelled Beijing to assume direct control) provided a template for Deng to envision Hong Kong's (and Taiwan's) reunification with China in the 1980s. See Qi, *Deng Xiaoping yu Xianggang huigui*, 213–32.
2 *DXN*, vol. 2, 917–18.
3 Cheng Linsheng, *Deng Xiaoping 'Yiguo liangzhi' sixiang yanjiu* [A Study of Deng Xiaoping's Thinking about 'One Country, Two Systems'] (Shenyang: Liaoning renmin chubanshe, 1992), 142–3; Wei and Liu, *Deng Xiaoping lilun fazhan shi*, 293–7.
4 Dong Yuzheng and Dong Li, *Deng Xiaoping GangAo zhanlue sixiang yanjiu* [A Study of Deng Xiaoping's Strategic Thinking about Hong Kong and Macao] (Dongguan: Guangdong keiji chubanshe, 1997), 110–23; Guo Shengwei, *Deng Xiaoping waijiao moulue* [Deng Xiaoping's Diplomatic Strategy] (Beijing: Zhongyang wenxian chubanshe, 2008), 156–65.
5 See Alfred D. Wilhelm, Jr., *The Chinese at the Negotiating Table: Style and Characteristics* (Washington, DC: National Defence University Press, 1994); Paul H. Kreisberg, 'China's Negotiating Behaviour', in Thomas W. Robinson and David Shambaugh (eds), *Chinese Foreign Policy: Theory and Practice* (Oxford: Clarendon Press, 1995), 453–77.
6 Dong and Dong, *Deng Xiaoping GangAo zhanlue sixiang yanjiu*, 127–84; Zhang and Xu (eds), *Zhou Nan jiemi GangAo huigui*, 117.
7 Wei and Liu, *Deng Xiaoping lilun fazhan shi*, 305–6.
8 *Li Xiannian zhuan* [A Biography of Li Xiannian], vol. 2 (Beijing: Zhongyang wenxian chubanshe, 2009), 1295–7.
9 Xu Jiatun, *Xu Jiatun Xianggang huiyilu* [The Hong Kong Memoirs of Xu Jiatun], vol. 1 (Taipei: United Press, 1993), 122; Cottrell, *The End of Hong Kong*, 107, 113.
10 Cradock, *Experiences of China*, 175; Renwick, *A Journey with Margaret Thatcher*, 82.
11 Meyer, *Getting Our Way*, 154.
12 TNA, PREM 19/1053 Part 4, Holmes to Coles, 26 November 1982; Cradock, *Experiences of China*, 172.
13 CAC, GBR/0014/DOHP 83, Interview with David Clive Wilson (Lord Wilson of Tillyorn), 19 September 2003, p. 42.
14 CAC, GBR/0014/DOHP 15, Interview with Sir Robin McLaren, 31 July 1996, pp. 17–18; GBR/0014/DOHP 26, Interview with Sir Percy Cradock, 4 November 1997, p. 23.
15 TNA, CAB 148/229, Cabinet secretary note, 14 October 1983; PREM 19/1058 Part 9, Armstrong to Coles, 5 October 1983; PREM 19/1058 Part 9, Coles to Armstrong, 6 October 1983.
16 TNA, PREM 19/1053 Part 4, HK to FCO, no. 1334, 18 November 1982.
17 BLO, MSS.Ind.Ocn.s.328, Interview with Sir S.Y. Chung, file 328/2, tape 5, side 1, pp. 198–9.
18 TNA, PREM 19/791 Part 3, Holmes to Coles, 20 October 1982.

19 CAC, GBR/0014/DOHP 26, Interview with Sir Percy Cradock, 4 November 1997, p. 28.
20 Chung, *Hong Kong's Journey to Reunification*, 50–1.
21 TNA, PREM 19/790 Part 2, Beijing to FCO, no. 611, 30 September 1982.
22 Meyer, *Getting Our Way*, 151.
23 TNA, PREM 19/790 Part 2, FCO to Beijing, no. 466, 1 October 1982.
24 TNA, PREM 19/790 Part 2, Beijing to FCO, no. 620, 5 October 1982.
25 TNA, PREM 19/790 Part 2, Coles to Thatcher, 5 October 1982.
26 TNA, PREM 19/791 Part 3, Beijing to FCO, no. 672, 19 October 1982.
27 TNA, PREM 19/1053 Part 4, Holmes to Coles, 12 November 1982.
28 TNA, PREM 19/1053 Part 4, HK to FCO, no. 1354, 22 November 1982; Chung, *Hong Kong's Journey to Reunification*, 63–4.
29 TNA, FCO 21/2219, Coles to Holmes, 23 November 1982.
30 TNA, PREM 19/1053 Part 4, Beijing to FCO, no. 817, 4 December 1982.
31 TNA, PREM 19/1053 Part 4, Record of call on Yao Guang by Cradock on 26 January 1983.
32 TNA, PREM 19/1053 Part 4, Pym to Thatcher, 27 January 1983.
33 TNA, PREM 19/1053 Part 4, Beijing to FCO, no. 133, 9 February 1983.
34 TNA, PREM 19/1053 Part 4, Beijing to FCO, no. 134, 9 February 1983.
35 TNA, PREM 19/1053 Part 4, Pym to Thatcher, 16 February 1983; FCO, 'Future of Hong Kong: The next stage', 11 February 1983.
36 TNA, PREM 19/1054 Part 5, Record of discussion on 7 March 1983.
37 TNA, PREM 19/1054 Part 5, Pym to Thatcher, 8 March 1983.
38 TNA, CAB 128/77, CC(83)8th Conclusions, 10 March 1983.
39 TNA, PREM 19/1054 Part 5, Thatcher to Zhao, 10 March 1983.
40 TNA, PREM 19/1054 Part 5, Beijing to FCO, no. 269, 23 March 1983.
41 TNA, PREM 19/1054 Part 5, Holmes to Coles, 14 April 1983.
42 Lu, *Lu Ping koushu Xianggang huigui*, 21; Li, *Huigui de lichen*, 104–5.
43 *DXN*, vol. 2, 899–900.
44 Wang, *Liao Chengzhi Zhuan*, 542.
45 Dong and Dong, *Deng Xiaoping GangAo zhanlue sixiang yanjiu*, 60.
46 *DXN*, vol. 2, 901–2.
47 TNA, PREM 19/1055 Part 6, Beijing to FCO, no. 439, 12 May 1983.
48 TNA, PREM 19/1055 Part 6, Beijing to FCO, no. 416, 9 May 1983.
49 TNA, PREM 19/1055 Part 6, Beijing to FCO, no. 418, 9 May 1983.
50 TNA, PREM 19/1055 Part 6, Beijing to FCO, no. 426, 10 May 1983.
51 TNA, CAB 128/77, CC(83)18th conclusions, 12 May 1983.
52 Li Yunying and Chang Xiaole, *Shige yu waijiao: Zhou Nan waijiao shengya ceji* [Poetry and Diplomacy: A Side Note on the Diplomatic Career of Zhou Nan] (Xianggang: Ganglong chubanshe, 2004).
53 TNA, PREM 19/1055 Part 6, Beijing to FCO, no. 517, 3 June 1983.
54 TNA, PREM 19/1055 Part 6, Beijing to FCO, no. 518, 6 June 1983; Beijing to FCO, no. 570, 21 June 1983.
55 TNA, PREM 19/1055 Part 6, Beijing to FCO, no. 580, 23 June 1983.
56 TNA, PREM 19/1055 Part 6, Coles to Holmes, 27 June 1983.

57 Qi, *Deng Xiaoping yu Xianggang huigui*, 100–1; *DXN*, vol. 2, 915–16.
58 TNA, PREM 19/1055 Part 6, Beijing to FCO, no. 599, 28 June 1983; Beijing to FCO, no. 601, 28 June 1983.
59 TNA, PREM 19/1056 Part 7, Holmes to Coles, 1 July 1983.
60 TNA, PREM 19/1056 Part 7, Record of discussion between Thatcher and governor and Executive Council unofficial members on 4 July 1983.
61 Cottrell, *The End of Hong Kong*, 109.
62 TNA, PREM 19/1056 Part 7, Beijing to FCO, no. 663, 12 July 1983.
63 TNA, PREM 19/1056 Part 7, FCO to Beijing, no. 421, 6 July 1983; Beijing to FCO, no. 664, 12 July 1983.
64 TNA, PREM 19/1056 Part 7, Beijing to FCO, no. 670, 13 July 1983.
65 TNA, PREM 19/1056 Part 7, Beijing to FCO, no. 671, 13 July 1983.
66 TNA, PREM 19/1056 Part 7, Beijing to FCO, no. 667, 13 July 1983.
67 TNA, PREM 19/1056 Part 7, Beijing to FCO, no. 678, 15 July 1983; Fall to Coles, 20 July 1983.
68 TNA, PREM 19/1056 Part 7, Coles to Fall, 22 July 1983.
69 TNA, PREM 19/1055 Part 6, HK to FCO, no. 624, 5 May 1983.
70 TNA, PREM 19/1056 Part 7, Beijing to FCO, no. 710, 25 July 1983.
71 TNA, PREM 19/1056 Part 7, Beijing to FCO, no. 718, 26 July 1983.
72 TNA, PREM 19/1056 Part 7, Beijing to FCO, no. 715, 26 July 1983.
73 TNA, PREM 19/1056 Part 7, Beijing to FCO, no. 711, 25 July 1983; Beijing to FCO, no. 719, 26 July 1983.
74 TNA, PREM 19/1056 Part 7, Parsons to Coles, 27 July 1983.
75 TNA, PREM 19/1056 Part 7, 'The legal system of Hong Kong', 29 July 1983; 'The economic system of Hong Kong', 29 July 1983; 'The monetary system of Hong Kong', 29 July 1983; 'The financial system of Hong Kong', 29 July 1983.
76 TNA, PREM 19/1056 Part 7, HK to Beijing, no. 413, 29 July 1983; Beijing to FCO, no. 751, 2 August 1983.
77 TNA, PREM 19/1056 Part 7, Beijing to FCO, no. 741, 29 July 1983; Beijing to FCO, no. 758, 3 August 1983.
78 Cottrell, *The End of Hong Kong*, 113.
79 *Li Xiannian nianpu*, vol. 6, 206.
80 *Ibid.*, 214–15.
81 *Li Xiannian zhuan*, vol. 2, 1299.
82 Xu, *Xu Jiatun Xianggang huiyilu*, vol. 1, 100.
83 TNA, PREM 19/1057 Part 8, Beijing to FCO, no. 879, 10 September 1983; *DXN*, vol. 2, 931–2.
84 TNA, PREM 19/1057 Part 8, Note of meeting on 5 September 1983.
85 TNA, PREM 19/1057 Part 8, FCO to Beijing, no. 618, 20 September 1983.
86 TNA, PREM 19/1057 Part 8, Beijing to FCO, no. 927, 22 September 1983.
87 TNA, PREM 19/1057 Part 8, Beijing to FCO, no. 932, 23 September 1983.
88 TNA, PREM 19/1057 Part 8, HK to Ottawa, no. 11, 26 September 1983; PREM 19/1057 Part 8, HK to New York, no. 12, 27 September 1983; PREM 19/1058 Part 9, Beijing to FCO, no. 987, 5 October 1983; Qi, *Deng Xiaoping yu Xianggang huigui*, 106–7.

89 Clayton, 'From Laissez-faire to "Positive Non-Interventionism"'.
90 Catherine R. Schenk, *The Decline of Sterling: Managing the Retreat of an International Currency, 1945–1992* (Cambridge: Cambridge University Press, 2010), 340, 349–51, 353.
91 TNA, PREM 19/1057 Part 8, HK to FCO, no. 1435, 29 September 1983; Cottrell, *The End of Hong Kong*, 124–5.
92 TNA, PREM 19/1057 Part 8, FCO to HK, no. 997, 30 September 1983; PREM 19/1057 Part 8, Kerr to Turnbull, 30 September 1983; PREM 19/1058 Part 9, Kerr to Turnbull, 6 October 1983; Nigel Lawson, *The View from No. 11: Memoirs of a Tory Radical* (London: Bantam Press, 1992), 522–3.
93 TNA, PREM 19/1058 Part 9, HK to FCO, no. 1522, 13 October 1983.
94 TNA, PREM 19/1058 Part 9, Walters to Thatcher, 20 October 1983.
95 TNA, PREM 19/1057 Part 8, Beijing to FCO, no. 937, 24 September 1983.
96 TNA, PREM 19/1057 Part 8, New York to Hong Kong, no. 006, 27 September 1983.
97 TNA, PREM 19/1058 Part 9, Howe to Thatcher, 1 October 1983.
98 TNA, PREM 19/1058 Part 9, Howe to Thatcher, 4 October 1983.
99 TNA, PREM 19/1058 Part 9, Record of meeting on 5 October 1983.
100 Aitken, *Margaret Thatcher*, 424.
101 TNA, PREM 19/1058 Part 9, Record of discussion between Thatcher and Youde and EXCO unofficial members on 7 October 1983.
102 TNA, PREM 19/1058 Part 9, FCO to Beijing, no. 669, 7 October 1983.
103 TNA, PREM 19/1058 Part 9, Beijing to FCO, no. 1028, 14 October 1983.
104 *Li Xiannian zhuan*, vol. 2, 1300.
105 TNA, PREM 19/1058 Part 9, Beijing to FCO, no. 1050, 19 October 1983; Beijing to FCO, no. 1058, 20 October 1983; Beijing to FCO, no. 1054, 20 October 1983.
106 TNA, PREM 19/1058 Part 9, Beijing to FCO, no. 1057, 20 October 1983.
107 TNA, PREM 19/1058 Part 9, Beijing to FCO, no. 1068, 21 October 1983.
108 TNA, PREM 19/1058 Part 9, Howe to Thatcher, 24 October 1983.
109 TNA, CAB 148/229, Minutes of meeting of Cabinet Defence and Overseas Policy Committee, Sub-Committee on Hong Kong, OD(K)(83)1st meeting, 25 October 1983.
110 *DXN*, vol. 2, 941–2.
111 TNA, PREM 19/1059 Part 10, Beijing to FCO, no. 1160, 8 November 1983; Cottrell, *The End of Hong Kong*, 131.
112 TNA, PREM 19/1059 Part 10, Beijing to FCO, no. 1161, 8 November 1983.
113 TNA, PREM 19/1059 Part 10, HK to FCO, no. 1699, 9 November 1983.
114 TNA, PREM 19/1059 Part 10, FCO to Athens, no. 460, 9 November 1983.
115 TNA, PREM 19/1059 Part 10, Beijing to FCO, no. 1188, 14 November 1983; Beijing to FCO, no. 1196, 15 November 1983.
116 TNA, PREM 19/1059 Part 10, Beijing to FCO, no. 1192, 15 November 1983.
117 TNA, PREM 19/1059 Part 10, Beijing to FCO, no. 1199, 16 November 1983.
118 TNA, CAB 148/229, Minutes of meeting of Sub-Committee on Hong Kong on 17 November 1983, OD(K)(83)2nd meeting, 18 November 1983.

119 TNA, PREM 19/1059 Part 10, Beijing to FCO, no. 1257, 28 November 1983.
120 TNA, PREM 19/1059 Part 10, Beijing to FCO, no. 1309, 7 December 1983; Beijing to FCO, no. 1314, 8 December 1983.
121 TNA, PREM 19/1059 Part 10, Howe to Thatcher, 12 December 1983.
122 TNA, CAB 148/229, Minutes of meeting of Sub-Committee on Hong Kong on 13 December 1983, OD(K)(83)3rd meeting, 19 December 1983.
123 TNA, PREM 19/1059 Part 10, Cradock to Howe, 12 December 1983.
124 Moore, *Margaret Thatcher*, vol. 2, 19.

5

Negotiating autonomy and continuity, 1984

New teams, redefined objectives

As 1984 dawned, Percy Cradock was succeeded by Richard Evans, the new UK ambassador to China, as the British chief negotiator in the Hong Kong talks. Cradock became the prime minister's foreign affairs adviser at Number 10, and was concurrently deputy under secretary of state in the FCO with responsibility for Hong Kong.[1] On the Chinese side, Vice Foreign Minister Yao Guang was replaced by Zhou Nan, assistant foreign minister supervising West European affairs. The FCO saw Zhou, who had been involved in informal talks with Cradock about Hong Kong in 1983, as a 'very bright' diplomat with 'excellent English' and 'a more sophisticated operator than Yao'.[2] Although each session would still last for two days, Zhou wanted more frequent informal contact in order to allow both sides to grasp each other's position.[3]

China was cautiously optimistic about reaching an agreement with Britain. General Secretary Hu Yaobang spoke to French journalists in late January, saying that the Hong Kong talks had 'made progress' because both sides had 'adopted a wise attitude, a forward-looking attitude'. But more time was needed to discuss certain 'detailed questions'.[4] To Deng Xiaoping, 1984 was a critical year. As he had told Thatcher in September 1982, an agreement on Hong Kong ought to be reached in two years' time, lest China unilaterally announce its plan. What was at stake was not only the resolution of the Hong Kong question, but also the wider implications for the Taiwan question and Sino-American relations. It was during 1984 that Deng publicly announced the 'one country, two systems' model, originally designed for Taiwan. Deng was acutely aware of the 'harmful' effect of the Taiwan Relations Act on China's policy of peaceful reunification.[5] Although 1983–84 could be deemed the 'golden years' of Sino-American cooperation since normalisation, as symbolised by high-level visits, expanded trade, and advanced technology transfer, mutual mistrust between the two countries remained high. During the visit of President Ronald Reagan to China between 26 April and 1 May 1984, for instance, US security officials had found five listening devices hidden in the rooms where the president and his close advisers were lodged.[6] Thinking from a strategic and global perspective, Deng was determined to bring the Hong Kong talks to a successful conclusion by the latter part of 1984.

After abandoning 'any British link of authority', the Thatcher government redefined its negotiating objectives while trying to get the unofficial members of Hong Kong's Executive Council on board. On 16 January 1984, Sze-yuen Chung led a delegation of ten unofficials (their third mission of its kind) along with Governor Edward Youde to 10 Downing Street for consultation. Thatcher confided to the visitors that the current British objectives were to secure 'the highest degree of autonomy for Hong Kong', to get China to accept 'the principle of minimum change in the Hong Kong systems', and to seek 'maximum assurances' from Beijing so as to maintain domestic and international confidence. Chung suggested, and Thatcher agreed, that the definition of the British objective regarding assurances should include the phrase 'for at least 50 years after 1997'. Nevertheless, to instil a sense of realism in Chung, Thatcher pointed out that there could be 'no absolute guarantee of Chinese behavior after 1997 any more than there was now'. Rather, Britain should 'pin down the Chinese to an international reputation for integrity': if they failed to negotiate a satisfactory agreement, there would be 'effects on their international prestige and on Taiwan and American opinion'.[7]

Thatcher's emphasis on the importance of autonomy and continuity for post-1997 Hong Kong should be put in a historical context. While London possessed sweeping constitutional powers, Hong Kong had been enjoying a great degree of autonomy since the late 1950s: the UK–Hong Kong relationship was characterised by negotiation, bargaining, and mutual concessions. The tradition of trusting 'the man on the spot' due to geographical distance and lack of parliamentary interest; Hong Kong's prosperity and huge sterling reserves; and Britain's retreat from empire and reorientation towards Europe: all these were factors behind Hong Kong's growing autonomy or 'long decolonisation'. The colonial governor was able to resist metropolitan demands for social reform, such as housing and labour laws. Hong Kong's autonomy was best shown in the financial and economic sphere: the government drew up its own budget, maintained a free dollar market (which created an economic anomaly within the Sterling Area), and managed its external commercial relations (such as international trade negotiations). Its sterling holdings enabled Hong Kong to bargain for the retention of British troops in the 1960s, at a time when the UK government was contemplating a military withdrawal from east of Suez. Following the 1967 devaluation of the pound which resulted in a heavy loss for its official sterling reserves,

Hong Kong managed to secure, from London in 1968, an agreement that guaranteed against losses from any future devaluation, and to achieve complete monetary independence from Britain by adopting a floating rate regime in 1974.[8] Between 1974 and early 1979, the bargaining between the left-wing Labour governments and Governor Murray MacLehose was particularly intense: the latter resisted welfare state-style reforms, such as minimum wages and working-class representation in the legislature.[9]

It is worth noting that, for all the limits of social reform, the MacLehose era was a period of change and progress in Hong Kong: more public housing, more new towns, free primary and secondary education, and an independent commission against corruption. In 1981, the MacLehose government published a white paper on district administration, proposing the introduction of District Boards, partially elected by constituencies, in urban areas in 1982. The British intended to develop representative government in Hong Kong, at a time when they were deliberating over its future. Thus, although Thatcher talked of 'minimum change' in Hong Kong's systems after 1997, the political system was moving towards a degree of democracy in the 1980s – an issue that the Chinese would raise objections to during the Hong Kong talks.[10]

Working papers and draft agreements

During the eighth round of talks on 25–26 January 1984, the Chinese and the British discussed the working papers on Hong Kong's various systems handed over by the latter. Zhou Nan and his deputy, Lu Ping, made detailed comments on the four working papers concerning the monetary system, lifestyle, freedoms and rights of the individuals, the economy, and the legal system, respectively. There was no major discrepancy in the two sides' views.[11]

The Chinese asked the British to produce as quickly as possible all the working papers. They envisaged that discussions of agenda item one (arrangements after 1997) should be completed by the end of March, while those of items two (arrangements up to 1997) and three (transfer of sovereignty) should be conducted as rapidly as possible.[12] As the private secretary to the foreign secretary told his counterpart at Downing Street, China wanted 'a quick agreement on the main principles', while Britain hoped to 'include as much detail as possible' so that 'conditionality is safeguarded'.[13] Thatcher found Chinese pressure for rapid negotiation 'rather worrying'.[14]

At the ninth round of talks on 22–23 February, the British and Chinese delegations discussed in detail the working papers on the public service and defence, but made 'limited progress'. On the former, Zhou Nan suggested that the terms of service and pension rights of serving and retired public officers would be maintained after 1997. He was adamant that the posts of secretaries in the SAR government should be filled by 'citizens of Chinese nationality who held permanent Hong Kong identity cards'. Yet British and other foreign nationals could be employed to serve as 'advisers in organs at all levels within the SAR'. Zhou described the defence working paper as 'the worst' document the British had ever tabled because it 'infringed the Chinese premise'. China vehemently rejected the British suggestion that 'in normal circumstances', no Chinese troops should be stationed in Hong Kong after 1997. Nevertheless, he assured Richard Evans that the Chinese would be 'prudent and circumspect about exercising their right to station forces in Hong Kong'.[15]

On 27 February, the Cabinet's Sub-Committee on Hong Kong met to consider the negotiating strategy. On the timetable of negotiation, Geoffrey Howe first reminded ministers of the Chinese intention to announce the arrangements for Hong Kong in September. He noted that Governor Youde and the unofficial members hoped that the September announcement would be 'interim in nature', allowing time for its provisions to be digested by the Hong Kong people and for a final agreement to be reached some time in 1985. Evans, with whom Howe sided, thought that the Chinese deadline of September should be 'taken very seriously'. Concerned that a unilateral Chinese statement would 'damage confidence' in Hong Kong, Howe argued that Britain's primary objective should be the issue of a joint statement in September which was 'as binding as possible on the Chinese', but which made clear that 'the agreement was conditional upon its ratification by the British Parliament'. Ratification would be forthcoming only when China had 'taken the necessary steps to enshrine the provisions of the agreement into the basic laws [sic]', the SAR's mini-constitution. Besides, Howe believed that it was essential to 'begin the process of informing opinion in Hong Kong and elsewhere as to the likely content of a joint agreement'. He proposed to visit Hong Kong to make a public statement on the talks in late April. Thatcher endorsed Howe's proposals.[16]

The Chinese, too, reviewed their negotiating strategy. Deng Xiaoping approved a speech which President Li Xiannian planned to deliver at a cross-departmental meeting about Hong Kong and Macao affairs on 1 March.[17] Li said that although the Sino-British talks had 'achieved some progress', China should not rule out the prospect of no agreement and even of 'disturbances' in Hong Kong. The previous year (1983), the British had played 'the confidence card' and 'the economic card', causing the slide in the Hong Kong dollar. If there were 'serious disturbances' in Hong Kong, China should reconsider the timing and method of recovering Hong Kong.[18]

China's sensitivity to Britain playing 'the confidence card' was aroused by the debate on the Lobo motion in Hong Kong's Legislative Council. In late February, Roger Lobo, senior unofficial member, had decided to table a motion which deemed it essential that any proposal for the future of Hong Kong should be debated in the council before any final agreement was reached.[19] After learning of Lobo's proposed action, Zhou Nan summoned Evans to the Ministry of Foreign Affairs, claiming that the resolution of the Hong Kong question was 'a bilateral matter between the British and Chinese governments', and that China would never accept 'the concept of the three legged stool'. The Lobo motion, Zhou criticised, would be 'unfavourable to the smooth progress of the talks'. Evans replied that it was 'not a question of the British government playing the public opinion card or any other card'. Constitutionally, any member of the council was free to table a motion on any subject, and Lobo's was a 'procedural' (not substantive) motion.[20] During the debate on the Lobo motion on 14 March, twenty legislators voiced their opinions on Hong Kong's future, concluding that 'no settlement which fails to engender trust can possibly preserve our stability and prosperity'.[21]

Back in Beijing, the tenth round on 16–17 March focused on the working papers on constitutional arrangements and shipping. The former noted that post-1997 government structures should 'involve a high degree of continuity'. The chief executive should be 'elected in accordance with procedures approved by the Legislative Council', and then be 'formally appointed by the Central Government'. The Legislative Council should be 'selected by an elective process'.[22] During the talks, Zhou Nan stressed that Hong Kong's political system after 1997 would be defined under the Basic Law to be drafted by the Chinese government, and as such no decision could be taken until after the enactment of the Basic Law. Zhou added that constitutional developments before 1997 should not conflict with the future provisions of the Basic Law, and should be discussed in advance with the Chinese government. He did not take issue with the working paper on shipping.[23]

The topic of Hong Kong's pre-1997 constitutional development was addressed in a memorandum by Howe to Thatcher dated 19 March. As the talks would soon enter agenda item two, the issue became more urgent, and it was essential to keep the process of constitutional reform under Britain's own control and to prevent China from claiming 'the right of veto'. Howe noted that as policy formulation in Hong Kong was currently based on 'consultation and consensus', the Hong Kong governor and the Executive Council had agreed to 'build on existing structures and to proceed slowly towards indirect elections giving the possibility of moving to direct elections in the 1990's'. Accordingly, Howe recommended that Hong Kong should move progressively to a system under which the Legislative Council would be indirectly elected under a collegiate system and by functional groups. Howe did not envisage making a decision on direct elections before the beginning of the 1990s.[24] Thatcher agreed that Britain should establish 'a significant measure of self-government in Hong Kong well before 1997'. This would 'foster a sense of responsibility among the Hong Kong population' and 'make it more difficult for the Chinese to set aside autonomous arrangements after 1997'.[25]

In late March, the FCO produced a draft agreement on Hong Kong. As a basis for discussion, the draft was a 'maximalist' agreement. The main text of the draft agreement set out the British understanding of the principles underpinning the establishment of the SAR, while the annexes drew upon the working papers and a separate Chinese statement laid down the 'twelve-point' plan.[26] When the Sub-Committee on Hong Kong convened on 26 March, Howe pointed out that the negotiations were 'at a critical stage'. Howe argued that the British aims should be to 'reach as detailed an Agreement as possible', and to link ratification of the agreement to the enactment of the Basic Law. But as the Chinese expected to take three to four years to draft the Basic Law, Howe proposed that Parliament would ratify the agreement after signature, but 'on the understanding that an Order in Council would be required in 1997 to effect the actual transfer of sovereignty and administration'. This 'two-stage process of legislation' – that is, 'Parliament ratifying the Agreement but not giving it effect until much later' – would also be 'a means of putting pressure on the Chinese to deliver the full terms of the Agreement in the drafting of their Basic Law'. Concerning the form of an agreement, Howe was doubtful that the precedent mentioned by the Chinese of the 1972 Shanghai Communiqué, in which the US and Chinese governments simply set out their respective positions on Taiwan, would be 'appropriate or adequate'. Howe said that the British draft agreement was 'full and detailed', but it would most likely encounter 'strong Chinese objections'. Howe proposed to pass the draft agreement on to the Chinese before his planned visit to China so as to give them adequate time to study the text. The Sub-Committee approved his proposals.[27]

Also on 26 March, the eleventh round of talks started in Beijing, during which the British ran into difficulties with the Chinese over a range of issues. Commenting on the working paper on civil aviation, Zhou Nan recalled point six of the 'twelve-point' plan, which stated that post-1997 Hong Kong would remain 'a free port and a separate tariff area', adding that the 'basic spirit' of this was applicable to civil aviation. But the term 'exclusive authority' in relation to the SAR government used in several places in the working paper was 'obviously contrary to the principle of sovereignty'. According to relevant international conventions on civil aviation, Zhou explained, 'a state had complete and exclusive sovereignty over the air space above its territory'. The SAR government would need to 'obtain authority from the central government in handling any major issues about external civil aviation relations which involved sovereignty', albeit that the central government would 'take account of the special needs and economic interests of the SAR'. Hong Kong's present system of civil aviation management and those airlines currently operating in Hong Kong could be maintained after 1997. In response, Evans explained that 'arrangements concerning air traffic rights were an integral aspect of economic relations with foreign countries'. As such, the starting point for the British working paper was point ten of the 'twelve-point' plan. The two sides, moreover, had sharp differences over the questions of nationality and constitutional matters. Zhou asserted that China did not recognise 'dual nationality for Chinese nationals' (which included all Hong Kong residents of Chinese descent). After 1997, the existing rights of BDTCs in Hong Kong should cease, and no new British passport should be issued to Chinese nationals there. On Hong Kong's constitutional arrangements after 1997, Zhou made it plain that it was 'not realistic' to expect that the bilateral agreement between China and Britain would 'cover the full detail of the government structure of the SAR' before the promulgation of the Basic Law.[28]

A day after the eleventh round of talks, an event in Hong Kong threatened to derail the talks. On 28 March, Jardine Matheson, a traditional British *hong*, announced the relocation of its legal domicile from Hong Kong to Bermuda. In view of the political uncertainty over Hong Kong, Bermuda, a UK overseas territory, would offer better legal protection for the company.[29] Shocked by the Jardine decision, China accused Britain of making yet another attempt to 'play the economic card' by withdrawing capital from Hong Kong.[30] The Thatcher government appeared to have no prior knowledge of the Jardine decision, but this was not the case for the Hong Kong governor. In a memorandum to the prime minister dated 30 March, John Coles noted that Youde had been 'told a week ago', but he 'did not inform London and [was] very contrite about not having done so'.[31] Interestingly, Sze-yuen Chung thought that Jardine's announcement was 'good for Hong Kong as a whole at that moment of time' because 'it did show the Chinese that foreign investors are mobile'.[32]

To Howe, there had been a hardening of the Chinese attitude in the last two rounds.[33] They wished to start discussing agenda item two (arrangements prior to 1997) in April, with constitutional development, internal security, and the localisation of the civil service as likely subjects.[34] Thatcher was concerned that the British were 'being pushed rapidly towards partial Chinese control in Hong Kong long before 1997'.[35] At the meeting of the Sub-Committee on Hong Kong on 3 April, Howe argued that while it was important to not allow the Chinese to 'take over or undermine the Hong Kong pattern of Government through consultation over pre-1997 arrangements', it would be desirable to discuss with them a range of pre-1997 issues in order to 'achieve the greatest possible degree of continuity of systems'. In particular, as the Chinese had indicated that any British proposal for constitutional development before 1997 should not conflict with the Basic Law, discussion might provide the British with 'a useful means of influencing the drafting of the Basic Law itself'. Besides, ministers considered how to handle the forthcoming visit to Britain of the unofficial members of Hong Kong's Executive Council. Howe believed that the unofficials' views on Britain's negotiating tactics had been based on 'a number of misconceptions', including the assumption that Britain had made no progress in the talks. He wished to correct their misconceptions.[36]

During their fourth mission to London, the unofficial members along with the governor met with Thatcher and Howe on 6 April. Sze-yuen Chung could not hide his unhappiness about the timetable for reaching agreement. Early in the year, when the unofficials had been asked to accept that an interim agreement would be announced in September, it was based on the understanding that there would be 'no agreement without a draft Basic Law'. But now Britain decided to have a final agreement by September, and to ratify it without waiting for the promulgation of the Basic Law. The unofficials were also alarmed by the Chinese unwillingness to 'commit themselves to a detailed agreement' during the eleventh round. Howe responded that the British government and the unofficials were 'united in trying to get the best possible agreement for Hong Kong', but 'similarly [they] had to face the realities together'. Thatcher confided to the unofficials that Britain had indeed 'obtained an important Chinese concession with regard to the continuation of any agreement for 50 years'. With pragmatism getting the better of her, Thatcher reminded the unofficials that 'the Chinese could, if they chose, simply do nothing and wait until the end of the [New Territories] lease'. Yet they continued to negotiate because they 'wanted stability and prosperity in Hong Kong, were concerned about their standing in world opinion and wished to set the right precedent for Taiwan'.[37]

Shortly after the unofficials' departure from London, the twelfth round of talks took place in Beijing on 11–12 April. Starting agenda items two and three, Zhou Nan offered some basic Chinese ideas about arrangements for the transitional period and for the transfer of government. During the transitional period, Britain would 'have full responsibility for maintaining economic and social stability in Hong Kong', while China would 'actively cooperate' with the British. As the Hong Kong dollar would continue to circulate after 1997, Zhou suggested that Britain should 'keep China informed of the issue of currency, of the management and use of the Exchange Fund, and of the circumstances of note issuing banks'. The Hong Kong branch of the Bank of China should become 'a member of the advisory commission on the Exchange Fund and one of the presidents of the Hong Kong Association of Banks'. Significantly, Zhou stated that it would be necessary to set up 'a permanent Sino-British joint group or committee in Hong Kong during the transition period'. As 'a liaison body and not an organ of power', it aimed to 'coordinate implementation of the Sino-British agreement' and to 'discuss concrete measures for the smooth transfer of government'. As for the transfer of government, Zhou envisioned that the transitional period would be roughly divided into two stages. From now till about 1993 – that is, before the promulgation of the Basic Law – Britain should 'create the conditions for an orderly transfer of government and provide China with detailed information about the work of various Hong Kong Government departments'. During this period, China would formulate the Basic Law. Between about 1994 and the end of June 1997, China and Britain should, 'through consultation, reform step by step the legislative, administrative and judicial arrangements in Hong Kong to bring them into line with the [requirements] of the Basic Law'. In response, Evans said that Zhou had made 'a very important statement', and Britain would study it carefully.[38]

In his report to the FCO, Evans argued that the Chinese proposals for the transitional period 'go far beyond the limited machinery and scope of consultation which officials and ministers were contemplating in late March'. He found it unacceptable that the Chinese 'should be consulted on all important matters between conclusion of an agreement and 1997'.[39] Howe agreed that Zhou's proposals diverged very sharply from the British concepts of 'continuity' and 'autonomous administration'. During the transitional period, it would not be necessary to 'undertake substantial changes in the laws, administrative arrangements or other fields, since this would negate the concept of continuity'. Nor should Britain agree to establish 'any machinery before 1997 which could give the impression that the central people's government were preparing to administer Hong Kong rather than to leave administration to the people of the territory'.[40]

Immediately after the twelfth round, Evans called on Zhou at the Foreign Ministry to hand over the annexes to the draft agreement, and to discuss the latter which had been submitted to the Chinese earlier.[41] Zhou put it bluntly that the British draft agreement was 'fundamentally unacceptable' and could not be taken 'as a basis for negotiation'. The main problem was that it was 'a clear attempt to negate and limit Chinese sovereignty over Hong Kong', and Britain was 'trying to turn the future SAR into some sort of independent political entity'. Article 1, for example, 'contained nothing on the restoration of Hong Kong by the United Kingdom to China, nor on the assumption by China of sovereignty and the right of administration in 1997'. At this juncture, Zhou introduced the Chinese draft agreement, consisting of a draft joint declaration, draft notes, and a draft protocol. Zhou regarded a joint communiqué or joint declaration as appropriate, with the 1972 Shanghai Communiqué between China and the United States serving as a point of reference. On content, Zhou stressed that Britain and China should 'first and foremost solve the central question of sovereignty in explicit and unequivocal terms'. Accordingly, the first article of the draft joint declaration stipulated that Britain would 'restore the Hong Kong area' to China on 1 July 1997, and China would 'resume the exercise of its sovereignty'. To Zhou, the joint declaration should 'focus on major principles and not be a document containing details'. An annex to the joint declaration, taking the form of an exchange of notes, would 'amplify the implications of the 12 guidelines in the light of the talks'. Lastly, a protocol on arrangements for the transitional period set out 'the principles which would ensure an orderly transfer of government' and the work of the Sino-British joint group.[42]

Assessing the Chinese counter-draft on the eve of Howe's China visit, R. D. Clift, head of the FCO's Hong Kong Department, noted that the draft joint declaration 'binds the UK to restore Hong Kong to China but does not bind China to implement either its 12 points or the elaboration contained in the exchange of notes'. Nevertheless, as 'a first bid', the Chinese draft 'could, with extensive adaptation, form the basis of an acceptable agreement': after all, it did 'contain a provision for detail additional to the 12 points'. Clift proposed that during his visit, Howe should begin by arguing for the British draft and, if China rejected it, make preliminary comments on the Chinese draft, before suggesting referring both documents to the negotiators in the next round of talks.[43]

Howe's visit to China: timetable

As part of his Far Eastern trip including Korea and Japan, Howe arrived in Beijing on the afternoon of 15 April. His official party of nineteen people included Lady Howe (Elspeth), Principal Private Secretary L. V. Appleyard, Assistant Under Secretary of State David Wilson, and Percy Cradock.[44] During his all-day meeting with Foreign Minister Wu Xueqian on 16 April, Howe started with a general statement that the British draft agreement 'unequivocally met Chinese requirements of principle', by making it clear that 'Hong Kong would be administered under the Chinese constitution'. On the timetable of negotiation, Howe explained 'the Parliamentary constraints' on the timing of signature and ratification. He argued strongly that the conclusion of a draft agreement in September could meet the Chinese desire for making an announcement on Hong Kong by then, and would allow for parliamentary debate on the agreement in November and for signature before the end of the year. For his part, Wu found the British draft agreement 'unacceptable' because it was 'ambiguous on the question of transfer of sovereignty'. Wu asserted that the 'twelve-point' guidelines for Hong Kong 'were an internal affair and not to be treated as something for approval by another country or taken as the result of negotiation'. The Basic Law would take the 'twelve-point' guidelines as 'its basis', and 'the agreement would be reflected in it'. However, the British draft agreement 'attempted to define its details', and indeed the British side was 'seeking to replace the Basic Law with the agreement'. To Wu, the Chinese draft agreement was 'clear cut and reasonable' concerning the 'restoration of Hong Kong to China'. The text of the agreement should cover mainly 'major issues of principle', while 'specific issues' could be dealt with in the annexes. On the timetable, Wu believed that it was 'entirely possible' to conclude discussion of an agreement in May or June, and to afford the British Parliament 'ample time' to complete the necessary constitutional procedures before the signing of the agreement in September. On the pre-1997 arrangements, Wu disagreed that the proposed Sino-British joint group could 'give the impression of condominium in Hong Kong'. Rather, as 'a liaison body', the joint group's task would be to 'coordinate the implementation of the agreement' during the transitional period.

Howe regarded the Chinese draft agreement as unacceptable: it appeared to 'visualise legal obligations only on the British side', with no provision for post-1997 arrangements that matched 'HMG's obligation to transfer sovereignty'. On the timetable, Howe said that it would not be possible to complete discussion by May or June, although Britain hoped to move as quickly as possible. Concerning the link between the agreement and the Basic Law, Howe understood that the Basic Law would be 'an internal Chinese affair'. But as the Chinese side had indicated that the drafting process would 'take some time', the British believed that it was necessary to give Hong Kong people 'clear and precise assurances about their future'. Turning to the transitional period, Howe accepted that many issues, such as land leases, required consultation before 1997. But he had difficulties with the Chinese proposal for a joint group, which would 'give the impression that China was proposing, or preparing, to send people to administer Hong Kong or that a condominium was being established'. Howe, moreover, expressed concern about 'the Chinese suggestion for step by step reform of the legislative, judicial and administrative arrangements to bring them into line with the Basic Law'. Although Britain saw 'a need for some changes', it attached great importance to 'the continuity of systems', and the Chinese suggestion could 'imply major changes'. After a recess, Wu agreed that both the British and Chinese drafts should remain on the table for further discussion.

Howe then raised three outstanding issues – nationality, constitutional development, and the public service. On nationality, Howe said that Britain hoped to create a new category of British nationality to allow Hong Kong's

BDTCs to retain their existing rights under another name, which would have 'no colonial connotations'. Howe stressed that this would only be 'a transitional arrangement' as in general British nationality was transmissible for one generation only. Wu, however, emphasised the fundamental principle that China did 'not recognise dual nationality'. As regards constitutional development, Howe pointed out that the British draft agreement 'embodied the concept of continuity of government structure' while not precluding 'necessary changes'. Howe hoped that China could provide 'a clear expression of the autonomy which the legislature and executive of the future SAR would enjoy'. Wu responded that the composition, functions, and procedures of the SAR government would be defined in the Basic Law, but it was impossible to define them at present. Lastly, on the public service, Howe suggested that after 1997 British and other foreign nationals should not be excluded from any post 'simply because of their race'. Wu replied that British and other foreign nations with permanent ID cards could be employed to serve 'as advisers or officers up to the rank of deputy secretary in certain departments'. But the chiefs of principal departments and the commissioner of police should be 'Chinese nationals with permanent Hong Kong ID cards, nominated by the SAR government and approved by the central people's government'. Wu concluded that 'mutual understanding had been enhanced' through 'friendly and frank discussions'.[45]

On the following day, Howe met with Ji Pengfei, state councillor and head of the Hong Kong and Macao Affairs Office, and Premier Zhao Ziyang separately. While the atmosphere of the meetings was friendly, both Ji and Zhao pressed hard on the timetable and content of the agreement and the proposal for a joint group. Ji insisted that the agreement should 'only cover matters of principle and not too much detail', but there would be an annex, which would be 'equally valid and binding'.[46] When they met in the afternoon, Zhao similarly assured Howe that both the agreement and the annexes would 'have binding force and be equally valid'.[47]

On the morning of 18 April, Howe was granted an interview with Deng Xiaoping in the Great Hall of the People. During the ninety-minute conversation, Deng was 'friendly and ebullient', yet remained firm on key issues. Deng began by stressing 'the future continuity of Chinese policies'. Looking at economic policies 'for 20 or even 30 to 50 years ahead', Deng said that these policies were 'not personal' to him, but, if the path was correct, would 'long outlast him'. The Chinese assurance that Hong Kong's systems would 'remain unchanged for 50 years' should be seen in that context. At this juncture, Deng made an important concession about the issue of timetable. Recognising that London had to 'respect Parliament and give them time to consider the matter', Deng would not object to the British proposal for publishing a draft agreement by September and signing it by the year's end.

Nevertheless, Deng insisted that the agreement should deal with 'matters of principle': if it contained 'too many details', 'errors might be made'. Deng added that an annex in the form of an exchange of notes would deal with the detail, but 'excessive detail was not good'. Commenting on the transitional period, Deng showed 'considerable anxiety' and 'could not take it for granted that the next 13 years would be peaceful'. Notwithstanding his hope for 'no trouble', Deng had already 'noted some signals', for example, Jardine's decision to move its headquarters to Bermuda. Although he accepted that 'Jardine's move had not been encouraged by HMG', it showed that 'some businessmen were playing a damaging role', and some people might try to 'leave Hong Kong in a mess for the future SAR government'. Deng claimed that China 'had no information about monetary policies in H[ong]K[ong], and very little about land leases'. He worried about a 'wholesale flight of capital' from Hong Kong. Deng saw the imperative of a joint group in Hong Kong in order to 'increase China's knowledge and create conditions for the handover'. The joint group would be set up in Hong Kong, but its meeting could rotate between Hong Kong, Beijing, and London. Howe agreed to explore the idea of a 'rotating group'.

Deng, moreover, talked about Hong Kong's future leaders. With the proposed joint group in mind, Deng said that the British and Chinese should 'consult together on choosing candidates to be future officials', adding that they should be 'patriots, i.e. stand for China's resumption of sovereignty'. Besides, Deng asserted that in 1997 China would send 'a small armed force' to Hong Kong, its presence being 'a symbol of sovereignty' and 'a factor for stability'. Worrying that the presence of Chinese troops might have 'an adverse effect on confidence', Howe proposed that 'an internal security force' be established instead. Howe asked China to be 'prudent and circumspect and voluntarily refrain from stationing forces' in Hong Kong. Deng replied that there was no time to discuss the issue.[48] In Howe's impression, Deng was 'certainly a sharp negotiator, despite appearances to the contrary'.[49] On the way to the airport for a flight to Hong Kong, Howe was accompanied by Zhou Nan, who expressed his hope that Britain would recognise 'the positive moves' made by Deng about the timetable.[50]

Upon his arrival in Hong Kong on 18 April, Howe spent the first two days meeting with the governor, UMELCO, and business and social leaders.[51] On the morning of 20 April, Howe made his 'unveiling statement' at the Legislative Council chamber. While being aware of 'the problems and anxieties for the people of Hong Kong which arise from the confidentiality of the negotiations', Howe said that the expiry of the New Territories Lease, which covered 92 per cent of the territory, was 'a fact we could not and cannot ignore'. Howe asserted that 'it would not be realistic to think of an agreement that provides for continued British administration in Hong Kong after 1997'. Rather, it was imperative to focus on 'other ways of securing the assurances necessary for the continuity of Hong Kong's stability, prosperity and way of life'. Specifically, the British had been seeking 'a high degree of autonomy' for Hong Kong under Chinese sovereignty. Howe revealed that, as the Chinese government had stated publicly that Hong Kong people would administer Hong Kong after 1997, in the years immediately ahead, the political system of Hong Kong would be 'developed on increasingly representative lines'. Although Britain and China were still some way off reaching an agreement, Howe concluded, 'a good deal of progress' had been made, and there was 'a will on both sides to bring our work to fruition in an agreement'.[52] There followed a question-and-answer session with the press.[53]

The press coverage of Howe's statement was 'generally favourable', not least because it helped remove uncertainty over Hong Kong's future.[54] Although the Hang Seng Index went down forty-five points on 24 April, the loss was just little more than the gain in the previous week.[55] Still, Governor Youde was aware that underlying concerns remained within the society. The middle and richer classes had 'hoped, however illogically, for the retention of some residual form of British administration or involvement'. But Howe's statement could not but contribute to 'a degree of anti-British feeling' and the trend of emigration from Hong Kong to the Western world.[56]

In reporting to Thatcher about his visits to China and Hong Kong, Howe noted that the outcome was 'less negative' than he had expected. Although the Chinese had rejected the British draft agreement, 'their acceptance of the idea of an agreement binding on both sides, with an equally binding annex', was something that Britain could build on. While the Chinese proposal for a joint group contained 'obvious dangers', Howe also saw 'opportunities for educating the Chinese about the way in which Hong Kong functions'. By ensuring that the Chinese were kept informed of pre-1997 institutional changes in Hong Kong, the joint group would enable Britain 'to some extent to condition Chinese thinking about the Basic Law'.[57]

Winning hearts and minds

After Howe had made an 'unveiling statement' about the talks in Hong Kong, the Thatcher government sought to win over public opinion at home. A parliamentary debate on Hong Kong's future was scheduled for mid-May. Between 10 and 15 May, Sze-yuen Chung led a UMELCO delegation to London with a view to lobbying ministers and MPs before the debate. Against the will of Governor Youde, Chung had released a UMELCO statement to the press on the eve of his departure.[58] The statement made it plain that although the unofficial members, appointed by the governor, could make 'no claim to representative status', they had been in touch with all sectors of the community, and as such were 'in a position to reflect the views and wishes of Hong Kong people'. The statement spelt out four conditions or requests that would determine the acceptability of the agreement by Hong Kong. The agreement should contain 'full details of the proposed administrative, legal, social and economic systems applicable after 1997'; provide 'adequate and workable assurances that the terms of the agreement will be honoured'; state that the Basic Law would incorporate the provisions of the agreement; and guarantee to safeguard the rights of British nationals in Hong Kong.[59]

China's propaganda machine lambasted the UMELCO statement as 'an attempt to obstruct the conclusion of an agreement by the Chinese and British governments on the Hongkong issue at an early date'.[60] Howe worried that the unofficials' public statement would have 'an unhelpful impact on the negotiations with the Chinese'. It was also feared that Chung would press for a right of abode in Britain.[61] As it turned out, the UMELCO delegation received a hostile reception in Britain. Chung suspected that the FCO might have briefed the British press and scared parliamentarians off about the UMELCO visit, whose alleged aim was to 'lobby for the immigration of a few million British colonial subjects in Hong Kong to their crowded country'.[62] On 15 May, a day before the House of Commons debate, the UMELCO delegation was received by Thatcher. Chung stressed that the delegation was 'not here to make demands but to reflect the wishes, fears and feelings of the Hong Kong people about their future'. Thatcher said that she did understand 'the basic fears of the people of Hong Kong', but it was also important that the unofficials 'should not put Peking in a position where it lost face'. The pragmatic prime minister stressed that Britain was 'not seeking an agreement for its own sake', but 'life was a question of alternatives'. In response, Chung sounded a warning: 'To transfer land was one thing. To transfer people was another.'[63]

The House of Commons debate started at about 7 pm on 16 May. Howe began by paying tribute to 'the very important contribution' that the unofficial members made to the administration of Hong Kong. He mentioned, though, that the UMELCO statement was 'issued entirely on their own initiative', and its terms were 'not the subject of any prior consultation with the Government, either in London or in Hong Kong'. Howe defended Britain's negotiating approach by arguing that assurances for continuity and autonomy for Hong Kong could best be provided by 'a detailed and binding agreement'. On the sensitive issue of nationality, Howe said that neither this Parliament, nor the next, would 'favour changes which stimulated emigration from Hong Kong to the United Kingdom or elsewhere'. About twenty-two MPs took part in the debate, lasting until midnight, which demonstrated remarkable unanimous support for Howe's approach. Denis Healey (Leeds, East), shadow foreign secretary, spoke of 'the realities' that Britain should recognise if the talks were to be successful. With his experience as defence secretary in the 1960s, he claimed that China had 'never needed to use troops to take over Hong Kong or to break international law'. He believed that China 'tried to smooth the way of the talks', and 'wished Hong Kong to continue its present economic situation and political and social freedoms' after 1997. Edward Heath (Old Bexley and Sidcup), an old friend of China, congratulated Howe on 'the frankness with which he stated the real position' of Hong Kong.[64] As Baroness Young, the FCO's minister of state, reported to Cabinet ministers on 17 May, the MPs who had spoken had 'revealed widespread sympathy for the people of Hong Kong, combined with a recognition that the realities of the situation left the Government no alternative but to continue to work for a full, detailed and binding agreement with China'.[65]

With both Houses of Parliament demonstrating support for the government,[66] Thatcher and her ministers considered the next step in the negotiation. On 23 May, the Sub-Committee on Hong Kong agreed to the establishment of a joint group, on the strict understanding that it would not be based in Hong Kong but would meet as necessary in London, Hong Kong, and Beijing. To Howe, as China would 'try to meddle' in Hong Kong affairs regardless of Britain's disagreement, the establishment of the joint group might 'well provide a means of controlling Chinese interference as long as its terms of reference are carefully drawn up'.[67] During the fifteenth round of talks on 30–31 May, Evans proposed a 'peripatetic joint group' with tightly defined functions. Zhou Nan, however, reiterated Deng's view that the group should be set up in Hong Kong but might rotate to meet in Beijing, London, and Hong Kong. Besides, Evans and Zhou discussed the creation of a working group to consider documents submitted by both sides with a view to reaching agreement as soon as possible.[68] In the sixteenth round on 12–13 June, it was decided that a working group would meet full-time between rounds of formal talks. David Wilson, assistant under secretary of state responsible for Asia and the Pacific in the FCO, would lead the British team of the group, while Ambassador Ke Zaishuo would head the Chinese team.[69]

Deng Xiaoping deliberately chose to speak in public in order to make China's position on Hong Kong crystal clear. During the second session of the Sixth NPC and of the Sixth Chinese People's Political Consultative Conference on 25 May, Deng sought to quash a rumour that China would not station troops in Hong Kong after 1997. Speaking to Hong Kong and Macao journalists covering the proceedings, Deng asserted that the Chinese leader[70] who reportedly made such a claim had 'talked nonsense' and did not represent 'the Central's view'. As Hong Kong was 'Chinese territory', Deng asked rhetorically 'why can't [China] station troops there?'.[71] To win the hearts and minds of Hong Kong residents, Deng received a Hong Kong industrial and commercial delegation on 22 June. In front of the cameras, Deng enunciated the policy of 'one country, two systems'. After resuming the exercise of China's sovereignty over Hong Kong in 1997, Deng proclaimed, Hong Kong's current social, economic, and legal systems as well as its way of life would remain unchanged for fifty years. Apart from stationing troops in Hong Kong, China would not assign officials to the SAR government.[72] When receiving the delegation of Sze-yuen Chung and two other unofficial members the following day, Deng's tone was harsher. In front of journalists from Hong Kong, Deng welcomed Chung to Beijing 'in [his] individual capacity': he vehemently opposed a 'three legged stool' in the Sino-British bilateral talks. A stern-faced Deng lectured the visitors on China's Hong Kong policy, while dismissing the existence of a crisis of confidence in the territory.[73]

To Howe, Deng's 'dismissive attitude' towards the three unofficial members was 'neither helpful to confidence within Hong Kong nor to progress in the negotiations', which had been 'erratic' in recent rounds. The issue of the joint group remained the main stumbling block to an agreement. Howe argued that it might be sensible to make a concession on the location of the joint group in Hong Kong in return for 'important concessions' by China, for example, over the terms of the draft agreement. He proposed to make another visit to Beijing in late July. At its meeting on 17 July, the Sub-Committee on Hong Kong endorsed Howe's proposed visit. Howe would carry with him a message by Thatcher to Zhao Ziyang, suggesting that the question of location of the joint group be put aside for the present while discussions continued on its composition, functions, and powers, as well as on post-1997 arrangements.[74]

Howe's second China visit: the joint group

Howe's visit was scheduled for 27–31 July. Before his arrival in Beijing, Howe would have a twenty-four-hour stopover in Hong Kong on 26 July with the aim of consulting the Executive Council. He would return to the city following the China visit in order to make a public statement.[75] The Chinese leadership attached great importance to Howe's visit, regarding it as a make-or-break moment in the protracted negotiations. Just before Howe set off for Hong Kong, on 24–25 July the nineteenth round of talks was held in Beijing, during which the Chinese side tabled the revised draft joint declaration, among other issues.⁷⁶ During informal contact with Evans after the formal session, Zhou Nan revealed the Chinese disappointment about the absence of 'British flexibility' over the joint group. Referring to reports in the British press that Howe was considering a further visit to Beijing in September, Zhou confided to Evans that 'all senior Chinese leaders would be very busy in September', and would not be able to receive foreign visitors. Thus, Howe's visit in two days' time was 'very important': unlike his April visit, 'the stakes were higher and the time for the achievement of an agreement was shorter'.⁷⁷

In essence, the year 1984 marked the thirty-fifth anniversary of the founding of the PRC. Deng Xiaoping was eager to reach an agreement on Hong Kong in time for an announcement to the Chinese people about its retrocession on the national day.⁷⁸ On 27 July (the day Howe arrived in Beijing), at Premier Zhao's suggestion, Zhou Nan went to the holiday resort of Beidaihe to meet with Deng, who was relaxing there. Deng asserted that China should make a 'non-principled compromise' to the British.⁷⁹ The joint group should be based in Hong Kong, but its name could be changed and the timing of location could be flexible. On the latter, Deng said that it did 'not matter' if the joint group was set up two years after the entry into force of the agreement and terminated two years after China had recovered Hong Kong in 1997. Deng asked Zhou to try to reach an agreement on that basis. Besides, Deng suggested expediting the drafting of the Basic Law, which should be completed by 1990 and preferably earlier.⁸⁰

While Zhou was receiving instructions from China's paramount leader, Howe arrived in Hong Kong to consult with the Executive Council. The unofficial members regarded the setting up of the joint group in Hong Kong as 'a high price to pay' for an agreement. Nevertheless, after a long discussion, a general consensus emerged that 'tying the Chinese down on terms of reference and deferring the establishment of the joint group in Hong Kong until 1993 would make location in Hong Kong bearable'. Moreover, prolonging the operation of the joint group beyond 1997 would represent 'a major reassurance' by Beijing.⁸¹ Indeed, that the joint group should continue for certain years before and after 1997 was the idea of Maria Tam, an unofficial and a barrister: she called it a 'mirror image'.⁸²

Upon his arrival in Beijing in the late afternoon of 27 July, Howe's party (consisting of Percy Cradock and David Wilson, among others) was escorted to the Diaoyutai State Guesthouse, where Howe could 'feel like home' following his April trip.⁸³ The next morning, Howe had a session with Wu Xueqian. He handed over a copy of Thatcher's letter to Zhao Ziyang and the British draft on the joint group, while giving a full presentation of the outstanding issues.⁸⁴ But it was the private lunch meeting between Cradock and Zhou Nan that really began to unlock the deadlock over the joint group.

Having just returned from Beidaihe with Deng's fresh instructions, Zhou made an important offer that China was prepared to defer establishing the joint group in Hong Kong for two years after the signing of the agreement (that is, 1987), and to allow the group to continue its work until 2000. But it could in no circumstances accept deferment of location in Hong Kong until 1993 as the British proposed. Significantly, Zhou said that the Chinese leaders 'could not wait beyond this visit to achieve a solution of this issue', nor would it 'bargain further'. 'If [Britain] could not accept this offer during the visit', he warned, 'the Chinese would withdraw the offers they had made, and the negotiations as a whole would fail'.[85]

In-between the morning and afternoon sessions with Wu Xueqian, the British briefly discussed Zhou's offer in the garden of the Diaoyutai State Guesthouse. Cradock considered Zhou's offer as a serious one.[86] But Howe hoped to make further progress. When the session resumed in the afternoon, Wu said that if Britain agreed to the Chinese proposal, he would make 'substantial concessions' by preparing to state explicitly, in the Chinese draft protocol, that the 'Joint Liaison Group' (as it was now called) would 'not be an organ of power' and would 'not have a supervisory role'.[87] In a restricted session with Wu on the morning of 29 July, Howe said that Britain hoped to defer moving the joint group to Hong Kong until 1989. Wu, however, proposed 1988. As regards the termination date, Wu said that the year 2000 was 'a beginning of a new era', and thus China did not want its work to continue after that date. Besides, Howe proposed, and Wu agreed, that two working groups should meet as soon as possible to finalise the paper on the joint group and the main outstanding points on the main agreement.[88]

On Thatcher's instruction,[89] Howe made a last-ditch effort to press for 1989, but Wu proposed 1 January 1988 instead. This prompted Howe to suggest 1 July 1988 as the effective date, for this would 'split the difference on a year' and would be 'the same time of the year as the expiry of the [New Territories] Lease in 1997'.[90] When receiving Howe on 30 July, Zhao Ziyang accepted the date of 1 July 1988 as 'a big concession made to meet the British wishes'. In addition, Zhao welcomed the news that the Wilson–Ke working group had just agreed on the language of the key parts of the main agreement, to the effect that the joint declaration and its annexes would be both 'legally binding' and their contents would be 'stipulated in the Basic Law'. Zhao thanked Howe for conveying Thatcher's message to him, which demonstrated 'her friendly attitude and statesmanship'. With agreement on the most important question, Zhao said, it would not be difficult to settle the outstanding issues.[91]

Howe met with Deng Xiaoping on the morning of 31 July. Having just returned to Beijing from his summer resort at Beidaihe, and with the deadlock over the joint group broken, Deng could afford starting with a joke: 'You can see my skin has gone brown, like an African ... I have changed my nationality.'[92] But during the ninety-minute conversation, Deng also had important messages to communicate to Britain. Deng said that the two sides had 'almost reached agreement on the Hong Kong question', with 'only small details' remaining, and their achievement would 'set an example to the world'. Deng expressed his strong conviction that the concept of 'one country, two systems' would work in Hong Kong. But he was 'very concerned' about the period before 1997. Deng spelt out his 'five hopes', including that the Hong Kong government would not 'discourage a wholesale flight of capital'. (It appeared that Deng still failed to grasp the nature of Hong Kong's capitalism.) At the end, Deng proclaimed that China had 'the highest trust in the Secretary of State and the Prime Minister', while thanking Thatcher for her contribution to the resolution of the Hong Kong question. Deng extended an invitation to the Queen to visit China. Howe returned the compliment to the Chinese: 'The Hong Kong negotiations without Zhou Nan would be like a Chinese banquet without *mao-tai*.'[93]

From Beijing, Howe flew to Hong Kong in the late afternoon of 31 July. At the Executive Council meeting on the following morning, Sze-yuen Chung and other unofficials praised Howe for securing from the Chinese 'a major achievement', particularly concerning the joint group. Provided that the outstanding issues, like the nationality question, were resolved satisfactorily, Chung had 'high hopes' that the final agreement would be acceptable to the Hong Kong people.[94]

Finalising the annexes: constitution, nationality, civil aviation, land leases

Following Howe's fruitful China trip, the Hong Kong negotiation entered its endgame. The twenty-first round took place on 22–23 August, covering land leases, nationality, and the schedule of the outstanding issues. But the Chinese remained intransigent on key issues.[95] Intense negotiations over the annexes to the main agreement were being conducted by the Wilson–Ke working group and by a newly created 'ad hoc group' (whose title was chosen to distinguish it from the working group) led by Robin McLaren and Lu Ping.[96] The working group discussed the legal system and rights and freedoms of Hong Kong people, reaching satisfactory agreements on both counts.[97] But it failed to make a breakthrough on constitutional arrangements after 1997. The Chinese were reluctant to endorse an elective process for the selection of the chief executive.[98]

The McLaren–Lu ad hoc group worked on the annexes about land leases, civil aviation, and nationality. On land leases, the British aimed to seek Chinese agreement to recognise existing leases and new leases running beyond 1997. The Chinese proposed the establishment of a land commission to consider the total amount of new land leases to be granted before 1997, and a reasonable division of income from leases between the present Hong Kong government and the future SAR government. Concerning civil aviation and nationality, both of which touched upon the sensitive issue of sovereignty in Beijing's eyes, the British and Chinese negotiators had serious disagreement (see below).[99]

Another issue that needed to be resolved was the timing of ratification of the agreement. For the Thatcher government, before ratification by Parliament, domestic legislation was needed – the passage of a short bill to enable British sovereignty over Hong Kong to be transferred to China by an Order in Council at a future date. Due to the exigencies of the parliamentary timetable for the 1984–85 session, the earliest possible date for ratification was thought to be 30 June 1985. But it was impossible to be 'absolutely certain' that Parliament could pass the aforementioned bill and then ratify the agreement by that date.[100] During the twenty-second round of talks on 5–6 September, Evans proposed 30 June 1985 as the deadline for the exchange of instruments on ratification, while hoping to qualify that date by adding the words 'subject to completion of necessary procedures in national legislatures'. Seeing a period of six months as 'too long', however, Zhou Nan insisted on a definite date for ratification and avoidance of 'conditional language'.[101] After receiving his preliminary report on the first day of the talks, Howe instructed Evans to inform Zhou that the British government undertook to 'make every effort to ensure that legislation is passed in time to allow ratification by 30 June 1985'.[102] On the second day, Zhou remained unconvinced, warning that Evans' proposal would 'put the talks at risk'.[103] The communiqué issued at the end of the session did not specify a date for the next meeting.[104] (The twenty-second round turned out to be the last session.)

To resolve the outstanding issues, Howe proposed, and Thatcher agreed, to send a message to Wu Xueqian about the slow progress in negotiation.[105] At 8 pm on 8 September, Evans called on Zhou to deliver Howe's message. In his letter, Howe first talked about 'the spirit of give and take' shared by the two sides. Nevertheless, he was increasingly concerned about the lack of progress on a number of issues since his July visit. On nationality, the British government faced 'enormous political difficulties' regarding the question of transmissibility. It hoped that Hong Kong's BDTCs should retain the right to transmit their status to their children 'for one generation only'. Howe highlighted two 'fundamental questions of principle' regarding British passports. Despite the Chinese proposal that all new British passports should be issued before 30 June 1997, Howe worried that a very large number of applications before that date would impose 'an intolerable bureaucratic burden' on Britain. Notwithstanding the Chinese proposal for the use of the words 'travel documents', Howe stressed the importance of a reference to 'British passports' in the annex on nationality. Howe suggested that if the two sides were able to reach agreement on the two passport issues, Britain would be prepared to take a second look at the question of transmissibility. As for post-1997 constitutional arrangements, Britain hoped that the chief executive would be elected, whereas the Chinese position was that he should be 'elected or selected by consultation'. Howe was willing to accept the Chinese position, provided that the agreement would state that the legislature would be 'selected by an elective process' and that the chief executive would be 'accountable to the legislature'.

On the question of civil aviation, China had so far refused to delegate standing authority to the SAR government to conclude air service agreements after 1997, which was deemed the prerogative of the central government. (Ironically, Britain, treating colonial Hong Kong as a 'domestic airport', controlled all air traffic rights.) Britain, on the other hand, saw civil aviation within the context of Hong Kong's autonomy in external economic relations, while hoping to protect the interests of Cathay Pacific Airways, the local airline owed by Swire Pacific. In his letter, Howe argued that Cathay Pacific had 'a key role to play in the future prosperity of Hong Kong', and thus the airline would need 'the assurance that the SAR will continue to have adequate control of the air services network'. Finally, on the date of ratification of the agreement, Howe stated that Britain was prepared to drop the additional qualifying words in the draft agreement, while assuring China that it would do all in its power to ensure that the necessary legislative steps were completed by 30 June 1985. At the end of his message, Howe offered to come to China again to resolve the outstanding issues if necessary.[106]

Deng Xiaoping, too, was concerned about the slow pace of negotiations. If Britain and China could not resolve the outstanding issues, it risked 'the collapse of the entire structure' that had been built over a long period.[107] At this juncture, Deng conceived the Hong Kong question from a wider strategic perspective. On the morning of 8 September (before Evans called on Zhou that evening), Deng had an interview with the visiting Italian leader of the Senate. Deng said that with regard to the problem of national unification, China had a 'Hong Kong question' and a 'Taiwan question'. To resolve both questions, China thus put forward the method of 'one country, two systems'. Deng said that the Chinese were currently in talks with the British about Hong Kong, and 'could reach agreement'. Deng, moreover, talked of China's disputes with Japan over the Diaoyu Islands and with some Southeast Asian countries over the Spratly Islands, disputes that could be resolved by 'war' or by 'peaceful negotiation'. Deng asserted that the 'one country, two systems' formula, together with 'joint development' of contested lands (while putting the sovereignty issue aside), were both methods to resolve international disputes.[108] In short, Deng was eager to demonstrate to the world that the Hong Kong question could be peacefully resolved due to the wider implications for Taiwan and other international conflicts.

Wu Xueqian's reply to Howe's message came on 11 September. On the nationality issue, Wu suggested that the British government could issue 'some form of British travel documents' to persons who currently held the BDTC status before 30 June 1997, but not after that date. He further proposed that if Britain withdrew the proposals for issuing new British 'travel documents' after 1997 and for allowing the transmissibility of nationality to the next generation, China would accept that Britain could refer to the new documents as 'passports' in the British memorandum. Concerning constitutional arrangements, Wu noted from Howe's message that Britain was willing to accept the Chinese position that the chief executive should be 'selected by election or consultation'. In these circumstances, China was prepared to state in annex one that the legislature should be 'selected by an elective process', and that the executive should be 'accountable to the legislature'. On the question of ratification, Wu said that China would agree that the joint declaration could state that the exchange of instruments of ratification should take place in Beijing before 30 June 1985. Finally, Wu confided to Evans that the 'concessions and compromises' that he offered had been approved by Premier Zhao and other leaders. Thus, Britain should 'not let specific issues postpone conclusion of the talks', for there were 'not many days left'.[109]

When the Sub-Committee on Hong Kong convened on 12 September, Howe updated ministers on the exchange of messages with Wu. Howe said that Wu had accepted the British proposals for constitutional arrangements and the deadline for ratification. On defence, however, there had been no significant change to the Chinese position on the stationing of troops in Hong Kong after 1997. On nationality, while the British offer to drop transmissibility had prompted China to accept the use of the word 'passports' in the British memorandum, Beijing remained adamant that no such documents could be issued after 30 June 1997. Howe proposed a compromise solution: although 30 June 1997 should be the 'deadline for applications' for new passports, 'the process of actually issuing the documents could continue after that date'.[110]

Howe sent a second message to Wu on 13 September. After appreciating the 'positive spirit' of Wu's reply, Howe spelt out the still outstanding issues. On civil aviation, Howe hoped that the Chinese side would be more flexible. As for the Chinese insistence on the issue of British passports before 30 June

1997, Howe proposed that Britain would continue to accept applications for new passports until that date, but those applications which had been received but not processed by then should be dealt with later as quickly as possible. Finally, Howe raised his concern about the Chinese proposal for 'extensive revision, involving changes both of language and substance, of the whole of Annex 1' (China's 'basic policies' regarding Hong Kong). While not excluding consideration of 'changes of grammar or punctuation', Howe stressed that the British side simply could not reopen 'issues of substance' after months of negotiation to reach agreement.[111]

Wu replied within three days, on 16 September. In his message, Wu noted that the two sides had basically reached agreement on civil aviation. (At last, Beijing agreed that in order to maintain Hong Kong's status as an international and regional aviation centre, the Chinese government would authorise the SAR government to negotiate or revise air service agreements, except for air services to, from, or through mainland China.)[112] Concerning British passports, Wu insisted that the British government should issue them before 30 June 1997, lest it create 'very great political difficulties' for China. As for Howe's concern about the revised Annex 1, Wu believed that the changes proposed by the Chinese side were 'reasonable' and were fully 'in accordance with procedure'. Wu expressed his full confidence that China and Britain would be able to 'reach an historic agreement at an early date'.[113]

On 17 September, the working group and the ad hoc group finally agreed on all the texts for the joint declaration and the three annexes (China's 'basic policies' regarding Hong Kong, the Joint Liaison Group, and land leases, respectively).[114] The nationality issue was covered by an exchange of memoranda. According to the British memorandum, from 1 July 1997, all former BDTCs would be eligible to retain 'an appropriate status' which, 'without conferring the right of abode in the United Kingdom', would entitle them to continue to use passports issued by the UK government. Those passports would be issued before 1 July 1997, except for eligible persons born on or after 1 January 1997 but before 1 July 1997, who would obtain passports up to 31 December 1997.[115] On 19 September, the draft agreement was submitted to both the British and the Chinese governments for approval.[116] In a memorandum to Thatcher, Howe opined that this was 'the best agreement [Britain] could have achieved in all the circumstances'. The Joint Declaration and its annexes were 'unequivocally a binding international agreement'. They contained 'sufficient detail and clarity' about post-1997 arrangements that would 'command the confidence of the people of Hong Kong', as well as 'a provision that its terms will be stipulated in the basic law'. To Howe, the final agreement represented 'major concessions by the Chinese' on many issues, such as deferment of the joint group's location in Hong Kong and elections in the SAR legislature.[117]

Thatcher received a delegation of the unofficial members of Hong Kong's Executive Council in order to hear their views on the draft agreement. On behalf of all unofficials, Sze-yuen Chung made a statement. Recalling the UMELCO statement issued last May, Chung said that the draft agreement 'falls short of meeting completely all our requirements', such as the lack of 'precise details' about the government structure and the withdrawal of transmissibility of nationality. But 'what is the alternative?', he asked. Rejecting either 'no agreement' or 'the likelihood of a unilateral declaration by the Chinese', the unofficials believed that the people of Hong Kong would 'accept the reality of the unpalatable alternative'. Chung stated that this was 'a reasonable agreement, the best that can be achieved, and one which we can commend to the people of Hong Kong in good conscience'. Nevertheless, in commending it to Hong Kong, the unofficials hoped that the British government could give assurances on four points, including maintaining 'a credible and effective government' in Hong Kong over the next thirteen years and ensuring that 'the Basic Law will conform with the terms of the agreement'. Thatcher responded that Chung's statement on commending the agreement to Hong Kong people 'in good conscience' 'meant a great deal to her'. To her, 'Britain's responsibility in the matter of Hong Kong's future was a moral one'.[118]

Signing the Joint Declaration

On 26 September in Beijing, Zhou Nan and Evans initialled the Joint Declaration. It was time to test the acceptability of the draft agreement in Hong Kong. On the same day, the Hong Kong government published a white paper (which featured a short introduction, the Joint Declaration and its annexes, and explanatory notes), inviting public comments. An Assessment Office was established with the remit of providing an accurate assessment of opinion on the draft agreement. An independent monitoring team would observe the work of the office. By the time the consultation period ended on 15 November, the Assessment Office had received written submissions by all the major representative bodies, such as the Legislative Council and all eighteen District Boards, and by 679 organisations and 1,815 individuals. Meanwhile, it had taken into account the findings of twenty-three opinion polls of varying sizes. On 23 November, the Assessment Office presented its report to the governor, concluding that 'most of the people of Hong Kong' found the draft agreement 'acceptable'. Nevertheless, while the report noted the general acceptance of the draft agreement, the assessors were also drawn to expressions of concern and anxiety by some sections of the Hong Kong community – for example, the Law Society of Hong

Kong about the uncertainty over the Basic Law and the Meeting Point (a political pressure group) concerning the pace of democratisation.[119] Above all, Hong Kong residents had been informed from the outset that the draft agreement could only be accepted or rejected, but could not be revised or re-negotiated. The fate of Hong Kong had been sealed by Britain and China in secret negotiations.

On 5 December, the House of Commons debated the Hong Kong agreement. Thirty-six MPs spoke in turn, covering such issues as the joint group, nationality, and representative government. After outlining how the Joint Declaration and its annexes constituted a 'comprehensive', 'detailed', and 'legally binding international agreement', Howe asserted that the next twelve years would be 'crucial' for Hong Kong, and that Britain would need to 'achieve progress in constitutional development' while 'keep[ing] constantly in mind the unique circumstances of Hong Kong, and its future position as a special administrative region of the People's Republic of China'. (On 21 November, the Hong Kong government had published a white paper on further development of representative government in Hong Kong.)[120] Denis Healey, shadow foreign secretary, said that the general acceptance of the agreement had demonstrated 'the realism of the people of Hong Kong', who acknowledged 'the impossibility of changing an agreement made by two Governments'. He agreed that Hong Kong should move towards 'more representative government' in the next twelve years. Edward Heath regarded the Joint Declaration as 'a realistic agreement'. As somebody who had 'dealt with the Government of the People's Republic in private business in the City', Heath said that he had always found the Chinese 'meticulous in carrying out agreements made since the revolution'. Last but not least, Enoch Powell, an anti-immigration MP (South Down) of the Ulster Unionist Party, took issue with the exchange of memoranda on nationality. It was 'one thing for the Government to say that the new status [for Hong Kong's BDTCs] will not give these people the right of abode in the United Kingdom'; it was 'another to ignore the increasing pressure that will be brought to bear on the United Kingdom' for resettling them on the grounds of 'humanity and urgency' in the event of crises. After about four and a half hours, the FCO's minister of state, Richard Luce, rounded up the debate by strongly commending the Hong Kong agreement to the House, which unanimously approved it.[121] Five days later, on 10 December the House of Lords held its debate on Hong Kong, and similarly endorsed the agreement.[122]

All this set the scene for Thatcher's visit to Beijing to sign the agreement. To Cradock, her signature would 'give the agreement the maximum authority'.[123] At 9 am on 19 December, Thatcher's party attended the welcoming ceremony, hosted by Premier Zhao Ziyang, in Tiananmen Square. A nineteen-gun salute was fired, and Thatcher accompanied by

Zhao walked along the red carpet to inspect the guard of honour. What followed was a packed programme of separate talks with four members of the Politburo Standing Committee on a single day.[124] During her meeting with Zhao, Thatcher talked about the British government's commitment to implementing the Joint Declaration in every aspect and its hope that China would 'solicit opinion from a wide range of people in Hong Kong' in the drafting of the Basic Law. She mentioned the development of representative government in Hong Kong, which would 'give the people the experience which they needed to run their own administration after 1997'. Zhao expressed his appreciation for Thatcher's 'vision and statesmanship' during the negotiations. He said that 'the Basic Law would define the government structure, the form of legislature and the method of selection of the Chief Executive', and as such the Chinese government 'was not prepared to make any comment on constitutional development during the transitional period'.[125] Thatcher 'left it at that'. (As she recollected later, 'it was as far as I felt it was prudent to go at this meeting'.)[126] Thatcher informed Zhao that the Queen was very happy to accept in principle the invitation to visit China, probably in the second half of 1986. Zhao in turn confirmed his acceptance of her invitation to visit Britain in June 1985.[127]

It was her conversation with Deng Xiaoping, a little over two years after their first encounter, that was of most symbolic significance. Following her note card which highlighted, among other points, 'congratulate on concept of one country/two systems',[128] Thatcher said that 'the stroke of genius in the negotiations had been the concept of "one country, two systems"', which, although being '[d]eceptively simple', had been 'the key that had unlocked the future'. In response, Deng gave 'credit' to 'Marxist historical dialectics, or to "seeking truth from the facts"'. In view of some people's doubts about China's policy, Deng hoped to inform Thatcher and indeed the whole world that 'China had always honoured its commitments'. With her strong conviction in free-market capitalism, Thatcher said that Deng's concept was a 'great design' that 'would work because capitalist Hong Kong worked very well now and it was not going to be changed after 1997'. She had full confidence that 'the agreement would be honoured'. When discussing international issues, Deng asked Thatcher to send his congratulations to US President Ronald Reagan on his re-election. (Thatcher would travel to Camp David to meet with Reagan after her China visit.) Importantly, Deng asked the prime minister to convey his hope that 'China and the US would cooperate in solving the question of Taiwan' during Reagan's second term, particularly if the president found the concept of 'one country, two systems' 'desirable'. After all, the concept had been 'devised originally to solve the Taiwan and not the Hong Kong question'. Thatcher warmly agreed, adding that the United States 'had welcomed the Hong Kong agreement'.[129]

The signature ceremony took place in the western hall of the Great Hall of the People at 5:30 pm. With Deng and top officials from both sides witnessing the occasion from behind the signing table, and a hundred guests from Hong Kong and local and overseas journalists observing on the side, Zhao and Thatcher inked both the English and Chinese versions of the Joint Declaration and then exchanged the signed instruments. They exchanged the memoranda on nationality. Then, the two leaders made speeches, and all participants and guests marked the occasion with champagne. The entire ceremony lasted for thirty minutes.[130] This was followed by the welcoming banquet for some four hundred guests.[131] After the banquet, Howe had a separate meeting with Wu Xueqian to discuss some outstanding points from the negotiations. Howe proposed that Britain and China should jointly register the Joint Declaration at the UN during the next year's General Assembly session, a proposal that Wu agreed to consider.[132]

Conclusion

It took twenty-two rounds of formal talks for Britain and China to reach an agreement on Hong Kong's future. Beginning in 1984, the plenary sessions were supplemented by frequent informal contact between the chief negotiators of the two teams, and from mid-June onwards by the intense meetings of the working group and later the ad hoc group. Now that the Thatcher government had conceded both sovereignty and administrative rights to China, the principal British negotiating objectives shifted to securing the highest degree of autonomy for post-1997 Hong Kong, minimum changes to its systems, and maximum Chinese assurances as stipulated in a detailed and binding agreement. By producing the working papers on Hong Kong's various systems as the basis for discussion, the British aimed to 'educate the Chinese in the realities of how Hong Kong worked'.[133] Some of the ideas of the working papers eventually found their way into the annexes to the Joint Declaration.

The British had to overcome many hurdles between the eighth and the twenty-second rounds. The first hurdle was the Chinese deadline of September 1984 and their threat to make a unilateral announcement on Hong Kong's future if no agreement was reached by then. The Thatcher government was pulled in another direction by the unofficial members of Hong Kong's Executive Council, who wanted nothing more than an interim agreement in September. Concerned that the breakdown of talks would seriously damage confidence in Hong Kong, Howe decided to visit Beijing in April to resolve the timetable dispute, and other issues, with the Chinese leaders. With the personal intervention of Deng Xiaoping, who had made a compromise, it was agreed that an initial agreement would be initialled in September and then be considered by the British Parliament, before the signing of the agreement by the end of 1984. Another obstacle in the negotiations was the Chinese proposal for creating a joint group in Hong Kong to discuss important issues during the transitional period. Fearful of the prospect of a condominium in Hong Kong before 1997, Thatcher and particularly the unofficial members resisted establishing such a group in Hong Kong. Another visit by Howe to China in July, and further concessions by Deng, were required to break the impasse over the joint group. As 1 October 1984 marked the thirty-fifth anniversary of the founding of the PRC, Deng, desperate to wrap up the talks by September, regarded Howe's visit as a 'make-or-break' moment. As Robin McLaren recollected: 'In the end the [September] deadline probably worked more in our favour than in theirs because the Chinese ... were the ones who were in a hurry.'[134] By agreeing to defer the establishment of the joint group in Hong Kong until mid-1988, and to prolong its life until 2000, Deng broke the back of the negotiations.

Above all, the protracted and difficult negotiations resulted from China's sensitivity to everything that had to do with sovereignty on the one hand, and on the other Britain's concern about the acceptability of the agreement in Parliament and Hong Kong. From the wording of the draft agreement to nationality and the stationing of troops, the Chinese insisted that the principle of China's sovereignty over Hong Kong be fully and explicitly recognised by Britain. Eventually, the negotiations were brought to a successful conclusion under 'the spirit of give and take'. By exchanging messages with Wu Xueqian in early and mid-September, Howe managed to resolve the outstanding issues in time for initialling the agreement on 26 September. To Howe and Thatcher, the Joint Declaration and its annexes, which were detailed and binding and whose provisions would be stipulated in the Basic Law, were the best deal possible. The Hong Kong agreement was not the result of a one-sided retreat or capitulation by Britain; indeed, the Chinese also made concessions, such as assurances that Hong Kong's capitalist system would remain 'unchanged for 50 years' and that the SAR legislature would be constituted by 'elections'. It is fair to conclude that, on balance, Britain had made more compromises to China than the other way round. The unofficial members were right to argue that the people of Hong Kong could not but 'accept the reality of the unpalatable alternative' to British rule. According to a local independent opinion survey in late November, 51 per cent of the respondents was 'very pleased and very reassured' or 'generally pleased' with the draft agreement; but 41 per cent expressed that they 'can't be reassured until the agreement is implemented', with the remaining respondents not believing in or not knowing the agreement.[135]

As Christopher Meyer, FCO spokesman who accompanied Thatcher and Howe to Beijing in December 1984, argued: from the outset, Britain had to 'negotiate from a position of weakness', and the aim was to 'abandon sovereignty's form in return for keeping its substance'.[136] In 1984 the 'substance' was no longer British administration, but the Common Law, individual freedom, and above all a capitalist system insulated from socialist China. In this sense, Thatcher's Britain had 'punched above its weight' by giving substance to Deng's otherwise vague 'twelve-point' plan for Hong Kong. The diplomacy of 'education' had yielded positive results at last.

Notes

1. SJC, Papers of Percy Cradock, Cradock/B/4, FCO to Beijing, no. 895, 19 December 1983.
2. TNA, PREM 19/1262 Part 11, Ricketts to Coles, 6 January 1984.
3. See Li and Chang, *Shige yu waijiao*, 162.
4. Zheng Zhongbing (et al.), *Hu Yaobang nianpu ziliao changbian* [Long Series of Materials on the Chronicle of Hu Yaobang], vol. 2 (Hong Kong: Time International Publishing, 2005), 895.
5. *DXN*, vol. 2, 961.
6. Mann, *About Face*, 134, 147–8.
7. TNA, PREM 19/1262 Part 11, Record of meeting with EXCO unofficial members on 16 January 1984.
8. Goodstadt, *Uneasy Partners*, 49–70; Ray Yep (ed.), *Negotiating Autonomy in Greater China: Hong Kong and Its Sovereign Before and After 1997* (Copenhagen: NIAS Press, 2013).
9. Yep and Lui, 'Revisiting the golden era of MacLehose and the dynamics of social reforms'.
10. The issue of Hong Kong's democratisation will be discussed more fully in Chapter 7.
11. TNA, PREM 19/1262 Part 11, Beijing to FCO, no. 131, 25 January 1984.
12. TNA, PREM 19/1262 Part 11, Beijing to FCO, no. 132, 25 January 1984.
13. TNA, PREM 19/1262 Part 11, Ricketts to Coles, 31 January 1984.
14. TNA, PREM 19/1262 Part 11, Coles to Ricketts, 2 February 1984.
15. TNA, PREM 19/1263 Part 12, Ricketts to Coles, 24 February 1984; Beijing to FCO, no. 303, 22 February 1984; Beijing to FCO, no. 321, 24 February 1984.
16. TNA, CAB 148/241, OD(K)(84)2nd meeting, 27 February 1984.
17. *DXN*, vol. 2, 964.
18. *Jianguo yilai Li Xiannian wengao* [Manuscripts of Li Xiannian since the Founding of the PRC], vol. 4: January 1977–April 1992 (Beijing: Zhongyang wenxian chubanshe, 2011), 249–50.
19. Chung, *Hong Kong's Journey to Reunification*, 78.
20. TNA, PREM 19/1263 Part 12, Beijing to FCO, no. 358, 1 March 1984.

21 Chung, *Hong Kong's Journey to Reunification*, 80–1.
22 TNA, PREM 19/1263 Part 12, Hong Kong Department, Working Paper on constitutional arrangements and central government structures, 3 February 1984.
23 TNA, PREM 19/1263 Part 12, Ricketts to Coles, 21 March 1984; Beijing to FCO, no. 501, 16 March 1984.
24 TNA, PREM 19/1263 Part 12, Howe to Thatcher, 19 March 1984; Hong Kong to FCO, no. 682, 14 March 1984.
25 TNA, CAB 148/241, Limited circulation annex to OD(K)(84)1st meeting, 11 January 1984.
26 TNA, PREM 19/1263 Part 12, Howe to Thatcher, 21 March 1984; Hong Kong Department, Draft agreement, 16 March 1984.
27 TNA, CAB 148/241, OD(K)(84)3rd meeting, 26 March 1984.
28 TNA, PREM 19/1263 Part 12, Beijing to FCO, no. 584, 27 March 1984.
29 The decision to relocate the corporate headquarters was also related to a complete restructuring of Jardine, which had a diverse portfolio of businesses and subsidiaries in the early 1980s. Feng, *Xianggang yingzi caituan,* 293–302.
30 Li and Chang, *Shige yu waijiao,* 169.
31 TNA, PREM 19/1263 Part 12, Coles to Thatcher, 30 March 1984.
32 BLO, MSS.Ind.Ocn.s.328, Interview with Sir S.Y. Chung, file 328/2, tape 7, side 1, p. 296.
33 TNA, PREM 19/1264 Part 13, Appleyard to Coles, 5 April 1984.
34 TNA, PREM 19/1263 Part 12, Howe to Thatcher, undated (but probably 29 March 1984).
35 TNA, PREM 19/1263 Part 12, Coles to Appleyard, 30 March 1984.
36 TNA, CAB 148/241, Limited circulation annex to OD(K)(84)4th meeting, 3 April 1984; PREM 19/1264 Part 13, Howe to Thatcher, 2 April 1984.
37 TNA, PREM 19/1264 Part 13, Record of meeting with EXCO Unofficial Members on 6 April 1984.
38 TNA, PREM 19/1264 Part 13, Beijing to FCO, no. 702, 11 April 1984.
39 TNA, PREM 19/1264 Part 13, Beijing to FCO, no. 703, 11 April 1984.
40 TNA, PREM 19/1264 Part 13, FCO to Beijing, no. 374, 11 April 1984.
41 TNA, PREM 19/1263 Part 12, Hong Kong Department, Draft agreement, 16 March 1984.
42 TNA, PREM 19/1264 Part 13, Beijing to FCO, no. 739, 13 April 1984; Draft joint declaration proposed by China, attached in Beijing to FCO, no. 740, 13 April 1984.
43 TNA, PREM 19/1264 Part 13, Clift to FCO private secretary, 13 April 1984.
44 TNA, FCO 40/1653, Conference section, Protocol Department, 'Administrative arrangements for the visit of the secretary of state for foreign and commonwealth affairs to China, Korea, Japan and Hong Kong, 14–28 April 1984'.
45 TNA, PREM 19/1264 Part 13, Beijing to FCO, no. 759, 16 April 1984.
46 TNA, PREM 19/1264 Part 13, Beijing to FCO, no. 764, 17 April 1984.
47 TNA, PREM 19/1264 Part 13, Beijing to FCO, no. 765, 17 April 1984.
48 TNA, PREM 19/1264 Part 13, HK to FCO, no. 1057, 18 April 1984; *DXN,* vol. 2, 970.

49 Howe, *Conflict of Loyalty*, 372.
50 TNA, PREM 19/1264 Part 13, HK to FCO, no. 1058, 18 April 1984.
51 TNA, PREM 19/1264 Part 13, HK to FCO, nos. 1078 and 1079, 19 April 1984.
52 TNA, PREM 19/1264 Part 13, Statement by Howe in Hong Kong, 20 April 1984.
53 'Foreign secretary faces the media', *South China Morning Post* (21 April 1984).
54 TNA, PREM 19/1264 Part 13, HK to FCO, no. 1099, 21 April 1984.
55 TNA, PREM 19/1264 Part 13, Bone to Coles, 24 April 1984.
56 TNA, FCO 40/1667, HK to FCO, no. 1178, 1 May 1984.
57 TNA, PREM 19/1265 Part 14, Howe to Thatcher, 1 May 1984.
58 TNA, PREM 19/1265 Part 14, HK to Beijing, no. 375, 9 May 1984; FCO to HK, no. 839, 8 May 1984.
59 CAC, Papers of Jeremy Bray, Box 13, file 104/1056, Statement issued by unofficial members of the Hong Kong Executive and Legislative Councils on 9 May 1984; Also see Chung, *Hong Kong's Journey to Reunification*, 83–6.
60 TNA, FCO 40/1667 HKK040/1 Part E, Beijing to FCO, no. 910, 12 May 1984.
61 TNA, CAB 128/78/18, CC(84)18th Conclusions, 10 May 1984.
62 Chung, *Hong Kong's Journey to Reunification*, 86–90; Frank Ching, *Hong Kong and China: For Better or For Worse* (New York: The China Council of The Asia Society/The Foreign Policy Association, 1985), 26.
63 TNA, PREM 19/1265 Part 14, Record of discussion between Thatcher and UMELCO delegation on 15 May 1984.
64 *Hansard*, House of Commons Debates, vol. 60, 16 May 1984, cols. 417–18, 420–1, 423, 428–9.
65 TNA, CAB 128/78/19, CC(84)19th Conclusions, 17 May 1984.
66 On the House of Lords debate on Hong Kong, see *Hansard*, House of Lords Debates, vol. 452, 21 May 1984, cols. 101–31.
67 TNA, CAB 148/241, OD(K)(84)6th meeting, 23 May 1984; PREM 19/1265 Part 14, Howe to Thatcher, 18 May 1984.
68 TNA, PREM 19/1265 Part 14, Beijing to FCO, no. 1014, 31 May 1984; Note on the fifteenth round of negotiations on the future of Hong Kong, 1 June 1984.
69 TNA, PREM 19/1265 Part 14, Beijing to FCO, no. 1104, 13 June 1984.
70 In *Deng Xiaoping nianpu* and Zhou Nan's memoir, the name of the Chinese leader was not mentioned. (*DXN*, vol. 2, 978; Zhang and Xu (eds), *Zhou Nan jiemi GangAo huigui*, 146–8) But according to the British archival record and Xu Jiatun's memoir, the said Chinese leader was Huang Hua, vice chairman of the NPC and former foreign minister. Another leader making a similar claim was General Geng Biao. (TNA, PREM 19/1265 Part 14, Appleyard to Powell, 21 June 1984; Xu, *Xu Jiatun Xianggang huiyilu*, vol. 1, 107–8)
71 TNA, PREM 19/1265 Part 14, HK to FCO, no. 1429, 25 May 1984; *DXN*, vol. 2, 978.
72 *DXW*, vol. 3, 58–61; *DXN*, vol. 2, 982–4.
73 Chung, *Hong Kong's Journey to Reunification*, 98–101.
74 TNA, CAB 148/241, OD(K)(84)7th meeting, 28 June 1984; OD(K)(84)8th meeting, 17 July 1984.

75 TNA, FCO 40/1660, Beijing to FCO, no. 1360, 11 July 1984; FCO 40/1660, Clift to Cradock, 11 July 1984; CAB 128/79/5, CC(84)28th Conclusions, 26 July 1984.
76 TNA, PREM 19/1266 Part 15, Budd to Powell, 27 July 1984.
77 TNA, PREM 19/1266 Part 15, Beijing to FCO, no. 1622, 26 July 1984.
78 Chen, *Xianggang wenti tanpan shimo*, 239.
79 *Ibid.*, 240–1.
80 Zhang and Xu (eds), *Zhou Nan jiemi GangAo huigui*, 152–3; *DXN*, vol. 2, 988.
81 TNA, PREM 19/1266 Part 15, HK to FCO, no. 2140, 27 July 1984.
82 Chung, *Hong Kong's Journey to Reunification*, 110.
83 Howe, *Conflict of Loyalty*, 375.
84 TNA, PREM 19/1266 Part 15, Thatcher to Zhao, 23 July 1984; Howe, *Conflict of Loyalty*, 376.
85 TNA, PREM 19/1266 Part 15, Beijing to FCO, no. 1653, 28 July 1984; Chen, *Xianggang wenti tanpan shimo*, 242.
86 Cottrell, *The End of Hong Kong*, 160; Chen, *Xianggang wenti tanpan shimo*, 243.
87 TNA, PREM 19/1266 Part 15, Beijing to FCO, no. 1653, 28 July 1984.
88 TNA, PREM 19/1266 Part 15, Beijing to FCO, no. 1657, 29 July 1984.
89 TNA, PREM 19/1266 Part 15, FCO to Beijing, no. 907, 29 July 1984.
90 TNA, PREM 19/1266 Part 15, Beijing to FCO, no. 1666, 30 July 1984.
91 TNA, PREM 19/1266 Part 15, Beijing to FCO, no. 1677, 31 July 1984; Budd to Powell, 30 July 1984.
92 Cottrell, *The End of Hong Kong*, 162.
93 TNA, PREM 19/1266 Part 15, HK to FCO, no. 2176, 31 July 1984; *DXN*, vol. 2, 988–9; Howe, *Conflict of Loyalty*, 377.
94 TNA, PREM 19/1267 Part 16, HK to FCO, no. 2193, 1 August 1984.
95 TNA, PREM 19/1267 Part 16, Cartledge to Thatcher, 3 September 1984.
96 CAC, GBR/0014/DOHP 15, Interview with Sir Robin McLaren, 31 July 1996, p. 16; Li, *Huigui de lichen*, 128.
97 TNA, PREM 19/1267 Part 16, Cradock to Flesher, 24 August 1984.
98 TNA, PREM 19/1267 Part 16, HK to FCO, no. 2624, 3 September 1984; CAB 148/241, OD(K)(84)9th meeting, 4 September 1984.
99 TNA, PREM 19/1267 Part 16, HK to FCO, no. 2624, 3 September 1984; CAB 148/241, OD(K)(84)9th meeting, 4 September 1984.
100 TNA, CAB 148/241, OD(K)(84)9th meeting, 4 September 1984.
101 TNA, PREM 19/1267 Part 16, Beijing to FCO, no. 2098, 5 September 1984.
102 TNA, PREM 19/1267 Part 16, FCO to Beijing, no. 1099, 5 September 1984.
103 TNA, PREM 19/1267 Part 16, Beijing to FCO, no. 2133, 6 September 1984.
104 Chen, *Xianggang wenti tanpan shimo*, 253.
105 TNA, PREM 19/1267 Part 16, Howe to Thatcher, 6 September 1984; Powell to Appleyard, 7 September 1984.
106 TNA, PREM 19/1267 Part 16, FCO to Beijing, no. 1131, 8 September 1984; Li, *Huigui de lichen*, 116–18.

Negotiating autonomy and continuity, 1984   163

107 TNA, PREM 19/1267 Part 16, Beijing to FCO, no. 2195, 8 September 1984.
108 *DXN*, vol. 2, 993–4.
109 TNA, PREM 19/1267 Part 16, Beijing to FCO, no. 2256, 11 September 1984.
110 TNA, CAB 148/241, OD(K)(84)10th meeting, 12 September 1984.
111 TNA, PREM 19/1267 Part 16, FCO to Beijing, no. 1193, 13 September 1984.
112 Chen, *Xianggang wenti tanpan shimo*, 256–7; Xu, *Xu Jiatun Xianggang huiyilu*, vol. 1, 114–15.
113 TNA, PREM 19/1267 Part 16, Beijing to FCO, no. 2375, 16 September 1984.
114 TNA, PREM 19/1267 Part 16, Beijing to FCO, no. 2407, 17 September 1984.
115 Exchange of Memoranda, appended to Joint Declaration of the Government of the United Kingdom of Great Britain and Northern Ireland and the Government of the People's Republic of China on the Question of Hong Kong, 1984.
116 Howe, *Conflict of Loyalty*, 379.
117 TNA, PREM 19/1267 Part 16, Howe to Thatcher, 19 September 1984.
118 TNA, PREM 19/1267 Part 16, Record of meeting between Thatcher and unofficial members of the Executive Council on 19 September 1984; Chung speaking note, 19 September 1984.
119 Hong Kong Government, *Hong Kong 1985: A Review of 1984*, 20–1; TNA, PREM 19/1530 Part 17, Ricketts to Powell, 26 November 1984; 'Arrangements for testing the acceptability in Hong Kong of the draft agreement on the future of the territory', Report of the Assessment Office, two volumes, 29 November 1984.
120 See Chapter 7.
121 *Hansard*, House of Commons Debates, vol. 69, 5 December 1984, cols. 391, 397, 400–7.
122 See *Hansard*, House of Lords Debates, vol. 458, 10 December 1984, cols. 11–21.
123 TNA, FCO 40/1770, Cradock to Youde, 3 October 1984.
124 CAC, Papers of Baroness Thatcher, THCR 1/10/78, Protocol Department, Ministry of Foreign Affairs, 'Official visit of the right honourable Margaret Thatcher, prime minister of the United Kingdom of Great Britain and Northern Ireland to the People's Republic of China December 18–20, 1984'; TNA, PREM 19/1502, Briefing note 1: 'Formal welcoming ceremony'.
125 TNA, PREM 19/1502, Record of meeting between Thatcher and Zhao Ziyang on 19 December 1984.
126 Thatcher, *The Downing Street Years*, 493.
127 TNA, PREM 19/1502, Cradock to Howe, 4 January 1985.
128 CAC, Papers of Baroness Thatcher, THCR 1/10/78, 'Meeting with Deng Xiaoping'.
129 TNA, PREM 19/1502, Record of meeting between Thatcher and Deng Xiaoping on 19 December 1984; *DXN*, vol. 2, 1018–20.
130 CAC, Papers of Baroness Thatcher, THCR 1/10/78, Protocol Department, Ministry of Foreign Affairs, 'Official visit of the right honourable Margaret Thatcher, prime minister of the United Kingdom of Great Britain and Northern Ireland to the People's Republic of China December 18–20, 1984'; TNA, PREM 19/1503, Briefing note 2: 'Signature ceremony'.

131 CAC, Papers of Baroness Thatcher, THCR 1/10/78, Thatcher speech at the banquet in Beijing on 19 December 1984.
132 TNA, FCO 40/1673, Beijing to FCO, no. 3048, 19 December 1984.
133 TNA, FCO 40/1887, Youde to Howe, 3 July 1985.
134 CAC, GBR/0014/DOHP 15, Interview with Sir Robin McLaren, 31 July 1996, p. 18.
135 TNA, FCO 40/1728, 'Memo for Executive Council: SRH survey on the draft agreement', enclosed in Upton to Galsworthy, 10 December 1984.
136 Meyer, *Getting Our Way*, 154, 167.

6

Anglo-Chinese interactions and globalisation, 1985–86

At a time when the Hong Kong negotiation was underway in 1984, Deng Xiaoping was planning for the second wave of China's external opening. From 22 January to 16 February, Deng, accompanied by Politburo members Wang Zhen and Yang Shangkun, made inspection tours of the SEZs of Shenzhen, Zhuhai, and Xiamen, as well as Guangzhou and Shanghai. After two years of economic adjustment, the bottlenecks in agricultural and energy production had been overcome, prices had stabilised, and a trade surplus had been recorded. The reformist camp decided to seize the initiative from conservatives by tipping the balance between the plan and market.[1] Back in Beijing, on 24 February Deng called a meeting with General Secretary Hu Yaobang, Premier Zhao Ziyang, Yang, and others. 'The special economic zones are windows – windows onto foreign technology and new knowledge, and windows for showcasing the policy of openness', Deng declared. They could be 'very beneficial to us, not just in developing our economy and cultivating skills', but also in 'enhanc[ing] our nation's global impact'. Deng hinted that China might 'consider opening up some port cities, such as Dalian and Qingdao', which would 'not be called "special economic zones"' but could 'apply some of the policies that are being applied to special economic zones'.[2]

It was on the basis of Deng's remarks that Vice Premier Gu Mu convened a meeting with the governors of Guangdong, Fujian, and other provinces, the mayors of Shanghai and Tianjin, and forty or so departments of the State Council, lasting for twelve days. All participants agreed to open up a number of coastal cities reminiscent of the existing SEZs. With the Politburo's endorsement, on 4 May the Central Committee Secretariat and the State Council formally announced the opening of fourteen coastal cities, titled 'Economic and Technological Development Zones', including Shanghai, Tianjin, Dalian, Ningbo, Guangzhou, and so forth.[3] Foreign companies investing in these coastal cities would enjoy lower tax rates, duty-free import of components, and limited access to the domestic market.[4] There were more to come. On 10 February 1985, the Chinese government announced the creation of 'coastal economic open zones' along the Yangtze River Delta, the Minnan Delta, and the entire Pearl River Delta.[5] After inspecting Guangdong, Fujian, Zhejiang, and Jiangsu in late 1987 and early 1988, Zhao Ziyang declared a 'coastal development strategy', which aimed to create 'an export-oriented economy in the coastal regions to fully take advantage of opportunities offered by a global economy in transition'.[6]

In addition, Deng introduced comprehensive urban reform. In late June 1984, Deng, talking about foreign investment in China, uttered the term 'socialism with Chinese characteristics'. Although the CCP should 'uphold Marxism' and 'the path of socialism', it should 'combine with China's reality' to build 'socialism with Chinese characteristics'. Referring to the opening of the fourteen coastal cities, Deng said that 'attracting foreign capital can surely be an important supplement to the building of our nation's socialism'.[7] To echo Deng's remarks, Zhao redefined the nature of the Chinese economy. On 9 September, Zhao sent a letter to the Politburo Standing Committee about his ideas on reform of the economic structure. Essentially, what China practised was a 'planned economy', not a 'market economy'. Accordingly, China should 'gradually reduce the scope of compulsory planning and expand the scope of guidance planning'. On 20 October, the Third Plenum of the Twelfth Central Committee adopted a resolution on reform of the economic structure, affirming that China practised a 'planned commodity economy' rather than a 'market economy'. The government did not regard 'compulsory planning' as primary; instead, it favoured 'guidance planning' and the natural laws of demand and supply.[8]

The October decision was a landmark in Deng's reform, for it enabled the economy to gradually 'grow out of the plan'.[9] Even Chen Yun found it 'completely suitable for China's practical situation at present'. Now that China's economy was 'much bigger' and 'more complicated' than it had been fifty years ago, he argued, the method deemed suitable then might no longer be the case now.[10] In early 1986, the State Council, examining a report by a working conference at Shenzhen, confirmed that the establishment of the SEZs five years ago was 'correct'. The opening of coastal cities and economic structural reforms allowed China to 'observe and study the modern capitalist economy' and to 'develop expertise', which would have 'far-reaching' implications.[11]

It was against the backdrop of Deng's deepening reform that China and Britain reached an agreement on Hong Kong's future in late 1984. The successful resolution of the Hong Kong question provided the political context, and opened up opportunities, for intensified Anglo-Chinese economic relations. From the conclusion of economic cooperation and investment promotion agreements to exchange of high-level visits and support for China's admission to GATT, Thatcher and the FCO hoped to demonstrate that

Britain was a global trading nation, while strengthening the pro-Western orientation of the Chinese leadership. For all the British efforts to 'educate' the Chinese about free-trade globalisation, however, China's integration into the global capitalist system remained shallow by the end of 1986. As the world economy became more integrated and competitive, British companies were unable to capitalise on the favourable political atmosphere following the Hong Kong agreement to significantly increase their share of the China market.

Hong Kong agreement and China trade

During the summer of 1984, the FCO planning staff started drafting a planning paper on China in anticipation of reaching a satisfactory agreement on Hong Kong.[12] By mid-September, the first draft was completed.[13] But it was deemed too long and repetitive as well as too optimistic by Whitehall departments.[14] After considering the comments of all interested departments, Pauline Neville-Jones of the FCO planning staff submitted a final version of the planning paper to the foreign secretary's private secretary on 30 November. As she summarised the paper's conclusions, 'the Hong Kong Agreement will bring no automatic sea-change in our relations with China'. Britain should 'avoid explicit linkage between the Hong Kong Agreement and our expectations in regard to China': any improvements in Anglo-Chinese relations 'can and should be justified on their own merits'. Nevertheless, Britain could 'capitalise on the closer contacts, interest and goodwill that can be generated by the conclusion of the Agreement'. Besides, the potential benefit was a two-way process: 'the more genuine and broad-based an improvement we can achieve in general Sino-British relations, the better in turn will be the prospects for cooperation over Hong Kong itself'.[15] Geoffrey Howe did not bring the planning paper, which was deemed too lengthy, to the attention of Thatcher, who would visit Beijing to sign the Joint Declaration. But he wanted a copy to be included in his own briefing papers.[16]

If the British were planning for a new relationship with China amid progress in the Hong Kong talks, the Chinese, too, were eager to strengthen economic cooperation with Britain in line with Deng Xiaoping's deepening reform. On 26 September 1984, Robert Adley, a Tory MP (Christchurch), wrote to Thatcher about his recent meeting with the Chinese ambassador in London, who was 'extremely anxious to do what he can to bring about a dramatic improvement in Sino-British trade'. Adley got the impression that China wanted 'something fairly dramatic [and] fairly quickly', for it was the Chinese perception that 'many British companies were "rather conservative"'.[17] The FCO was cautious about making a 'dramatic initiative' to promote Sino-British trade following the Hong Kong agreement. Mark Elliott, head of the Far Eastern Department, perceived that Adley, who had 'a general interest in China' and had been 'active and outspoken (often unhelpfully)' about Hong Kong's future, might harbour 'the illusion that he has acted as some sort of intermediary with the Chinese over Hong Kong'. Although the successful conclusion of the Hong Kong negotiations 'may well indirectly present trade opportunities', it was imperative to 'avoid giving any impression that our handling of the Hong Kong issue has been or ever will be influenced by prospects of commercial gain'.[18] Peter Ricketts, Howe's private secretary, also had reservations about a '"dramatic" trade initiative', believing that in its commercial dealings with Britain and other countries, China was 'likely to continue to be swayed heavily by considerations of price and quality'.[19]

The Chinese gave more hints about their desire for increased trade with Britain. During his meeting with Ambassador Richard Evans on 19 October, Vice Foreign Minister Zhou Nan said that 'the proportion of China's external trade occupied by the U[nited]S[tates] and Japan did not reflect Chinese policy', and that 'China would like to see an increase in trade with Western Europe'. 'Now that the Hong Kong question was solved', Zhou claimed, 'the only major political obstacle to the development of Sino-British trade had been removed'. Referring to the recent visit to China by West Germany's Chancellor Helmut Kohl, which focused on commercial issues, Zhou asked whether the British prime minister would bring any concrete proposals to China later in December.[20] As the FCO's Far Eastern Department assessed it, the Chinese wished to 'reduce their growing technological dependence on Japan and the USA by increasing imports from W[estern] Europe'. Britain should 'exploit current Chinese goodwill'.[21]

Following Beijing's announcement on 'sweeping reforms of the urban economy', on 31 October John Boyd of the FCO wrote to the DTI about how to brief the prime minister on her China visit in December. Although Thatcher's visit should not be 'a trade promotion exercise', Boyd said, the government should consider seriously whether China's new reform would 'open up opportunities for British business'.[22] The Chinese appealed directly to Thatcher for British investment in China. Between 10 and 19 November, Jing Shuping, president of China International Economic Consultants whose main work was to attract foreign investment to China, paid a private visit to the UK as a special guest speaker at a commercially organised China conference in London.[23] During his brief call on Thatcher on 13 November, Jing said that 'the Chinese Government attached great importance to commercial cooperation with Western Europe'. 'Expectations of the Prime Minister's visit were high', Jing stressed. Thatcher replied that the 'main purpose' of her visit

Anglo-Chinese interactions and globalisation   169

was to sign the Hong Kong agreement, but '[o]nce that was done', Britain 'would, of course, wish to develop our commercial relations further'.[24]

Both the DTI and the Department of Energy were inclined to discuss commercial issues with the Chinese during Thatcher's visit in December.[25] Within the Cabinet, Lord Young, minister of state without portfolio, anxious to 'take advantage of any commercial spin-off from signature of the Hong Kong Agreement', suggested that 'a group of businessmen' should accompany Thatcher to the signature ceremony. However, the FCO objected to his suggestion on the grounds that 'it might be seen as selling Hong Kong for commercial advantage'.[26] Ministers finally decided that Thatcher 'should not take businessmen with her, to avoid displacing Hong Kong from centre of stage and giving impression of having done deal on Hong Kong for sake of UK commercial interests'. But they saw the 'importance of follow-up', or a business mission following Thatcher's visit.[27] It was decided that Lord Young should be the leader of that mission, and that he 'should move rapidly after the Prime Minister's visit to capitalise on the possible commercial advantages of the favourable atmosphere'.[28]

Thatcher believed that during her China visit, she would probably not have sufficient time to discuss specific commercial projects with the Chinese leaders. But she was content that 'the successful conclusion of the Hong Kong negotiations itself further strengthens the framework of political support necessary for the rapid growth of trade with China'.[29] When Thatcher arrived in Beijing in December, both Zhao Ziyang and Hu Yaobang supported the idea of a British trade mission. Hu added that they 'would personally intervene to ensure the success of the mission'.[30]

British defence sales and COCOM liberalisation

In early 1985, the FCO's Far Eastern Department defined the British objectives for China after the signing of the Hong Kong agreement: 'to work towards settling the future of Hong Kong; to encourage the development of a stable and pro-Western China; to increase British exports; [and] to promote exchanges and visits'.[31] According to the 1985 objectives of the Beijing Embassy, in the long term Britain should 'encourage China to maintain and expand the "open door" policy, with the objective of binding her further into the international economic and trading system'. The government should 'help British industry to obtain as large a share as possible of China's expanding import market', covering business and defence equipment sales. In the short term, Britain should finalise the negotiations for the Guangdong nuclear project and for an investment promotion and protection agreement, while taking the lead in trade liberalisation in COCOM meetings.[32]

The Thatcher government was eager to increase strategic exports to China. In February 1985, Thatcher agreed to a review of Britain's defence sales policy towards China.[33] Conducted by the MoD with detailed input from the FCO and the DTI, the review was submitted to the defence secretary on 24 May. The main thrust of the review was that 'a more liberal policy on defence sales to China' would 'fit well with our overall aim of promoting a more closely cooperative relationship with China', 'build on the success of the Hong Kong negotiations', and 'lead to an essential strengthening of China's military position vis a vis the Soviet Union' with 'a helpful effect on the global balance of power'. Between 1979 and 1983, the review recalled, applications to sell defence equipment had been judged against 'the criterion that the equipment should not upset, or have a significant effect on, the strategic balance in the area'. In 1983, Britain's defence sales to China amounted to about £1 million, restricted mainly to radar, sonar, and communications equipment. (After three years of negotiations, China decided to cancel the contracts with Marconi for the modernisation of two Luda-class destroyers worth £120 million.) The review pointed out that by 1985, 'the strategic threat to UK Home Base and UK Bases abroad from China is negligible given their current capabilities and intentions'. China's land-based strategic missiles, which had the range to strike Britain, were believed to be too small in number, while its strategic air force was modelled on the outdated Soviet medium bomber. China was 'unlikely in the foreseeable future to cease regarding USSR as her major strategic threat'. Concerning the threat to Hong Kong, the risks of a Chinese military intervention before 1997 was 'small' but remained a 'possibility'. Yet they would not be increased by British defence sales since China already had 'a more than adequate capability to occupy Hong Kong if she so chose'. On sales prospects, the review noted that, given the 'low priority' afforded to defence in Deng Xiaoping's Four Modernisations, Britain should target those areas in which China had a strong preference – 'all submarine equipment, including torpedoes, naval systems, avionics and airborne radar and missile technology'. On 29 May, Defence Secretary Michael Heseltine submitted the defence sales review to the prime minister. Both Thatcher and Howe, agreeing that the strategic threat from China to Britain and Hong Kong was 'negligible', approved the review's recommendations.[34]

When it came to defence sales or high-technology transfer to countries of the 'proscribed destinations', such as the Soviet Union and Communist China, the approval of COCOM was required. Back in 1980, Britain, arguing that China posed a 'lesser strategic threat' than did 'the other proscribed destinations', had proposed 'a formal differential in favour of China'. Although France (doubtful about China's continued openness to the West in the long term) and West Germany (concerned about being seen as discriminating against the Soviet Union) objected to a 'formal differential', they indicated that they would raise no objections to anything Britain might wish to export to China – thus, this was a 'tacit acceptance of a China differential'.[35] Besides, the United States had relaxed its controls on China. In 1983, President Ronald Reagan, recognising China's status as a 'friendly, non-allied country', moved China to the same country group as Europe, Japan, Australia, and so forth. Accordingly, licence applications for seven commodity categories in the 'green zone' which presented 'minimal national security risk' (such as computers and scientific instruments) would receive expeditious consideration by COCOM and routine approval by the US Commerce Department.[36] All this resulted in a dramatic increase in COCOM licence applications for China. In 1984, for instance, about 80–85 per cent of 3,237 cases were related to China.[37]

In early 1985, COCOM held a high-level meeting, and later ad hoc group meetings, to find ways of streamlining approval of China-related applications, so that its workload could focus on other 'proscribed destinations' like the Soviet Union.[38] The British had been a leading exponent of liberalisation of COCOM controls on China. To the FCO's Trade Relations and Exports Department, the removal of China from the COCOM control list would 'obviate a major difficulty that would otherwise face Hong Kong in 1997', when, as part of the PRC, Hong Kong would be liable to COCOM controls.[39] After months of deliberations, in December COCOM agreed to a partial relaxation of controls on China, permitting the licensing of some twenty-seven product categories (mainly computers, telecommunications equipment, and semi-conductors) at 'national discretion' without the need for COCOM's prior approval.[40]

Trade missions and high-level visits

As an economic 'follow-up' to the 1984 Hong Kong agreement, the trade mission led by Lord Young took place between 28 February and 9 March 1985. Young's delegation consisted of representatives of GEC, Cable and Wireless, British Aerospace, and Rolls-Royce, as well as Percy Cradock. Under the DTI's coordination, and with Thatcher 'taking a close personal interest' in its preparation, the mission aimed to 'build on good Sino-British political relations following the signature of the Hong Kong agreement to lay the foundations for an expansion of British exports to China'; to 'impress on appropriate Chinese contacts the excellence of what Britain has to offer in a number of sectors to whose development the Chinese attach priority', such as energy and transport; and to 'further the specific business interests of particular British companies'.[41] During his week-long stay in China, Young discussed with the Chinese the Guangdong nuclear project (see below) and the modernisation of the Tangshan coal mine, among other matters. Premier Zhao Ziyang, receiving Young's delegation on 4 March, said that with the successful resolution of the Hong Kong question, the Chinese government expected a big increase in Sino-British trade. To Zhao, China needed high technology, while Britain wanted overseas markets. Thus, the two countries should expand economic and technological cooperation on the basis of mutual benefit. Lord Young, for his part, hoped that Britain and China would become partners for comprehensive and long-term cooperation.[42]

During his visit, Young handed the draft of a new UK–China economic cooperation agreement to the Chinese for consideration. While the text was closely similar to the 1979 agreement, which was due to expire on 31 December 1985, the new agreement did not include 'a target figure for "joint economic activity" to be achieved by a specific deadline'.[43] As the FCO's Far Eastern Department lamented, the 'ludicrously unrealistic figure' of US$14 billion by 1985 in the current agreement would have meant 'an average of US$2 billion trade per year' during the whole period.[44] The new UK–China economic cooperation agreement was to be signed during the Chinese premier's visit to Britain three months later.

As the first stop of his Western European tour including West Germany and the Netherlands, Zhao Ziyang visited Britain between 2 and 8 June 1985. Back in 1979, Zhao, then first secretary in Sichuan Province, had toured Britain, where he had been deeply impressed by the British efforts to transform declining industries through modernisation.[45] In early 1984, Zhao had made an extensive tour of six Western European countries (on top of his visits to the United States and Canada). The Chinese government hoped that Europe could occupy a higher proportion of China's total foreign trade. As Deng Xiaoping told the former Conservative prime minister, Edward Heath, in mid-April, European countries were 'relatively open' to the question of technology transfer, and thus China was 'strengthening economic ties with Europe'.[46] From a wider strategic perspective, China's policy towards Europe was in line with its 'independent foreign policy', proclaimed in 1982, whereby China refrained from alignment with any state and opposed 'hegemonism'.[47] Deng believed that 'a strong and united Europe' would contribute not only to China's own development, but also to world peace and prevention of US–Soviet domination.[48] Here lay the convergence of strategic interests between China and Europe, of which Britain was seen as a key partner.

Coming as it did a week after the ratification of the Joint Declaration on Hong Kong, the Thatcher government had high expectations for the outcome of Zhao's visit. According to a FCO brief, the British aimed to 'impress on China Britain's value as a political and economic partner' and to 'underline the importance [Britain attached] to an outward looking, economically pragmatic China'.[49] It was decided that the level of reception accorded to Zhao should be comparable with the status given to Premier Hua Guofeng in 1979 and with the Chinese treatment of Thatcher in 1984. As Iain C. Orr of the Far Eastern Department put it: 'The Chinese attach particular importance to building on personal relationships, and accord great political significance to those between leaders'.[50] Zhao's party comprised Vice Premier Tian Jiyun, Foreign Minister Wu Xueqian, and Vice Foreign Minister Zhou Nan. During his week-long stay (five full days) in Britain, Zhao had two rounds of talks with Thatcher (plus the farewell call she paid to him); held separate meetings or engagements involving six Cabinet ministers; signed agreements on economic and nuclear cooperation; had lunch with the Queen at Buckingham Palace; made a major speech on Chinese foreign policy at Chatham House; and toured Scotland and Cambridge.[51]

On 3 June, Zhao received a guard of honour in the FCO Quadrangle, followed by a courtesy call on the prime minister at Downing Street. In their first formal session that afternoon, Thatcher welcomed Zhao by expressing her hope that the visit would 'open a new chapter of friendly relations between China and the United Kingdom'. Thatcher proposed to begin with the Hong Kong issue. She said that there appeared 'no major outstanding problems' at present, and the next step would be the drafting of the Basic Law or the SAR's mini-constitution. Thatcher mentioned that there was 'some demand in Hong Kong for a greater degree of participation in Government'. Zhao agreed that 'Sino-British relations were entering a new and historic period' – indeed, 'the best relations which [they] had ever had'. China 'wanted a mutually beneficial relationship on a long term basis'. On Hong Kong, Zhao stressed that China was 'committed to a firm, comprehensive and effective implementation of the Joint Declaration'. As there existed 'differing views' on Hong Kong's political institutions, Zhao suggested that the two foreign ministers might discuss the issue in detail (see Chapter 7).[52]

Thatcher and Zhao then moved on to East–West relations where they demonstrated convergent views on a number of issues. Thatcher shared her impression of Mikhail Gorbachev, the new Soviet communist party general secretary following the death of Konstantin Chernenko, who 'would give priority to domestic matters'. In view of this, Thatcher did not realistically expect early progress in the Geneva talks on arms control between the Soviet Union and the United States, but nonetheless hoped that the two sides would reaffirm the Anti-Ballistic Missile Treaty.[53] However, the future of the treaty had been rendered problematic by the Strategic Defence Initiative (SDI) announced by US President Ronald Reagan in early 1983. Thatcher was highly sceptical about Reagan's idea of a space-based defence system to intercept incoming Soviet strategic missiles. Thatcher confided to Zhao that the SDI would 'undermine nuclear deterrence', and it was 'impossible to monitor and control research'. Zhao, sharing Thatcher's fears, argued that China did not believe that the SDI was 'a purely defensive concept': rather, it would lead to 'a new escalation of the arms race'. Importantly, Zhao hoped to see 'a united and strong Western Europe which would take its destiny into its own hands', and which could 'exert pressure on the United States to be very prudent about the Strategic Defence Initiative'. On Sino-Soviet bilateral relations, Zhao revealed that economic relations had 'expanded recently', but Moscow had 'shown no flexibility on the three obstacles to improve political relations' – a Soviet withdrawal from Afghanistan, reduction of Soviet forces on the Chinese borders, and Vietnam's pullout from Cambodia. In response to Thatcher's enquiry about his assessment of the Cambodian problem, Zhao said that there seemed 'no early prospect of a Vietnamese withdrawal', but he believed that '[i]n the long term the burden would become insupportable for the Vietnamese'. Towards the end of the meeting, Zhao renewed the invitation to the Queen and Prince Philip to visit China, suggesting that October 1986 would be the best time. Thatcher, in turn, expressed her hope that General Secretary Hu Yaobang would take up her invitation to visit Britain.[54] The two-hour meeting was followed by the welcome dinner hosted by Thatcher in Zhao's honour.

When Thatcher and Zhao held the second round of talks two days later, the topic concentrated on economic issues. Thatcher recalled Lord Young's trade mission to China in the previous March, whose results she wanted to build on. She appreciated China's recent decisions to purchase British Aerospace's BAe 146 airliner (ten on order) and Short Brothers' SD360 aircraft (eight contracted). Thatcher said that Britain was considering offering a loan facility to China, and this was done in a committee under her own chairmanship. Zhao delightfully replied that British soft loans would be 'conducive to enlarging trade, especially in the case of large projects'. While hoping that 'Sino-British bilateral trade would gain an increasing share in the total volume of China's trade', Zhao nonetheless wished that Thatcher would recognise that 'competition was fierce particularly on prices'. Vice Premier Tian Jiyun ascertained that China's 'future priority areas' were energy, transport, and communications, with food processing being important too. He saw scope for Britain to 'play a big role' in China's development in these areas, 'provided British companies met the three conditions of readiness to transfer high technology, good quality and reasonable prices'. In defending Britain's international competitiveness, Thatcher endeavoured to link Sino-British relations to Hong Kong. She 'understood the need to be competitive', but hoped that 'China would also take account of a wider consideration': '[i]ncreased trade would show the rest of the world how well Britain and China were co-operating and reinforce the confidence created by the Hong Kong Agreement'. Zhao agreed that it was imperative to 'also take into account the political context'. 'If China considered economic factors alone', he explained, 'it would do business only with Japan' (thus implying that Britain was not competitive enough).

At Thatcher's invitation, Lord Young listed a number of areas and projects of particular interest to Britain – for example, the Ningbo steel complex, on which a British consortium led by Davy McKee had started discussions with the Chinese; the renovation of the Tangshan coal mine, on which a feasibility study had been completed by the National Coal Board with the DTI's financial support; and the Pilkington/Yaohua general glass joint venture, of which Pilkington would license to Yaohua its float glass technology for production in a newly constructed factory in Shanghai. Young emphasised that 'many British companies were anxious to go into joint ventures and were ready to transfer modern technology'.[55]

At this juncture, Thatcher brought up the Guangdong nuclear power station project. Since her 1982 China visit when she had personally raised the issue, the Chinese and Hong Kong governments had given their respective approval of the project based on an Anglo-French package. In late 1983, the Hong Kong Nuclear Investment Company and the Guangdong Nuclear Investment Company started negotiating for a joint venture contract. On 19 January 1985, the contract for establishing the Guangdong Nuclear Power Joint Venture Company was signed, with the Guangdong Nuclear Investment Company having a 75 per cent shareholding and the Hong Kong Nuclear Investment Company holding 25 per cent. Once completed, the Guangdong nuclear power station would supply Hong Kong with 70 per cent of the electricity generated each year.[56] At the signing ceremony in the Great Hall of the People, Deng Xiaoping described the Guangdong nuclear power plant as 'the largest joint venture' in China, a project that would 'further strengthen the economic links between the mainland and Hong Kong' and 'increase the confidence of Hong Kong people'.[57] The French company Framatome would be the supplier of the nuclear island, while Britain's GEC Turbine Generators would build the conventional island. Nevertheless, negotiations over the final contracts were far from straightforward. The main difficulties centred on the price of the GEC turbine generator and the terms of export credit offered by the British government. The Guangdong Nuclear Power Joint Venture Company bargained for a 25 per cent reduction from the original price of £300.484 million offered by GEC, on the grounds that this would be GEC's first experience in manufacturing such a huge turbine generator. GEC accepted a price reduction of 17 per cent only. During the negotiations over a financial package, the Bank of China (which would borrow a loan from a consortium of British banks on behalf of the Guangdong Nuclear Power Joint Venture Company) hoped that the

British government would give favourable export credit terms for the GEC contract. The Export Credits Guarantee Department of the British government was prepared to offer export credit facilities at an annual interest rate of 10 per cent, to be reduced to 9.5 per cent later.[58] In short, the Chinese and British were engaged in price bargaining before the Guangdong project could really get off the ground.

When meeting with Zhao on 6 June, Thatcher asked whether the Chinese government was ready to make a formal announcement on the Guangdong nuclear project. Zhao replied that 'discussion of the technical and commercial aspects of that project were virtually complete but negotiation on prices continued'. And there was 'the important question of the quality of the generators', for it would be 'the first time that GEC had produced generators of this size and the Chinese side were not fully confident they would be of the necessary quality'. Thatcher said that a 'fresh impetus' to the negotiations was needed so that outstanding matters could be settled rapidly. Moreover, Thatcher did not miss the chance to promote defence sales, such as submarines and torpedoes. She revealed that 'within COCOM, Britain had been in the forefront in trying to get a differential in favour of China'. Zhao expressed his gratitude for the British efforts, while hoping that Britain would continue to 'exert its influence in favour of further liberalisation leading to eventual abolition of COCOM restrictions for China'.[59]

Before Zhao's departure, Thatcher paid a farewell call on him at Claridges on the morning of 8 June. Having developed a rapport with the Chinese premier (one of her 'old friends'),[60] Thatcher presented Zhao with two signed photographs of him inspecting the guard of honour and with four ties chosen by her from Turnbull & Asser. Thatcher said that she would follow up the issues discussed during the visit, 'particularly those relating to trade matters'. She added that 'the increasing friendship and co-operation between Britain and China should be reflected in an increase in trade'. Zhao replied that 'his visit had furthered co-operation in all fields between China and Britain'. Thatcher was pleased that both sides had confirmed 'their determination to implement in full the Joint Declaration on Hong Kong'. She congratulated Zhao on making 'a highly successful visit'.[61]

The success of Zhao's visit was symbolised by the conclusion of two important agreements. On 3 June, Thatcher and Zhao signed the new UK–China agreement on economic cooperation, which entered into force on 1 January 1986 and lasted for five years. Accordingly, Britain and China should 'take all possible measures to create favourable conditions for strengthening economic co-operation' and 'for bringing about a rapid increase in their economic ties'; 'encourage firms, enterprises and organisations of both countries to take initiatives and measures' for enhancing business opportunities; and 'expand economic co-operation and exchanges involving technology transfers, manufacturing equipment and products', notably in such sectors as textiles, machine-building, oil and natural gas, aerospace, and telecommunications.[62] On the same day, Thatcher and Zhao also inked an agreement on the peaceful use of nuclear energy, which entered into force upon signature and lasted for fifteen years. Britain and China should seek to 'promote co-operation' over the following areas: 'underlying civil nuclear research' including reactor safety and radiation protection; 'consultancies related to the development of a power generation infrastructure, energy planning', and so forth; and 'hardware, including both nuclear and conventional island components and balance of plant'. The areas of cooperation under the agreement should be 'exclusively for peaceful purposes': nuclear material and technological information in the context of cooperation should 'not be used so as to result in any nuclear explosive device'.[63]

Towards the end of 1985, the price negotiations over the Guangdong nuclear project were given a boost by the personal intervention of Zhao Ziyang and Thatcher. In late October, Zhao conveyed, via the Chinese ambassador in London, a message to Thatcher, expressing his hope that the prime minister would 'further exert influence' on the GEC negotiators so that they would 'further reduce the price' of the conventional island.[64] By that time, the Chinese had demanded a price reduction of 20 per cent, while GEC offered a 18 per cent reduction, thus leaving a gap of £6 million.[65] In her reply to Zhao dated 7 November, Thatcher noted that 'a flexible approach on both sides' was necessary in order to bring the negotiations to a successful conclusion. She stressed that GEC had 'already gone a very long way' towards meeting the Guangdong Nuclear Power Joint Venture Company's position on price cuts, and that the offer of 9.5 per cent interest rate on loans to the Bank of China represented 'the best financial terms' Britain could 'defend internationally'. Thatcher hoped that the Chinese government would 'use its influence to moderate the Joint Venture Company's demands'.[66] As a result of the two premiers' direct intervention, on 3 January 1986, the Guangdong Nuclear Power Joint Venture Company and the GEC Turbine Generators signed the memorandum of understanding on the price, commercial terms, and technical aspects of the GEC contract.[67] Meanwhile, on 6 January the British government and the Bank of China signed the memorandum of understanding on the financial terms in support of the project: the British loans, underwritten by the Export Credits Guarantee Department, would be repayable at an annual interest rate of 9.5 per cent over a period of fifteen years.[68] According to a DTI press release, the contracts for the Guangdong nuclear power station, valued at over £250 million, would create 'wide benefits' by maintaining 'many jobs in GEC and in many UK sub-contractors and suppliers' and by 'strengthen[ing] economic ties between China, Hong Kong and the United Kingdom'.[69] (It was not until 23 September that the Chinese and the British and French suppliers formally signed the key contracts for the nuclear and conventional islands, with construction work beginning in 1987).[70]

During Zhao's visit, Thatcher had pledged to offer soft loans to China. It came to fruition in mid-May 1986, when Zheng Tuobin, minister for foreign economic relations and trade, visited Britain to sign an agreement with Geoffrey Howe. Until then, Britain's aid to China had been restricted to a small programme of technical cooperation, started in 1983, to pay for British consultants to advise the Chinese government and industry on technical matters. The British regarded the programme as a success, but the Chinese wanted British soft loans, especially because other European countries like France and West Germany were already providing them. Signed on 15 May, the financial agreement between Britain and China provided for development loans worth £300 million, payable at 5 per cent over twenty years.[71] As Thatcher remarked during Zheng' courtesy call a day earlier, it was 'important that trade should expand as rapidly as possible as an earnest [sic] of the friendly relations between the two countries', and the soft loans agreement would help 'sustain trade with China'. Zheng regarded the terms of loan facilities offered by Britain as 'favourable'. He stressed that China 'attached high priority to expanding trade with the European Community including the UK'.[72]

During the same visit, Zheng and Howe also signed an agreement on investment promotion and reciprocal protection. The two sides agreed to 'encourage and create favourable conditions' for investment in their respective countries, and to accord 'fair and equitable treatment' as well as 'the most constant protection and security' to foreign investors. The agreement guaranteed 'the right to transfer freely to the country where [investors] reside their investments and returns', although this would be 'subject to the right of each Contracting Party in exceptional balance of payment difficulties and for a limited period to exercise equitably and in good faith powers conferred by its laws'.[73] All in all, the agreements on soft loans and investment protection, together with the 1985 agreements on economic cooperation and nuclear energy, provided a strong legal and institutional framework for Anglo-Chinese trade, investment, and technological cooperation.

To keep up the momentum of high-level exchanges, the Thatcher government enthusiastically welcomed General Secretary Hu Yaobang to Britain between 8 and 12 June. As Thatcher told Hu in her invitation letter, there were 'many friends of China here who will be anxious to meet you'.[74] To the FCO, Hu's would be a rather 'unusual visit' – 'the first ever by a purely party leader' who did not hold any government position. The FCO was inclined to aim for 'a more philosophical emphasis than for Premier Zhao's visit' in 1985. It was suggested that the prime minister should discuss with

Hu 'theoretical/ideological aspects of British and Chinese politics and cultural outlooks', highlighting 'parallels as well as differences between Britain and China'. In fact, the Chinese government had requested 'a strong cultural element': Hu was 'personally very keen on Shakespeare, and especially wanted to go to Stratford'. One of the highlights of Hu's trip was the confirmation of a new scholarship scheme, originally proposed by Y. K. Pao, to increase the number of Chinese postgraduate students in Britain.[75] The main British objective for Hu's visit was to demonstrate to China that 'the West is fully committed to the success of China's modernisation and opening to the world, with Britain making a large practical contribution'.[76] The FCO was eager to 'make a more lasting and positive impression on the Chinese than is made by [Britain's] European partners/competitors'.[77]

From Beijing's perspective, Britain was the first stop of Hu's tour of Western Europe, which also included West Germany, France, and Italy. In what was his first time to set foot on European soil, Hu aimed to 'extensively publicise China', 'support the unity and independence of Europe', and 'promote the trend towards multipolarity'. To him, there was 'no conflict of fundamental interests' between China and Western Europe.[78] As far as his trip to Britain was concerned, Hu hoped to enhance understanding, expand cooperation, and promote world peace. The successful resolution of the Hong Kong question had created 'the favourable condition' for the development of Sino-British relations 'at a higher level'.[79] Hu's entourage of about thirty people included Vice Premier Li Peng and Vice Foreign Minister Zhou Nan.

Thatcher received Hu Yaobang and Li Peng at Downing Street on the afternoon of 9 June. They began with the topic of Hong Kong, where 'both sides were satisfied with progress on Hong Kong and agreed on the need to maintain confidence'. There was a meeting of minds on the Soviet strategic threat, too. Thatcher said that, as far as a second Reagan–Gorbachev summit was concerned, it should 'produce practical results and not be simply a goodwill session like the Geneva summit' of 19–20 November 1985.[80] In particular, it would need to conclude agreements on arms control, with the most promising areas being chemical weapons and Intermediate-Range Nuclear Forces (INF). Concerning the INF talks (which started in Geneva in late 1981), Thatcher argued that Britain 'sought a global solution', one that would not allow the Soviet Union to move weapons from Europe to Asia. She 'did not wish to export our security problems to Asia or to increase the threat to China from the Soviet Union'. Hu offered his views: 'The greatest dilemma facing the Soviet Union was how both to develop the national economy and maintain military parity with the United States. The Soviet Union wanted the best of both worlds.' Commenting on Sino-Soviet relations, Hu revealed that although economic relations were 'going relatively smoothly', political relations did not have 'the slightest sign of any improvement', with Moscow proposing summit meetings and signature of 'hollow documents such as military non-aggression pacts' but without showing an interest in 'tackling practical questions'. Hu remarked that the Soviets needed to remove the three obstacles to Sino-Soviet normalisation, including forcing Vietnam to pull out from Cambodia. Thatcher agreed that it was 'a tragedy that Vietnam was still occupying Cambodia'. On Sino-American relations, Hu hoped that the Reagan administration would urge Taiwan to agree to exchange with China in the fields of postal services, air links, trade, and shipping. Thatcher commented that Sino-American relations would continue to improve. Turning to Sino-British relations, Li welcomed the recent British decision to grant China some £300 million of development loans. Li hoped that economic relations would be 'expanded further', but it would require Britain to import 'more goods' from China, provide 'more development loans', and set up 'more joint ventures'. Thatcher responded by highlighting Britain's 'lead in securing relaxation of COCOM rules in China's favour'.[81]

Prior to the Thatcher–Hu meeting, Li Peng, who was responsible for energy matters, had had a separate meeting with Secretary of State for Trade and Industry Paul Channon in the morning,[82] and with Secretary of State for Energy Peter Walker over lunch at Hyde Park Hotel. Realising that energy was one of China's development priorities, Walker stated that Britain and China had 'many common energy interests'. Following his China visit back in 1983, Walker had created an office within his department specifically to deal with energy matters with China. Li replied that China 'valued the co-operation of UK oil companies in the development of their offshore resources', and hoped that the exploration in the South China Sea would soon yield results. To underscore the British success in this field, Walker referred to the history of the North Sea Oil, which had experienced 'an initial period of disappointment' but then 'a number of significant oil discoveries'. He revealed that British Petroleum still regarded China as 'a promising area', so much so that it would press on with its exploration programme.[83]

When discussing the Guangdong nuclear project (the final contracts were yet to be signed), Li wondered if the Chernobyl accident in the Soviet Union in April had affected Britain's nuclear power programme.[84] Walker stressed that the UK reactors were of 'a considerably different design', and thus there was 'no direct relevance'. Commenting on the impact of Chernobyl on Hong Kong, Li said that the nuclear power station at Daya Bay would be the 'biggest single UK/Chinese collaboration', and that China 'attached great importance to proceeding with further nuclear development in order to increase its electricity capacity'. In the wake of the Chernobyl disaster, China had reviewed its nuclear policy, but concluded that the reactor system under planning was based on 'significantly different technology' from that used by the Soviets. Li recognised 'the strength of public feelings' in Hong Kong raised by the accident. He lamented that local opposition to the Daya Bay nuclear power station,[85] only fifty kilometres from Hong Kong, was 'causing some difficulty for the China Light and Power Company'. It would be helpful for the British government to 'use its influence to smooth out some of these difficulties'.[86]

On the same day, Li and Howe along with Y. K. Pao put their signatures to the memorandum of understanding on the Sino-British Friendship Scholarship Scheme, worth £35 million over ten years. The aim was to bring about 400 Chinese postgraduate students and researchers each year to Britain, with Pao and China each meeting two-fifths of the total cost and Britain paying the remainder.[87] At the welcoming banquet for Hu's party after the signing of the memorandum, Thatcher praised this 'innovative' scheme, which was due to 'the imagination and characteristic generosity of Sir Y. K.'. To impress the guests, she quoted a line from the 'Analects' of Confucius and asked rhetorically: 'Is it not a delight that friends should visit from afar?' Thatcher welcomed Li back to Britain as 'an old and valued friend', who had made an 'enormous contribution' to strengthening Sino-British economic cooperation over the years. Thatcher, moreover, attested that she had been 'lucky enough' to visit China three times and to observe the 'historic changes' that had been taking place. She wanted the Chinese leaders to see the qualities in Britain, which was 'a society on the move: inventive and flexible'. Thatcher concluded by proclaiming that 1986 was 'an exceptional year for Britain and China': Hu's current visit would be followed by the 'historic occasion' of the Queen's visit in October.[88] Hu said that the Queen would be 'accorded a grand and warm welcome by the Chinese people'.[89]

The royal tour of China

The first visit to China by a reigning monarch between 12 and 19 October was of great symbolic significance. Unlike her aversion to visiting the Soviet Union, Queen Elizabeth II had been wanting to go to China for years.[90] The visit 'set the seal on the warm friendship' between Britain and China, and helped 'provide a foundation for the building of ever closer contacts'.[91] During their week-long stay in China, the Queen and the Duke of Edinburgh had a packed programme, featuring visits to five cities, meetings with four of the five members of the Politburo Standing Committee, attendance of two state banquets, and sight-seeing. Not only did the Queen get the opportunity to see China, but the Chinese people, perhaps over a million, enthusiastically lined the streets to get a glimpse of the British monarch.[92]

On Sunday 12 October at 5 pm, the British Airways *TriStar* carrying the Queen touched down at Beijing Airport. The motorcade then brought the Queen and the Duke of Edinburgh to the Diaoyutai State Guesthouse No. 18, the most lavish accommodation there which had just been renovated in time for the visit.[93] On the morning of 13 October, in Tiananmen Square, the Queen was officially welcomed by President Li Xiannian, the official head of state, with a gun salute and an inspection of the guard of honour. During a chat in the Great Hall of the People following the welcoming ceremony, Li said that England 'was not unknown to the Chinese people, because it had been the cradle of the Industrial Revolution'. Li congratulated Geoffrey Howe, who accompanied the royal party, on 'playing such a splendid part in the Hong Kong settlement'.[94] At night, a lavish state banquet in the Queen's honour was given by Li, which featured a ten-course feast including such Chinese delicacies as sea slug, shark's fin, and lychee or 'dragon's eyes'. The Queen delivered a speech at the banquet:

> Today relations between the United Kingdom and the People's Republic of China are closer than they have ever been. This owes much to the settlement worked out between us for the future of Hong Kong. Both our countries are committed to doing everything possible to maintain Hong Kong's continued stability and prosperity.

The Queen announced that fellowships worth £1 million would be made available to Chinese scientists to allow them to conduct research in British laboratories over the next three years. For his part, Li proclaimed that the Queen's visit was 'an important milestone in the annals of Sino-British relations'.[95]

At the state banquet, Howe took the occasion to discuss concrete issues with Premier Zhao Ziyang, who was sitting next to him. Zhao 'gave a lengthy description of the success in the Chinese economy'. China had been 'able to sell off small enterprises, such as shops', and it was now considering moving to 'share ownership of larger scale enterprises'. Howe 'was struck by the extent to which [Zhao] paid tribute to privatisation and contracting out'. Commenting on the recent Reagan–Gorbachev summit at Reykjavik, Iceland (11–12 October),[96] Zhao believed that Gorbachev 'had over-reached himself', and the breakdown of the summit without agreement 'would have done himself substantial damage at home'. In particular, Zhao criticised, 'Gorbachev had bargained on being able to persuade the US to drop SDI' in exchange for the elimination of all strategic nuclear weapons within ten years – a link that was rejected by Reagan. Although China was 'hostile to the SDI', Zhao thought that 'a deal here could have been in the making' had it not been for Gorbachev's political miscalculation. In this regard, Zhao 'was very struck by the similarity of British and Chinese perceptions of many of the issues under discussion'. (True, Thatcher was alarmed by the proposals at Reykjavik because the elimination of all nuclear weapons would leave Western Europe vulnerable to preponderant Soviet conventional forces, and call into question Britain's own Trident deterrent.)[97] Howe agreed that, 'as independent nuclear powers and members of the Security Council', Britain and China 'had many common interests', and the two sides should continue to hold expert talks.[98]

On 14 October, the Queen accompanied by Howe and Ambassador Evans met with General Secretary Hu Yaobang in Zhongnanhai. After some courteous exchanges (during which 'the Duke of Edinburgh got visibly bored'), Hu said that 'China is a vast country', but there were 'not so many modernized things to see', just 'a lot of historical relics'. Thereafter, the Queen was greeted by Deng Xiaoping in the Diaoyutai State Guesthouse. 'Thank you for coming to see an old man such as me', said Deng. The Queen replied that Deng, aged 82, was younger than her mother.[99] Deng remarked that with the successful resolution of the Hong Kong question, the task now was to 'strive for developing the friendly cooperative relationship between the two states [and] enhancing friendship between the peoples of the two countries'.[100]

The royal party left Beijing for Shanghai on the morning of 15 October. The Queen performed a spectator piece of street theatre by walking along downtown Shanghai, where she was reportedly greeted by as many as two million Chinese residents. The mayor of Shanghai welcomed the Queen and the Duke of Edinburgh with a lunchtime banquet. At night, the Queen hosted a return banquet for President Li Xiannian and his wife, who had broken diplomatic protocol by coming from the capital for the event, held on board the Royal Yacht *Britannia*.[101] *Britannia* had demonstrated its 'potential as a trade platform' a day ago, when a 'sea day seminar', organised by the British Overseas Trade Board, was held off Shanghai.[102] Co-chaired by James Cleminson (chairman of the British Overseas Trade Board) and Eric Sharp (president of the Sino-British Trade Council and chairman of Cable and Wireless), the seminar participants were Chinese trade officials and representatives of British companies in the fields of energy, transport, telecommunications, and food processing.[103] The 'sea day' trade seminar was followed by a 'land day' in Peace Hotel, Shanghai.[104] Overall, twenty-five projects were discussed, and sixteen contracts signed.[105]

From Shanghai, the Queen's party made it to Xi'an, Shannxi, on 16 October. The Queen was fascinated with the famous terracotta warriors guarding the tomb of the first Chinese emperor in the excavated pit. Even Prince Philip demonstrated great interest in the clay figures.[106] But in Xi'an, the Duke got embroiled in an episode that might have derailed the Queen's trip. When meeting with a group of students from Edinburgh University (of which he was chancellor), the Duke was told that they were in Xi'an for one year as part of their language course. The Duke, as one student told a reporter later, then uttered rather offensive words: 'If you stay here much longer you'll go back with slitty eyes.' The British press was quick to make the most of the Duke's unfortunate 'slitty eyes' remarks. At a stormy press conference later, the Queen's press secretary, Michael Shea, did not deny that such remarks had been made, but argued that the Duke had taken part in 'a conversation that was "jokey, highly agreeable (and) fun"'. Shea 'reproached the press for dwelling on "trivia"', claiming that 'reporters should concentrate on the success of the visit'.[107] Howe decided to speak to Wu Xueqian, who, however, 'professed ignorance of the whole trivial affair'. Wu simply brushed the Duke's comments aside by saying: 'We know that he is a sincere man.'[108]

Arriving in Guangzhou, her final stop, on 18 October, the Queen was welcomed by a Chinese crowd of an estimated million along the streets.[109] In her farewell reception on board *Britannia*, the Queen presented every Chinese official with an autographed photo of her and Prince Philip.[110] Thus ended a week-long tour of China full of hospitality and symbolism. *Britannia* then carried the Queen and the Duke to Hong Kong, which they had first visited in 1975. For three days from 21 to 23 October, the Queen met with Hong Kong politicians and lay residents, and visited a number of institutions and places like the new headquarters of the Hongkong Bank and the Shatin racecourse. She wanted to demonstrate Britain's continuing commitment to Hong Kong's future.[111]

As the British Embassy in Beijing assessed it, the Chinese government had given the royal visit 'a very high profile', and all the Chinese leaders had been 'extremely friendly' to the Queen.[112] Nevertheless, Ambassador Evans was sensible enough to be sceptical that the visit had 'increased the Chinese propensity to be influenced by our views on the future of Hong Kong or on international issues'. Nor did he take it for granted that the visit had 'brought about any increase in the readiness of Chinese agencies to buy British goods or services'. Rather, the Chinese would continue to be influenced by 'price, quality and the availability of soft finance, technology, counter-trade and offset' when it came to commercial dealings with Britain.[113]

China's globalisation and GATT

Evans was right not to take the China market for granted in the age of globalisation. Indeed, Britain faced intense competition from the United States, Japan, and West Germany. Among Western countries, the United

States played a more important role in China's reform and globalisation than did Britain. The mid-1980s witnessed the deepening of US–China relations in economic, strategic, and cultural aspects following the establishment of diplomatic relations. Total bilateral trade more than tripled, from US$2,316.3 million in 1979 to US$7,876.3 million by 1986. The United States became China's third largest trading partner (albeit suffering from a massive trade deficit since 1986), after Hong Kong and Japan. Strategically, the United States and China continued their collaboration against the Soviet threat (for example, by sharing intelligence), notwithstanding Gorbachev's 'new thinking' in Soviet foreign policy and Beijing's tentative moves towards Sino-Soviet rapprochement. The two military establishments expanded working-level exchanges. Cultural and academic exchanges flourished, with increasing numbers of new visas issued annually to Chinese students and scholars entering the United States and more US foundations (like the Ford Foundation) opening offices in China.[114] For all Thatcher's aspirations to shape China's reforms, Britain was no match for the United States in terms of economic performance and military prowess. Although Britain remained 'the world's sixth-largest economy' in the early 1980s, it was 'now just an ordinary, moderately large power, not a Great Power', according to Paul Kennedy.[115]

As a result of Deng's second wave of opening since 1984, British merchandise exports to China (mainly machinery, scientific instruments, chemicals, textile fibres, and aeroplanes) increased from about £160 million in 1983 to £317 million the following year, and to £400 million in 1985, thus resulting in a modest surplus.[116] In 1985, Britain accounted for just 2.31 per cent of China's total imports, and was outperformed by Japan (25.62 per cent), the United States (10.35 per cent), and West Germany (6.11 per cent).[117] Only 0.5 per cent of Britain's total exports went to China that year.[118] In 1986, British exports soared another 25 per cent to £500 million, but their share of China's total imports remained about 2 per cent.[119] Thus, although Britain's exports to China had increased in value terms over the years, its share of the China market had not substantially changed.

The volume of British investment in China was miniscule. According to the Chinese Ministry of Foreign Economic Relations and Trade, the value of contracts involving foreign direct investment was estimated to be US$16.2 billion during 1979–85, with US$5.85 billion being recorded in 1985 or an increase of 120.7 per cent over 1984. There were 2,300 'equity joint ventures' (1,300 of which were established in 1985), 3,700 'contractual joint ventures' (1,500 in 1985), and 120 wholly foreign-owned ventures (46 in 1985).[120] Nevertheless, the Chinese were disappointed that by early 1986 there were comparatively few joint ventures in key economic sectors such as transport and energy. Rather, almost 70 per cent of the joint ventures were in production industries (mainly light industry and textiles), and 30 per cent in service industries (especially hotels). Around 80 per cent of foreign investment had come from Hong Kong, with the remaining 20 per cent in descending order from the United States, Japan, and Western Europe. Of the 2,300 joint venture projects, only one-third were actually in operation by early 1986.[121] About twenty British companies were investing in China. For example, GEC Telecommunications established a joint venture with Sichuan Posts & Telecommunications concerning rural telephone exchanges; Trafalgar House/Costain cooperated with the Guangdong authorities over the Hong Kong–Guangzhou toll super highway including a bridge; and Balfour Beatty was involved in the Guangdong nuclear project by supplying overhead transmission lines and substations (on top of GEC's building of the conventional island).[122] Britain's utilised foreign direct investment stood at US$71.6 million in 1985, which was higher than that of West Germany (US$24.1 million) and France (US$32.5 million) within the European Community – but was much lower than that of the United States (US$370 million).[123]

In essence, China's approach to foreign direct investment had been one of 'exploration' until 1986. It was characterised by lack of experience, inadequacy of central guidance, and low quality of foreign investment.[124] The promulgation of the law on joint ventures in July 1979 notwithstanding, the business environment remained difficult for foreigners due to a host of factors: the non-convertibility of the Chinese currency (the *renminbi*), limited access to the domestic market, and unclear definition of property rights.[125] As the FCO's economic advisers assessed it: 'Joint ventures have proved highly unattractive to foreign investors due to very hard case-by-case bargaining on terms by the Chinese and difficulties of foreign exchange repatriation'.[126] Moreover, foreign business people were put off by 'the poor technical quality of workforce' and 'the inflated value the Chinese place on their inputs into the joint venture, especially land and premises'.[127] In 1986, the Chinese government endeavoured to improve the investment environment, particularly for export-oriented, technologically advanced joint ventures. On 11 October, the State Council announced twenty-two regulations on encouraging foreign investment, including lower land use fees, new access to a limited foreign currency market, and simplified processing of investment applications.[128]

If British business people lacked confidence in making profits in China, the Chinese government appeared to be sceptical about the competitiveness of UK companies. During Lord Young's third trade mission to China on 10–17 November, Zhao Ziyang said that 'economic and commercial relationships between China and the United Kingdom were developing rapidly'. But China wanted to see 'greater inward investment by UK companies;

greater collaboration and greater levels of exports to the UK'. Zhao 'praised the quality of UK products but stressed the need for them to be priced as keenly as those of competing countries'. Young agreed that 'to be successful in China the prices of UK industry needed to be competitive', adding that 'UK products were now highly competitive following the upward movements in the value of the Yen'. He said that the British would 'do what they could to help China export more to the United Kingdom', but their efforts were limited by the fact that 'quotas and tariffs were set by the European Community' and that 'the UK was a market economy'.[129]

To expand its exports, China was eager to join GATT. As Premier Zhao argued in early 1986, with the opening of the fourteen coastal cities and the three coastal regional zones, the reform was 'expanding and deepening', and thus China's admission to GATT was both necessary and important.[130] Signed by twenty-three countries on 30 October 1947, and entered into force on 1 January 1948, GATT aimed to remove state barriers to trade in goods. GATT was predicated on an implicit 'liberal understanding' shared by the original signatories, particularly the United States and Britain. All contracting parties of GATT were expected to liberalise trade, enforce property rights and contracts, and limit the government's role in the economy – in short, to adopt a market economy.[131] Besides, it was the neoliberal assumption that economic liberalisation would lead to the rise of the middle class and demands for democracy. In essence, the founding and operation of GATT was closely entangled with the Cold War. For all its claims of inclusivity and universality, as Francine McKenzie argues, GATT became 'a western-dominated forum' and 'a pillar and instrument of the "free world"'.[132]

Back in November 1984, China had been granted permanent observer status in the GATT Council. On 10 July 1986, China informed the director general of GATT of its intention to resume its status as a contracting party to GATT.[133] By that time, China operated a dualistic trade regime. On the one hand, the opening of the SEZs, coastal cities, and regional zones was intended to increase China's exports and attract foreign direct investment. On the other hand, a system of tariffs and non-tariff barriers was established to protect the domestic market and state trading corporations. To insulate the critical sectors of the economy from international competition, China imposed high import tariffs on some products like TV sets, licensed trading rights, and used quotas to regulate imports. A dual price system existed, and China's currency was non-convertible.[134] To Deng Xiaoping, China's approach to GATT was inextricably linked to its 'status as a transition economy that is also a developing country'.[135] China insisted on being accorded 'developing country' status, whereby state intervention to protect infant industries and state-owned enterprises would be more tolerated, and a longer transition period for compliance with GATT rules would be allowed.¹³⁶

China's desire to join GATT presented Britain, and other Western developed countries, with a dilemma. Besides the legal question about the method of admission – whether China could simply resume the 'vacant seat' (as a result of the Republic of China's withdrawal from GATT in 1950) without making a fresh application, or if it would need to apply and negotiate the terms of accession – the British had to ponder the issue from both the foreign policy and trade policy angles. According to a joint paper by the FCO and the DTI in late 1985, although there were 'strong political arguments' for Britain to respond positively to China's desire to join GATT, 'accommodating a state trading country of China's size and economic potential into the GATT framework would pose problems' and 'offer few compensating advantages in the trade field'. From the perspective of foreign policy, China's accession to GATT would 'help to reinforce outward-looking tendencies in the Chinese hierarchy and to educate it in the workings of the world open trading system'. Besides, it would serve British interests in Hong Kong, for 'a harmonious relationship with China' would provide 'the best context for the smooth implementation of the Hong Kong agreement'. Yet the joint paper recognised that China's membership of GATT would have an 'important disadvantage', in that it would encourage the Soviet Union to apply for accession. The latter's admission, however, would 'change the whole nature of the GATT', which would 'risk becoming a forum for East-West and North-South disputes at the expense of its original functions'.

If the British saw advantages in China's accession to GATT from foreign policy perspectives, this was less the case from trade policy angles. To the FCO and the DTI, China was 'a state trading country', whose commercial practices were 'in the last analysis incompatible with the principles underlying the GATT system'. As 'an open, market-orientated trading system', GATT took, for example, 'subsidy' and 'dumping' seriously. But in China, 'prices are not determined in the market'. Although some 'state trading countries', such as Czechoslovakia, Poland, and Hungary, were members of GATT, and the protocols of accession did contain special terms, 'the East-West trade of the East European economies is too small to have had any significant disruptive effect on the GATT system'. However, the economic implications of China's accession to GATT would be huge. While China's present share of world trade was 'relatively small' (1.23 per cent in 1983), its potential was 'vast', and would for the foreseeable future be centred in 'areas of particular sensitivity in international trade, particularly for the developed countries', such as textiles and light industrial goods. Last but not least, in applying for GATT accession, China demanded that it be accepted as a 'developing country'. If so, the British worried, China would be able to 'claim a special treatment accorded under Part IV of the GATT', benefiting from 'all the commitments made by developed contracting parties to reduce trade barriers without having to reciprocate'. The joint paper concluded that it was 'most improbable that Chinese membership could in practice be prevented – even if this were thought desirable'. 'In economic and GATT terms', there would probably be 'more disadvantages than advantages'; but these considerations should not be 'decisive factors' provided that China could be brought to 'accept terms which adequately reflected her state-trading status'.[137]

After China had formally applied for GATT membership in July 1986, the position of the FCO and the DTI was such that Britain should not seek to lobby against it, 'given the political penalites [sic] that might involve not least in relation to Hong Kong'. Although Chinese membership was 'probably undesirable in terms of the balance of interest within GATT', Britain could 'mitigate the disadvantages provided that terms are agreed which adequately reflect China's state-trading status'.[138]

By the mid-1980s, China had achieved only 'shallow integration into the world economy'.[139] The degree of China's engagement with the global economy could be measured in terms of its market share of world trade and the size of its foreign trade as a proportion of gross domestic product (GDP). In 1986, China's share of world exports was only 1.8 per cent, notwithstanding the rapid growth of its exports since 1979. But if ranked among developing countries, China was the fourth largest exporter (rising from eighth place in 1980), accounting for approximately 5.6 per cent of all their exports. China captured 8.2 per cent of developing countries' total imports, making itself the largest developing market.[140] The ratio of China's foreign trade to GDP had grown rapidly, from less than 10 per cent in 1978 to 19.88 per cent by 1986. China's 1986 figure was comparable to the United States, which had a trade–GDP ratio of 16.86 per cent, and to Japan's ratio of 18.15 per cent.[141]

From a wider perspective, China's attitude towards GATT accession should be understood in the context of Deng's pursuit of 'independent globalisation'. If the United States and Britain expected China to embrace the implicit 'liberal understanding' of GATT (a market economy), Deng hoped to seize the opportunities for foreign trade and technology transfer, and yet to control or restrain those aspects of globalisation that undercut state sovereignty.[142] Instead of the wholesale importation of Western concepts of 'development', Deng's opening policy showed 'the negotiated acceptance of market ideas and global norms … on Chinese terms'.[143] China did not hesitate to uphold its sovereign rights to protect state-owned enterprises, impose tariffs on foreign countries, and maintain controls on foreign exchange. In pursuing the policy of reform, Deng aimed to build 'socialism with Chinese characteristics', while opposing 'bourgeois liberalisation'.[144] The primary goal of seeking GATT membership was to create a strong Chinese economy and to strengthen the party-state – a political goal that was more important than an ideological commitment to 'pure market liberalism'.[145] As events were to show, it would take fifteen years of protracted negotiations for China to join the World Trade Organisation, the successor to GATT.[146]

Conclusion

During 1984, Deng Xiaoping's second wave of economic opening and the conclusion of the Hong Kong negotiations set the stage for a new and closer relationship between Britain and China. Prior to the signing of the Joint Declaration in December, the Thatcher government had been contemplating how to capitalise on a Hong Kong agreement to promote Anglo-Chinese trade. The FCO rejected making a dramatic economic initiative as it did not want to create the impression that Britain was selling Hong Kong for commercial advantage – or 'kowtowing' to China. In fact, the Chinese were as eager as the British to build on the Hong Kong agreement: that trade should reflect the political relationship. With the resolution of the Hong Kong question, Britain and China actively engaged in the process of 'post-colonial' globalisation. Thatcher and British diplomats hoped to 'educate' the Chinese in the norms of the global trading system while reinforcing the pro-Western orientation of the Chinese leadership.

Anglo-Chinese relations in 1985–86 were characterised by high-level mutual visits, increased civilian trade, the relaxation of British defence sales, a convergence of strategic views on the Soviet threat, and cultural exchanges involving students and researchers. The nature of Anglo-Chinese economic interactions was transformed, in that exchange of goods was supplemented by intensified economic and technological cooperation. The British invested and set up joint ventures in China, transferring high-tech and managerial skills in the process. One of the most significant British projects was the Guangdong nuclear power plant, which involved triangular cooperation among China, UK companies like GEC, and Hong Kong's CLP. Anglo-Chinese interactions were facilitated by a framework of bilateral agreements covering economic cooperation, investment promotion, peaceful use of nuclear technology, and provision of British soft loans. These agreements were signed during the high-profile visits of the Chinese leaders and the Queen. Personal relationship and political symbolism mattered deeply to China. After having co-signed the Joint Declaration on Hong Kong and having met on three occasions between 1982 and 1985, Thatcher developed a rapport with Zhao Ziyang, the liberal reformer whom she would never forget even after her retirement from politics.¹⁴⁷ The Chinese warmly reciprocated the British friendship when the Queen made a royal tour of China in 1986. Anglo-Chinese relations were closer and better than at any time since diplomatic normalisation in 1972.

To Thatcher and the FCO, Britain was well placed to meet China's development priorities, namely energy, transport, telecommunications, and industrial renovation. When meeting with Chinese leaders and trade officials, Thatcher, Lord Young, and Peter Walker all endeavoured to 'sell' the achievement of UK companies to China, for example, the North Sea oil experience of British Petroleum in relation to South China Sea offshore oil exploration. In the age of globalisation, the Chinese, while hoping to reduce their economic dependence on the United States and Japan, wanted Britain to offer competitive prices. During the years-long negotiations over the Guangdong nuclear project, the Chinese were conscious of driving a hard bargain. Although Thatcher believed that Britain was a competitive global trading nation, the reality was such that, by the close of 1986, UK companies had been unable to secure a larger share of the China market than she and the DTI might have expected following the Hong Kong agreement. Thatcher's aspirations for 'Global Britain' turned out to be unrealistic and largely unsuccessful.

In opening China to foreign trade and investment, and in applying for GATT membership, Deng envisioned a strategy of 'independent globalisation'. Unlike Thatcher's brand of neoliberal globalisation, Deng stressed the primacy of sovereignty and socialism in China's engagement with the outside world. Seeing China as a 'developing country', Deng and particularly conservatives like Chen Yun found it imperative to protect the domestic market and to regulate the flows of trade through a system of tariffs and non-tariff barriers. These measures, however, clashed with the 'liberal understanding' of GATT and the rules of a market economy. But it was Deng's attitude towards democratisation, in China and in Hong Kong, that best captured the two competing visions of globalisation, as we will examine in the next chapter.

Notes

1 Naughton, *Growing Out of the Plan*, 175–7.
2 Li, *Breaking Through*, 176–7; Gu, *Gu Mu huiyi lu*, 346–7.
3 Li, *Breaking Through*, 180–6; Gu, *Gu Mu huiyi lu*, 350.
4 Zhong Jian, Guo Maojia, and Zhong Ruoyu (eds), *Zhongguo Jingji Tequ wenxian ziliao* [Archival Materials on China's Special Economic Zones], vol. 2 (Beijing: Shehui kexue wenxian chubanshe, 2010), 67–71.
5 Gu, *Gu Mu huiyi lu*, 356–7; Reardon, *A Third Way*, 186–96.

6 Zhao, *Prisoners of the State*, 149–50; Reardon, *A Third Way*, 226–46.
7 Zhonggong zhongyang wenxian yanjiushi (ed.), *Gaige kaifang sashi nian zhongyao wenxian xuanbian* [Important Selected Documents on Thirty Years of Reform and Opening], vol. 1 (Beijing: Zhongyang wenxian chubanshe, 2008), 335.
8 ZZW, vol. 2, 484–508.
9 Naughton, *Growing Out of the Plan*, 178.
10 *Chen Yun wenxuan*, vol. 3, 337.
11 Zhong Jian, Guo Maojia, and Zhong Ruoyu (eds), *Zhongguo Jingji Tequ wenxian ziliao* [Archival Materials on China's Special Economic Zones], vol. 1 (Beijing: Shehui kexue wenxian chubanshe, 2010), 156.
12 TNA, FCO 21/2622, Elliott to Harding, 10 August 1984.
13 TNA, FCO 21/2623, Planning paper: 'The UK–Chinese relationship', attached in Bailes to Boyd, 14 September 1984.
14 TNA, FCO 21/2636, Hart to Woolley, 5 October 1984; Galsworthy to Bailes, 5 October 1984.
15 TNA, FCO 21/2636, Neville-Jones to Private Secretary, 30 November 1984.
16 TNA, FCO 21/2636, Neville-Jones to Elliott, 4 December 1984.
17 TNA, FCO 21/2695, Adley to Thatcher, 26 September 1984.
18 TNA, FCO 21/2695, Elliott to Boyd, 12 October 1984.
19 TNA, FCO 21/2695, Ricketts to Flesher, 17 October 1984.
20 TNA, FCO 21/2695, Beijing to FCO, no. 2625, 19 October 1984.
21 TNA, FCO 21/2695, Orr to Boyd, 26 October 1984.
22 TNA, FCO 21/2695, Boyd to Corley, 31 October 1984.
23 TNA, FCO 21/2695, 'Essential facts', enclosed in Ricketts to Powell, 9 November 1984.
24 TNA, FCO 21/2695, Powell to Ricketts, 13 November 1984.
25 TNA, FCO 21/2696, Corley to Boyd, 9 November 1984; FCO 21/2695, Morphet to Boyd, 2 November 1984.
26 TNA, FCO 21/2696, Jenkinson to Elliott, 22 November 1984.
27 TNA, FCO 21/2696, Elliott to Wilson, 23 November 1984.
28 TNA, FCO 21/2696, Elliott to Wilson, 29 November 1984.
29 TNA, FCO 21/2696, Thatcher to Tracey, 13 December 1984.
30 TNA, FCO 21/2696, Beijing to DTI, no. 295, 20 December 1984.
31 TNA, FCO 21/2977, Elliott to Wilson, 29 March 1985.
32 TNA, FCO 21/3309, '1985 post objectives – Peking', attached in Orr to Wilson, 19 February 1986.
33 TNA, FCO 21/3025, Elliott to Wilson, 28 May 1985.
34 TNA, PREM 19/1682, Powell to Mottram, 1 June 1985; FCO 21/3025, Appleyard to Powell, 3 June 1985; FCO 21/3025, 'China: Review of UK policy on the sale of defence and militarily relevant equipment', attached in Davidson to Elliott, 24 May 1985.
35 TNA, FCO 21/3027, Quayle to Ashton, 22 February 1985; FCO Trade Relations and Exports Department, 'Strengthening COCOM: China case policy', 30 January 1985.

36 TNA, FCO 21/3383, Pares to Fletcher-Cooke, 17 December 1986; Meijer, 'Balancing Conflicting Security Interests', 18–21.
37 TNA, FCO 21/3027, FCO Trade Relations and Exports Department, 'Strengthening COCOM: China case policy', 30 January 1985.
38 TNA, FCO 21/3027, Paris to FCO, no. 117, 8 February 1985; Paris to FCO, no. 330, 19 April 1985; Smith to Hall, 10 June 1985.
39 TNA, FCO 21/3027, Quayle to Ashton, 22 February 1985.
40 Meijer, 'Balancing Conflicting Security Interests', 26–7.
41 TNA, FV 14/200, DTI memo: 'Initiating paper on the visit to China by minister without portfolio, 27 February to 9 March 1984', attached in Hall to Rossiter, 21 January 1985.
42 Wang, *Qishi niandai yilai de ZhongYing guanxi*, 157.
43 TNA, FCO 21/3036, Hall to PS/Minister for trade, 22 February 1985.
44 TNA, FCO 21/3036, Orr to Wilson, 10 May 1985.
45 *Zhao Ziyang wenji, 1975–1980: Sichuan* [Collected Works of Zhao Ziyang, 1975–1980: Sichuan] (Hong Kong: Chinese University Press, 2018), 748–61.
46 *DXW*, vol. 3, 119.
47 *Ibid.*, 56–7.
48 Guo, *Deng Xiaoping waijiao moulue*, 129; Jiang, *Daguo jiaoliang*, 7, 9.
49 TNA, PREM 19/1426, Brief: 'Bilateral relations: General'.
50 TNA, FCO 21/3002, Burrough to Jasper and Gibbs, 4 March 1985; Orr to Wilson, 22 March 1985.
51 TNA, PREM 19/1426, Brief: 'Programme'; FCO 21/3011, Elliott to Thomson, 5 July 1985.
52 TNA, FCO 21/3010, Record of conversation between Thatcher and Zhao Ziyang on 3 June 1985.
53 The Anti-Ballistic Missile Treaty was concluded in 1972 and was amended by a 1974 protocol, which allowed the United States and the Soviet Union to 'deploy one static ABM system with up to one hundred launchers in defence of either an Inter-Continental Ballistic Missile silo field or the national capital'. Thatcher, *The Downing Street Years*, 464–5.
54 TNA, FCO 21/3010, Record of conversation between Thatcher and Zhao Ziyang on 3 June 1985.
55 TNA, FCO 21/3010, Record of meeting between Thatcher and Zhao Ziyang on 6 June 1985.
56 China Light and Power Company, *Annual Report 1984*, 11; China Light and Power Company, *Annual Report 1985*, 13.
57 *DXN*, vol. 2, 1025.
58 TNA, PREM 19/1502, Beijing to DTI, no. 291, 19 December 1984; FCO 21/3044, Brief for meeting with Chinese ambassador about Guangdong nuclear project, October 1985.
59 TNA, FCO 21/3010, Record of meeting between Thatcher and Zhao Ziyang on 6 June 1985.
60 Thatcher, *Statecraft*, 158.
61 TNA, FCO 21/3011, Powell to Ricketts, 8 June 1985.

62 TNA, FCO 21/3036, Agreement between the government of the UK and the government of the PRC on economic cooperation, 3 June 1985.
63 TNA, AB 65/1583, Agreement between the government of the UK and the government of the PRC for cooperation in the peaceful use of nuclear energy, 3 June 1985.
64 TNA, FCO 21/3044, Ricketts to Powell, 30 October 1985.
65 TNA, FCO 21/3044, Far Eastern Department background note, 30 October 1985.
66 TNA, FCO 21/2982, Thatcher to Zhao Ziyang, 7 November 1985.
67 TNA, PV 13/126, Memorandum of understanding between Guangdong Nuclear Power Joint Venture Company and GEC Turbine Generators Ltd. concerning negotiations on the proposed conventional island contract, 3 January 1986.
68 TNA, PV 13/126, Memorandum of understanding between the British government and the Bank of China on the financial terms in support of the GEC contract, 3 January 1986.
69 TNA, PV 13/126, DTI to Beijing, no. 9, 6 January 1986.
70 Dangdai Zhongguo congshu bianji weiyuanhui (ed.), *Dangdai Zhongguo de dianli gongye* [Contemporary China: Power Industry] (Beijing: Dangdai Zhongguo chubanshe, 2009), 609.
71 TNA, FO 93/23/80, Agreement between the government of the UK and the government of the PRC concerning the financial arrangement relating to development loans, 15 May 1986.
72 TNA, PREM 19/1682, Powell to Gilbertson, 14 May 1986.
73 TNA, FO 93/23/79, Agreement between the government of the UK and the government of the PRC concerning the promotion and reciprocal protection of investments, 15 May 1986.
74 TNA, FCO 21/3342, Thatcher to Hu Yaobang, 16 September 1985.
75 TNA, FCO 21/3344, FCO to Beijing, no. 337, 22 April 1986; FCO 21/3345, Culshaw to Powell, 21 May 1986.
76 TNA, FCO 21/3350, FCO to Beijing, no. 572, 13 June 1986.
77 TNA, FCO 21/3342, Orr to Beston, 3 February 1986.
78 Zhang Liqun, Zhang Ding, Yan Ruping, Tang Fei, and Li Gongtian (eds), *Hu Yaobang (1915–1989)* [Hu Yaobang, 1915–1989], vol. 3 (Beijing: Beijing lianhe chuban gongsi, 2015), 882, 884.
79 Zheng (et al.), *Hu Yaobang nianpu ziiao changbian*, vol. 2, 1098.
80 At the Geneva summit, Reagan and Gorbachev had sharp differences over the SDI. Thatcher, *The Downing Street Years*, 470; William Taubman, *Gorbachev: His Life and Times* (London: Simon & Schuster, 2018), 278–91.
81 TNA, FCO 21/3349, Record of meeting between Thatcher and Hu Yaobang on 9 June 1986.
82 TNA, FCO 21/3349, Channon's meeting with Li Peng on 9 June 1986.
83 TNA, FCO 21/3349, Peter Walker's discussions with Li Peng on 9 June 1986.
84 On 26 April 1986, a sudden surge of power during a reactor systems test caused a fire and destroyed unit 4 of the nuclear power station at Chernobyl, Ukraine, resulting in the release of large amounts of radiation into the environment.

85 See Herbert S. Yee and Wong Yiu-chung, 'Hong Kong: The Politics of the Daya Bay Nuclear Plant Debate', *International Affairs*, 63: 4 (Autumn 1987), 617–30.
86 TNA, FCO 21/3349, Peter Walker's discussions with Li Peng on 9 June 1986.
87 Sohmen, *Y. K. Pao*, 176–7.
88 TNA, FCO 21/3347, Speech by Thatcher at dinner in honour of Hu Yaobang, 9 June 1986.
89 Zheng (et al.), *Hu Yaobang nianpu ziiao changbian*, vol. 2, 1099.
90 Robert Hardman, *Queen of the World: The Global Biography* (London: Arrow Books, 2019), 24, 435.
91 TNA, FCO 21/3474, Beijing to FCO, no. 2038, 22 October 1986.
92 TNA, FCO 21/3475, Evans to Howe, 10 November 1986.
93 'Queen brings new warmth to Peking', *The Times* (13 October 1986); Jiang, *Daguo jiaoliang*, 129.
94 'Queen smiles in a Chinese culture haze', *Guardian* (14 October 1986).
95 'Dragon's eyes fit for a Queen', *The Times* (14 October 1986); *Li Xiannian zhuan*, vol. 2, 1277.
96 See Taubman, *Gorbachev*, 294–304; Thatcher, *The Downing Street Years*, 470–1.
97 Renwick, *A Journey with Margaret Thatcher*, 158; Cradock, *In Pursuit of British Interests*, 68–9.
98 TNA, FCO 21/3474, Beijing to FCO, no. 1987, 14 October 1986.
99 'Great Wall stormed by Queen', *The Times* (15 October 1986); 'Queen gets top status tour', *Guardian* (15 October 1986).
100 *DXN*, vol. 2, 1145.
101 'A riot of colour for the Queen', *The Times* (16 October 1986); *Li Xiannian zhuan*, vol. 2, 1277.
102 Hardman, *Queen of the World*, 365.
103 TNA, FCO 21/3470, Seminar on board Her Majesty's Yacht Britannia off Shanghai on 14 October 1986: 'Sino-British trade and economic cooperation'.
104 'China beckons, but will Britain respond?', *Guardian* (16 October 1986).
105 TNA, FCO 21/3402, Lord Young's meeting in Ministry of Foreign Economic Relations and Trade, 11 November 1986.
106 'Parade of the guards', *Guardian* (17 October 1986).
107 'Duke in storm over "ghastly" remarks', *Guardian* (17 October 1986).
108 Howe, *Conflict of Loyalty*, 381.
109 'Typhoon Philip breezes through the storm', *Observer* (19 October 1986).
110 'State visit to China a success', *The Times* (20 October 1986); Jiang, *Daguo jiaoliang*, 133.
111 TNA, FO 972/160, Government House, HK, 'Royal visit to Hong Kong, 1986', 1 December 1986.
112 TNA, FCO 21/3474, Beijing to FCO, no. 2037, 22 October 1986.
113 TNA, FCO 21/3475, Beijing to FCO, no. 2136, 12 November 1986.
114 Harding, *A Fragile Relationship*, 146–7, 150–2, 166, 364.
115 Paul Kennedy, *The Rise and Fall of the Great Powers: Economic Change and Military Conflict from 1500–2000* (New York: Vintage Books, 1989), 425.

116 TNA, FCO 98/2439, FCO background brief: 'China's foreign trade', July 1985; FCO 21/3309, Evans to Howe, '1985 annual review: China', 20 January 1986.
117 Tang Renwu and Ma ji, *Zhongguo jingji gaige sanshi nian: Duiwai kaifang juan* [Thirty Years of China's Economic Reform: Volume on External Opening] (Chongqing: Chongqing daxue chubanshue, 2008), 116.
118 TNA, FCO 21/3477, Masefield to Wilson, 7 October 1986.
119 TNA, FCO 21/3688, Evans to Howe, '1986 annual review: China', 26 January 1987.
120 'Equity joint venture' has the status of a legal entity, in which the foreign and domestic partners have a stake and share profits and risks. 'Contractual' or 'cooperative joint venture' does not necessarily have the status of a legal entity, with rights and profit distribution contractually defined. TNA, FCO 40/1982, Annex I to Report by Economic Analysis Division, Economic Services Branch: 'Different forms of foreign investment in China', 16 October 1986.
121 TNA, FCO 21/3398, Wye to Ashton, 29 January 1986.
122 TNA, PREM 19/1682, 'China projects: UK list (as at 17 March 1986)'.
123 Markus Taube, 'Economic Relations between the PRC and the States of Europe', *The China Quarterly*, 169 (March 2002), 98; Harding, *A Fragile Relationship*, 368.
124 Yin Zhongming (et al.), *Zhongguo jingji gaige sanshi nian: Waijngmao juan* [Thirty Years of China's Economic Reform: Volume on Foreign Economic Trade] (Chengdu: Xinan caijing daxue chubanshe, 2008), 103.
125 Chung Chen, Lawrence Chang, and Yimin Zhang, 'The Role of Foreign Direct Investment in China's Post-1978 Economic Development', in Linda Yueh (ed.), *China and Globalization: Critical Concepts in Economics*, vol. 1: *Globalization and Chinese Growth (Part 1)* (Abingdon, Oxon: Routledge, 2013), 118–20.
126 TNA, FCO 21/3398, Hallett to Ashton, 23 April 1986.
127 TNA, FCO 21/3398, Parton to Fletcher-Cooke, 6 August 1986.
128 *Zhongguo Jingji Tequ wenxian ziliao*, vol. 2, 76–8; Shaun Breslin, *China and the Global Political Economy* (Basingstoke: Palgrave Macmillan, 2007), 85–6.
129 TNA, FCO 21/3402, Lord Young's meeting with Zhao Ziyang, 12 November 1986.
130 *ZZW*, vol. 3, 254.
131 Petros C. Mavroidis and André Sapir, *China and the WTO: Why Multilateralism Still Matters* (Princeton, NJ: Princeton University Press, 2021), 5, 102, 162–3.
132 Francine McKenzie, *GATT and Global Order in the Postwar Era* (Cambridge: Cambridge University Press, 2020), 101.
133 Harold K. Jacobson and Michel Oksenberg, *China's Participation in the IMF, the World Bank, and GATT: Toward a Global Economic Order* (Ann Arbor, MI: The University of Michigan Press, 1990), 92–4.
134 Naughton, *The Chinese Economy*, 382–7; Nicholas R. Lardy, *Integrating China into the Global Economy* (Washington, DC: Brookings Institution Press, 2002), 32–55.

135 L Yueh, 'The Rise of China', in Linda Yueh (ed.), *China and Globalization: Critical Concepts in Economics*, vol. 3: *China's External Impact and Future Growth in a Globalized World Economy (Part 1)* (Abingdon, Oxon: Routledge, 2013), 4.
136 Margaret M. Pearson, 'The Case of China's Accession to GATT/WTO', in Lampton (ed.), *The Making of Chinese Foreign and Security Policy in the Era of Reform*, 337–70.
137 TNA, FCO 98/2439, 'China and the GATT', enclosed in Shepherd to Spencer, 7 November 1985.
138 TNA, FCO 98/2877, Shepherd to Renwick, 23 July 1986.
139 Lardy, *Integrating China into the Global Economy*, 5–6.
140 Jacobson and Oksenberg, *China's Participation in the IMF, the World Bank, and GATT*, 11–12.
141 Men Honghua, *Zhongguo duiwai kaifang zhanlue (1978–2018 nian)* [China's Strategy of Foreign Opening, 1978–2018] (Shanghai: Shanghai renmin chubanshe, 2018), 246–7.
142 Keith, *Deng Xiaoping and China's Foreign Policy*, 56.
143 Gewirtz, *Unlikely Partners*, 274–5.
144 *DXW*, vol. 3, 194–7.
145 Pearson, 'The Case of China's Accession to GATT/WTO', 360.
146 See Li, *Breaking Through*, 377–83; C. Pei and L. Peng, 'Responsibilities of China after Accession to the WTO', in Yueh (ed.), *China and Globalization*, vol. 3, part 1, 66–79.
147 Thatcher, *Statecraft*, 192.

7

Democratisation and its limits, 1985–89

With the proclamation of the Universal Declaration of Human Rights by the UN in 1948, and the conclusion of the International Covenants of Political and Civil Rights and of Economic, Social, and Cultural Rights in 1966 (both of which came into force in 1976), human rights concerns became a key feature of the foreign policy of Western democracies.[1] In the 1980s, the triumph of neoliberalism, which linked free markets to political freedom,[2] in the United States and Britain provided further momentum to 'the rights revolution'. Margaret Thatcher and Ronald Reagan worked together to encourage 'a democratic tide around the world: in Asia, Latin America, Africa, and even the new stirrings in Eastern Europe and the Soviet Union'.[3] With the ascendancy of Mikhail Gorbachev in the Soviet Union in 1985, the prospects for democratic transition looked bright. By advocating 'perestroika' (restructuring) and 'glasnost' (openness), Gorbachev wanted to develop 'a social democratic variant of socialism'.[4] Thatcher was impressed by Gorbachev's political reform. When the Soviet president visited Britain in early April 1989, Thatcher professed in the welcoming dinner that 'economic change can only come about as a result of political change'.[5] To her, it 'takes longer to change a country economically than it does politically, particularly when that economic change involves changing central control into much more in personal initiative and enterprise'.[6] Thus, it was perhaps 'easier' for communist governments to start with political reform.[7]

Thatcher was not unaware that Deng Xiaoping's China had 'started on limited economic reform first'. By 1989, it was 'beginning to succeed in producing more goods for the people—on a limited scale certainly'.[8] It was the neoliberal assumption that globalisation and modernisation would make China increasingly Westernised, with the adoption of the rule of law and democratic institutions as the eventual outcome.[9] The violent suppression of the Chinese student protests at Tiananmen Square on 4 June, however, shattered that assumption. Nevertheless, Thatcher was a 'pragmatic neoliberal', and her commitment to democratic promotion abroad was not absolute. In view of the collapse of communism in Eastern Europe, Thatcher and the

FCO preferred evolutionary change to radical revolution, not least due to the implications for Gorbachev's position.[10] Similarly, they responded to the Tiananmen crisis in a pragmatic fashion.

The first section of this chapter focuses on Thatcher's approach to democratic promotion in China, and the second on her approach to that in Hong Kong.

Democratic promotion in China

Deng Xiaoping's political reform?

Britain and other EEC member states had high expectations that Deng Xiaoping's economic reform would lead to political liberalisation in China.[11] Yet the Thatcher government adopted a low-key and prudent attitude towards democracy and human rights issues in China. During General Secretary Hu Yaobang's visit to Britain in 1986, despite Amnesty International's briefings on Chinese political prisoners, Thatcher 'had spoken only in generalities with Hu over the matter'.[12] Not only Britain but also the United States preferred 'private diplomacy' to public condemnation of human rights violations in China. Due to strategic considerations, they regarded the Soviet Union as the 'greatest violator of human rights' in the world. Besides, it was believed that China should be given time to improve its legal system and behaviour, and that a tougher approach by the West would backfire by discrediting the reformers vis-à-vis the conservatives within the Chinese leadership.[13]

About six months following his 1986 visit to Britain, Hu Yaobang was forced to resign from his position due to Deng Xiaoping's gradual loss of confidence in his ability to deal with first 'spiritual pollution' and then 'bourgeois liberalisation'.[14] Encouraged by Fang Lizhi, a prominent astrophysicist at Hefei University in Anhui, to campaign for genuine elections to local assemblies, and against the backdrop of high inflation and rampant official corruption, students demonstrated in Hefei in December 1986. The demonstrations spread to other cities, including Shanghai, Tianjin, and Beijing, and lasted until mid-January 1987. As Deng talked of the harmful impact of 'bourgeois liberalisation', some people in China had advocated 'wholesale Westernisation', which in effect 'negated the leadership of the Chinese Communist Party and socialism'. All this affected China's political stability.[15] Consequently, the liberal-minded Hu, who was sympathetic towards the student protests, was purged by Deng. On 16 January, an enlarged meeting of the Politburo appointed Zhao Ziyang, then premier, as acting general secretary.[16] As the FCO's Far Eastern Department assessed it, Hu's purge was 'the most serious setback since Deng took over the reins in

1978'. Although statements by Beijing stressed that economic reform would continue uninterrupted, 'the pace of the programme, particularly on political reform, is bound to be affected'.[17]

The Thirteenth Party Congress, held between 25 October and 1 November 1987, confirmed the position of Zhao Ziyang as general secretary. In delivering his political report, Zhao provided a theoretical justification for the present policy while outlining the direction of future reform, particularly political reform. The CCP's basic line was summarised as 'one centre and two basic points'. The central task for China was economic development, while the two basic points underpinning it were adherence to the Four Cardinal Principles and persistence in the policy of reform and opening up. Moreover, Zhao put forward a theory of 'the primary stage of socialism'. As China was in an initial stage of socialist transformation, it was 'totally freed from the restrictions of orthodox socialist principles'.[18] Significantly, Zhao proposed political reform, the essence of which was separation of party and government. He outlined some measures, such as dividing government servants into fixed-term political appointees and permanent civil servants recruited by examination, and abolishing party leading groups in governmental organs.[19]

At its final session, the Thirteenth Party Congress elected a new Central Committee. Nine members of the Twelfth Politburo were not re-elected to the Thirteenth Central Committee, including Li Xiannian, Chen Yun, and Deng himself. The new Central Committee as a whole was smaller than the one elected in 1982, and the average age of its members was lower. At the First Plenary Session of the Thirteenth Central Committee on 2 November, a new Politburo Standing Committee was elected, comprising five members including General Secretary Zhao Ziyang and Acting Premier Li Peng (who became premier on 25 March 1988). Among the semi-retired elders, Deng kept only one formal post, as chairman of the Central Military Commission.[20] It is worth noting that at the plenum, a resolution was passed to the effect that Deng should be consulted on 'any matters of great importance' due to his 'political wisdom and experience'.[21]

In Ambassador Richard Evans' assessment, the personnel changes represented 'almost a clean sweep of the older generation', and the transition to 'a more technocratic, reform-minded leadership'. The new Politburo Standing Committee showed 'signs of balance between more liberal minded and the more bureaucratic wings in the party' – the former represented by Zhao Ziyang and the latter by Li Peng. Nevertheless, to Evans, it would be 'a mistake to talk about the "triumph" or "apotheosis" of the reformers'. It remained to be seen whether the elder leaders really would refrain from interfering in politics.[22] On the political reform proposed by Zhao, Evans envisaged that there would be 'plenty of room for foot-dragging', and the

Chinese people would 'have to wait a long time for anything we would call democracy'.[23]

In his political report, Zhao had provided a blueprint for reforming the political institution. According to Guoguang Wu, who had worked as an editor of the *People's Daily* and participated in the policy advisory group on political reform in the 1980s, Zhao was a 'liberal statesman' who 'valued institutionalization of political conduct and rule of law'. His concept of democracy 'combines socialism with liberal democracy, or something that falls into the ideational tradition of social democracy, opposing both state [or Party-state] and management dictatorships'.[24] If Zhao was an advocate of social democracy, the political reform Deng had in mind was more limited in scope. Deng had given four speeches about the issue in the autumn of 1986, focusing on eliminating bureaucratism and improving efficiency.[25] But by the year's end, the student protests (as mentioned earlier) propelled Deng to intensify the struggle against 'bourgeois liberalisation', which was synonymous with 'taking the capitalist road'.[26] As Zhao recollected later, Deng did not think in terms of the 'democratization of politics', but just 'a kind of administrative reform' involving only 'specific regulations, organization, methodology, and general morale', with the primary aim of making the party and the government more efficient.[27] Above all, Deng privileged stability and prosperity over democracy. During the visit to China by US President George Bush on 26 February 1989, Deng stressed the significance of a 'stable political environment' for China's economic reform. If the Chinese just sought 'the forms of democracy', they would achieve neither democracy nor economic development, but would only 'throw the country into turmoil'.[28]

A serious threat to China's stability began to unfold on 15 April 1989, when Hu Yaobang, the former party general secretary, died of a heart attack in hospital. What happened next was the transformation of Chinese students' mourning of their beloved leader into a broad-based pro-democracy movement in Beijing and in a large number of cities like Shanghai, Changsha, and Xi'an. After almost a decade of reform, the Chinese economy had witnessed profound improvement, but there was also growing public dissatisfaction with such problems as soaring inflation, rampant corruption, and social inequality. The broadcast of the television series *Heshang* (River Elegy), which explored the sources of China's backwardness and its authoritarian political culture, in mid-1988 had led to a rising tide of 'cultural fever' among students and intellectuals. Against the backdrop of a 'crisis of faith' in communism, hundreds of thousands of university students in Beijing and from other provinces converged at Tiananmen Square from late April to early June. They petitioned for dialogue with top officials, encamped inside the square, conducted hunger strikes, and called for political reform.[29]

In Zhongnanhai, a power struggle ensued in response to the large-scale student protests. On the one side were hardliners Li Peng and Yang Shangkun, who regarded the students' activities as a threat to the CCP leadership. On the other end was reformer Zhao Ziyang, who recognised the patriotic nature of the students' demands and saw 'the need to resolve the matter in a cool, reasonable, restrained, and orderly manner based on the principles of democracy and law'.[30] Taking advantage of Zhao's departure from Beijing for North Korea, the hardliners issued the first official verdict, in the form of a *People's Daily* editorial on 26 April, that the student demonstrations were 'premeditated and organized turmoil with anti-Party and anti-socialist motives'.[31] On 17 May, the Politburo Standing Committee held an enlarged meeting, which Deng attended. Despite Zhao's plea for compromise, it decided to impose martial law in Beijing.[32] Rather than being 'manipulated' by 'hard-liners' who had won a factional battle against 'reformers', according to Jeremy Brown, 'Deng himself decided that the student movement was turmoil that had to be crushed by force'.[33]

One of the reasons why Deng did not heed Zhao's advice was related to the visit to China by Mikhail Gorbachev on 15–18 May. Having been involved in the handling of the Sino-Soviet split in the late 1950s and early 1960s, Deng regarded his historic summit with Gorbachev as the high point of his long career. Although Sino-Soviet relations had improved since 1982, the symbolism of Gorbachev's visit (including a 'handshake', if not 'bear-hug', with the Soviet president) still mattered deeply to the eighty-five-year-old paramount leader.[34] However, Gorbachev arrived at a time when Tiananmen Square was being occupied by tens of thousands of students. In consequence, the grand welcoming ceremony had to move from the square to Beijing Airport. As the US ambassador in China opined, Deng was 'being personally humiliated by the student demonstrations'.[35] Worse still, during his conversation with Gorbachev on 16 May, Zhao had revealed the confidential decision of the First Plenum of the Thirteenth Central Committee that 'in all big questions [all party comrades] should turn to [Deng] as to a leader'.[36]

Before the formal imposition of martial law on 20 May, Zhao made last-ditch efforts to avoid confrontation by visiting the students in hospital (who were hospitalised as a result of their hunger strikes) and in Tiananmen Square. On the other hand, Beijing residents courageously blocked the PLA soldiers from entering the city. The Chinese troops had no choice but to withdraw to Beijing's surrounding areas for regrouping. The result was a two-week-long stalemate, until the night of 3 June. On the order of Deng and Yang, the PLA units forced their way into Tiananmen Square, firing on protesters in the process. By the early morning of 4 June, the soldiers had occupied the square. Although most of the students encamped inside the

Democratisation and its limits, 1985–89 203

square had withdrawn peacefully, the crowd resisting the troops from without had suffered heavy casualties. The exact number of deaths is unknown, but might range between hundreds and thousands.[37]

Condemning but not isolating China

The Thatcher government had been closely monitoring the unfolding of events in Beijing. In the Cabinet meetings in late April and early May, Geoffrey Howe reported on the restraint exercised by the Chinese authorities and the lack of military intervention so far. He appeared to be more critical of the students' tactics: 'It was unlikely that the students would obtain the political reforms they wanted by this means, whatever the continuing prospects for the economic reform programme.'[38]

The violent suppression of demonstrators on the night of 3–4 June, however, sent shockwaves through the British government, prompting Thatcher to respond immediately. On Sunday 4 June, Thatcher put out a statement on China:

> We are all deeply shocked by the news from Peking and appalled by the indiscriminate shooting of unarmed people. It is a reminder that, despite some recent easing of East/West tensions, a very great gulf remains between the democratic and the communist societies.

What happened in China was of 'particular concern' to Britain because of 'our responsibility for Hong Kong and our obligation – which we share with the Chinese Government under the Joint Declaration – to safeguard Hong Kong's future stability and prosperity'. Aware of 'the deep anxiety presently felt by people in Hong Kong', Britain would 'continue to stand by its commitment to a secure future for Hong Kong', while feeling 'confident that the Chinese Government also will continue to abide by their obligations under the 1984 Agreement'.[39] The following day, Howe summoned the Chinese chargé d'affaires in London to the FCO. Howe asserted that 'the British Government and people were united in condemning the merciless treatment of peaceful demonstrators, and deeply deplored the use of force to suppress the democratic aspirations of the Chinese people'.[40]

Significantly, Howe announced a number of measures about China and Hong Kong in the House of Commons on 6 June. 'In present circumstances', Howe proclaimed, 'there can be no question of continuing normal business with the Chinese authorities'. The British government decided to suspend all scheduled ministerial exchanges and all high-level military contact with China, and to ban all arms sales to China. Given the implications of the Beijing events for Hong Kong, Howe indicated that consultations about the drafting of the Basic Law had been suspended. He revealed that the British government was 'conducting a thorough examination of the programme for advancing and consolidating effective democracy in Hong Kong' before 1997 (see the next section). Regarding the 'slaughter in Peking' as 'a tragic setback to the campaign for democracy', Howe called for the House to send a 'united message' to China that '[e]conomic prosperity and personal liberty go hand in hand', and that the Chinese people would 'not forever tolerate government by repression'.[41]

Emotions were running high in the House of Commons. Gerald Kaufman (Manchester Gorton), shadow foreign secretary, 'condemn[ed] outright and in the strongest terms the abominable massacres which have been perpetrated in Beijing'. While expressing support for the suspension of arms sales, Kaufman called for the government to examine 'the possibility of cancelling all other exports to China, including exports of vehicles which could be used for repression of the civilian population'. He asked whether Howe would consult the other EEC members in order to ensure 'firm and concerted action', and whether Britain would consider taking action in the UN. David Howell (Guildford), chair of the Foreign Affairs Select Committee and a former Conservative minister, was appalled by 'the atrocities and butchery in Peking'. He urged Howe to remind Beijing of 'its obligations to maintain the stability, growth and prosperity of Hong Kong', not only 'now and up to 1997, but for 50 years thereafter and in perpetuity'. Paddy Ashdown (Yeovil), the Liberal Democrat leader, asked if Howe could try to 'build up international support for the joint declaration, perhaps through the medium of the United Nations'.[42] On the same day, in the House of Lords, Minister of State Lord Glenarthur made a similar statement on the events in China and the implications for Hong Kong.[43]

The British public was shocked by the carnage of Tiananmen Square shown on their television screens. On 5 June, the *Daily Mail* ran a commentary titled 'The Slaughter of the Innocents', with another piece reporting that 'China's Bloody Sunday' had left 'up to 2,600 pro-democracy demonstrators dead'.[44] An editorial of *The Times* wrote that the 'vicious massacre' in Tiananmen Square had 'earned China's leadership the fear and contempt of its own people and pariah status in the world'. While China had since 1979 been 'given the benefit of the doubt by Western governments', partly for 'geopolitical reasons' and partly because of 'the lure of its huge market', such 'optimism' about political liberalisation could 'no longer be justified' now.[45] A reader wrote to the editor of *The Times*, which printed the letter on 7 June, that Britain should 'stop kow-towing to the unelected, unrepresentative murderers in the Forbidden City', and that it was 'not too late to retreat from the shame that would well follow the implementation of the [Hong Kong] agreement as it now stands'.[46] Even the British left associated with the Society for Anglo-Chinese Understanding and the Communist Party of Great Britain condemned the killings at Tiananmen Square.[47]

While Thatcher and Howe issued statements expressing outrage on the Tiananmen bloodshed and suspended ministerial and military exchanges with China, they had no intention of going beyond these measures, at a time when the situation in Beijing remained in flux. As Howe told MPs on 6 June, it was 'important to maintain diplomatic, commercial and other human contacts, so far as is safe and possible, with the people and Government of China in order to try and retain the opportunity for recreating their previous open disposition'. Howe firmly believed that nothing should be done that would precipitate 'any increase in the isolation of the People's Republic of China'.[48] In essence, the FCO adopted a 'dual track approach' towards China. On the one hand, Britain 'used every appropriate opportunity to bring home to the Chinese leadership the revulsion felt in Britain at their brutal suppression of the democracy movement'. On the other, London was eager to convey the message that it was 'not our intention totally to isolate China within the international community'. Rather, Britain was ready to 'continue those aspects of [its] bilateral relations which primarily benefit the Chinese people (normal commercial trade and exchange programmes involving private individuals)', and to 'resume discussion with the Chinese of issues such as Hong Kong and Cambodia where British interests are directly at stake and China's cooperation is a prerequisite for political progress to be made'. In Ambassador Alan Donald's words, Britain's China policy should be 'both realist and opportunist'.[49]

The Thatcher government's restrained response was shared by the US administration. Having served as the US ambassador to the UN, the chief of the US Liaison Office in Beijing, and the head of the Central Intelligence Office in the 1970s, and as Reagan's vice-president in the 1980s, President George Bush had extensive foreign policy experience. He saw himself as a China expert, capable of conducting personal diplomacy with Deng Xiaoping in the pursuit of US interests.[50] On 5 June, Bush telephoned Thatcher, saying that he had just announced suspension of weapons sales and military contact with China, while deploring the use of violence by the Beijing authorities.[51] Bush acknowledged that his response was 'quite restrained and would not keep his critics, particularly those on the right, happy'. But before going any further, he wished to 'touch base' with the prime minister. Importantly, Bush was 'anxious to keep links to the Chinese Government open', to which Thatcher agreed.[52]

The British struggled to find out who was in charge in Zhongnanhai. Howe told the Cabinet on 8 June that 'Chinese leaders had been conspicuously absent from public view or the media in recent days'. There were reports that Deng had been 'ill'.[53] Then on the night of 9 June, Deng appeared on Chinese television. Addressing the generals and senior officers responsible for enforcing martial law in Beijing, Deng asserted that the 'turmoil' in Tiananmen Square had developed into a 'counter-revolutionary rebellion'. It was 'bound to occur sooner or later', and was 'determined by both the large international environment and China's own (small) environment'. Deng blamed the chaos on a 'handful of bad people', whose aims were to overthrow the CCP and the socialist system. Deng gave an assurance that China would continue its reform and opening up.[54] According to Ambassador Donald, Deng's address could mark 'the repudiation of the policies, particularly political and economic reform put forward by Zhao Ziyang' at the 1987 Thirteenth Party Congress.[55] Howe agreed that Deng's remarks 'pointed to more conservative economic policies, with slower growth and a renewed emphasis on central planning'. The Chinese economy seemed likely to 'take a step backward', Howe feared, although Beijing was trying its best to 'emphasise a return to normality'.[56]

Even before the June Fourth crackdown, Deng had hand-picked Jiang Zemin, then party secretary in Shanghai, to replace Zhao as the party general secretary.[57] The Fourth Plenum of the Thirteenth Central Committee, held on 23–24 June, confirmed the appointment of Jiang as general secretary and a six-member Politburo Standing Committee including Premier Li Peng. The plenum, moreover, passed a resolution on the mistakes committed by Zhao, who was formally dismissed from all his posts (and was placed under house arrest until his death).[58] In Howe's opinion, Jiang Zemin was 'the surprise choice to replace Zhao Ziyang'. It remained unclear how much influence Jiang would wield, given that the veterans Deng Xiaoping and Yang Shangkun were still on the scene. What is clear was that 'Chinese policy remained to pursue economic liberalisation without having to concede political liberalisation'.[59]

After clearing Tiananmen Square by force, the Chinese government turned to political reprisals against student leaders and dissidents, with rounds of arrests, trials, and executions. In response, Britain, both acting unilaterally and working closely with major international partners, 'condemned very strongly the continuing repression while avoiding a complete cut-off in contacts and lines of communication with China'.[60] The European Community had invested hopes in Deng's economic reform, but after Tiananmen it was forced to 'put the relationship with China into a broader political and human rights context'.[61] Back on 6 June, the European Council had issued a joint statement in Madrid and Brussels, condemning 'the violent repression used against peaceful demonstrators' and suspending all high-level contact.[62] When meeting at Madrid on 26–27 June, 'the Twelve' made a further statement on China, requesting Beijing to 'take into account the hopes for freedom and democracy deeply felt by the population'. The EEC decided to place an embargo on arms trade with China, postpone new cooperation projects, scale down cultural and scientific exchange programmes, and prolong visas to the Chinese students in Europe who wished to stay.[63] When the Group of Seven summit was held in Paris on 14–16 July, it was announced that all World Bank loans to China (which was the bank's largest single borrower) were postponed.[64] Moreover, the seven leading industrialised powers issued a strong statement, condemning 'the violent suppression in China in defiance of human rights'. They looked to the Chinese government to 'create conditions which will avoid their isolation and provide for a return to cooperation based upon the resumption of movement towards political and economic reform, and openness'.[65]

Nevertheless, the Thatcher government had no appetite to isolate China. Britain did 'not break off diplomatic relations with China', said Thatcher in a press conference, for it had 'a special interest with China, as well as Japan, and that special interest is our responsibility for the people of Hong Kong right to 1997'.[66] Indeed, the FCO had been seeking an opportunity to resume high-level contact with China as soon as possible. On 30 July, John Major, who had just replaced Howe as foreign secretary in the latest Cabinet reshuffle (the latter being 'demoted' to the posts of leader of the House of Commons and deputy prime minister), had a meeting with Chinese Foreign Minister Qian Qichen, inherited from Howe's diary, on the fringes of the twenty-nation peace conference on Cambodia in Paris. This allowed the pair to exchange views on Anglo-Chinese bilateral relations and Hong Kong, which impacted on each other. Major found Qian a 'modern diplomat', who was 'quietly inflexible'. Qian 'knew the strength of China's position in law over Hong Kong', yet also 'recognised the damage the Tiananmen Square massacre had done to his country abroad'.[67] Qian, for his part, regarded Major as a 'rising star' with a bright political future. When discussing the drafting of the Basic Law, Major suggested revising the article about the stationing of Chinese troops in Hong Kong after 1997, but Qian opposed this. Major agreed to resume the work of the Joint Liaison Group, which had been unilaterally suspended by Britain in June.[68] To Major, the meeting was 'civilised and relatively straightforward'. Although 'sharp differences were registered', he and Qian 'readily identified a way ahead and established a dialogue' between the two countries.[69]

During the annual meeting of the UN General Assembly on 27 September, Major continued to pursue Britain's 'dual track' policy towards China. He told the General Assembly that 'millions of us around the world were shocked to see Chinese troops kill and wound their fellow citizens on the orders of their own Government'. But the measures taken by Britain in response were 'not ... intended to isolate China'. Rather, Britain hoped to 'see China return to genuine reform and to repair the damage done to its international relations'.[70] On the margins of the proceedings, Major had 'useful discussions' with Qian Qichen on a bilateral basis.[71] Reflecting on his short, three-month tenure as foreign secretary (he was appointed chancellor of the exchequer on 26 October following Nigel Lawson's sudden resignation), Major believed that Britain 'had re-established relations with China after Tiananmen Square',[72] despite their continuing disagreement on Hong Kong's democratisation (see the next section).

Not only Britain, but other EEC member states, Japan, and the United States also sought to tread a fine line between condemnation and continued relations with China post-Tiananmen. Fearful of losing the China market to their competitors, West Germany and France opposed full sanctions on China.[73] Japan advocated the resumption of small-scale World Bank loans to China as early as October.[74] After barely a little over two weeks of the June Fourth crackdown, President Bush sent a handwritten letter to Deng Xiaoping, suggesting a special mission to China to conduct 'completely frank talks'.[75] On the weekend of 1–2 July, Bush's national security adviser, Brent Scowcroft, accompanied by Deputy Secretary of State Lawrence Eagleburger, secretly visited China. The message Bush wanted to convey was that the United States hoped to preserve its long-term relationship with China and to remove its sanctions; but due to domestic public pressure, this could not be achieved unless Beijing took steps to lift the martial law and to end the repression of dissidents.[76] In early December, Bush asked Scowcroft to undertake a second mission to China.[77]

The second Scowcroft mission came just a week after Thatcher had sent her own special envoy, Percy Cradock, to China to discuss the Hong Kong question. The political impact of Tiananmen on Hong Kong was tremendous, to which we now turn.

Democratisation in Hong Kong

Representative government and the Basic Law

As mentioned earlier, on 6 June 1989, Geoffrey Howe announced in Parliament that the British government intended to accelerate the pace of democratisation in Hong Kong. Prior to the 1980s, the British had contemplated but decided not to introduce democracy in Hong Kong due to a host of factors: China's opposition to political reform, which was seen as a path to Hong Kong's eventual independence;[78] the apparent political apathy of Hong Kong people, who wanted either to avoid entanglement with Chinese politics (the refugee generation) or to focus on money-making (the postwar baby boom generation);[79] and the colonial authorities' co-option of Chinese elites into an extended network of advisory bodies, thereby achieving what could be called 'administrative absorption of politics'.[80] With the emergence of a Hong Kong identity in the 1970s,[81] nonetheless, many university students, intellectuals, teachers, and social workers participated in social movements, such as recognition of Chinese as the official language and the 'Defend the Diaoyu Islands' campaign. With the onset of the Hong Kong question in the 1980s, more local residents were drawn into political debates. A number of political groups sprang up, for example, the Hong Kong Prospect Institute and the Meeting Point. Unlike the expatriate-dominated political organisations of the 1950s and 1960s, these new political groups were formed mainly by locally born Chinese in the service profession (like education, social work, and journalism).[82] Many of the founding members of the Meeting Point had been involved in the student and social movements in the 1970s. During the Hong Kong negotiations, the Meeting Point members – and other moderate, middle-class democrats – became so-called 'democratic reunionists', who supported Hong Kong's return to China under democracy and local autonomy.[83]

Against the backdrop of the emergence of the Hong Kong question and of an affluent middle class, in 1982 the British had taken the first step to develop representative government in Hong Kong. New District Boards, modelled on the existing local advisory bodies in the New Territories, were introduced in urban areas, with about one-third of the members of the boards elected by constituencies.[84] In 1984, the Thatcher government decided to speed up the development of representative government in Hong Kong. On 21 November, the Hong Kong government issued a white paper which proposed introducing indirect elections in the Legislative Council in 1985, while promising a further review in 1987. The total number of seats in the council in 1985 would be increased from forty-six to fifty-six, with official membership reduced from sixteen to ten, appointed unofficial members cut from thirty to twenty-two, and twenty-four members indirectly elected. Twelve of the latter would be elected by electoral college constituencies (consisting of directly elected representatives at the District Board and the Urban Council), and the other twelve by nine functional constituencies (such as commercial, industrial, and labour).[85]

In essence, the Thatcher government adopted a pragmatic and gradual approach to democratisation in Hong Kong, which could be attributed to two factors. In the short term, Thatcher and the FCO needed to 'sell' the Joint Declaration to Parliament, which alone had the power to authorise the relinquishment of Britain's sovereignty over Hong Kong.[86] As Private Secretary Charles Powell told Thatcher, Hong Kong's white paper on representative government would 'slightly accelerate the constitutional changes', which would be 'useful in Parliamentary debate on the Hong Kong agreement'.[87] In the long term, it was believed that the installation of a fully representative system in Hong Kong before 1997 would be the most effective way of preventing China's interference in Hong Kong affairs after the handover. In this vein, Britain apparently supported democracy in Hong Kong not on its own merits, but as a means to an end. At a personal level, Thatcher, while being firmly committed to individual freedom, harboured a 'neoliberal suspicion of democracy', which made her favour governance by elites and experts over parliamentary decision-making and power.[88]

The second factor was the attitude of UMELCO. Coming mainly from the business and other professional sectors, the unofficial members privileged economic prosperity and social stability over universal suffrage (the latter of which might lead to populist policies and high taxation). On the eve of the parliamentary debate on the Sino-British Joint Declaration, in late November 1984, Sze-yuen Chung and Roger Lobo led a UMELCO mission to London.[89] In a statement issued to the Thatcher government, while welcoming the development of a 'more representative form of government', the unofficials stressed that 'Hong Kong is not an independent state and can never be', and as such 'Parliamentary government as practised in the West, featuring adversarial politics, is not necessarily suited to Hong Kong'. Rather, Hong Kong should 'devise its own unique style of representative government, building on the proven elements which have been responsible for Hong Kong's success'.[90]

In 1985, the Hong Kong government enacted a new Legislative Council (Powers and Privileges) Ordinance. It aimed to empower the Legislative Council, soon including indirectly elected members, in line with the development of representative government. Accordingly, the ordinance defined 'certain powers, privileges and immunities' of legislative councillors, including freedom of speech and debate in the council, immunity from civil or criminal proceedings, and the power to summon witnesses to give evidence.[91] In addition, a monthly stipend of HK$8,500 (approximately £900) for UMELCO was introduced, so that the 'less well off' members of the Hong Kong community would not be deterred from standing for election.[92] The first indirect election of twenty-four seats in the Legislative Council took place on 26 September, with 'very high' voter turnout. Most of the elected candidates were professionals,[93] including Martin Lee, a liberal lawyer who contested the election in the legal functional constituency, and Szeto Wah, a democratic activist who ran for the education functional constituency. According to the post-mortem of the FCO's Hong Kong Department: 'The Hong Kong Government seems thus far to have achieved its aim of introducing gradual reform, based on existing representative institutions, without provoking explicit expressions of Chinese concern at the process.'[94]

While the British were developing representative government in Hong Kong, the Chinese commenced the drafting of the Basic Law with a view to writing into law the provisions of Annex 1 (China's basic policies regarding Hong Kong) to the Joint Declaration. Ji Pengfei, director of the State Council's Hong Kong and Macao Affairs Office, was entrusted with the overall task of drafting the Basic Law, with Vice Director Li Hou and Secretary General Lu Ping assuming day-to-day supervision of the process. A Basic Law Drafting Committee was formed, comprising fifty-nine members, thirty-six of whom came from the mainland and twenty-three from Hong Kong. While most of them came from a business background, the Hong Kong members of the committee also included elected Legislative councillors Martin Lee and Szeto Wah. A Basic Law Consultative Committee, consisting of 180 members from Hong Kong, was also set up to canvass local opinion.[95] The first full meeting of the Basic Law Drafting Committee was held in Beijing on 1 July 1985, during which a deadline was set for completing the writing of the Basic Law by early 1990. At its second full meeting on 18–22 April 1986, the committee established five special groups, each co-convened by a mainland member and a Hong Kong member, to undertake detailed drafting work about the different chapters of the Basic Law.[96]

Among the five special groups, the Special Group on Political Structure faced the most daunting task. The Sino-British Joint Declaration had only vague references to democracy, with the nature of the franchise unspecified. According to its Annex 1, the chief executive of the SAR should be 'selected by election or through consultations', whereas the legislature should be constituted by 'elections'. Indeed, when the working group led by David Wilson and Ke Zaishuo finalised the text of Annex 1 at the eleventh hour in September 1984, the Chinese side had proposed to change the wording concerning the selection of the Legislative Council, from 'an elective process' to 'elections'. As Wilson reflected after retirement: 'That formula was a point for dispute later, never specifying what sort of elections.'[97] Likewise, Sze-yuen Chung recollected that while the word 'election' in English was in the plural, the Chinese language did not have 'any plural or singular'. But 'at that time no one questioned what was meant by "elections" – what the plural signified, and whether it was the normal universal suffrage or direct, indirect, or functional'.[98] Consequently, the pro-business and pro-democracy members of the Basic Law Drafting Committee had vigorous debates about the scope and pace of democratisation in Hong Kong.[99]

It was Beijing that called the shots. To Zhou Nan, the chief Chinese negotiator of the Joint Declaration in 1984, the political system of the SAR should be executive led, and democracy should be gradually introduced in Hong Kong.[100] Lu Ping interpreted the meaning of the chief executive being 'accountable' to the legislature in terms of the present relationship between the governor and the Legislative Council, which was characterised by 'legislative consultation' rather than the legislature as the centre of decision-making.[101] Above all, Deng Xiaoping held the conviction that Hong Kong's political system should not be 'completely Westernised'. Hong Kong should not copy the Western model of 'separation of the three powers'. On the relationship between the central government and the SAR government (which was the remit of a separate special group), Deng argued that it was wrong to assume that Hong Kong affairs would be managed entirely by Hong Kong people, with Beijing playing no role at all. After 1997, Hong Kong residents could still 'criticise' the CCP or China, but if they turned their words into 'action' the central government would have no choice but to intervene. This was especially so if they attempted to 'convert Hong Kong into an anti-mainland base under the pretext of "democracy"'.[102]

Beijing feared that the development of representative government during the transitional period would turn Hong Kong into a de facto 'independent political entity' by 1997.[103] In a conversation with Geoffrey Howe on 4 June 1985, Foreign Minister Wu Xueqian said that although China was 'not opposed in principle to increasing participation in government by Hong Kong residents', the British government 'should be very prudent in its approach to democratisation'. Wu asked rhetorically that 'the Hong Kong people had not for a long time been particularly concerned about democratic rights'. If Britain introduced democracy 'with undue haste', it would be 'possible for a small and unrepresentative body of people to fish in muddy waters', which would have 'an adverse effect on Hong Kong's stability and prosperity'.[104] At a press conference on 21 November, Xu Jiatun, director of the Hong Kong branch of the NCNA, asserted that the development of representative government should be based on the Joint Declaration, but there was 'a tendency to deviate' from that agreement.[105] By 'pre-empting' China's promulgation of the Basic Law, Xu criticised, the British wanted the Basic Law to 'converge with the fait accompli' of democracy in Hong Kong, with a view to achieving 'drastic changes for thirteen years' (1984–97) and then 'no changes for fifty years' (1997–2047).[106]

Xu's remarks drove home to the British and Hong Kong governments the need for 'convergence' between the review of representative government and the drafting of the Basic Law. This would require consultation and cooperation between the two sides. After Britain and China had exchanged instruments ratifying the Joint Declaration on 27 May 1985 (and simultaneously registered it at the UN on 13 June of that year), the Joint Liaison Group was established to implement the agreement and to ensure a smooth transfer of government in 1997. The first few meetings of the Joint Liaison Group were held in a 'friendly and co-operative atmosphere', with the two sides reaching agreement on a number of issues such as Hong Kong's status as a separate contracting party to GATT.[107] At Li Hou's suggestion, the topic of Hong Kong's political system was added to the agenda of the group.[108]

Although Beijing had long insisted that the drafting of the Basic Law was primarily a Chinese responsibility, through the Joint Liaison Group and normal diplomatic channels, the Chinese actually welcomed British views and information, incorporating some of their ideas into the drafting process.[109] The FCO's Hong Kong Department was sanguine about Anglo-Chinese cooperation, arguing that Britain should 'use the [Joint Liaison] Group constructively ... both to educate the Chinese and to make the transfer of sovereignty as smooth as possible'.[110]

During the Queen's China visit in mid-October 1986, Ji Pengfei had a conversation with Geoffrey Howe about Hong Kong. Ji said that concerning the question of representative government, China considered it best for the 1987 review 'not to take place or to be delayed'. But realising that the Hong Kong government had already committed to it, China hoped that the review 'did not refer to direct elections', or, if mentioned, it should state that 'no decisions were taken'. Ji explained that 'Hong Kong opinion was divided' over the issue of political institution. After publication of the draft Basic Law, scheduled for 1988, 'the picture would be clearer', and a British review could then be undertaken. Howe agreed that the issue required 'prudent handling to avoid any shocks'. But the Hong Kong government 'must not be seen to renege on commitments because of criticism or pressure from the Chinese side'. Howe stressed that neither Hong Kong nor London had 'any preconceived views about direct elections'. The possibility of direct elections would be referred to in the 1987 review 'in the most balanced and prudent way'.[111]

In September and December 1986, Governor Edward Youde paid working visits to China to discuss Hong Kong affairs. The Chinese reiterated their hope that the British did not mention direct elections in the 1987 review.[112] Sadly, it was during his second visit that Youde died in his sleep on the night of 4–5 December. A statement issued by 10 Downing Street expressed deep distress for the passing of Youde, 'an outstanding civil servant who had worked selflessly for Hong Kong's interests'.[113] The Thatcher government appointed David Wilson, then assistant under secretary of state responsible for Asia and the Pacific and an experienced China hand, as the twenty-seventh governor of Hong Kong.[114]

In a memorandum to Thatcher dated 4 March 1987, Howe proposed to give China an analytical paper, setting out the pros and cons of different sorts of representative government but without pointing to any conclusions. Based on a chapter of the draft green paper (to be published by the Hong Kong government), the FCO paper considered the composition and selection of the Legislative Council, particularly the issue as to whether to introduce direct elections. If so, the options included introduction in 1988, agreement in principle but no introduction in 1988, and inclusion of directly elected seats in 1988 through replacement of those members elected by the electoral college constituencies.[115] With Thatcher's agreement, Howe handed over the paper to Wu Xueqian on the occasion of the world economic meeting at Berne, Switzerland, on 27 March. Although Wu 'did not give ground on the central Chinese concern' that Britain should 'not include the issue of direct elections' in the 1987 review, 'his request to that effect was not put with much conviction'. Howe had a further meeting with Wu in Bangkok, Thailand, on 21 April. This time, 'Wu did not press for omission of direct elections from the review, but he was more explicit than before in seeking [Britain's] specific agreement not to introduce direct elections in 1988' – a request that Howe declined.[116]

On 27 May the Hong Kong government released a green paper on representative government, inviting the public to respond by 30 September. A Survey Office was established to collect public views, and two independent monitors were appointed to oversee the office's work. A week before the end of the consultation period, both Howe, when meeting with Wu Xueqian in New York, and Governor David Wilson, when holding talks with Zhou Nan in China, briefed the Chinese in strict confidence on the likely outcome of the review. They proposed that if a majority of the public supported direct elections 'in principle', they would be introduced in 1991 or 1992. In reply, the Chinese suggested that 'if direct elections were not introduced until after the promulgation of the Basic Law, the Chinese Government would see that there was appropriate provision for them in the Basic Law'. In other words, China would not object to direct elections as long as the British did not introduce them in 1988. As Howe delightedly informed Thatcher, here was 'a highly satisfactory outcome', for Britain could secure 'the introduction of a measure of direct elections well ahead of 1997 with Chinese support and a guarantee of their survival thereafter'.[117] Thatcher agreed, attaching particular importance to Beijing's agreement to provide for direct elections in the Basic Law.[118]

By the time the consultation period ended, the Survey Office had received 124,228 submissions from individuals and 605 submissions from associations. Meanwhile, 164 public opinion surveys of various sorts had been conducted, and twenty-one signature campaigns collecting over 200,000 signatures had been launched. The white paper, published on 11 February 1988, noted that there was wide support for the principle of introducing direct elections in the Legislative Council, but the respondents were 'divided over the timing' of introduction. It concluded that a majority opposed direct elections in 1988. Instead, it proposed ten directly elected seats in geographically based single-seat constituencies in 1991.[119] Nonetheless, there appeared to be manipulation of figures by the colonial authorities. In campaigning against direct elections before 1990, pro-Beijing groups had prepared identical pre-printed letters, and asked their supporters to sign and then submit them to the Survey Office. Whereas these form letters opposing direct elections were accepted as individual submissions, 'the tens of thousands of signatures on a joint petition from the democratic lobby in support of direct elections counted as only one single submission'.[120] When Howe made a statement about the white paper in Parliament, the shadow foreign secretary dismissed it as 'a very timid White Paper', which 'does little more than tinker with the status quo'. Not only would direct elections not take place until 1991, but the proposal for only 18 per cent of the legislative seats or ten members was distinctly inadequate. Dr John Marek, a Labour MP (Wrexham), asked if Howe was aware of his 'sell-out' of Hong Kong, which 'caused considerable disappointment and a sense of betrayal among a large section of the Hong Kong community'.[121] There was a perception that the British government was 'kowtowing' to Beijing.

No sooner had Britain and China reached a private understanding about direct elections (or lack thereof) in 1988 than the Basic Law Drafting Committee released the first draft of the Basic Law in April. As there remained significant differences between the pro-business and pro-democracy members over the SAR's political system, the first draft, designed for solicitation of opinions, basically listed a number of alternative models for the selection of the chief executive and for the election of the Legislative Council.[122] After a period of public consultation, by late 1988 Louis Cha Leung-yung, the Hong Kong convenor of the Special Group on Political Institution, came up with what he called a 'mainstream model'. He proposed a fifteen-year timetable for democratisation based on the 'principle of gradual and orderly progress'. Accordingly, only 27 per cent of the Legislative Council (about sixteen members in an envisaged sixty-seat body) would be directly elected in 1997, a proportion that would be increased gradually to 50 per cent by the third and fourth terms of the council. The first three terms of the chief executive would not be directly elected, but selected by an Election Committee. A review of selecting the fourth chief executive would be conducted in 2011. After further changes, Cha's model formed the basis of the relevant chapter of the second draft of the Basic Law. Published by the NPC on 21 February 1989, the people of Hong Kong were given five months to comment on the draft Basic Law.[123] As Percy Cradock reported to Thatcher, the political system proposals in the draft Basic Law 'swing too much in the direction of conservative Hong Kong opinion'.[124]

British responses to the crisis of confidence

But the political situation in Hong Kong changed rapidly in view of the student pro-democracy movement in China. After the imposition of martial law in Beijing, on 21 May 1989 an estimated one million Hongkongers, unprecedented in the city's history, took to the streets in support of the Chinese students' cause. Another march, similar to the size of the first one, was held the following week. The All Hong Kong Alliance in Support of the Patriotic Democratic Movement in China (AHKA), an umbrella coalition of pro-democracy groups and activists, was established in Hong Kong. Chaired by Szeto Wah, an elected Legislative councillor and a Basic Law Drafting Committee member, the alliance helped furnish money, tents, and other supplies to the student protesters at Tiananmen Square.[125] Hong Kong's confidence was badly shaken by the June Fourth killings. The Hang Seng Index plunged a massive 582 points (losing 22 per cent of its value) on 5 June; there were runs on China-owned banks and panic buying in supermarkets; and the Hong Kong police resorted to tear gas to control a riot by hooligan elements in Kowloon on the night of 6–7 June.[126]

In response to the Beijing events, the Thatcher government suspended formal contact with the Chinese in the Joint Liaison Group and in the Land Commission. It suggested that China should postpone the promulgation of the Basic Law, scheduled for the spring of 1990.[127] (Beijing only agreed to extend the consultation period to the end of October.) To restore confidence in Hong Kong, Thatcher decided to '[move] rapidly to establish representative government based on direct elections, so that such representative government would be in place by 1997 and harder for the Chinese authorities to destroy'.[128] Clearly, Thatcher saw value in the instrumental use of democracy as a weapon against China's intervention in Hong Kong affairs after the handover. Although the 1988 white paper had proposed ten directly elected seats in 1991, and the second draft of the Basic Law envisaged an increase to a total of fifteen by 1997, the attitude of Hong Kong people towards democracy had shifted fundamentally in the light of the events in China. The Executive and Legislative Councils unanimously agreed that the number of directly elected seats in the Legislative Council should be doubled, from ten to twenty, in 1991, and should reach 50 per cent of the council by 1997. Local democrats clamoured for half of the legislative seats to be directly elected in 1991, and universal suffrage for the whole house by 1995.[129]

In Britain, MPs across the political spectrum, too, called for wider democracy in Hong Kong. After Howe had made a statement on China/Hong Kong on 6 June, Shadow Foreign Secretary Gerald Kaufman asked the government to urgently consider 'the possibility of bringing forward the elections [in the Legislative Council] scheduled for 1991 if possible to this year, but certainly to no later than next year', with a 'higher proportion' of its members directly elected. This would be a 'signal to the people of Hong Kong of our concern for their assured democratic future', he stressed. Paddy

Ashdown, the Liberal Democrat leader, urged Howe to consider the establishment by 1991 of a Legislative Council with at least half the seats directly elected. Other members in the House similarly spoke of their support for faster democratisation in Hong Kong – for example, Sir Peter Blaker of the Tories (Blackpool South), Dr Jeremy Bray of the Labour Party (Motherwell South), and Dr John Marek, also a Labour MP (Wrexham).[130]

Nevertheless, there were limits to Britain's democratic promotion in Hong Kong. As veteran Sinologist Percy Cradock reminded Thatcher, it was essential to 'avoid rapid, emotional responses' to the Tiananmen events.[131] Instead, Britain needed to 'strike a fine balance between on the one hand condemnation of the barbarities and on the other the need before long to do business with the regime in the interests of Hong Kong and of ourselves'. To Cradock, Britain 'did not conclude the [Hong Kong] Agreement with Deng because we thought he was a liberal'. Rather, it was because he 'ruled China and had in consequence the power to hurt or help Hong Kong'. As for the demands for accelerated democratisation, although Britain should 'keep in step with Hong Kong opinion', it also needed to 'take account of the risk that Peking reaction, particularly at the present time, would be hostile'. Cradock suggested that the matter be 'best handled by a quiet approach in Peking after the present turmoil has died down'.[132]

In response to the crisis of confidence, the Thatcher government contemplated providing Hong Kong's BDTCs with a right of abode in Britain. Back in 1986, the promulgation of the Hong Kong (British Nationality) Order provided for BDTCs to become British National (Overseas) (BN(O)) citizens by virtue of a connection with Hong Kong. In accordance with the nationality memorandum of the Sino-British Joint Declaration, BN(O) passport holders were permanent residents of, and had the right of abode in, Hong Kong.[133] Shocked by the Tiananmen carnage, in mid-June 1989, Dame Lydia Dunn and Allen Lee, senior unofficial members of the Executive and Legislative Councils, respectively, flew to London to lobby for Hong Kong's cause.[134] Calling on Thatcher on 23 June, Dunn opined that the people of Hong Kong were now facing 'an anxious time' and 'desperately needed support and reassurance', one way of which was to offer 'citizenship or right of abode for the 3.25 million BDTC passport holders'. Dunn stressed that she did not believe that the 'vast majority' of them would ever come to Britain, but an offer by London could have a 'calming effect'. Thatcher, while expressing her understanding of 'the feelings in Hong Kong', replied that 'there was no way she could offer citizenship to the 3.25 million BDTC passport holders'. Instead, Thatcher confided to Dunn that the British government was considering how to 'introduce greater flexibility on right of abode for certain categories of people in Hong Kong', some of whom could be Crown servants, entrepreneurs ready to invest in Britain, and other categories too.[135]

To reassure the Hong Kong people, Howe visited the territory between 2 and 4 July. He spoke of accelerating the pace of democratisation, while revealing that Britain would introduce a Bill of Rights for Hong Kong.[136] Howe made it plain that it was impossible for Britain to grant a right of abode to more than three million BDTC passport holders in Hong Kong, but the government was considering urgently a scheme which would make some provision for categories of people who wanted assurances.[137] During his visit, Howe was confronted with demonstrations and strong representations from UMELCO, businessmen, professionals, civil servants, and students, all of whom saw the right of abode in Britain as 'an insurance policy'.[138]

The Thatcher government could not meet Hong Kong's demands out of fear of non-white immigration to Britain. When it came to the globalisation of migration, race and domestic politics took precedence over the free movement of people in Thatcher's mind. On 10 July, Howe and Home Secretary Douglas Hurd sent a joint memorandum to Thatcher, recommending that up to 250,000 BDTCs (including dependents) be included in either a citizenship scheme or a combined citizenship/entry certificate scheme (the former was preferred).[139] Thatcher, however, had 'substantial reservations' about the proposed figure.[140] She was concerned about the 'effect on domestic public opinion', for the admission of a further 250,000 people from Hong Kong would increase the non-white population by 10 per cent.[141] (As a resident in Enoch Powell's constituency wrote to her anti-immigration MP, Hong Kong immigrants, while being seen as 'hardworking and law abiding', would 'also bring numerous problems' to an 'overcrowded' Britain.)[142] Moreover, Howe and Hurd's proposal that the scheme should be based on 'criteria other than rank or wealth' was at odds with Thatcher's emphasis on 'the economic benefit which immigrants might bring to the British economy through their entrepreneurial skills and ability to generate employment'.[143]

With the appointment of David Waddington as home secretary, who was 'much stricter on immigration' than Hurd,[144] and after lengthy discussions in Whitehall, the Cabinet met on 19 December to discuss a citizenship scheme for Hong Kong. The scheme aimed to 'persuade key people to remain in Hong Kong not to bring them to Britain'. It was decided that up to 50,000 heads of household (approximately 225,000 beneficiaries including dependents) could apply for full British citizenship without the need to leave Hong Kong. Under four categories of eligible applicants, the selection would be based on a 'points system' which gave more weight to entrepreneurs and professionals than to senior civil servants and 'vulnerable' individuals.[145] The following day, Hurd, now foreign secretary, announced the 'selection scheme' in the House of Commons. (Despite criticisms by some anti-immigration MPs, the British Nationality (Hong Kong) Act was promulgated on 26 July 1990.)[146]

Subverting China and internationalising Hong Kong?

To Beijing, the political fallout of Tiananmen on Hong Kong worked both ways. Back on 11 July, when receiving the Hong Kong members of the Basic Law Drafting and Consultative Committees, the new CCP general secretary, Jiang Zemin, had famously quoted a Chinese literary saying: 'Well water does not mix with river water.' Just as China ('river water') would not impose socialism on Hong Kong, Jiang asserted, so too should Hong Kong ('well water') not bring its capitalist way to the mainland.[147] More explicit warnings were delivered by Li Hou and Lu Ping in mid-November, when they gave interviews to Hong Kong reporters about the Basic Law. Li revealed that consideration was being given to adding provisions to the Basic Law to 'prohibit Hong Kong from becoming a base for subversion against the C[entral]P[eople's]G[overnment] and the socialist system'. He worried that 'the internationalisation of Hong Kong' would lead to 'foreign political forces' using Hong Kong to 'subvert' the Chinese government. Li warned against 'a rush towards democratisation' in Hong Kong, for it could create problems for 'convergence with the Basic Law'.[148]

In essence, Hong Kong's support for the Chinese student protests in the summer had hardened Beijing's attitude towards the Basic Law. Prior to the Tiananmen crisis, Beijing had been willing to accept many changes in the drafting process. For example, the requirement for a law against 'subversion' against China in the first draft had been deleted from the second draft, whose article 23 merely referred to offences that were already covered by existing laws in Hong Kong. But after 4 June, the mainland and pro-Beijing Hong Kong members of the Basic Law Drafting Committee brought the clause back to the final draft, with the addition of two further offences banning any activities in Hong Kong by, or with links with, foreign political organisations.[149] Beijing was particularly sensitive to the activities of AHKA, fearing a 'demonstration effect' on China – or the prospect of a 'peaceful evolution into democracy promoted by Hong Kong influences entering China through Guangdong Province'.[150] Consequently, Szeto Wah, AHKA's chairman, was expelled from the Basic Law Drafting Committee. After Beijing's brutal suppression of the student protests, Szeto and core members of AHKA undertook so-called 'Operation Yellow Bird' – a covert operation that facilitated the escape of Chinese students and dissidents from the mainland to the Western world by providing money to their smugglers, temporary accommodation in Hong Kong, and assistance in liaison with foreign governments about resettlement opportunities. (As Szeto recollected later, about 300–400 people had been rescued under 'Operation Yellow Bird'.)[151] While it might not have had full knowledge of AHKA's covert operations at the time, Beijing was so concerned about Hong Kong being turned into an anti-communist base that it brought pressure to bear on the British to outlaw AHKA, but to no avail.[152] Although Governor Wilson was aware that it would be 'very dangerous ... if Hong Kong became a centre for an underground movement dedicated to the overthrow of the Chinese Government',[153] as long as AHKA did not contravene Hong Kong laws it would be allowed to exist.

China, moreover, did not look with favour on Britain's efforts to mobilise international support for Hong Kong. During the European Council meeting in Madrid on 26–27 June 1989, the Twelve issued a statement on China with a reference that 'the recent events have caused great anxiety in Hong Kong'.[154] When the G7 summit took place in Paris on 14–16 July, the seven industrialised powers called for China to 'do what is necessary to restore confidence' in Hong Kong, recognising that 'the continuing support of the international community will be an important element in the maintenance of confidence in Hong Kong'.[155] During the Commonwealth heads of government meeting in Kuala Lumpur between 18 and 24 October, a communiqué with a reference to Hong Kong was issued: leaders of the Commonwealth states acknowledged 'the concerns of the people of Hong Kong', and agreed that 'those in a position to do so would assist in any way possible in promoting the continued prosperity of Hong Kong'.[156]

Beijing's propaganda machine lambasted Britain for playing the 'internationalisation card'. On 20 November, the *People's Daily* issued an editorial, criticising that recently 'senior British officials had used the so-called confidence crisis in Hong Kong to advocate internationalising the Hong Kong question'. These officials had claimed that 'since Hong Kong was a multi-national centre it ought to become an international economic centre insulated from mainland China'. China 'rejected the internationalisation of Hong Kong', which was 'Chinese territory'.[157] Three days later, the *People's Daily* carried a report on an article published earlier by Hong Kong-based *Wen Wei Po*. The article contended, from a legal perspective, that 'the position of Hong Kong as an international centre and the internationalisation of the Hong Kong issue were distinct issues'. The former was 'accepted by China and its continuation would be guaranteed after 1997', but the latter was 'in breach of the J[oint] D[eclaration] and the norms of international law'.[158]

Confronted with the demands for accelerated democratisation in Hong Kong on the one hand, and on the other Beijing's hardened attitude towards the Basic Law, Thatcher decided to send Percy Cradock as her personal emissary to China. On 4 December, Cradock, accompanied by Robin McLaren, assistant under secretary of state focusing on the Far East, and later joined by Ambassador Alan Donald, flew to Beijing in secret. His main purpose was to hand a formal letter from Thatcher to General Secretary

Jiang Zemin. In her letter, Thatcher stated that she hoped to 'reverse the trend of deterioration of the two countries' relations and restore the good communications of the past'. She stressed that Britain would continue to 'follow strictly the Joint Declaration', and it had 'no intention to use Hong Kong as a base of subversion' or to 'internationalize' the Hong Kong question. But facing 'huge pressure to "increase substantially" the quota of the directly elected members of the Hong Kong Legislative Council in 1991 – pressure that she could not ignore' – Thatcher hoped that 'China would keep in step with the UK's arrangement when drafting the Basic Law'.[159]

On his second day in Beijing, Cradock was received by Jiang Zemin for nearly two hours. Claiming that China 'had done nothing to harm Britain' but London had imposed sanctions on China, Jiang told Cradock that he had 'hard evidence of funds from Hong Kong being used to provide tents and general support for the demonstrators in Tiananmen Square' in the previous summer. While not denying Hong Kong's financial assistance to the Chinese students, Cradock gave an assurance that Britain had 'no intention of allowing Hong Kong to be used as a base to subvert the authority of the Chinese government'. In response to charges that Britain was attempting to 'internationalize' the Hong Kong question, Cradock reassured Jiang that Britain regarded Hong Kong as a 'bilateral issue' between London and Beijing, albeit adding that Hong Kong was 'a great financial and commercial centre, with links with many countries'.[160] Significantly, Cradock argued that 'Sino-British relations should be treated as a whole': 'if there were any difficulties in any aspect, progress could hardly be achieved in the overall relationship between Britain and China'. He suggested that if the two sides could reach an agreement on the issue of direct elections in Hong Kong's Legislative Council, 'the door to restoring good relations was open'. That is to say, 'the issue of the election in Hong Kong became a precondition for normalizing our relations'. Jiang, however, rejected such a linkage, which was likened to 'exerting pressure' on China.[161]

When meeting with Foreign Minister Qian Qichen on the last day of his visit, Cradock asked for China's 'flexibility' about the Basic Law, particularly Hong Kong's political system, so as to reflect the changing Hong Kong opinion since the Tiananmen events. Britain hoped that the Legislative Council should have at least twenty (not ten) directly elected seats in 1991, and a correspondingly larger number (than fifteen) in 1995. To Qian, there was a private understanding between China and Britain, reached in 1988, concerning Hong Kong's democratic development. Qian asked Cradock to convey a message to Thatcher: that the British and Chinese governments 'should strictly abide by the principles of the Joint Declaration', and that 'in the interest of Hong Kong's stability and prosperity matters already discussed and decided on should not be lightly altered'.[162]

In Cradock's assessment of the outcome of his mission, he noted that the discussions were 'civilized, though tough', and the two sides agreed on 'the need to look beyond recent events, to maintain contact and to restore a degree of co-operation, both in the wider international sphere and, more particularly, over Hong Kong'. But on the specific issue of Hong Kong's democratisation, there was no consensus on the number of directly elected legislative seats in 1991.[163] At a deeper level, Cradock believed that there was 'a profound suspicion on the Chinese side of Western-style democracy as a force for political change and instability, even chaos'. Worse still, the collapse of communist regimes in Poland (coincidentally, on 4 June), Hungary, East Germany, and Czechoslovakia added to Beijing's fears.[164] Deng Xiaoping had been closely observing the trend of 'upheaval' in Eastern Europe and the Soviet Union since the summer.[165] Deng and the conservatives believed that the United States and some Western countries were trying to promote the 'peaceful evolution' of socialist countries towards capitalism.[166] The revolutionary change in Eastern Europe vindicated Deng's use of force against the Chinese demonstrators back in June. The weakening of Soviet influence as a result of Gorbachev's political reform convinced Deng to avoid similar political liberalisation in China.[167]

About two weeks after Cradock's secret visit, Jiang sent a formal reply to Thatcher. While 'praising the UK's positive attitude toward China', Jiang stated that the final version of the Basic Law would 'not differ much' from the current draft. If the number of directly elected legislative seats was 'greatly exceeded', it would be 'difficult to accord with the Basic Law'. Nevertheless, Jiang's letter hinted that there was still 'a possibility of revising the draft', and 'the door [for Sino-British discussion] was not completely closed'.[168] Finally, the deadlock over Hong Kong's democratisation was broken after the exchange of seven communications between Qian Qichen and Douglas Hurd between 18 January and 12 February 1990. China agreed that the Legislative Council would have eighteen directly elected seats in 1991 – a modest number out of sixty seats, but an advance from the original ten – and twenty directly elected seats in 1997 – or 33 per cent of the council, which however would steadily increase to twenty-four seats in 1999 and thirty in 2003. Meanwhile, the British and Chinese agreed on the so-called 'through train' arrangement for Legislative councillors elected in 1995, who, after satisfying certain requirements, could serve a full four-year term until 1999. On 4 April, the NPC promulgated the Basic Law of the SAR. The composition of the Legislative Council corresponded with the latest exchanges between Hurd and Qian. The first chief executive would be selected by a broadly representative Selection Committee, but the 'ultimate aim' was selection by 'universal suffrage' according to 'the principle of gradual and orderly progress'.[169]

Similar to Thatcher's instrumental approach to democratic promotion in Hong Kong, China saw democracy as a means to an end, namely to ensure the success of 'one country, two systems'.[170] By agreeing to make Hong Kong's political system more democratic than what the drafts of the Basic Law had allowed prior to 4 June – and much more open than the Leninist party-state on the mainland – Deng Xiaoping and Jiang Zemin hoped to maintain prosperity and stability in Hong Kong, while harnessing the capital and skills of local people to serve China's modernisation.

Conclusion

The Thatcher government took a pragmatic, gradualist, and instrumental approach to democratic promotion in China and Hong Kong. When Deng Xiaoping launched the policy of reform in 1979, Britain, along with other Western countries, had high hopes that economic openness would ultimately bring about political liberalisation. Personally, Thatcher believed in evolutionary change rather than radical revolution. By pursuing a policy of constructive engagement with China, Britain hoped to bolster the reform-minded leaders while 'educating' them in democratic principles and international norms. Nevertheless, Deng was a 'pragmatic Leninist', who believed in administrative reform rather than political system reform.[171] The 1989 Tiananmen crackdown dashed all hopes for a liberal and democratic China. It demonstrated that Deng's vision of globalisation, which put sovereignty and stability above individual freedom and political rights, was very different from the neoliberal variant of Thatcher and Reagan. In response to the June Fourth tragedy, the Thatcher government resorted to a dual-track approach to managing the frosty relationship with China and the confidence crisis in Hong Kong. Thatcher 'oppose[ed] linking human rights issues in China with trade issues' as 'it would be counter-productive to slow down the rate of progress towards an open, free economy by seeking to cut China off from trade, investment and outside influence, since there are roads to freedom'.[172] Thus, Britain suspended high-level political contact, military sales, and financial loans to China, but there was no rupture of diplomatic relations or imposition of full sanctions. The FCO stuck to a policy of engagement with China, not least due to Britain's responsibility for the Hong Kong people right up to 1997.

Since 1984, the Thatcher government had been accelerating the development of representative government in Hong Kong, which was regarded as the best way of preventing China's interference in Hong Kong affairs after 1997. But the Chinese demand for 'convergence' with the Basic Law put a limit on Britain's democratic promotion in Hong Kong. As a result, Britain could not but negotiate with China over the pace of Hong Kong's democratisation. But in view of the Tiananmen crisis, the Thatcher government was under pressure from both the Hong Kong populace and British parliamentarians to accelerate the process of democratisation. Yet Thatcher's 'instincts' told her that 'this was the wrong time' to exert pressure on China. As she explained in her memoir: 'The Chinese leadership was feeling acutely apprehensive', and a forceful British attempt would have 'provoked a strong defensive reaction that might have undermined the Hong Kong Agreement'. Rather, Britain 'needed to wait for calmer times before considering moves towards democratization within the scope of the agreement'.[173] China became suspicious of British motives in Hong Kong, thanks to Thatcher's efforts to mobilise international support for the city and the colonial authorities' tolerance of the activities of AHKA. Fears about the 'internationalisation' of the Hong Kong question and the creation of an anti-communist base on its doorstep hardened China's attitude towards the Basic Law, whose drafting process reached its final stage in late 1989.

Did Thatcher and the FCO unashamedly 'kowtow' to China? Or did they pragmatically make the most of a difficult situation in 1989? In Parliament and within Hong Kong society, there were emotional talks about Britain's 'sell-out' and 'betrayal', be it about the slow pace of Hong Kong's democratisation or the Thatcher government's reluctance to grant British citizenship to Hong Kong residents.[174] Instead of 'kowtowing' to China in secret, though, Britain issued public statements to condemn and imposed limited sanctions on Beijing. When John Major, as foreign secretary, resumed high-level contact with Qian Qichen in late July, and Cradock, as Thatcher's special envoy, visited China for secret talks in early December, they were not practising 'appeasement' in the style of Neville Chamberlain – that is, sacrificing the interests of a small place (Hong Kong) in order to satisfy the ambitions of the more powerful country (China). If anything, Cradock saw the linkage between Hong Kong and China the other way round: only by resolving the dispute over Hong Kong's political system could Anglo-Chinese relations be improved. What Cradock aimed to achieve was to persuade, or 'educate', the Chinese leaders that Hong Kong's attitude towards democracy had changed since 4 June, and their accommodation of local political aspirations was essential to restoring confidence in the territory and normalcy in Anglo-Chinese relations. Cradock's quiet diplomacy did not immediately bear fruit, but it was followed by the exchange of seven communications between Douglas Hurd and Qian in early 1990, which broke the impasse over Hong Kong's direct elections. As Cradock said of the 1990 understanding some years later, 'this was done with Chinese agreement, because that was the only way the improvements would outlast 1997'.[175]

Notes

1 Yongjin Zhang and Barry Buzan, 'China and the Global Reach of Human Rights', *The China Quarterly*, 241 (March 2020), 171–2.
2 Cronin, *Global Rules*, 148–9. It is paradoxical that neoliberal theorists are 'profoundly suspicious of democracy': 'Governance by majority rule is seen as a potential threat to individual rights and constitutional liberties.' Harvey, *A Brief History of Neoliberalism*, 66.
3 MTF, Speeches at White House state banquet (Thatcher and Reagan), 16 November 1988, www.margaretthatcher.org/document/107384.
4 Brown, *The Human Factor*, 234.
5 MTF, Thatcher speech at dinner for Gorbachev, 6 April 1989, www.margaretthatcher.org/document/107630deng.
6 MTF, Thatcher press conference in Tokyo, 21 September 1989, www.margaretthatcher.org/document/107772.
7 MTF, Thatcher press conference in Moscow, 23 September 1989, www.margaretthatcher.org/document/107776.
8 *Ibid.*
9 Ikenberry, *A World Safe for Democracy*, 263; Jacques, *When China Rules the World*, 12, 16.
10 See Moore, *Margaret Thatcher*, vol. 3, 484–6, 491–2; Brown, *The Human Factor*, 278–87.
11 Thomas Christiansen, Emil Kirchner, and Uwe Wissenbach, *The European Union and China* (London: Red Globe Press, 2019), 7.
12 Rosemary Foot, *Rights beyond Borders: The Global Community and the Struggle over Human Rights in China* (Oxford: Oxford University Press, 2000), 95.
13 *Ibid.*, 92, 109–10; Zhang and Buzan, 'China and the Global Reach of Human Rights', 173.
14 On the gradual falling out between Deng and Hu, see Pantsov with Levine, *Deng Xiaoping*, 395–403.
15 *DXN*, vol. 2, 1180.
16 Bao, Chiang, and Ignatius (eds), *Prisoner of the State*, 161–82.
17 TNA, FCO 21/3698, Sullivan to Private Secretary, 19 January 1987.
18 Bao, Chiang, and Ignatius (eds), *Prisoner of the State*, 204–8. Quote on 206.
19 Richard Baum, 'Zhao Ziyang and China's "Soft Authoritarian" Alternative', in Guoguang Wu and Helen Lansdowne (eds), *Zhao Ziyang and China's Political Future* (Abingdon, Oxon: Routledge, 2008), 111; TNA, PREM 19/2597, Beijing to FCO, no. 1831, 26 October 1987.
20 TNA, PREM 19/2597, Beijing to FCO, no. 1896, 2 November 1987; Bao, Chiang, and Ignatius (eds), *Prisoner of the State*, 208–11.
21 Bao, Chiang, and Ignatius (eds), *Prisoner of the State*, 46.
22 TNA, PREM 19/2597, Beijing to FCO, no. 1904, 3 November 1987.
23 TNA, PREM 19/2597, Beijing to FCO, no. 1831, 26 October 1987.
24 Guoguang Wu, 'Democracy and Rule of Law in Zhao Ziyang's Political Reform', in Wu and Lansdowne (eds), *Zhao Ziyang and China's Political Future*, 52.

25 See *DXW*, vol. 3, 176–80.
26 *Ibid.*, 123–5.
27 Bao, Chiang, and Ignatius (eds), *Prisoner of the State*, 247.
28 *DXN*, vol. 2, 1267.
29 Chen Jian, 'Tiananmen and the Fall of the Berlin Wall: China's Path toward 1989 and Beyond', in Jeffrey A. Engel (ed.), *The Fall of the Berlin Wall: The Revolutionary Legacy of 1989* (New York: Oxford University Press, 2009), 106–9.
30 Bao, Chiang, and Ignatius (eds), *Prisoner of the State*, 19.
31 *Ibid.*, 10.
32 *DXN*, vol. 2, 1276–7.
33 Jeremy Brown, *June Fourth: The Tiananmen Protests and Beijing Massacre of 1989* (Cambridge: Cambridge University Press, 2021), xii.
34 On Sino-Soviet normalisation and the Deng–Gorbachev summit, see Sergey Radchenko, *Unwanted Visionaries: The Soviet Failure in Asia at the End of the Cold War* (New York: Oxford University Press, 2014), 161–7.
35 James Lilley with Jeffrey Lilley, *China Hands: Nine Decades of Adventure, Espionage, and Diplomacy in Asia* (New York: PublicAffairs, 2004), 301, 309.
36 The Wilson Center Digital Archive, 'Excerpts from conversation between Mikhail Gorbachev and Zhao Ziyang', 16 May 1989, http://digitalarchive.wilsoncenter.org/document/119290.
37 According to Brown, the number of deaths could be as low as 478, as high as 3,000, or somewhere in between. Brown, *June Fourth*, xiii.
38 TNA, CAB 128/93, CC(89)15th Conclusions, 27 April 1989; CC(89)16th Conclusions, 4 May 1989.
39 TNA, PREM 19/2597, Thatcher statement on recent events in Beijing, 4 June 1989.
40 *Hansard*, House of Commons Debates, vol. 154, 6 June 1989, col. 30.
41 *Ibid.*, cols 30–2.
42 *Ibid.*, cols 32–5.
43 *Hansard*, House of Lords Debates, vol. 508, 6 June 1989, cols 744–55.
44 'The slaughter of the innocents', *Daily Mail* (5 June 1989); 'Angry crowds launch their fightback', *ibid.*
45 'Message from the Square', *The Times* (5 June 1989).
46 Letters to the Editor, *The Times* (7 June 1989).
47 Buchanan, *East Wind*, 220–1.
48 *Hansard*, House of Commons Debates, vol. 154, 6 June 1989, cols 33, 43–4.
49 TNA, FCO 21/4196, Millington to McLaren, 10 October 1989.
50 Jeffrey A. Engel (ed.), *The China Diary of George H. W. Bush: The Making of a Global President* (Princeton, NJ: Princeton University Press, 2008); Kristina Spohr, *Post Wall, Post Square: Rebuilding the World after 1989* (London: William Collins, 2019), 28–30.
51 Lilley, *China Hands*, 324; Mann, *About Face*, 196.
52 TNA, PREM 19/2597, Powell to Wall, 5 June 1989; MTF, Memo of conversation, 5 June 1989, 12:02–12:09 pm, Oval Office, www.margaretthatcher.org/document/149365.

53 TNA, CAB 128/93, CC(89)20th Conclusions, 8 June 1989.
54 'Address to officers at the rank of general and above in command of the troops enforcing martial law in Beijing', 9 June 1989, *DXW*, vol. 3; TNA, PREM 19/2597, Cradock to Powell, 9 June 1989.
55 TNA, PREM 19/2597, Beijing to FCO, no. 1104, 10 June 1989.
56 TNA, CAB 128/94, CC(89)22nd Conclusions, 22 June 1989.
57 *DXN*, vol. 2, 1281–2.
58 *Ibid.*, 1282–3.
59 TNA, CAB 128/94, CC(89)23rd Conclusions, 29 June 1989.
60 TNA, CAB 128/94, CC(89)22nd Conclusions, 22 June 1989.
61 Christiansen, Kirchner, and Wissenbach, *The European Union and China*, 75.
62 Secretariat-General of the Commission (ed.), *Bulletin of the European Communities*, 22: 6 (1989), Annex II: Declaration on China, 87.
63 *Ibid.*, 17.
64 Mann, *About Face*, 197; Foot, *Rights beyond Borders*, 117.
65 TNA, PREM 19/2634, Declaration on China at the G7 summit in Paris, 15 July 1989.
66 MTF, Thatcher press conference in Tokyo, 21 September 1989, www.margaretthatcher.org/document/107772.
67 John Major, *The Autobiography* (London: HarperCollins, 2020), 119–20.
68 Qian Qichen, *Ten Episodes in China's Diplomacy* (New York: HarperCollins, 2006), 256.
69 Major, *The Autobiography*, 120.
70 United Nations Digital Library, Forty-fourth Session of General Assembly, Provisional verbatim record of the eighth meeting at headquarters, New York, 27 September 1989, https://digitallibrary.un.org/record/76242?ln=en.
71 TNA, CAB 128/94, CC(89)30th Conclusions, 5 October 1989.
72 Major, *The Autobiography*, 129.
73 Christiansen, Kirchner, and Wissenbach, *The European Union and China*, 15.
74 Qian, *Ten Episodes in China's Diplomacy*, 149–50.
75 *DXN*, vol. 2, 1282.
76 Mann, *About Face*, 206–9; The National Security Archive, The George Washington University, National Security Archive Electronic Briefing Book No. 16, 'Tiananmen Square, 1989: The Declassified History', Document 33, State Department document entitled 'Themes', 29 June 1989, https://nsarchive2.gwu.edu/NSAEBB/NSAEBB16/#d33.
77 See Mann, *About Face*, 218–23; *DXN*, vol. 2, 1304–5.
78 Pepper, *Keeping Democracy at Bay*.
79 Gordon Matthews, Eric Kit-wai Ma, and Tai-lok Lui, *Hong Kong, China: Learning to Belong to a Nation* (London: Routledge, 2008), 27–35.
80 Ambrose Yeo-chi King, 'Administrative Absorption of Politics in Hong Kong: Emphasis on the Grass Roots Levels', *Asian Survey*, 15: 5 (May 1975), 422–39.
81 Tsang, *A Modern History of Hong Kong*, 190–6.
82 Alvin Y. So, *Hong Kong's Embattled Democracy: A Societal Analysis* (Baltimore, MD and London: The Johns Hopkins University Press, 1999), 67.

83 Ho-fung Hung, *City on the Edge: Hong Kong under Chinese Rule* (Cambridge: Cambridge University Press, 2022), 124–5, 154–6.
84 Pepper, *Keeping Democracy at Bay*, 189.
85 *White Paper: The Further Development of Representative Government in Hong Kong* (Hong Kong: Government Printer, November 1984).
86 During the parliamentary debate on the Sino-British Joint Declaration on 5 December, at least nineteen MPs spoke of the need for a more representative system in Hong Kong, most of whom favoured a gradual process. TNA, FCO 40/1796, 'MP's comments on constitutional development in Hong Kong over past 12 months', enclosed in Galsworthy to Wilson, 24 October 1985.
87 TNA, PREM 19/1530 Part 17, Howe to Thatcher, 8 November 1984.
88 Harvey, *A Brief History of Neoliberalism*, 66, 76, 82.
89 Chung, *Hong Kong's Journey to Reunification*, 122–6.
90 TNA, PREM 19/1503, Statement issued by the unofficial members of the Hong Kong Executive and Legislative Councils on 29 November 1984, 'The future of Hong Kong'.
91 TNA, FCO 40/1813, 'The Legislative Council (Powers and Privileges) Ordinance 1985, No. 35 of 1985', enclosed in Wing to Howe, 5 July 1985.
92 TNA, FCO 40/1795, Galsworthy to Wilson, 20 May 1985.
93 TNA, T 450/481, HK to FCO, no. 2030, 27 September 1985.
94 TNA, FCO 40/1796, Galsworthy to PS/Renton, 7 October 1985.
95 Xu, *Xu Jiatun Xianggang huiyilu*, vol. 1, 153, 156–64.
96 Li, *Huigui de lichen*, 144–5; Danny Gittings, *Introduction to the Hong Kong Basic Law*, 2nd edition (Hong Kong: Hong Kong University Press, 2016), 21.
97 CAC, GBR/0014/DOHP 83, Interview with David Clive Wilson (Lord Wilson of Tillyorn), 19 September 2003, pp. 42–3, www.chu.cam.ac.uk/media/uploads/files/Wilson.pdf.
98 BLO, MSS.Ind.Ocn.s.328, Interview with Sir S.Y. Chung, file 328/2, tape 8, side 2, p. 349.
99 Xu, *Xu Jiatun Xianggang huiyilu*, vol. 1, 184–92.
100 Zhang and Xu (eds), *Zhou Nan jiemi GangAo huigui*, 174–5.
101 Xu, *Xu Jiatun Xianggang huiyilu*, vol. 1, 185; Lu, *Lu Ping koushu Xianggang huigui*, 66.
102 *DXN*, vol. 2, 1179.
103 Gao Wanglai, *Daguo tanpan moulue – ZhongYing Xianggang tanpan neimu* [The Negotiating Strategy of Great Power: An Inside Story of Sino-British Negotiation over Hong Kong] (Beijing: Shishi chubanshe, 2012), 131, 143.
104 TNA, FCO 21/3010, Record of meeting between Howe and Wu Xueqian on 4 June 1985.
105 TNA, FCO 40/1814, Secretary (General Duties) to Powell, undated, attaching Addenda to the summary of media reports on constitutional reforms in Hong Kong.
106 Xu, *Xu Jiatun Xianggang huiyilu*, vol. 1, 173.
107 TNA, FCO 40/2210, 'Annual report on Hong Kong 1985–86', presented to Parliament by Howe, February 1987.

108 Li, *Huigui de lichen*, 190.
109 Xu, *Xu Jiatun Xianggang huiyilu*, vol. 1, 154; Li, *Huigui de lichen*, 190; Chung, *Hong Kong's Journey to Reunification*, 161.
110 TNA, FCO 40/1887, Galsworthy to Youde, 1 August 1985.
111 TNA, PREM 19/1796, Beijing to FCO, no. 1989, 14 December 1986.
112 Li, *Huigui de lichen*, 192.
113 TNA, PREM 19/2230, FCO to HK, no. 2796, 5 December 1986.
114 TNA, PREM 19/2230, Powell to Galsworthy, 5 January 1987.
115 TNA, PREM 19/2230, Howe to Thatcher, 4 March 1987.
116 TNA, PREM 19/2230, Howe to Thatcher, 6 May 1987.
117 TNA, PREM 19/2727, Howe to Thatcher, 2 October 1987; Li, *Huigui de lichen*, 195.
118 TNA, PREM 19/2727, Powell to Galsworthy, 5 October 1987.
119 TNA, PREM 19/2727, Drafts of the key chapters of the white paper, attached in Howe to Thatcher, 6 January 1988.
120 Ming K. Chan, 'Decolonization without Democracy: The Birth of Pluralistic Politics in Hong Kong', in Friedman (ed.), *The Politics of Democratization*, 164–5.
121 *Hansard*, House of Commons Debates, vol. 127, 10 February 1988, cols 355, 357.
122 Gittings, *Introduction to the Hong Kong Basic Law*, 23–4.
123 Li, *Huigui de lichen*, 168–71.
124 TNA, PREM 19/2727, Cradock to Thatcher, 21 February 1989.
125 Szeto Wah, *Da jiang dong qu: Szeto Wah huiyilu* [The Great River Flows Eastward: The Memoir of Szeto Wah] (Hong Kong: Oxford University Press, 2011), 297–9.
126 TNA, PREM 19/2728, HK to FCO, no. 1862, 6 June 1989; CAB 128/93, CC(89)20th Conclusions, 8 June 1989.
127 TNA, PREM 19/2728, HK to FCO, no. 1887, 7 June 1989.
128 TNA, PREM 19/2728, Powell to Thatcher, 7 June 1989.
129 Xu, *Xu Jiatun Xianggang huiyilu*, vol. 2, 416–19.
130 *Hansard*, House of Commons Debates, vol. 154, 6 June 1989, cols 32–3, 35–6, 38–9.
131 Cradock, *Experiences of China*, 225.
132 TNA, PREM 19/2728, Cradock to Thatcher, 12 June 1989.
133 TNA, FCO 40/2210, 'Annual report on Hong Kong 1985–86', presented to Parliament by Howe, February 1987.
134 Lydia Dunn was made a life peer in the Queen's 1989 New Year Honours List.
135 TNA, PREM 19/2728, Memorandum of conversation between Thatcher and Lydia Dunn and Allen Lee, 23 June 1989.
136 In 1968 Britain had signed the International Covenant on Civil and Political Rights, which took effect in 1976 and was also applied to Hong Kong that year. But as of mid-1989, the colonial authorities had not started local legislation. In March 1990, the Hong Kong government introduced a Bill of Rights, incorporating the spirit of the covenant, which was passed in June 1991. Wang Fengchao, *Xianggang zhengzhi fazhan licheng (1843–2015)* [The Course

of Development of Hong Kong's Political Institutions, 1843–2015] (Hong Kong: Chung Hwa Book (HK), 2017), 91–3.
137 TNA, CAB 128/94, CC(89)24th Conclusions, 6 July 1989.
138 TNA, PREM 19/2728, Howe/Hurd to Thatcher, 10 July 1989.
139 TNA, PREM 19/2728, Howe/Hurd to Thatcher, 10 July 1989.
140 TNA, PREM 19/2728, Powell to Walters, 11 July 1989.
141 TNA, PREM 19/2728, Appleyard to Thatcher, 14 July 1989.
142 CAC, Papers of Enoch Powell, POLL 3/2/1/76, Reid to Powell, 23 June 1989; Powell's private secretary to Reid, 29 June 1989.
143 TNA, PREM 19/2728, Appleyard to Thatcher, 14 July 1989.
144 Moore, *Margaret Thatcher*, vol. 3, 572–3; Hurd, *Memoirs*, 531.
145 TNA, CAB 128/94, CC(89)39th Conclusions, 19 December 1989.
146 CAC, Papers of Enoch Powell, POLL 3/2/1/76, Statement by Hurd to House of Commons, 20 December 1989; Moore, *Margaret Thatcher*, vol. 3, 574–5, 584.
147 Yuan Qiushi, *Xianggang huigui dashiji* [A Chronicle of the Return of Hong Kong] (Hong Kong: Joint Publishing (HK), 2015), 93.
148 TNA, FCO 40/2672, HK to FCO, no. 2484/3836, 20 November 1989. Also see FCO 40/2673, HK to FCO, no. 3849, 21 November 1989.
149 Gittings, *Introduction to the Hong Kong Basic Law*, 26–7.
150 Edward Friedman, 'Introduction', in Friedman (ed.), *The Politics of Democratization*, 10.
151 Szeto, *Da jiang dong qu*, 339–48.
152 Xu, *Xu Jiatun Xianggang huiyilu*, vol. 2, 394–6; MTF, CIA Electronic Reading Room, CIA memo: 'China-HK-UK: Negotiations to resume', 2 August 1989, www.margaretthatcher.org/document/149413.
153 TNA, FCO 40/2797, Wilson to Major, 27 July 1989.
154 Secretariat-General of the Commission (ed.), *Bulletin of the European Communities*, 22: 6 (1989), Annex II: Declaration on China, 17.
155 TNA, PREM 19/2634, Declaration on China at the G7 summit in Paris, 15 July 1989.
156 MTF, Thatcher press conference after the Kuala Lumpur Commonwealth summit, 24 October 1989, www.margaretthatcher.org/document/107802.
157 TNA, FCO 40/2673, Beijing to FCO, no. 2032, 20 November 1989.
158 TNA, FCO 40/2673, Beijing to FCO, no. 2051, 23 November 1989.
159 Qian, *Ten Episodes in China's Diplomacy*, 257–8.
160 Cradock, *Experiences of China*, 229–30.
161 Qian, *Ten Episodes in China's Diplomacy*, 258.
162 Cradock, *Experiences of China*, 230–1; Qian, *Ten Episodes in China's Diplomacy*, 259.
163 Cradock, *Experiences of China*, 229, 232.
164 Ibid., 231–2.
165 *DXN*, vol. 2, 1286–8.
166 Ibid., 1289; Harding, *A Fragile Relationship*, 235–7.
167 Radchenko, *Unwanted Visionaries*, 180, 196.
168 Qian, *Ten Episodes in China's Diplomacy*, 258–9.

169 Li, *Huigui de lichen*, 199–203; Wang, *Xianggang zhengzhi fazhan licheng*, 70–5.
170 Lau, *Xianggang de dute minzhulu*, 70.
171 Shambaugh, *China's Leaders*, 95, 325.
172 Thatcher, *The Path to Power*, 530.
173 Thatcher, *The Downing Street Years*, 495.
174 William Shawcross, *Kowtow!* (London: Chatto & Windus, 1989), 9–10, 42.
175 SJC, Papers of Percy Cradock, Cradock/B/10, 'Argument does not hold water', published in *South China Morning Post* (30 September 1996).

Conclusion

Before we draw some conclusions, it is necessary to examine the impact of the Tiananmen crisis on China's application for accession to GATT. How the Thatcher government saw the issue in 1989 reflected its perception of China's role in economic globalisation amid political repression at home.

China and GATT, 1989

Shortly after China's announcement on its intention to join GATT, in 1987 a working party was established with the remit of developing a draft protocol of accession.[1] During the first phase of negotiation, the Chinese government submitted a memorandum on China's foreign trade regime to the working party,[2] which then addressed a series of questions to Beijing.[3] By December 1988, the Chinese had provided their replies and additional information to the working party.[4]

During the second phase of negotiation in early 1989, the European Community, the United States, and Canada all expressed concerns that China's foreign trade regime diverged from 'GATT's open market principles'. Although Beijing maintained that China was seeking to establish a 'planned market (or commodity) economy', developed countries were sceptical about 'the true meaning of this contradiction in terms'.[5] To Britain, China's foreign trade system was 'not yet GATT-compatible' since it retained 'too many State Trading features'. But 'considerable efforts towards reform' had been made, and this progress should be welcomed and further encouraged. Admission to GATT of 'an economy of the size and with the potential of China's' would undoubtedly have 'a major influence on the future of the whole GATT system'. Britain attached importance to a number of GATT provisions that China should embrace: a 'market based pricing system'; transparency; useable safeguards against China's 'export surges endangering particularly sensitive sectors of the UK economy'; and transitional arrangements. To the DTI, the protocol of accession should be properly negotiated, including China's demands for 'less developed country' status in GATT.[6]

The Tiananmen crackdown on 4 June, however, cast a shadow on the GATT negotiations. The main question was whether the next working party meeting, scheduled for 11–12 July, should go ahead. The United States was inclined to hold a 'very short meeting', while finding 'technical reasons for not prolonging it'.[7] Britain believed that GATT was 'not the right place to make political gestures'. But appalled by the events in Beijing, Britain was 'not conducting business as usual' with China, and thus saw some logic in postponing the working party meeting.[8] It was decided that the chairman of the working party would talk informally with the Chinese, suggesting that, given the uncertain economic situation in China, a poorly attended meeting would not be worthwhile. The July meeting of the working party was thus postponed to a later date (unspecified).[9]

By early September, as the FCO instructed the UK mission in Geneva, '[u]ncertainty remained about the future of economic reform in China'.[10] On the 14th, the working party met informally, without the participation of the Chinese delegation, and decided that Beijing should provide a clear statement about the situation in the economic and trade field in the past months.[11] The Chinese statement was duly submitted to the GATT Secretariat on 10 November. It stated that in September 1988 the Chinese government had decided to 'readjust the economy' for a period of three years or more. At the same time, 'reform measures would be deepened and improved and the open policy unswervingly implemented'. The statement provided supplementary data on China's foreign trade regime – for example, the total value of imports and exports in the first nine months of 1989 saw an increase of 14.3 per cent over the corresponding period of the previous year. It concluded that China's economy was 'turning for the better', with excessively high growth slowed down, over-expanded capital construction curbed, and inflation checked.[12]

China still had a long way to go to conform with the provisions of GATT, not least due to the dualism (plan and market) in its trading system. The Tiananmen crisis had the effect of slowing down the multilateral negotiations over China's GATT accession. The neoliberal expectation that China would become an open and democratic country suffered a serious setback in 1989. As Thatcher told the leaders of the member states of the Commonwealth in October, there always existed 'the risk that the clock will be put back again', and the Tiananmen events were 'a reminder that Communism will not necessarily lie down and die quietly'.[13] Nevertheless, after a decade of reform and opening up, China was increasingly entangled with the process of economic globalisation. Between 1978 and 1989, China's exports had grown at the average annual nominal rate of 17 per cent (in terms of the US dollar); and the ratio of exports to GDP had risen sharply from 5 to 13 per cent.[14]

In retrospect, the Tiananmen crisis did not propel China to disengage from the global economy. Although the Jiang Zemin government adopted economic retrenchment policies and debated the future of reform, there was no turning back the clock.[15] As the semi-retired Deng Xiaoping advised his comrades in late 1989, China should observe the international situation coolly and patiently, while concentrating on the practical task of development at home[16] – advice that could be summarised as 'keep a low profile and bide your time'. In 1992, Deng once again put economic reform high on the agenda of the Chinese government by making a high-profile tour of the Shenzhen SEZ, whose achievement he affirmed.

Globalisation and Anglo-Chinese relations

In 1979, Margaret Thatcher came to power with the determination to reverse Britain's relative economic decline and to restore its greatness on the world stage. She harboured the vision of what her Conservative successors decades later would call 'Global Britain', in that the UK would actively engage with the world rather than confining itself to Europe or accepting a post-imperial fate. Influenced by neoliberalism, Thatcher saw the globalisation of free trade as essential to her project of 'Global Britain'. In this regard, Thatcher could not afford to ignore the Far East, where some of the world's fastest growing economies were located. Deng Xiaoping's opening up of China since late 1978 provided a golden opportunity for Thatcher to recast Britain as a global trading nation. To Thatcher and the FCO, Britain was well placed to satisfy China's development priorities in such fields as energy, telecommunications, transport, and industrial renovation. Given the experience of UK companies, such as British Petroleum and GEC, they believed that Britain enjoyed a competitive edge over other countries in the scramble for the China market. Besides, the Thatcher government supported China's accession to GATT in principle. Founded on an implicit 'liberal understanding' that all contracting parties should break down trade barriers and embrace a market economy, GATT played a crucial role in the globalisation of free trade. By helping to integrate China into the rules-based international economic order, Thatcher hoped to strengthen the pro-Western orientation of the Chinese leadership while allowing Britain to compete freely in the global economy.

To strengthen Anglo-Chinese economic relations, the Thatcher government concluded a series of economic cooperation and investment agreements with China, liberalised defence sales, invited Premier Zhao Ziyang and

General Secretary Hu Yaobang to Britain for high-level talks, and used the Queen's China visit as a charm offensive. In negotiating business deals with Britain and other countries, the Chinese were highly conscious of price and quality. If anything, China's price bargaining showed that it embraced market competition and global economic interdependence. Through high-level visits, and during the Hong Kong negotiations (which aimed to 'educate' the Chinese about how capitalist Hong Kong worked), the British played a part in the Chinese learning of the norms of the global capitalist system. Deng's principle of 'seeking truth from facts' informed China's 'global learning'. In the 1980s, China became a *'system-maintaining'* and *'system-exploiting'* power rather than one that sought to 'reform or transform the existing international system', according to Samuel Kim.[17] Margaret M. Pearson similarly observes: 'Learning occurred directly through channels of influence, such as the need for China to adopt [GATT] standards in order to join the organization, and indirectly as more and more Chinese officials became convinced that deeper economic integration was both beneficial and necessary.'[18] Nevertheless, the process of Chinese learning took time. For conservatives like Chen Yun, who were influenced by economic nationalism, foreign competition was potentially harmful to the domestic economy.[19] All this explained the ebbs and flows (or the *'shou-fang'* cycles) of Deng's reform, between state-oriented and market-oriented policies, since 1979.

Above all, Deng's vision of globalisation clashed with Thatcher's neoliberal variant. To Deng, China's embrace of economic globalisation did not mean Westernisation or adoption of liberal democracy. Rather, Deng put a premium on national sovereignty and the political dominance of the CCP. What China pursued was 'independent globalisation' or 'independent opening': it held the initiative of determining the scope and pace of engaging with the global economy. Although Deng argued that socialist countries could also practise a 'market economy', China would not adopt 'capitalism' but rather use the market mechanism to build a 'socialist market economy'. When applying for accession to GATT in 1986, Beijing insisted on China's status as a 'developing country'. Accordingly, China would need to regulate the flows of trade through a system of tariffs and non-tariff barriers, protect domestic industries through subsidies, and maintain financial stability through price controls. To Britain and other developed countries, however, Deng's China still retained many 'state trading' features. As of 1989, China's foreign trade system was not yet GATT-compatible.

It was Deng's attitude towards democracy that sharply highlighted the two competing visions of globalisation. If neoliberals assumed that China's economic reform would ultimately lead to political liberalisation, Deng saw development and modernisation as essential to the construction of 'socialism with Chinese characteristics'. From the closing of the Democracy Wall in 1979 to the struggle against 'bourgeois liberalisation' in late 1986, Deng found it imperative to uphold the Four Cardinal Principles. When Premier Zhao Ziyang advocated political reform in 1987, Deng thought primarily in terms of administrative reform in order to make the party-state more efficient. The brutal suppression of the Chinese student protests on 4 June 1989 vividly showed how far Deng was prepared to go in preserving the legitimacy of the CCP. As far as Hong Kong's democratisation was concerned, Deng's attitude was more pragmatic and flexible, however. After hard bargaining with Britain, China gave its blessing to the introduction of direct elections in the Legislative Council in 1991, if not earlier. By making provision for direct elections in the Basic Law, promulgated in 1990, China hoped to ensure the success of 'one country, two systems' in Hong Kong after the handover. In this vein, support for democracy became a means to an end.

If Deng picked and chose which aspects of globalisation he wanted, Thatcher, too, lacked an absolute commitment to all facets of globalisation. If Deng was a 'pragmatic Leninist',[20] Thatcher could be deemed a pragmatic neoliberal. Having a neoliberal suspicion of democracy (or governance by majority rule), Thatcher subordinated democratic promotion abroad to other foreign policy objectives. In 1989, Thatcher and the FCO preferred evolutionary change to radical revolution in Eastern Europe. While Britain had 'a deep interest in freedom in Eastern Europe', Cradock argued, there was 'an interest in stability which in the final analysis overrode it'.[21] In other words, Thatcher hoped to win the European Cold War through constructive engagement with Gorbachev's Soviet Union. Thatcher and Cradock saw China in a similar light. After the Tiananmen crackdown, Britain condemned but did not isolate China. Notwithstanding the neoliberal assumption that economic reform would encourage political liberalisation, Thatcher's diplomacy of engagement was aimed primarily at reinforcing the pro-Western orientation of China rather than promoting democracy as such. In the wake of the June Fourth tragedy, the Thatcher government sought to restore normalcy in Anglo-Chinese relations as soon as possible, not least due to Britain's responsibility to Hong Kong up to 1997. Nevertheless, Thatcher's moral commitment to the Hong Kong people did not include British citizenship and immigration rights. Influenced by racial prejudice and domestic politics, Thatcher opposed granting a right of abode in Britain to most Hong Kong Chinese, both in 1981 and in 1989. While enthusiastically embracing the globalisation of trade and markets, Thatcher resisted the free movement of people (save entrepreneurs) in an increasingly connected world.

The global history of Anglo-Chinese interactions in the 1980s, then, demonstrates that globalisation was not a linear, uniform, and inevitable process. There were competing visions of globalisation, and there were different roads to modernity. Not only did Deng survive the Tiananmen crisis in 1989, but, with hindsight, he and his successors would turn China into an economic powerhouse in the twenty-first century.

Hong Kong's 'long decolonisation'

The 'long decolonisation' of Hong Kong commenced in the 1960s. It was not a declared policy or any master plan by London, but rather a protracted and complicated process of changes in the UK–Hong Kong relationship. Perceptions of British interests in Hong Kong shifted in relation to events and developments in the metropole (for example, decisions on defence cuts, which made Hong Kong indefensible), within the colony (like the 1967 leftist riots, which triggered London's long-term planning for Hong Kong), and at the international level (such as Britain's entry into the EEC, which rendered Hong Kong's status anomalous). Although Hong Kong remained a Crown Colony, by the 1970s the colonial government effectively enjoyed financial and administrative autonomy from London. The home government did not give constant instructions to the governor. Nor could it 'coerce' Hong Kong into 'buying British' or adopting policies that went against local interests. As Governor Murray MacLehose recollected: 'There was dialogue with London, sometimes intense, sometimes none at all, but never instruction.'[22] What British ministers and diplomats wanted most was that Hong Kong was 'administered well', and would not become 'a subject of criticism either in the U.K. or the world, or with China'.[23]

Against the backdrop of globalisation, whose contemporary phase started in 1945 and was intensified by Reagan's and Thatcher's neoliberal policies and Deng's opening up of China in the 1980s, the UK–Hong Kong relationship deviated further from the pattern of 'vertical' integration characteristic of empire. (Both the system of imperial/Commonwealth preference and the Sterling Area had been disbanded in the early 1970s when Britain joined the EEC and floated the pound.) As an international financial, manufacturing, and communications centre, Hong Kong became a 'global city' that maintained strong 'horizontal' connections and networks with the United States, Japan, and Southeast Asian countries. The economic globalisation of Hong Kong did not make *de jure* decolonisation inevitable, however. On the contrary, Thatcher was determined to hold on to Hong Kong when she visited Beijing to discuss its future in September 1982. Nevertheless, Britain could no longer take the imperial connection for granted when it came to trade and commerce with Hong Kong in the age of intensified globalisation. Empire conferred no commercial advantage on UK companies, which needed to grasp the opportunities in the competitive Hong Kong market.[24]

All this meant that in 1982 Thatcher was not motivated by Hong Kong's economic value to Britain per se. In Beijing, Thatcher took pains to stress to Deng that Britain did not obtain revenue from Hong Kong. The main question is why Thatcher was eager to retain Hong Kong, and, after two years of negotiations, why the Iron Lady was 'for (re)turning'.

The legal validity of the three treaties governing Hong Kong's status might be one factor. As a lawyer, Thatcher firmly believed that Britain's sovereign claims over Hong Kong rested on the Treaty of Nanking and the two Conventions of Peking. Nonetheless, Thatcher was pragmatic enough to recognise that Britain could not ultimately rely on the legal argument to resolve the Hong Kong question. It was not merely because Deng regarded the three treaties as 'unequal' and invalid, while proclaiming to recover the whole of Hong Kong in 1997. As Thatcher told the unofficial members in 1982, 'the important point was not whether the treaties were unequal but what was to be done about them. Even if they were regarded as valid there would still be a problem'.[25] As 92 per cent of the territory of Hong Kong was obtained under a ninety-nine-year lease in 1898, Britain deemed it unviable to retain the remaining 8 per cent of the territory when the New Territories Lease expired in 1997. The significance of legal considerations, indeed, lay in the fact that Thatcher was opposed to unilateral abrogation of international treaties. During her visit to Beijing, Thatcher thus sought Deng's agreement to open talks to resolve the Hong Kong question by mutual agreement.

Thatcher's China visit came just three months after Britain's triumph in the Falklands War. The euphoria of victory might have emboldened Thatcher to seek continued British rule in Hong Kong beyond 1997. Yet pragmatism quickly got the better of the 'emotional Margaret'. The Iron Lady did not need the Chinese to remind her that Hong Kong was not the Falkland Islands, and China not Argentina. As a FCO brief put it in 1982: 'Kowloon and Hong Kong militarily indefensible but in any case China could throttle economically'.[26] In other words, a military solution to the Hong Kong problem was never on the table.

If the legal and military arguments for retaining the colony were not strong enough, Thatcher did see a moral obligation to the people of Hong Kong. To hand over British territory, as David Wilson recollected, to 'a Communist government, which she thoroughly disliked, was even worse'.[27] During the Hong Kong negotiations, Percy Cradock and Richard Evans took pains to stress Britain's moral obligations to Hong Kong residents, much to the annoyance of the Chinese. The latter accused Britain of being hypocritical due to the alleged economic benefits it extracted from Hong Kong. Thatcher also saw British subjects in the Falkland Islands through a moral lens.[28] In a Chequers meeting in the midst of the Falklands War, Thatcher asked rhetorically whether the FCO was prepared to 'hand over people who believed in democracy to a dictatorship'. She would 'never abandon' the Falkland islanders, who were 'British', and would never fail to uphold 'the principle of self-determination'.[29] The similarities between the Falkland and Hong Kong cases end here, however. While the Thatcher government was willing to accord the Falkland islanders a right to veto any deal between Britain and Argentina, the right of self-determination was denied to the people of Hong Kong (given China's principled objection).

If, in 1982, Thatcher found it morally wrong to hand over capitalist Hong Kong to communist China, her feeling of pride in Hong Kong's achievement, and her conviction in free-market capitalism generally, paradoxically explained why she agreed to sign the Joint Declaration in late 1984. Thatcher firmly believed that Hong Kong's success owed much to British institutions and values. During the 'first phase' of talks with the Chinese from October 1982 to June 1983, the British refused to yield on the issue of both sovereignty and administration, arguing that only British rule could sustain confidence in Hong Kong. When the 'second phase' of talks started in July 1983, the British negotiating objective shifted to trading sovereignty for administration. Notwithstanding Cradock's tactics of 'finessing' the British administrative link, the Chinese still refused to enter into detailed discussions until Cradock stated, in November, that Britain envisaged 'no link of authority' between the UK and Hong Kong after 1997.

From the eighth to twenty-second rounds in 1984, the principal objectives of the Thatcher government were to negotiate for a high degree of autonomy for Hong Kong, the continuity of its system after 1997, and a detailed and binding agreement that stipulated China's policies regarding Hong Kong. In producing working papers as the basis for discussion, the British aimed to 'educate' the Chinese about how capitalist Hong Kong worked. Specifically, they sought to preserve the 'substance' of British rule – the Common Law, freedom, and capitalism – as much as possible, while abandoning the 'forms' of sovereignty and administration. After tough bargaining and mutual compromises with the Chinese, the British managed to incorporate the key ideas of the working papers into the annexes to the main agreement. While the Joint Declaration was less than 1,200 words long, Annex 1 concerning China's basic policies ran to over 4,500 words.[30] Once she became satisfied that after 1997 Hong Kong would maintain its capitalist way of life for fifty years, enjoy a high degree of autonomy, select (some of) its legislative councillors by 'elections', and so forth, Thatcher agreed to put her signature to the Joint Declaration in December 1984. By preserving its capitalist system insulated from socialist China, Thatcher was optimistic that Hong Kong would continue to flourish after the relinquishment of British sovereignty. And Britain would be in a position to compete effectively in Hong Kong's globalised markets.

The diplomacy of education

As a study of diplomatic history, this book seeks to assess the success and failure of Thatcher's diplomacy of decolonisation and globalisation. Former British diplomats naturally lauded the Joint Declaration as 'a significant achievement for British diplomacy',[31] and 'the best agreement that could have been reached given the realities of power'.[32] In managing Hong Kong's decolonisation, and in dealing with communist China, Thatcher was more pragmatic than her rhetoric and confrontational style might suggest. Being pragmatic in the tradition of the British foreign establishment was, however, tainted by the collective memories of 'appeasement' and 'kowtow'. If Thatcher and British diplomats regarded the Joint Declaration as an achievement, the majority of Hong Kong people, which in 1982 had preferred continual British administration, accepted it out of a sense of inevitability and powerlessness. The draft Hong Kong agreement made available for public consultation in late 1984 could not be revised or re-negotiated. During the secret negotiations, the wishes of Hongkongers were never a decisive factor for Britain (which gauged public opinion largely through the lens of the elitist unofficial members) and China (with Deng Xiaoping believing that he knew enough of local voices by receiving delegations of 'patriotic' Chinese). Fears about Hong Kong's future did not completely dissipate after the conclusion of the agreement.[33] Such fears resurfaced in 1989, when the Tiananmen crackdown sent shockwaves through Hong Kong society. The Thatcher government's refusal to grant British citizenship to Hong Kong residents, and to support wider democracy in the Legislative Council, led to accusations of a British 'sell-out' and 'betrayal'. Instead of 'kowtowing' to Beijing, government critics called for a tougher response to the June Fourth events.[34]

It is true that Thatcher, Howe, and Cradock could not but accept the 'realities behind diplomacy'.[35] On Hong Kong, the Chinese apparently held all the cards in the negotiations. The British had to constantly retreat from their previously held positions, until they conceded both sovereignty and administration to China. Insofar as China's external orientation was concerned, Thatcher was far from successful in pursuing the agenda of neoliberal globalisation. By 1989, China remained a state-trading system, while not buying more British goods than UK companies might hope for. The Tiananmen crackdown not only shattered all hopes for the emergence of a democratic China, but also called into question Beijing's commitment to freedom and autonomy in Hong Kong under the Joint Declaration. Nevertheless, if 'appeasement' meant sacrificing the interests of a small country in order to protect the British national interest (such as averting war), there is no evidence to suggest that the Thatcher government intentionally struck a 'bad' deal on Hong Kong's future with a view to, for example, improving the prospects for British exports to China. Subconsciously, Thatcher and British diplomats might have created a favourable political atmosphere for Anglo-Chinese economic interactions after successfully resolving the Hong Kong question. (Indeed, the Chinese urged Thatcher to capitalise on the signing of the Joint Declaration to expand bilateral trade.) But this was a far cry from saying that Britain sold Hong Kong for commercial advantage. If the British conceived any linkage between Hong Kong and China, they appeared to prioritise (not sacrifice) the former. Shortly after Thatcher's China visit in September 1982, the FCO contemplated whether to make an economic gesture to Beijing in order to improve the atmosphere of talks on Hong Kong. In the aftermath of the 1989 Tiananmen crackdown, Cradock, secretly visiting Beijing, suggested to Jiang Zemin that only by resolving the dispute over Hong Kong's direct elections could Anglo-Chinese relations be improved.

Just as the revisionist historiography of Britain's appeasement policy in the 1930s has questioned the simplified portrayal of Neville Chamberlain as the 'guilty man' dictated by Britain's 'decline',[36] so too was Thatcher's China policy not simply determined by Britain's diminishing power and relative economic decline since 1945. Rather, the structural constraints on British diplomacy were mediated through the policy choices of Thatcher, Howe, and Cradock. What they pursued was not a policy of 'appeasement' or confrontation, but a diplomacy of 'educating' China. By 'educating', it meant to reshape China's (inaccurate) preconceptions and (limited) knowledge about how free-market capitalism worked in Hong Kong, and how adherence to the norms of the global trading system was vital to China's admission to GATT. No doubt the process of Chinese learning was complicated and gradual. And China was receptive to British ideas and advice only when they served its national interests. Still, through a diplomacy of engagement and negotiation, Thatcher and the FCO were able to resolve the Hong Kong question peacefully by late 1984, deepen Anglo-Chinese relations thereafter, and prevent China's total isolation following the Tiananmen crackdown in 1989. An alternative approach – 'gunboat diplomacy', for instance – would have propelled China to take over Hong Kong unilaterally, to acquire goods and technology from Britain's competitors, and to eliminate what remains of FCO influence on Beijing's decision-making.

Did Thatcher make a difference in British diplomacy? Lacking foreign affairs experience and being preoccupied with domestic economic issues during her first term, Thatcher could not but rely on Foreign Secretary Carrington and, as far as Hong Kong was concerned, the likes of Cradock. During the Hong Kong negotiations, Thatcher was apparently persuaded (or 'educated') by the FCO to accept the inevitable. Cradock believed that the prime minister was 'prepared to compromise under extreme persuasion, in order to achieve a practical result'.[37] As John Campell writes: 'It was Cradock who persuaded her – reluctantly – to shift her ground.'[38] Nevertheless, I argue that Thatcher also convinced herself that a capitalist Hong Kong insulated from socialist China would continue to flourish after 1997, pragmatism being one side of her personality. As David Wilson recalled in an oral interview: 'when it really came to the crunch [Thatcher] was pragmatic and sensible'.[39] Rather than being led by the nose by the FCO, the industrious Thatcher 'took an interest' in the Hong Kong talks, reading 'all the key telegrams and other papers' and making herself available to the unofficial members during their numerous missions to London.[40] Thatcher felt strongly for the unofficials in a way that career diplomats like Cradock did not. As Lydia Dunn told Thatcher's authorised biographer, Thatcher 'was perhaps alone among the British team in understanding that Hong Kong was a human issue, not just a diplomatic one'.[41] To reassure the unofficials, Thatcher insisted on a detailed and binding agreement and on postponing the joint group's move to Hong Kong for as long as possible. Through her determination, bluffing, and at times 'unreasonableness', Thatcher pushed the Chinese to the limit, and helped secure a better deal for Hong Kong than any of her foreign secretaries and diplomats had initially expected.[42]

Thatcher's agency in the Hong Kong negotiations, and in Britain's China policy, was vindicated by the fact that the Chinese 'felt great admiration for her because she was the Iron Lady'.[43] Deng Xiaoping had 'the highest trust' in Thatcher.[44] Despite her hostility to communism, Thatcher, for her part, was quite impressed by Deng's immense authority: a chain-smoking and spitting tiny figure who exerted absolute control over a vast country of 1.3 billion people.[45] That said, Thatcher and Deng reached a deal on Hong Kong not because of any sentimental bond between themselves, but out of a sense of realism they shared. It was Zhao Ziyang with whom Thatcher truly developed a rapport. As her private secretary wrote of the 1982 China visit, Thatcher 'had got on well' with Zhao, and '[t]his mattered, because a good personal relationship would assist in a happy outcome to the talks'.[46] Not only did she eventually co-sign the Joint Declaration with Zhao, but Thatcher was also eager to work with the liberal reformer to advance Anglo-Chinese economic relations. Even after Zhao's house arrest due to the 1989 crisis, and after her own retirement from politics in 1992, Thatcher, when visiting Beijing to meet several dignitaries, continued to ask to see her 'old friend' (but to no avail).[47]

Ultimately, Thatcher's aspirations, sheer will, and courage could not hide the realities of British power in a world dominated or shaped by a resurgent United States, a nuclear-armed Soviet Union, an increasingly integrated European Community (despite Thatcher's dislike of monetary and political union), and the rising Asian powers, principally Japan and China. Strategically, China attached more importance to the United States and the Soviet Union than to Britain in the last phase of the Cold War. Economically, Britain managed to secure only a modest share of the China market. On Hong Kong, the promulgation of the Basic Law in early 1990 marked a new phase in the transitional period, during which China's role in Hong Kong politics became increasingly important. The local business and political elites who had supported British colonial rule gradually shifted their allegiance to China in the lead-up to Hong Kong's handover. By the time she left office in November 1990, Thatcher's vision of 'Global Britain' – a global trading nation that looked beyond the shores of the Isles and Europe to engage with the rising China – was only partially fulfilled, if at all.

1989 to 2019

Thirty years after the Tiananmen crackdown, in June 2019 the attempt by SAR Chief Executive Carrie Lam to introduce a bill allowing extradition of fugitives to and from mainland China caused serious political unrest in Hong Kong and a rapid deterioration of Anglo-Chinese relations. The protests against the extradition bill escalated into large-scale pro-democracy demonstrations, often accompanied by violent clashes between young radicals and police officers. Just as Deng Xiaoping had talked of 'the large international environment' behind the Chinese student demonstrations in 1989, so too did the 2019 Hong Kong protests occur against the international backdrop of US President Donald Trump's trade war against China and growing Western fears about the rise of China under Xi Jinping. In 2020, Beijing responded to what it saw as US efforts to instigate a 'colour revolution' in Hong Kong in the previous year[48] by imposing a national security law, which banned treason, secession, sedition, and subversion, on the city. Seeing the sweeping national security law as a 'clear breach' of the 1984 Sino-British Joint Declaration,[49] the Boris Johnson government introduced a BN(O) visa scheme, which allowed over three million Hong Kong residents with BN(O) status and their dependents to live, work, and study in the UK for five years as a pathway to British citizenship. China, in turn, accused Britain of violating its promises by giving the right of abode in Britain to Hongkongers. In 2021, Beijing revamped the SAR's electoral system in order to ensure that only 'patriots' could govern Hong Kong. The pro-establishment bloc won all but one legislative seats in the election later that year, and in May 2022 John Lee Ka-chiu, the sole candidate, was elected as the fifth chief executive by the pro-Beijing Election Committee.

This book has traced the long-term origins of Hong Kong's current predicament and the resultant difficulties in Anglo-Chinese relations. Between 1984 and 2022, we witness the conclusion and then violation (both actual and alleged) of the Joint Declaration concerning Hong Kong's autonomy and democracy; the reversal of UK immigration policy towards Hong Kong, from denial of a right of abode to the generous BN(O) visa scheme; and the transformation of Anglo-Chinese relations, from 'golden era' to mutual mistrust and accusations. It is tempting to conclude, with the benefit of hindsight, that Thatcher should not have trusted Deng Xiaoping by handing over Hong Kong to communist China, and that the FCO's inclination towards 'appeasing' Beijing in the 1980s was vindicated by the rise of China (or the 'China threat') in the twenty-first century. Nonetheless, although historical writing is as much about the present as it is about the past, there is the danger of using the past to serve the present. Any objective assessment of British diplomacy during the Thatcher years should be set in its proper historical context. In the 1980s, no politician or commentator could have predicted that China would become an economic superpower under a strongman that could challenge US hegemony, that Britain would leave the European Community/Union and look east, and that a significant number of Hong Kong citizens would embrace confrontational means in the fight for democracy and against the 'one country, two systems'. On the latter, Thatcher and Cradock were perhaps 'right to be wrong' about the (in)compatibility between Chinese sovereignty and Hong Kong's autonomy, inherent in Deng's creative formula.

Notes

1. GATT Digital Library 1947–1994, Stanford Libraries, Stanford University (hereafter GDL), 'Working party on China's status as a contracting party', L/6191, 19 June 1987, https://exhibits.stanford.edu/gatt/catalog/gs805nk6409.
2. GDL, Memo on China's foreign trade regime, L/6125, 18 February 1987, https://exhibits.stanford.edu/gatt/catalog/fd408nh7406.
3. McKenzie, *GATT and Global Order in the Postwar Era*, 99.
4. GDL, The Secretariat note, Spec(88)13/Add.4, 9 December 1988, https://exhibits.stanford.edu/gatt/catalog/rr250dc2201.
5. TNA, FCO 21/4255, Geneva to FCO, no. 132, 2 March 1989; FCO 21/4255, Sankey to Bayne, 21 February 1989; GDL, The Secretariat note, Spec(88)13/Add.5, 9 June 1989, https://exhibits.stanford.edu/gatt/catalog/jv202fb4293.
6. TNA, FCO 21/4255, DTI paper: 'China and GATT', 1 June 1989.
7. TNA, FCO 21/4255, Geneva to DTI, teleletter NFR, 15 June 1989.
8. TNA, FCO 21/4255, Geneva to DTI, 23 June 1989.
9. TNA, FCO 21/4255, Geneva to FCO, no. 412, 30 June 1989.

Conclusion 245

10 TNA, FCO 21/4255, FCO to Geneva, no. 237, 11 September 1989.
11 TNA, FCO 21/4255, Vereker to Johnson, 14 September 1989.
12 GDL, Communication from China, Spec(88)13/Add.6, 10 November 1989, https://exhibits.stanford.edu/gatt/catalog/vc816gs1159.
13 MTF, Thatcher speech to Commonwealth summit (global trends and prospects), 18 October 1989, www.margaretthatcher.org/document/107792.
14 Sung, *The China–Hong Kong Connection*, 61–2.
15 Joseph Fewsmith, *China since Tiananmen: From Deng Xiaoping to Hu Jintao*, 2nd edition (Cambridge: Cambridge University Press, 2008), 21–47; Naughton, *The Chinese Economy*, 98–9.
16 *DXN*, vol. 2, 1286–8.
17 Kim, 'Thinking Globally in Post-Mao China', 193, 203 (original emphasis).
18 Pearson, 'The Case of China's Accession to GATT/WTO', 367–8.
19 *Ibid.*, 360.
20 Shambaugh, *China's Leaders*, 95.
21 Cradock, *In Pursuit of British Interests*, 104.
22 BLO, MSS.Ind.Ocn.s.377, Transcript of interviews with Lord MacLehose of Beoch, 1989 and 1991, tape 5, p. 197.
23 *Ibid.*, tape 10, p. 507.
24 TNA, FCO 40/1157, Nott to Carrington, 19 February 1980.
25 MTF, Record of meeting between Thatcher and UMELCO on 27 September 1982, www.margaretthatcher.org/document/122627.
26 TNA, FCO 21/2214, FCO paper: 'Future of Hong Kong', 23 July 1982.
27 CAC, GBR/0014/DOHP 83, Interview with David Clive Wilson (Lord Wilson of Tillyorn), 19 September 2003, p. 44.
28 Ezequiel Mercau, *The Falklands War: An Imperial History* (Cambridge: Cambridge University Press, 2019), 64–5.
29 Nicholas Henderson, *Mandarin: The Diaries of an Ambassador 1969–1982* (London: Weidenfeld and Nicolson, 1994), 462.
30 Gittings, *Introduction to the Hong Kong Basic Law*, 17.
31 Meyer, *Getting Our Way*, 167.
32 Hurd, *Memoir*, 529.
33 'It's OK … but a couple of fears still remain', *South China Morning Post* (27 September 1984); 'Dissenting voices raise issues on HK's future', *Hong Kong Standard* (29 September 1984).
34 Shawcross, *Kowtow!*, 9–10.
35 Paul Kennedy, *The Realities Behind Diplomacy: Background Influences on British External Policy 1865–1980* (London: Fontana Press, 1985).
36 See Aster, 'Appeasement'.
37 Cradock, *In Pursuit of British Interests*, 22.
38 Campell, *Margaret Thatcher*, vol. 2, 316.
39 CAC, GBR/0014/DOHP 83, Interview with David Clive Wilson (Lord Wilson of Tillyorn), 19 September 2003, p. 44.
40 CAC, GBR/0014/DOHP 15, Interview with Sir Robin McLaren, 31 July 1996, pp. 17–18.

41 Moore, *Margaret Thatcher*, vol. 2, 103.
42 *Ibid.*, p. 19; Aitken, *Margaret Thatcher*, 424.
43 Moore, *Margaret Thatcher*, vol. 2, 97.
44 TNA, PREM 19/1266 Part 15, HK to FCO, no. 2176, 31 July 1984.
45 Moore, *Margaret Thatcher*, vol. 2, 102; Renwick, *A Journey with Margaret Thatcher*, 85.
46 TNA, PREM 19/962 Part 2, Coles note, 24 September 1982.
47 Thatcher, *Statecraft*, 158.
48 'Chinese official warns Hong Kong protesters against "color revolution"', *New York Times* (7 August 2019), www.nytimes.com/2019/08/07/world/asia/hong-kong-protests-china-violence.html.
49 'Guidance: Six-monthly report on Hong Kong: July to December 2020', 10 June 2021, www.gov.uk/government/publications/six-monthly-report-on-hong-kong-july-to-december-2020/six-monthly-report-on-hong-kong-july-to-december-2020.

Bibliography

Archival sources

The National Archives, Kew, Surrey, UK

AB 65	United Kingdom Atomic Energy Authority
BT 241	Board of Trade
BW 23	British Council: China
CAB 128	Cabinet: Minutes
CAB 133	Cabinet Office: Commonwealth and International Conferences and Ministerial Visits to and from the UK
CAB 134	Cabinet: Miscellaneous Committees
CAB 148	Cabinet Office: Defence and Overseas Policy Committees and Sub-Committees
CO 129	Colonial Office: Hong Kong
CO 1030	Colonial Office and Commonwealth Office: Far Eastern Department and successors
DEFE 69	Ministry of Defence (Navy)
FCO 21	Foreign and Commonwealth Office: Far Eastern Department
FCO 40	Foreign and Commonwealth Office: Hong Kong Department
FCO 98	Foreign and Commonwealth Office: European Integration Department (External)
FO 93	Foreign and Commonwealth Office: Protocols of Treaties
FO 371	Foreign Office: Political Departments
FO 972	Foreign and Commonwealth Office: Research Department
FV 14	Ministry of Technology
PV 12	Department of Industry
PV 13	Department of Industry and Department of Trade and Industry
T 450	HM Treasury
PREM 16	Prime Minister's Office: Correspondence and Papers, 1974–1979
PREM 19	Prime Minister's Office: Correspondence and Papers, 1979–1997

Bodleian Library, University of Oxford, Oxford, UK

Uncatalogued Papers of Lord Callaghan
Conservative Party Archive
Interview with Sir S. Y. Chung, 1989 and 1990, MSS.Ind.Ocn.s.328
Interview with Lord MacLehose of Beoch, 1989 and 1991, MSS.Ind.Ocn.s.377

Churchill Archives Centre, Churchill College, Cambridge, UK

British Diplomatic Oral History Programme:
GBR/0014/DOHP 83, Interview with David Clive Wilson (Lord Wilson of Tillyorn), 19 September 2003; GBR/0014/DOHP 26, Interview with Sir Percy Cradock, 4 November 1997; GBR/0014/DOHP 15, Interview with Sir Robin McLaren, 31 July 1996
Papers of Baroness Thatcher
Papers of Enoch Powell
Papers of Jeremy Bray
Papers of Michael Stewart

The Library, St. John's College, Cambridge, UK

Papers of Percy Cradock

National Archives and Records Administration, College Park, Maryland, US

Record Group 59, Records of the Executive Secretariat, Conference Files, 1949–63

Public Records Office, Kwun Tong, Hong Kong

HKRS 70-8-356; HKRS 545-1-133-12; HKRS 1642-1-24; HKRS 1642-1-41; HKRS 1687-1-82

Digital archives

GATT Digital Library 1947–1994, Stanford Libraries, Stanford University
Margaret Thatcher Foundation Archive
The National Security Archive, The George Washington University
United Nations Digital Library
The Wilson Center Digital Archive

Newspapers

Daily Mail (UK)
Financial Times (UK)
Guardian (UK)
Hong Kong Standard (HK)
New York Times (US)
Observer (UK)
South China Morning Post (HK)
Sunday Telegraph (UK)
The Times (UK)

Published primary sources

Bao, Pu, Renee Chiang, and Adi Ignatius (eds. and trans.). *Prisoner of the State: The Secret Journal of Zhao Ziyang*. London: Pocket Books, 2010.
Lord Carrington. *Reflect on Things Past: The Memoirs of Lord Carrington*. London: Collins, 1988.
Chung, Sze-Yuen. *Hong Kong's Journey to Reunification: Memoirs of Sze-Yuen Chung*. Hong Kong: Chinese University Press, 2001.
Cowper-Coles, Sherard. *Ever the Diplomat: Confessions of a Foreign Office Mandarin*. London: HarperCollins, 2012.
Cradock, Percy. *Experiences of China*. London: John Murray, 1994.
—— *In Pursuit of British Interests: Reflections on Foreign Policy under Margaret Thatcher and John Major*. London: John Murray, 1997.
Editorial Committee for Party Literature, CCP Central Committee (ed.). *Selected Works of Deng Xiaoping*, vol. 3: *1982–1992*. Beijing: Foreign Languages Press, 1994.
Hansard, House of Commons Debates and House of Lords Debates.
Harris, Robin. *Not for Turning: The Life of Margaret Thatcher*. London: Bantam Press, 2013.
Heath, Edward. *The Course of My Life: My Autobiography*. London: Hodder and Stoughton, 1999.
Henderson, Nicholas. *Mandarin: The Diaries of an Ambassador 1969–1982*. London: Weidenfeld and Nicolson, 1994.
Howe, Geoffrey. *Conflict of Loyalty*. London: Macmillan, 1994.
Hurd, Douglas. *Memoirs*. London: Abacus, 2004.
Lawson, Nigel. *The View from No. 11: Memoirs of a Tory Radical*. London: Bantam Press, 1992.
Li, Lanqing, translated by Ling Yuan and Zhang Siying. *Breaking Through: The Birth of China's Opening-up Policy*. New York: Oxford University Press, 2009.
Lilley, James with Jeffrey Lilley. *China Hands: Nine Decades of Adventure, Espionage, and Diplomacy in Asia*. New York: PublicAffairs, 2004.
Major, John. *The Autobiography*. London: HarperCollins, 2020.
Meyer, Christopher. *Getting Our Way: 500 Years of Adventure and Intrigue: The Inside Story of British Diplomacy*. London: Phoenix, 2010.
Owen, David. *Time to Declare*. London: Penguin Books, 1992.
Qian, Qichen. *Ten Episodes in China's Diplomacy*. New York: HarperCollins, 2006.
Renwick, Robin. *A Journey with Margaret Thatcher: Foreign Policy under the Iron Lady*. London: Biteback Publishing, 2013.
Thatcher, Margaret. *The Downing Street Years*. London: HarperCollins, 1993.
—— *Statecraft: Strategies for a Changing World*. London: HarperCollins, 2003.
—— *The Path to Power*. London: Harper Press, 2011.
Wong, Man Fong. *China's Resumption of Sovereignty over Hong Kong*. Hong Kong: The David C. Lam Institute for East-West Studies, Hong Kong Baptist University, 1997.

Chinese primary sources

Chen Yun nianpu, xiuding ben [A Chronicle of Chen Yun, revised edition], vol. 2. Beijing: Zhongyang wenxian chubanshe, 2015.

Chen Yun wenxuan [The Selected Works of Chen Yun], vol. 3. Beijing: Renmin chubanshe, 1995.
Deng Xiaoping junshi wenxuan [The Selected Military Works of Deng Xiaoping], vol. 3. Beijing: Renmin chubanshe, 1993.
Deng Xiaoping nianpu, 1975–1997 [A Chronicle of Deng Xiaoping, 1975–1997], vols 1 and 2. Beijing: Zhongyang wenxian chubanshe, 2004.
Deng Xiaoping wenxuan [The Selected Works of Deng Xiaoping], vols 2 and 3. Beijing: Renmin chubanshe, 1993.
Gu Mu. *Gu Mu huiyilu* [Memoir of Gu Mu]. Beijing: Zhongyang wenxian chubanshe, 2009.
Huang Hua. *Qinli yu jianwen: Huang Hua huiyilu* [Experience and Observation: Memoir of Huang Hua]. Beijing: Shiji zhishi chubanshe, 2007.
Jiang Enzhu. *Daguo jiaoliang: ZhongOu guanxi yu Xianggang huigui qinli* [Great Power Contest: Witnessing Sino-European Relations and the Return of Hong Kong]. Beijing: Zhongxin chuban jituan, 2016.
Jianguo yilai Li Xiannian wengao [Manuscripts of Li Xiannian since the Founding of the PRC], vol. 4: January 1977–April 1992. Beijing: Zhongyang wenxian chubanshe, 2011.
Li Hou. *Huigui de lichen* [The Journey of Retrocession]. Hong Kong: Joint Publishing (HK), 1997.
Li Xiannian zhuan [A Biography of Li Xiannian], vol. 2. Beijing: Zhongyang wenxian chubanshe, 2009.
Lu Ping (with the collaboration of Qian Yijiao). *Lu Ping koushu Xianggang huigui* [Lu Ping Speaks on the Return of Hong Kong]. Hong Kong: Joint Publishing (HK), 2009.
Szeto, Wah. *Da jiang dong qu: Szeto Wah huiyilu* [The Great River Flows Eastward: The Memoir of Szeto Wah]. Hong Kong: Oxford University Press, 2011.
Xi Zhongxun wenji [The Collected Works of Xi Zhongxun], vol. 1. Beijing: Zhonggong dangshi chubanshe, 2013.
Xu Jiatun. *Xu Jiatun Xianggang huiyilu* [The Hong Kong Memoirs of Xu Jiatun], vol. 1. Taipei: United Press, 1993.
Ye Jianying nianpu, 1897–1986 [A Chronicle of Ye Jianying, 1897–1986], vol. 2. Beijing: Zhongyang wenxian chubanshe, 2007.
Zhang Chunsheng and Xu Yu (eds). *Zhou Nan jiemi GangAo huigui – ZhongYing ji ZhongPu tanpan taiqian muhou* [Zhou Nan's Leaks about the Return of Hong Kong and Macao to their Motherland – Sino-British and Sino-Portuguese Talks and their Background]. Xianggang: Zhonghua chubanshe, 2012.
Zhao Ziyang wenji, 1980–1989 [The Collected Works of Zhao Ziyang, 1980–1989], vol. 1: *1980–1982*; vol. 2: *1983–1984*; vol. 3: *1985–1986*. Hong Kong: Chinese University Press, 2016.
Zhao Ziyang wenji, 1975–1980: Sichuan [The Collected Works of Zhao Ziyang, 1975–1980: Sichuan]. Hong Kong: Chinese University Press, 2018.
Zheng Zhongbing (et al.). *Hu Yaobang nianpu ziiao changbian* [Long Series of Materials on the Chronicle of Hu Yaobang], vol. 2. Hong Kong: Time International Publishing, 2005.
Zhong Jian, Guo Maojia, and Zhong Ruoyu (eds). *Zhongguo Jingji Tequ wenxian ziliao* [Archival Materials on China's Special Economic Zones], vol. 1 and 2. Beijing: Shehui kexue wenxian chubanshe, 2010.
Zhonggong zhongyang wenxian yanjiushi (ed.). *Gaige kaifang sashi nian zhongyao wenxian xuanbian* [Important Selected Documents on Thirty Years of Reform and Opening], vol. 1. Beijing: Zhongyang wenxian chubanshe, 2008.

Chinese secondary works

Chen Dunde. *Xianggang wenti tanpan shimo* [Negotiations for the Hong Kong Question from Beginning to End]. Hong Kong: Chung Hwa Book (HK) Company, 2009.
Cheng Linsheng. *Deng Xiaoping 'Yiguo liangzhi' sixiang yanjiu* [A Study of Deng Xiaoping's Thinking about 'One Country, Two Systems']. Shenyang: Liaoning renmin chubanshe, 1992.
Dangdai Zhongguo congshu bianji weiyuanhui (ed.). *Dangdai Zhongguo de dianli gongye* [Contemporary China: Power Industry]. Beijing: Dangdai Zhongguo chubanshe, 2009.
Deng Kaisong and Lu Xiaomin (et al.). *Yue Guang guanxi shi 1840–1984* [A History of Guangdong–Hong Kong Relations 1840–1984]. Hong Kong: Qilin shuye youxian gongsi, 1997.
'Deng Xiaoping: Gaige shi Zhongguo de dierci geming' bianxie zu, *Deng Xiaoping: Gaige shi Zhongguo de dierci geming* [Deng Xiaoping: Reform is China's Second Revolution]. Beijing: Taihai chubanshe, 2017.
Deng Xiaoping ji waiguo shounao huitan lu [A Record of Deng Xiaoping's Meetings with Foreign Heads]. Beijing: Taihai chubanshe, 2011.
Dong Yuzheng and Dong Li. *Deng Xiaoping GangAo zhanlue sixiang yanjiu* [A Study of Deng Xiaoping's Strategic Thinking about Hong Kong and Macao]. Dongguan: Guangdong keiji chubanshe, 1997.
Feng Bangyan. *Xianggang yingzi caituan, 1841–1996* [British Business Groups in Hong Kong, 1841–1996]. Hong Kong: Joint Publishing (HK), 1996.
Gao Wanglai. *Daguo tanpan moulue – ZhongYing Xianggang tanpan neimu* [The Negotiating Strategy of Great Power: An Inside Story of Sino-British Negotiation over Hong Kong]. Beijing: Shishi chubanshe, 2012.
Guo Shengwei. *Deng Xiaoping waijiao moulue* [Deng Xiaoping's Diplomatic Strategy]. Beijing: Zhongyang wenxian chubanshe, 2008.
Li Yunying and Chang Xiaole. *Shige yu waijiao: Zhou Nan waijiao shengya ceji* [Poetry and Diplomacy: A Side Note on the Diplomatic Career of Zhou Nan]. Xianggang: Ganglong chubanshe, 2004.
Lu Dong Qing and Lu Shou Cai. *Xianggang jingji shi* [A History of Hong Kong Economy]. Hong Kong: Joint Publishing (HK), 2002.
Men Honghua. *Zhongguo duiwai kaifang zhanlue (1978–2018 nian)* [China's Strategy of Foreign Opening, 1978–2018]. Shanghai: Shanghai renmin chubanshe, 2018.
Mo Kai. 'Xiandai maoyi tixi de chengzhang licheng' ['The Course of Development of the Modern Trading System']. In Wang Gungwu (ed.), *Xianggang shi xinbian* [Hong Kong History: New Perspectives], vol. 1. Hong Kong: Joint Publishing (HK), 1997, pp. 281–323.
Qi Pengfei. *Deng Xiaoping yu Xianggang huigui* [Deng Xiaoping and the Return of Hong Kong]. Beijing: Xinhua chubanshe, 2004.
Qian Jiang. *Deng Xiaoping yu ZhongMei jianjiao fengyun* [Deng Xiaoping and the Winds and Clouds of Establishing Sino-American Diplomatic Relations]. Beijing: Zhonggong dangshi chubanshe, 2005.
Shenzhen shi shizhi bangongshi (ed.). *Zhongguo Gongchandang Shenzhen lishi dashiji, 1921–2011* [A Historical Record of Key Events of the Chinese Communist Party in Shenzhen, 1921–2011]. Shenzhen: Shenzhen baoye jituan chubanshe, 2012.
Su Xing (et al.). *Deng Xiaoping shehuizhuyi shichang jingji lilun yu Zhongguo jingji tizhi zhuangui* [Deng Xiaoping's Theory of Socialist Market Economy and

the Changing Trajectory of China's Economic Institution]. Beijing: Renmin chubanshe, 2008.
Tang Renwu and Ma ji. *Zhongguo jingji gaige sanshi nian: Duiwai kaifang juan* [Thirty Years of China's Economic Reform: Volume on External Opening]. Chongqing: Chongqing daxue chubanshue, 2008.
Wang Fengchao. *Xianggang zhengzhi fazhan licheng (1843–2015)* [The Course of Development of Hong Kong's Political Institutions, 1843–2015]. Hong Kong: Chung Hwa Book (HK), 2017.
Wang Hongxu. *Qishi niandai yilai de ZhongYing guanxi* [Sino-British Relations since the 1970s]. Harbin: Heilongjiang jiaoyu chubanshe, 1996.
Wang Junyan. *Liao Chengzhi Zhuan* [Biography of Liao Chengzhi]. Beijing: Renmin chubanshe, 2006.
Wang Weimin. *Bainian zhongying guanxi* [A Century of Sino-British Relations]. Beijing: Shiji zhishi chubanshe, 2006.
Wei Wei and Liu Ke. *Deng Xiaoping lilun fazhan shi* [A History of the Development of Deng Xiaoping Theory]. Beijing: Shanghai renmin chubanshe, 2004.
Xi Zhongxun zhuzheng Guangdong bianweihui (ed.). *Xi Zhongxun zhuzheng Guangdong* [Xi Zhongxun Governs Guangdong]. Beijing: Zhonggong dangshi chubanshe, 2007.
Yang Jisheng. *Gaige niandai de zhengzhi douzheng* [Political Struggles during the Reform Years]. Hong Kong: Excellent Culture Press, 2004.
Yin Zhongming (et al.). *Zhongguo jingji gaige sanshi nian: Waijngmao juan* [Thirty Years of China's Economic Reform: Volume on Foreign Economic Trade]. Chengdu: Xinan caijing daxue chubanshe, 2008.
Yuan Qiushi. *Xianggang huigui dashiji* [A Chronicle of the Return of Hong Kong]. Hong Kong: Joint Publishing (HK), 2015.
Zhang Liqun, Zhang Ding, Yan Ruping, Tang Fei, and Li Gongtian (eds). *Hu Yaobang (1915–1989)* [Hu Yaobang, 1915–1989], vol. 3. Beijing: Beijing lianhe chuban gongsi, 2015.
Zheng Bijian (et al.). *Jingji quanqiuhua yu Zhongguo jingji jueqi* [Economic Globalisation and the Economic Rise of China]. Beijing: Zhonggong zhongyang dangxiao chubanshe, 2006.
Zhonggong Zhongyang wenxian yanjiushi (ed.). *Chen Yun duiwai kaifang sixiang xingcheng he fazhan* [The Formation and Development of Chen Yun's Thinking about External Opening]. Beijing: Zhongyang wenxian chubanshe, 2013.

Secondary sources

Aitken, Jonathan. *Margaret Thatcher: Power and Responsibility*. London: Bloomsbury, 2013.
Albers, Martin. *Britain, France, West Germany and the People's Republic of China, 1969–1982: The European Dimension of China's Great Transition*. London: Palgrave Macmillan, 2016.
Aldous, Richard. *Reagan and Thatcher: The Difficult Relationship*. London: Arrow Books, 2013.
Aster, Sidney. 'Appeasement: Before and after Revisionism'. *Diplomacy & Statecraft*, 19: 3 (2008), 443–80.
Baum, Richard. 'Zhao Ziyang and China's "Soft Authoritarian" Alternative'. In Guoguang Wu and Helen Lansdowne (eds), *Zhao Ziyang and China's Political Future*. Abingdon, Oxon: Routledge, 2008, pp. 109–21.

Benton, Gregor and Edmund Terence Gomez. *The Chinese in Britain, 1800–Present: Economy, Transnationalism, Identity*. Basingstoke: Palgrave Macmillan, 2008.
Bickers, Robert. 'The Colony's Shifting Position in the British Informal Empire in China'. In Judith M. Brown and Rosemary Foot (eds), *Hong Kong's Transitions, 1842–1997*. London: Macmillan, 1997, pp. 33–61.
―――― *Out of China: How the Chinese Ended the Era of Western Domination*. London: Allen Lane, 2017.
Brands, Hal. *Making the Unipolar Moment: U.S. Foreign Policy and the Rise of the Post-Cold War Order*. Ithaca, NY: Cornell University Press, 2016.
Breslin, Shaun. *China and the Global Political Economy*. Basingstoke: Palgrave Macmillan, 2007.
Brown, Archie. *The Human Factor: Gorbachev, Reagan, and Thatcher, and the End of the Cold War*. Oxford: Oxford University Press, 2020.
Brown, Jeremy. *June Fourth: The Tiananmen Protests and Beijing Massacre of 1989*. Cambridge: Cambridge University Press, 2021.
Brown, Kerry. *What's Wrong with Diplomacy? The Future of Diplomacy and the Case of the UK and China*. Melbourne: Penguin Group (Australia), 2015.
Buchanan, Tom. *East Wind: China and the British Left, 1925–1976*. Oxford: Oxford University Press, 2012.
Cahill, Damien and Martijn Konings. *Neoliberalism*. Cambridge: Polity Press, 2017.
Cannadine, David. *Margaret Thatcher: A Life and Legacy*. Oxford: Oxford University Press, 2017.
Carroll, John. *A Concise History of Hong Kong*. Hong Kong: Hong Kong University Press, 2007.
Chan, Ming K. 'Decolonization without Democracy: The Birth of Pluralistic Politics in Hong Kong'. In Edward Friedman (ed.), *The Politics of Democratization: Generalizing East Asian Experiences*. Boulder, CO: Westview Press, 1994, pp. 161–81.
Chen, Chung, Lawrence Chang, and Yimin Zhang. 'The Role of Foreign Direct Investment in China's Post-1978 Economic Development'. In Linda Yueh (ed.), *China and Globalization: Critical Concepts in Economics*, vol. 1: *Globalization and Chinese Growth (Part 1)*. Abingdon, Oxon: Routledge, 2013, pp. 116–37.
Chen, Jian. 'Tiananmen and the Fall of the Berlin Wall: China's Path toward 1989 and Beyond'. In Jeffrey A. Engel (ed.), *The Fall of the Berlin Wall: The Revolutionary Legacy of 1989*. New York: Oxford University Press, 2009, pp. 96–131.
Ching, Frank. *Hong Kong and China: For Better or for Worse*. New York: The China Council of The Asia Society/The Foreign Policy Association, 1985.
Chiu, Stephen and Tai-Lok Lui. *Hong Kong: Becoming a Chinese Global City*. London: Routledge, 2009.
Christiansen, Thomas, Emil Kirchner, and Uwe Wissenbach. *The European Union and China*. London: Red Globe Press, 2019.
Chu, Cindy Yik-yi. *Chinese Communists and Hong Kong Capitalists: 1937–1997*. New York: Palgrave Macmillan, 2010.
Clark, Greg. *Global City: A Short History*. Washington, DC: Brookings Institution Press, 2016.
Clayton, David W. 'From Laissez-faire to "Positive Non-Interventionism": The Colonial State in Hong Kong Studies'. *Social Transformations in Chinese Societies*, 9: 1 (2013), 1–20.
―――― 'Constructing Colonial Capitalism: The Public Relations Campaigns of Hong Kong Business Groups, 1959–1966'. In David Thackeray, Andrew Thompson, and Richard Toye (eds), *Imagining Britain's Economic Future,*

c.1800–1975: Trade, Consumerism and Global Markets. Cham: Palgrave Macmillan, 2018, pp. 231–51.
Cooper, James. Margaret Thatcher and Ronald Reagan: A Very Political Special Relationship. London: Palgrave, 2012.
Cottrell, Robert. The End of Hong Kong: The Secret Diplomacy of Imperial Retreat. London: John Murray, 1993.
Crafts, Nicholas. 'Economic Growth during the Long Twentieth Century'. In Roderick Floud, Jane Humphries, and Paul Johnson (eds), The Cambridge Economic History of Modern Britain, vol. 2: 1870 to the Present. Cambridge: Cambridge University Press, 2014, pp. 26–59.
Crafts, Nick. 'Reversing Relative Economic Decline? The 1980s in Historical Perspective'. Oxford Review of Economic Policy, 7: 3 (Autumn 1991), 81–98.
Crane, David. 'The Harrier Jump-Jet and Sino-British Relations'. Asian Affairs, 8: 4 (March–April 1981), 227–50.
Cronin, James E. Global Rules: America, Britain and a Disordered World. New Haven, CT: Yale University Press, 2014.
Darwin, John. Britain and Decolonisation: The Retreat from Empire in the Post-War World. London: Palgrave, 1988.
——— The Empire Project: The Rise and Fall of the British World-System. Cambridge: Cambridge Press, 2009.
——— Unfinished Empire: The Global Expansion of Britain. London: Allen Lane, 2012.
Dillon, Michael. Deng Xiaoping: The Man who Made Modern China. London: Tauris, 2015.
Dixon, David. 'Thatcher's People: The British Nationality Act 1981'. Journal of Law & Society, 10: 2 (Winter 1983), 161–80.
Eckes, Alfred E., Jr. and Thomas W. Zeiler. Globalization and the American Century. Cambridge: Cambridge University Press, 2003.
Edgerton, David. The Rise and Fall of the British Nation: A Twentieth-century History. London: Allen Lane, 2018.
Engel, Jeffrey A. (ed.). The China Diary of George H. W. Bush: The Making of a Global President. Princeton, NJ: Princeton University Press, 2008.
Evans, Eric J. Thatcher and Thatcherism. Abingdon, Oxon: Routledge, 2019.
Fellows, James. 'Britain, European Economic Community Enlargement, and "Decolonisation" in Hong Kong, 1967–1973'. International History Review, 41: 4 (2019), 753–74.
Ferguson, Niall. 'Introduction: Crisis, What Crisis?'. In Niall Ferguson, Charles S. Maier, Erez Manela, and Daniel J. Sargent (eds), The Shock of the Global: The 1970s in Perspective. Cambridge, MA: Harvard University Press, 2010, pp. 1–21.
———. The Square and the Tower: Networks, Hierarchies and the Struggle for Global Power. London: Penguin Books, 2018.
Fewsmith, Joseph. China since Tiananmen: From Deng Xiaoping to Hu Jintao, 2nd edition. Cambridge: Cambridge University Press, 2008.
Foot, Rosemary. Rights beyond Borders: The Global Community and the Struggle over Human Rights in China. Oxford: Oxford University Press, 2000.
Fravel, M. Taylor. Strong Borders, Secure Nation: Cooperation and Conflict in China's Territorial Disputes. Princeton, NJ: Princeton University Press, 2008.
Friedman, Edward (ed.). The Politics of Democratization: Generalizing East Asian Experiences. Boulder, NC: Westview Press, 1994.
Fukuyama, Francis. The End of History and the Last Man. London: Penguin, 1992.

Gerald, Hughes, R. *The Postwar Legacy of Appeasement: British Foreign Policy since 1945*. London: Bloomsbury Academic, 2014.

Gerstle, Gary. *The Rise and Fall of the Neoliberal Order: America and the World in the Free Market Era*. New York: Oxford University Press, 2022.

Gewirtz, Julian B. *Unlikely Partners: Chinese Reformers, Western Economists, and the Making of Global China*. Cambridge, MA: Harvard University Press, 2017.

Gittings, Danny. *Introduction to the Hong Kong Basic Law*, 2nd edition. Hong Kong: Hong Kong University Press, 2016.

Goodstadt, Leo F. *Uneasy Partners: The Conflict between Public Interest and Private Profit in Hong Kong*. Hong Kong: Hong Kong University Press, 2005.

Hamilton, Peter E. *Made in Hong Kong: Transpacific Networks and a New History of Globalization*. New York: Columbia University Press, 2021.

Hampton, Mark. *Hong Kong and British Culture, 1945–1997*. Manchester: Manchester University Press, 2017.

Harding, Harry. *A Fragile Relationship: The United States and China since 1972*. Washington, DC: Brookings Institution Press, 1992.

Hardman, Robert. *Queen of the World: The Global Biography*. London: Arrow Books, 2019.

Harvey, David. *Neoliberalism: A Brief History*. Oxford: Oxford University Press, 2007.

Hevia, James L. *Cherishing Men from Afar: Qing Guest Ritual and the Macartney Embassy of 1793*. Durham. NC: Duke University Press, 1995.

——— *English Lessons: The Pedagogy of Imperialism in Nineteenth-Century China*. Durham, NC: Duke University Press, 2003.

Hopkins, A. G. 'Introduction: Globalization – An Agenda for Historians'. In A. G. Hopkins (ed.), *Globalization in World History*. London: Pimlico, 2002, pp. 1–10.

——— 'Rethinking Decolonization'. *Past and Present*, 200 (August 2008), 211–47.

——— *American Empire: A Global History*. Princeton, NJ: Princeton University Press, 2018.

Hopkins, Tony. 'Macmillan's Audit of Empire, 1957'. In Peter Clarke and Clive Trebilcock (eds), *Understanding Decline: Perceptions and Realities of British Economic Performance*. Cambridge: Cambridge University Press, 1997, pp. 234–60.

Hung, Ho-fung. *City on the Edge: Hong Kong under Chinese Rule*. Cambridge: Cambridge University Press, 2022.

Hurst, Matthew. 'Britain's Approach to the Negotiations over the Future of Hong Kong, 1979–1982'. *International History Review* (published online 5 January 2022), DOI: 10.1080/07075332.2021.2024588.

Huntington, Samuel P. *The Third Wave: Democratization in the Late Twentieth Century*. Norman, OK: University of Oklahoma Press, 1993.

Ikenberry, G. John. *A World Safe for Democracy: Liberal Internationalism and the Crisis of Global Order*. New Haven, CT: Yale University Press, 2020.

Iriye, Akira. *China and Japan in the Global Setting*. Cambridge, MA: Harvard University Press, 1998.

Jackson, Ben. 'The Think-tank Archipelago: Thatcherism and Neo-liberalism'. In Ben Jackson and Robert Saunders (eds), *Making Thatcher's Britain*. Cambridge: Cambridge University Press, 2012, pp. 43–61.

Jacobson, Harold K. and Michel Oksenberg. *China's Participation in the IMF, the World Bank, and GATT: Toward a Global Economic Order*. Ann Arbor, MI: The University of Michigan Press, 1990.

Jacques, Martin. *When China Rules the World: The End of the Western World and the Birth of a New Global Order*, 2nd edition. London: Penguin Books, 2012.

Kapur, Harish. *Distant Neighbours: China and Europe*. London: Pinter Publishers, 1990.

Keith, Ronald. *Deng Xiaoping and China's Foreign Policy*. Abingdon: Routledge, 2018.

Kelly, Jason M. *Market Maoists: The Communist Origins of China's Capitalist Ascent*. Cambridge, MA: Harvard University Press, 2021.

Kennedy, Paul. *The Realities Behind Diplomacy: Background Influences on British External Policy 1865–1980*. London: Fontana Press, 1985.

——— *The Rise and Fall of the Great Powers: Economic Change and Military Conflict from 1500–2000*. New York: Vintage Books, 1989.

Kim, Samuel S. 'Thinking Globally in Post-Mao China'. *Journal of Peace Research*, 27: 2 (May 1990), 191–209.

King, Ambrose Yeo-chi. 'Administrative Absorption of Politics in Hong Kong: Emphasis on the Grass Roots Levels'. *Asian Survey*, 15: 5 (May 1975), 422–39.

King, Stephen D. *Grave New World: The End of Globalization, the Return of History*. New Haven, CT: Yale University Press, 2017.

Kreisberg, Paul H. 'China's Negotiating Behaviour'. In Thomas W. Robinson and David Shambaugh (eds), *Chinese Foreign Policy: Theory and Practice*. Oxford: Clarendon Press, 1995, pp. 453–77.

Lampton, David M. *Same Bed Different Dreams: Managing U.S.–China Relations 1989–2000*. Berkeley, CA: University of California Press, 2001.

Lardy, Nicholas R. *Integrating China into the Global Economy*. Washington, DC: Brookings Institution Press, 2002.

Lau, Pui-king. 'Economic Relations between Hong Kong and China'. In Joseph Y. S. Cheng (ed.), *Hong Kong in Transition*. Hong Kong: Oxford University Press, 1986, pp. 235–67.

Lewis, John Wilson and Xue Litai. *Imagined Enemies: China Prepares for Uncertain War*. Stanford, CA: Stanford University Press, 2006.

Lo, Yui Chim. 'The Last Stand of Colonialism? The Unofficial Members of the Executive and Legislative Councils and the Sino-British Negotiations over Hong Kong, 1982–1984'. *Journal of Imperial and Commonwealth History*, 48: 2 (2020), 370–94.

Louis, William Roger. 'Hong Kong: The Critical Phase, 1945–1949'. *American Historical Review*, 102: 4 (October 1997), 1052–84.

Lu, Ning. *The Dynamics of Foreign Policy Decisionmaking in China*. Boulder, CO: Westview Press, 1997.

Magee, Gary B. and Andrew S. Thompson. *Empire and Globalisation: Networks of People, Goods and Capital in the British World, c.1850–1914*. Cambridge: Cambridge University Press, 2010.

Mann, James. *About Face: A History of America's Curious Relationship with China, from Nixon to Clinton*. New York: Random House, 1999.

Mark, Chi-kwan. *Hong Kong and the Cold War: Anglo-American Relations 1949–1957*. Oxford: Oxford University Press, 2004.

——— 'Lack of Means or Loss of Will? The United Kingdom and the Decolonization of Hong Kong, 1957–1967'. *International History Review*, 31: 1 (March 2009), 45–71.

——— 'Development without Decolonisation? Hong Kong's Future and Relations with Britain and China, 1967–1972'. *Journal of the Royal Asiatic Society*, 24: 2 (2014), 315–35.

——— 'Crisis or Opportunity? Britain, China, and the Decolonisation of Hong Kong in the Long 1970s'. In Priscilla Roberts and Odd Arne Westad (eds), *China, Hong Kong and the Long 1970s: Global Perspectives*. London: Palgrave Macmillan, 2017, pp. 257–77.
——— *The Everyday Cold War: Britain and China, 1950–1972*. London: Bloomsbury Academic, 2017.
——— 'To "Educate" Deng Xiaoping in Capitalism: Thatcher's Visit to China and the Future of Hong Kong in 1982'. *Cold War History*, 17: 2 (June 2017), 161–80.
——— 'Decolonising Britishness? The 1981 British Nationality Act and the Identity Crisis of Hong Kong Elites'. *Journal of Imperial and Commonwealth History*, 48: 3 (2020), 565–90.
Matthews, Gordon, Eric Kit-wai Ma, and Tai-lok Lui. *Hong Kong, China: Learning to Belong to a Nation*. London: Routledge, 2008.
Mavroidis, Petros C. and André Sapir. *China and the WTO: Why Multilateralism Still Matters*. Princeton, NJ: Princeton University Press, 2021.
McKenzie, Francine. *GATT and Global Order in the Postwar Era*. Cambridge: Cambridge University Press, 2020.
Meijer, Hugo. 'Balancing Conflicting Security Interests: U.S. Defense Exports to China in the Last Decade of the Cold War'. *Journal of Cold War Studies*, 17: 1 (Winter 2015), 4–40.
Mercau, Ezequiel. *The Falklands War: An Imperial History*. Cambridge: Cambridge University Press, 2019.
Meyer, David R. *Hong Kong as a Global Metropolis*. Cambridge: Cambridge University Press, 2000.
Mills, Lawrence. *Protecting Free Trade: The Hong Kong Paradox, 1947–97*. Hong Kong: Hong Kong University Press, 2012.
Miners, Norman. *The Government and Politics of Hong Kong*, 2nd edition. Hong Kong: Oxford University Press, 1977.
Ming, Ruan. *Deng Xiaoping: Chronicle of an Empire*. Boulder, CO: Westview Press, 1994.
Mok, Florence. 'Chinese Illicit Immigration into Colonial Hong Kong, c. 1970–1980'. *Journal of Imperial and Commonwealth History*, 49: 2 (April 2021), 339–67.
Moore, Charles. *Margaret Thatcher: The Authorized Biography*, vol. 1: *Not for Turning*. London: Allen Lane, 2013.
——— *Margaret Thatcher: The Authorized Biography*, vol. 2: *Everything She Wants*. London: Allen Lane, 2015.
——— *Margaret Thatcher: The Authorized Biography*, vol. 3: *Herself Alone*. London: Allen Lane, 2019.
Munn, Christopher. *Anglo-China: Chinese People and British Rule in Hong Kong, 1841–1880*. Hong Kong: Hong Kong University Press, 2008.
Naughton, Barry. *Growing Out of the Plan: Chinese Economic Reform, 1978–1993*. Cambridge: Cambridge University Press, 1995.
——— *The Chinese Economy: Transitions and Growth*. Cambridge, MA: The MIT Press, 2007.
Ogle, Vanessa Ogle. 'Archipelago Capitalism: Tax Havens, Offshore Money, and the State, 1950s–1970s'. *American Historical Review*, 122: 5 (December 2017), 1431–58.
Osterhammel, Jürgen and Niels P. Peterson. *Globalization: A Short History*. Princeton, NJ: Princeton University Press, 2005.

Palmer, Dean. *The Queen and Mrs Thatcher: An Inconvenient Relationship*. Stroud, Gloucestershire: The History Press, 2016.

Pantsov, Alexander V. with Steven I. Levine. *Deng Xiaoping: A Revolutionary Life*. New York: Oxford University Press, 2015.

Paul, Kathleen. *Whitewashing Britain: Race and Citizenship in the Postwar Era*. Ithaca, NY: Cornell University Press, 1997.

Pearson, Margaret M. 'The Case of China's Accession to GATT/WTO'. In David M. Lampton (ed.), *The Making of Chinese Foreign and Security Policy in the Era of Reform*. Stanford, CA: Stanford University Press, 2001, pp. 337–70.

Pei, C. and L. Peng. 'Responsibilities of China after Accession to the WTO'. In Linda Yueh (ed.), *China and Globalization: Critical Concepts in Economics*, vol. 3: *China's External Impact and Future Growth in a Globalized World Economy (Part 1)*. Abingdon, Oxon: Routledge, 2013, pp. 66–79.

Pepper, Suzanne. *Keeping Democracy at Bay: Hong Kong and the Challenge of Chinese Political Reform*. Lanham, MD: Rowman & Littlefield, 2008.

Platt, Stephen. *Imperial Twilight: The Opium War and the End of China's Last Golden Age*. London: Atlantic Books, 2019.

Radchenko, Sergey. *Unwanted Visionaries: The Soviet Failure in Asia at the End of the Cold War*. New York: Oxford University Press, 2014.

Reardon, Lawrence C. *A Third Way: The Origins of China's Current Economic Development Strategy*. Cambridge, MA: Harvard University Asia Center, 2020.

Ritzer, George and Paul Dean. *Globalization: The Essentials*, 2nd edition. Hoboken, NJ: Wiley-Blackwell, John Wiley & Sons, 2019.

Roberti, Mark. *The Fall of Hong Kong: China's Triumph and Britain's Betrayal*. New York: John Wiley & Sons, Inc., 1996.

Roberts, Priscilla. 'Bringing the Chinese State Back In: The Role of Quasi-Private Institutions in Britain and the United States'. In Priscilla Roberts and Odd Arne Westad (eds), *China, Hong Kong and the Long 1970s: Global Perspectives*. London: Palgrave Macmillan, 2017, pp. 303–25.

Sandbrook, Dominic. *Who Dares Wins: Britain, 1979–1982*. London: Penguin, 2020.

Saunders, Robert. '"Crisis? What Crisis?" Thatcherism and the Seventies'. In Ben Jackson and Robert Saunders (eds), *Making Thatcher's Britain*. Cambridge: Cambridge University Press, 2012, pp. 25–42.

Sargent, Daniel J. *A Superpower Transformed: The Remaking of American Foreign Relations in the 1970s*. New York: Oxford University Press, 2015.

Sassen, Saskia. *The Global City: New York, London, Tokyo*. Princeton, NJ: Princeton University Press, 2001.

Schenk, Catherine R. 'Closing the Hong Kong Gap: The Hong Kong Free Dollar Market in the 1950s'. *Economic History Review*, 47: 2 (May 1994), 335–53.

——— *Hong Kong as an International Financial Centre: Emergence and Development, 1945–65*. London: Routledge, 2001.

——— 'The Empire Strikes Back: Hong Kong and the Decline of Sterling in the 1960s'. *Economic History Review*, 57: 3 (August 2004), 551–80.

——— *The Decline of Sterling: Managing the Retreat of an International Currency, 1945–1992*. Cambridge: Cambridge University Press, 2010.

Seldon, Anthony, with Jonathan Meakin and Illias Thoms. *The Impossible Office? The History of the British Prime Minister*. Cambridge: Cambridge University Press, 2021.

Shambaugh, David. *Beautiful Imperialist: China Perceives America, 1972–1990*. Princeton, NJ: Princeton University Press, 1991.

——— *China's Leaders: From Mao to Now*. Cambridge: Polity Press, 2021.
Shao, Wenguang. *China, Britain and Businessmen: Political and Commercial Relations, 1949–1957*. London: Macmillan, 1991.
Shawcross, William. *Kowtow!* London: Chatto & Windus, 1989.
Shepherd, John. *Crisis? What Crisis? The Callaghan Government and the British 'Winter of Discontent'*. Manchester: Manchester University Press, 2013.
Sheridan, Michael. *The Gate to China: A New History of the People's Republic & Hong Kong*. London: William Collins, 2021.
Slobodian, Quinn. *Globalists: The End of Empire and the Birth of Neoliberalism*. Cambridge, MA: Harvard University Press, 2020.
So, Alvin Y. *Hong Kong's Embattled Democracy: A Societal Analysis*. Baltimore, MD and London: The Johns Hopkins University Press, 1999.
So, Alvin and Yin-Wah Chu. *The Global Rise of China*. Cambridge: Polity, 2015.
Sohmen, Anna Pao. *Y K Pao: My Father*. Hong Kong: Hong Kong University Press, 2013.
Spohr, Kristina. *Post Wall, Post Square: Rebuilding the World after 1989*. London: William Collins, 2019.
Sung, Yun-wing. *The China–Hong Kong Connection: The Key to China's Open-Door Policy*. Cambridge: Cambridge University Press, 1991.
Taube, Markus. 'Economic Relations between the PRC and the States of Europe'. *The China Quarterly*, 169 (March 2002), 78–107.
Taubman, William. *Gorbachev: His Life and Times*. London: Simon & Schuster, 2018.
Tharoor, Shashi. *Inglorious Empire: What the British Did to India*. London: Penguin Books, 2017.
Thomas, Martin and Andrew S. Thompson. 'Rethinking Decolonization: A New Research Agenda for the Twenty-First Century'. In Martin Thomas and Andrew S. Thompson (eds), *The Oxford Handbook of the Ends of Empire*. Oxford: Oxford University Press, 2018, pp. 1–26.
Tomlinson, Jim. 'Thrice Denied: "Declinism" as a Recurrent Theme in British History in the Long Twentieth Century'. *Twentieth Century British History*, 20: 2 (2009), 227–51.
——— *Managing the Economy, Managing the People: Narratives of Economic Life in Britain from Beveridge to Brexit*. Oxford: Oxford University Press, 2017.
Tsang, Steve. *Democracy Shelved: Great Britain, China, and Attempts at Constitutional Reform in Hong Kong, 1945–1952*. Hong Kong: Oxford University Press, 1988.
——— *Hong Kong: An Appointment with China*. London: I.B. Tauris, 1997.
——— *A Modern History of Hong Kong: 1841–1997*. London: I.B. Tauris, 2003.
Vinen, Richard. *Thatcher's Britain: The Politics and Social Upheaval of the 1980s*. London: Pocket Books, 2010.
——— 'Thatcherism and the Cold War'. In Ben Jackson and Robert Saunders (eds), *Making Thatcher's Britain*. Cambridge: Cambridge University Press, 2012, pp. 199–217.
Vogel, Ezra F. *Deng Xiaoping and the Transformation of China*. Cambridge, MA: Harvard University Press, 2011.
Westad, Odd Arne. *The Global Cold War: Third World Interventions and the Making of Our Times*. Cambridge: Cambridge University Press, 2005.
——— *Restless Empire: China and the World Since 1750*. London: The Bodley Head, 2012.
Wilhelm, Jr., Alfred D. *The Chinese at the Negotiating Table: Style and Characteristics*. Washington, DC: National Defence University Press, 1994.

Wong, John D. 'Hong Kong Breaking into the International League: Cathay Pacific's Extension to Long-haul Routes, 1970s–1980s'. *International Journal of Asian Studies* (2021), 1–20.
Wong, Siu-lun. *Emigrant Entrepreneurs: Shanghai Industrialists in Hong Kong*. Hong Kong: Oxford University Press, 1988.
Wu, Guoguang. 'Democracy and Rule of Law in Zhao Ziyang's Political Reform'. In Guoguang Wu and Helen Lansdowne (eds), *Zhao Ziyang and China's Political Future*. Abingdon, Oxon: Routledge, 2008, pp. 32–57.
Yee, Herbert S. and Wong Yiu-chung. 'Hong Kong: The Politics of the Daya Bay Nuclear Plant Debate'. *International Affairs*, 63: 4 (Autumn 1987), 617–30.
Yep, Ray (ed.). *Negotiating Autonomy in Greater China: Hong Kong and Its Sovereign before and after 1997*. Copenhagen: NIAS Press, 2013.
Yep, Ray and Tai-Lok Lui. 'Revisiting the Golden Era of MacLehose and the Dynamics of Social Reforms'. *China Information*, 24: 3 (2010), 249–72.
Yueh, Linda. 'The Rise of China'. In Linda Yueh (ed.), *China and Globalization: Critical Concepts in Economics*, vol. 3: *China's External Impact and Future Growth in a Globalized World Economy (Part 1)*. Abingdon, Oxon: Routledge, 2013, pp. 3–13.
Zhang, Shu Guang. *Beijing's Economic Statecraft during the Cold War, 1949–1991*. Washington, DC: Woodrow Wilson Centre Press, 2014.
Zhang, Xiaoming. *Deng Xiaoping's Long War: The Military Conflict between China and Vietnam, 1979–1991*. Chapel Hill, NC: The University of North Carolina Press, 2015.
Zhang, Yongjin and Barry Buzan. 'China and the Global Reach of Human Rights'. *The China Quarterly*, 241 (March 2020), 169–90.
Zhou, Taomo. 'Leveraging Liminality: The Border Town of Bao'an (Shenzhen) and the Origins of China's Reform and Opening'. *Journal of Asian Studies*, 80: 2 (May 2021), 337–61.

Index

'48 Group' 22, 34

Adley, Robert 167–8
All Hong Kong Alliance in Support
 of the Patriotic Democratic
 Movement in China (AHKA) 216,
 219–20, 224
appeasement 6–7, 240–1
Appleyard, L. V. 139
Ashdown, Paddy 204, 217
Atkins, Humphrey 77

Bank of China 77, 137, 175, 177
Basic Law 134–8, 144, 147, 154,
 155, 156, 158, 173, 204, 207,
 210, 212, 214, 216, 219–23,
 236, 243
 Drafting Committee 211, 215, 219
Belstead, Lord 80
Boyd, John 168
Bremridge, John 116
Britain
 1978 scientific and technological
  cooperation agreement with
  China 28
 1979 air services agreement with
  China 35–6, 37
 1979 economic cooperation
  agreement with China 29, 30,
  37, 86, 95
 1979 education and cultural
  exchange agreement with
  China 36, 37
 1985 economic cooperation
  agreement with China
  172, 176

 1985 investment protection
  agreement with China 178
 1985 peaceful use of nuclear energy
  agreement with China 177
 competitiveness 3, 37, 175
 diplomatic relations with China
  17, 32, 48
 economic decline 2, 3, 18, 37,
  234
 educate China 7–8, 37, 78, 86,
  95, 101, 109, 114, 122, 123,
  143, 157, 190, 213, 223, 235,
  239, 241
 investment in China 185–6
 investment in Hong Kong 61
 kowtow to China 7, 224, 240
 Macartney Embassy to China 7
 sale of Harrier to China 26–7, 31–2,
  35, 37, 86
 trade with China 17, 26, 32–3, 86,
  87–8, 185
 trade with Hong Kong 10,
  60, 67
British Aerospace 31, 34, 171, 174
British Airways 62
British Dependent Territories Citizen
 (BDTC) 65, 141, 150, 217–18
British National (Overseas) (BN(O))
 217, 243, 244
British Nationality (Hong Kong) Act
 1990 218
British Nationality Act 1981 64–5,
 67, 79
British Petroleum 92, 180, 234
Brzezinski, Zbigniew 27
Bush, George 201, 205, 208

Index

Callaghan, James 2, 17, 18, 26, 27, 28, 29, 30, 50, 51, 54, 65
Cambodia 28, 174, 180, 205, 207
Cameron, David 1
Canada 172, 232
capitalism 3, 6
Carrington, Lord 19, 31, 55, 56, 58, 59, 60, 67, 77, 80, 241
Carter, Jimmy 27, 28, 32
Cathay Pacific Airways 62, 151
Cha, Louis 76, 215
Chamberlain, Neville 7, 224, 241
Channon, Paul 180
Chen Yun 24, 37, 86–7, 166, 200, 235
China Light and Power Company (CLP) 62, 91–3, 181
China Merchants Company 24
China, People's Republic of
  Democracy Wall 25, 37, 236
  political liberalisation 4, 199, 204, 206, 222, 235
  political reform 200, 201, 236
  Tiananmen Square crackdown 6, 7, 198, 202–3, 206, 208, 233, 236, 240, 241
China, Republic of 188
Chinese Communist Party (CCP) 6, 22, 166, 199
Chung Sze-yuen 81, 102, 110, 117–18, 131, 136, 137, 143–4, 146, 149, 154, 210, 211
Civil Aviation Administration of China 35
Cleminson, James 183
Clift, R. D. 139
Coles, John 79, 103, 136
Coordinating Committee for Multilateral Export Controls (COCOM) 27, 31, 169, 170–1, 176, 180
Cortazzi, H. A. H. 29, 36–7, 49
Cradock, Percy 17, 20–1, 30, 36, 50, 51, 53, 54, 55–6, 59, 78, 80, 88, 101, 102, 105, 108, 111, 112, 114, 116, 117, 118–21, 123, 130, 139, 155, 171, 208, 215, 217, 220–2, 224, 236, 238, 239, 240, 241, 244

decolonisation 9, 10, 47
democracy 2, 4, 5, 6, 18, 37, 187, 219, 222, 223
Deng Xiaoping 22–3, 50, 54, 56, 57, 59, 66, 75–7, 87, 93, 99, 100, 106, 107, 109, 111, 119, 120, 122, 130, 131, 133, 145–6, 147, 151–2, 157, 165–6, 170, 172, 175, 183, 187, 198, 199, 200, 201, 202, 205–6, 208, 212, 222, 223, 234, 235, 238, 240, 242, 243, 244
  on bourgeois liberalisation 190, 199
  on capitalism 25, 235
  cat theory 24
  and Edward Heath 78, 113–14, 172
  Four Cardinal Principles 25, 37, 236
  and Geoffrey Howe 141–2, 148
  globalisation 4, 223, 235
  independent globalisation 4, 25, 37, 189, 191
  and Lord Carrington 58
  and Margaret Thatcher 83–4, 156
  and Murray MacLehose 51–3
  reform and opening up 1, 23, 37, 63
  socialism with Chinese characteristics 4, 166, 190, 235
Donald, Alan 79, 205, 206, 220
Douglas-Home, Alec 17
Duke of Edinburgh 181, 183–4
Dunn, Lydia 81, 217, 242

Eagleburger, Lawrence 208
Elliott, Mark 168
European Economic Community (EEC) 47, 48, 61, 87, 199, 204, 206, 208, 237, 242
Evans, Richard 101, 130, 133, 134, 138, 150, 168, 183, 184, 200, 238

Falklands War 20, 78, 80, 238
Fang Lizhi 199
Fok Ying-tung 76
Foot, Michael 21
France 19, 22, 26, 33, 37, 77, 87, 88, 90, 170, 178, 179, 186, 208
free market 2, 4, 6, 18
free trade 2, 61
Friedman, Milton 18

General Agreement on Tariffs and
    Trade (GATT) 4, 61, 166, 191,
    212, 234, 241
  China's accession to 187–90,
    232–3
General Electric Company (GEC) 34,
    62, 88, 90, 91, 171, 175–6, 177,
    186, 234
Glenarthur, Lord 204
Global Britain 1, 10, 37, 191, 234, 243
globalisation 2–4, 5–6, 9–10, 48, 59,
    60, 61, 62, 64, 79, 184, 198, 218,
    233, 234, 236, 237
Goodhart, Charles 116
Gorbachev, Mikhail 173, 179, 182,
    185, 198, 202, 222
Grantham, Alexander 45
Great Britain–China Centre 22
Gu Mu 165
Guangdong nuclear power project
    88–91, 92, 93, 172, 175–6,
    177–8, 180, 186

Haddon-Cave, Philip 46
Hayek, Friedrich 18
Healey, Denis 145, 155
Heath, Edward 7, 18, 19, 78, 113, 145,
    155, 172
Heseltine, Michael 170
Hong Kong
  1967 riots 45, 47, 237
  autonomy 10, 47, 48, 61, 117,
    131, 237, 244
  Chinese immigration 35, 46, 52
  Convention of Peking 44, 238
  defence 47, 48, 237
  democracy 45, 48, 132, 204, 208–9,
    210, 211–12, 216, 224, 244
  emigration to Britain 21, 79, 80,
    144, 218
  as global city 9, 10, 59, 66, 237
  globalisation 9, 66, 237
  as international financial centre
    46, 60
  investment in China 63–4
  Korean War embargoes 45
  Legislative Council 45, 209,
    210, 211, 213–16, 221, 222,
    236, 240
  Letters Patent 44, 102
  long decolonisation 10, 47, 131,
    237
  long-term planning, full
    utilisation 45
  New Territories land leases
    50–7, 66
  New Territories Lease 4, 44, 49,
    118, 122
  Queen's visit 184
  representative government 132, 155,
    156, 209–10, 212, 223
  role in the Cold War 17, 45
  Royal Instructions 44, 102
  textile exports 46, 61
  trade with China 63
  Treaty of Nanking 44, 238
  unequal treaties 5, 45
Hong Kong and Macao Affairs
    Office 50, 76, 77, 100, 107,
    119, 211
Hong Kong and Shanghai Bank 62, 84,
    115, 184
Hong Kong dollar 46–7, 109,
    113, 114, 115–16, 120, 123,
    133, 137
Hong Kong negotiations
  Chinese troops stationed in Hong
    Kong 133, 142
  civil aviation 135–6, 151, 153
  constitutional arrangements 134,
    151, 152
  Cradock and Yao Guang 104–5,
    106–8, 109, 110–11, 112–13,
    114–15, 118–19, 121–2
  Cradock and Zhang Wenjin 103–4
  Cradock and Zhou Nan 108–9
  Evans and Zhou Nan 138–9,
    145, 150
  joint group 138, 140, 142,
    145, 148–9
  nationality 136, 140, 150–1, 152–3
  Wilson–Ke working group 145,
    148, 149
  working papers 132, 134,
    157, 239
Hong Kong, Sub-Committee on 102,
    119, 121, 122, 133, 135, 136,
    145, 146, 152

Howe, Geoffrey 7, 20, 111, 114, 116–17, 119–20, 121, 122, 123, 133, 134, 135, 136–7, 138, 142–3, 144, 146, 147, 150–1, 152–3, 155, 157, 158, 167, 178, 181, 182–3, 184, 203–4, 205, 206, 207, 208, 212, 213–14, 215, 216, 218, 240, 241
  visited China April 1984 139–42
  visited China July 1984 147–9
Howell, David 204
Hu Yaobang 23, 66, 76, 77, 130, 165, 169, 174, 183, 199, 201, 235
  visited Britain 1986 178–80
Hua Guofeng 17, 19, 23, 24, 28, 29, 30, 32, 36, 77, 86, 173
  visited Britain 1979 33–6, 37, 56
Huang Hua 53, 57, 104
Huang, Rayson 76
Hurd, Douglas 19, 218, 222, 224

Institute of Economic Affairs 3
International Monetary Fund (IMF) 3, 4
Italy 33, 36, 88, 179

Japan 1, 3, 23, 32, 34, 37, 45, 60, 64, 79, 87, 139, 168, 171, 184, 186, 207, 208, 237, 243
Jardine Matheson 62, 136, 142
Ji Pengfei 17, 100, 141, 211, 213
Jiang Zemin 206, 219, 221, 222, 223, 234, 241
Jing Shuping 168
Johnson, Boris 243
Joint Declaration, Sino-British 10, 153, 154, 155, 157, 158, 167, 172, 173, 176, 203, 209, 211, 212, 217, 220, 221, 239, 240, 243, 244
Joint Liaison Group 207, 212–13, 216
Joseph, Keith 18, 34, 62

Kadoorie, Lord Lawrence 88, 90, 93
Kan Yuet-keung 51
Kaufman, Gerald 204, 216
Ke Zaishuo 145, 211
Keswick, John 22
Kinnock, Neil 21
Kohl, Helmut 19, 168

Lam, Carrie 243
Lawson, Nigel 208
Lee Ka-chiu 243
Lee, Allen 217
Lee, Martin 210, 211
Li Hou 77, 211, 212, 219
Li Jusheng 49, 101, 111, 112
Li Ka-shing 76
Li Peng 179, 180–1, 200, 202, 206
Li Qiang 29, 30, 49–50, 51
Li Xiannian 29, 77, 100, 113, 119, 133, 182, 183, 200
Liao Chengzhi 50, 57, 76, 100, 104, 107
Liu Shaoqi 22
Liu Tianfu 92
Lobo, Roger 134, 210
Lu Ping 76, 101, 132, 149, 211, 219
Luce, Richard 155

Macao 48, 58, 59, 99
MacDonald, Malcolm 22
MacLehose, Murray 20, 48, 49, 50, 54, 56, 57, 64, 66, 132, 237
  visited China 1979 51–3
Macmillan, Harold 18, 47
Major, John 207–8, 224
Mao Zedong 17, 19, 22, 23, 25, 33, 36
Marek, John 215
Marshall, Walter 90, 93
May, Theresa 1
McLaren, Robin 149, 158, 220
Meeting Point 155, 209
Mitterrand, François 19
Multi-Fibre Arrangement (MFA) 61

neoliberalism 2, 3, 37, 187, 198
Neville-Jones, Pauline 167
New China News Agency (NCNA) 49, 50, 76, 85, 101, 104, 107, 111, 113, 119, 212
Nott, John 34, 35, 60

one country, two systems 76, 99–100, 124, 130, 146, 149, 151, 223, 236, 244
Orr, Iain C. 173
Owen, David 28, 50, 51, 54

Index

Palliser, Michael 32
Palmerston, Lord 44
Pao, Y. K. 92, 179, 181
Parkinson, Cecil 61
Parsons, Anthony 112
Peretz, David 116
Philip, Prince 174, 183, 184
post-colonial globalization 9
Powell, Charles 209
Powell, Enoch 155, 218
Pym, Francis 20, 80, 91, 94, 104, 105, 106, 111

Qian Qichen 207–8, 221, 222, 224
Queen Elizabeth II 156, 173, 174, 235
   visited China 1986 181–4, 213

Reagan, Ronald 2, 3, 75, 130, 156, 171, 173, 179, 182, 198, 205, 237
Ricketts, Peter 168
Roberts, Margaret Hilda 18
   see also Thatcher, Margaret
Rolls-Royce 26, 171

Scowcroft, Brent 208
Sharp, Eric 183
Shenzhen 23, 24, 63, 165, 234
Shultz, George 86
Singapore 3, 117
Sino-British Trade Council 21, 22, 34, 88, 183
Sino-Vietnamese Border War 26, 28–9
Society for Anglo-Chinese Understanding 22, 205
Song Zhiguang 55
Soviet Union 4, 17, 19, 22, 25, 26, 27, 29, 33, 34, 35, 75, 87, 171, 179, 180, 181, 188, 198, 199, 222, 236, 242
Special Administrative Region of Hong Kong (SAR) 99, 107, 135, 136, 211, 243
   chief executive 211, 215, 222
Special Economic Zone (SEZ) 4, 24, 86, 88, 165, 166, 187
Sterling Area 46, 47, 115, 131, 237
Stewart, Michael 22
Swire Pacific 62, 81
Szeto Wah 210, 211, 216, 219

Taiwan 17, 24, 50, 52, 58, 59, 66, 75, 77, 78, 99, 114, 130, 135, 151, 156, 180
Tam, Maria 147
Thatcher, Denis 18, 92
Thatcher, Margaret 1, 18, 55, 61, 64, 66, 67, 78, 79, 80, 81, 85, 90, 93, 94, 101, 102, 104, 105, 106, 109, 111, 114, 116–18, 120, 121, 122, 123, 124, 132, 133, 135, 136, 148, 166, 168, 169, 170, 171, 175, 178, 181, 183, 185, 198, 199, 203, 205, 207, 208, 209, 214, 216, 217, 218, 220–1, 223, 224, 233, 238, 239, 240, 241–3, 244
   capitalism 19, 78, 156, 239
   on communism 4
   democratic promotion 4, 198–9, 223, 236
   and Deng Xiaoping 83–4, 156
   globalisation 3, 19, 33, 37, 76, 191, 234, 236, 240
   and Hu Yaobang 179–80
   and Hua Guofeng 33–4, 35–6, 56
   Iron Lady 5, 6, 8, 238, 242
   neoliberalism 3, 11, 210, 234
   personality 6, 8, 101, 117, 242
   as pragmatic neoliberal 4, 198, 236
   and Ronald Reagan 2, 3, 19
   on socialism 5, 19
   and Unofficial Members of the Executive Council 110, 117–18, 131, 137, 154
   and Unofficial Members of the Executive Council and the Legislative Council (UMELCO) 80–1, 85, 144
   visited China 1977 19
   visited China 1982 1, 75, 76, 81–5, 91–3
   visited China 1984 155–7
   and Zhao Ziyang 81–3, 91–2, 156, 176–7, 190, 242
Thatcherism 6, 18, 79
Tian Jiyun 173, 174
Tibet 22, 58
Trench, David 45
Truman, Harry 45
Trump, Donald 243

United Nations 8, 198, 204
    Committee on Decolonisation 47
United States 2, 3, 6, 23, 25, 26, 28, 29, 31, 32, 34, 37, 46, 47, 50, 59, 60, 64, 75, 79, 86, 87, 90, 91, 114, 139, 156, 168, 171–3, 179, 184, 185, 186, 189, 198, 208, 222, 232, 233, 237, 242
Unofficial Members of the Executive Council and the Legislative Council (UMELCO) 65, 210, 218

Vance, Cyrus 27
Varley, Eric 28
    visited China 1979 29–30
Vietnam 28, 34, 174, 180
    Vietnamese refugees 28, 33

Waddington, David 218
Walker, Peter 180
Wang Kuang 49, 104
Wang Zhen 28, 29–30, 165
Wei Jingsheng 25
West Germany 19, 26, 32, 33, 37, 77, 87, 88, 90, 168, 170, 172, 178, 179, 184, 186, 208
Western Europe 23, 25, 34, 174, 179, 186
Whitelaw, William 64
Williams, Shirley 36
Wilson, David 20, 21, 51, 101, 139, 145, 211, 213, 214, 220, 238, 242
Wilson, Harold 17, 18, 47

World Bank 4, 207, 208
Wu Xueqian 116, 139, 141–2, 148, 150, 152–3, 157, 158, 173, 184, 212, 214

Xi Jinping 1, 243
Xi Zhongxun 24, 104
Xu Jiatun 76, 101, 113, 212

Yang Shangkun 24, 165, 202, 206
Yao Guang 101, 104, 112, 120–1, 122, 130
Ye Jianying 58–9, 77, 78, 99, 114
Youde, Edward 20–1, 79, 84, 101, 102, 105, 107, 111, 112, 114, 123, 131, 133, 136, 143, 213
Young, Baroness 145
Young, Lord 169, 171–2, 174, 175, 186
Young, Mark 45
Yu Qiuli 34

Zhang Wenjin 35, 81, 101, 103, 104
Zhao Ziyang 6, 23, 75, 77, 87, 93, 106, 141, 148, 152, 155, 165, 166, 169, 172, 177, 182, 186–7, 199–200, 202, 206, 234, 236
    and Margaret Thatcher 81–3, 91–2
    visited Britain 1985 172, 173–7
Zheng Tuobin 178
Zhou Enlai 17, 23, 24, 36
Zhou Nan 108, 130, 132, 134, 135, 137–8, 142, 147, 149, 150, 168, 173, 179, 211, 214

EU authorised representative for GPSR:
Easy Access System Europe, Mustamäe tee 50,
10621 Tallinn, Estonia
gpsr.requests@easproject.com

www.ingramcontent.com/pod-product-compliance
Lightning Source LLC
Chambersburg PA
CBHW051606230426
43668CB00013B/2006